# SIXTUS V

# THE HERMIT OF VILLA MONTALTO

# SIXTUS V

# THE HERMIT OF VILLA MONTALTO

W. T. SELLEY

**GRACEWING**

First published in 2011
by

Gracewing
2, Southern Avenue
Leominster
Herefordshire
HR6 0QF
www.gracewing.co.uk

All rights reserved. No part of this publication may be used, reproduced, stored in any retrieval system, or transmitted in any form, or by any means, electronic, mechanical, photocopying, recording or otherwise, without the written permission of the publisher.

© Literary Estate of W. T. Selley 2011

The right of W. T. Selley to be identified as the author of this work has been asserted in accordance with the Copyright, Designs and Patents Act 1988.

ISBN 978 085244 750 5

Cover design: Based on painting of Pope Sixtus V and his coat-of-arms

# Table of Contents

Table of Contents..................................................................v

Abbreviations......................................................................vii

Map of the Papal States and surrounding territories..........x

Preface................................................................................xi

CHAPTER 1: Fra Felice...........................................................1

CHAPTER 2: Called to Rome................................................25

CHAPTER 3: The Hermit of Villa Montalto..........................95

CHAPTER 4: The Conclave of Sixtus V...............................139

CHAPTER 5: Master of his House.......................................179

CHAPTER 6: A New Rome has Risen from the Ashes.........219

CHAPTER 7: The Worth of his Ambitions..........................255

CHAPTER 8: The Papal States and the Italian Peninsula...345

CHAPTER 9: Foreign Diplomacy and Final Days...............381

EPILOGUE: A Pope in a Hurry..................................................395

Bibliography.................................................................................401

Glossary.......................................................................................409

Appendix 1: Family Tree of Felice Peretti.................................414

Appendix 2 The Conclave of 1585..............................................415

Appendix 3 Monetary values and Papal coinage.....................419

Index of names............................................................................421

# *Abbreviations*

*Album generale*    A. Coccia, *Album generale ordinis fratrum minorum conventualium* (Roma: Curia Generalizia OFMConv, 1960).

AM    L. Wadding, *Annales Minorum seu trium Ordinum a S. Francisco institutorum, ab anno 1541 continuati a pluribus viris eruditis* (Rome : 1625–1660), 30 vols.

Bettenson    H. Bettenson, *Documents of the Christian Church* (Oxford: OUP, 1963).

Brown    H. F. Brown, *Calendar of State Papers Relating to English Affairs in the Archives of Venice 1581–1591*, Volume 8 (London: 1894).

*Bullarium*    *Bullarium Romanum* (Torino: 1857–1872), 16 vols.

Cardella    L. Cardella, *Memorie storiche de' cardinali della santa romana Chiesa scritte da Lorenzo Cardella parroco de' SS. Vincenzo*, ed. Anastasio alla Regola in Roma (Roma: Stamperia Paglierini, 1793), 9 vols..

CEHE    *The Cambridge Economic History of Europe* (Cambridge: CUP, 1966–1989), 8 vols.

CMH    J. E. E. Dalberg-Acton, A. W. Ward et. al., *Cambridge Modern History* (Cambridge: CUP, 1902–1912), 14 vols.

| | |
|---|---|
| Cugnoni | G. Cugnoni, "Documenti Chigiani concernenti Felice Peretti, Sisto V, come privato e come pontefice" in *Archivio della Società Romana di Storia Patria* 5(1882). |
| Delumeau | J. Delumeau, *Vie économique et sociale de Rome dans la seconde moitié du XVIe siècle* (Paris: De Boccard, 1957–1959), 2 vols. |
| DBI | *Dizionario Biografico degli Italiani* (Roma: Istituto dell'Enciclopedia Italiana, 1960– ). |
| EC | *Enciclopedia Cattolica* (Città del Vaticano:1948–1954), 12 vols. |
| Eubel | K. Eubel & G von Gulik, *Hierarchia Catholica Medii et Recientoris Aevi*. Volume III (1503–1592). (Munich: Sumptibus et Typis Librariae Regensbergianae, 1935). |
| Galli | P. A. Galli, *Notizie intorno alla vera origine, patria, e nascita del Sommo Pontefice Sisto V* (Ripatransone: Valenti, 1754). |
| Hübner | J. A. von Hübner, *The Life and Times of Sixtus the Fifth* (London: Longmans Green & Company, 1872), 2 vols. |
| Massimo | Marchese Massimo Taparelli Azeglio, *Recollections of Massimo D'Azeglio*. Trans. Count Andrea Maffei (London: Chapman & Hall, 1868). |
| Narducci | E. Narducci, *Catalogo di manoscritti ora posseduti da D. Baldassare Boncompagni* (Roma: 1892²). |
| NCE | *New Catholic Encyclopedia* (New York: McGraw Hill, 1966). |
| NCMH | *New Cambridge Modern History* (Cambridge: CUP, 1957–1979), 14 vols. |

*Abbreviations*

ODCC — F. L. Cross & E. A. Livingstone, *The Oxford Dictionary of the Christian Church* (Oxford: OUP, 1974).

Pastor — L. von Pastor, *The History of the Popes from the Close of the Middle Ages* (London: J. Hodges, 1938), 40 vols.

*Pont. Max.* — Anon, *Sixtus V Pontifex Maximus.* Written after the Pope's death. Archivio Segreto Vaticano, Armadio 11, Tomo 61, pp. 45–104.

Prodi — P. Prodi, *The Papal Prince: One Body and Two Souls. The papal monarchy in early modern Europe* (Cambridge: CUP, 1987), 2 vols.

Ranke — L. von Ranke, *History of the Popes: Their Church and State* (Oxford: OUP, 1875).

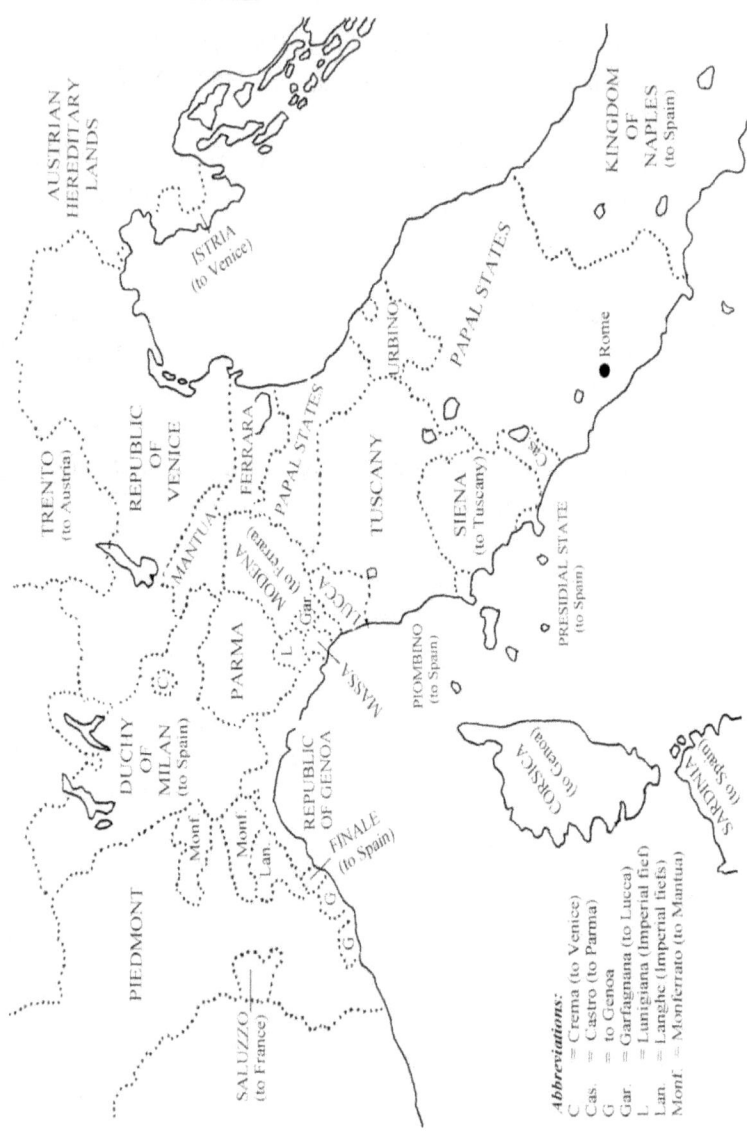

Map of the Papal States and surrounding territories at the time of Pope Sixtus V

# *Preface*

WHEN WE CONSIDER the life of a celebrity—especially a Pope who lived over four hundred years ago—we must not make the mistake of looking at his life with our modern attitudes and prejudices.

There were few Popes from religious orders, and in the previous centuries only Sixtus IV and Nicholas IV had come from the Franciscan Order as Sixtus V was to do. Benedict XII, Eugenius III and Lucius III were Cistercian; Gelasius II, Clement VI and Urban V, Benedictine; Hadrian IV, Augustinian and Innocent V, Benedict XI and Pius V, Dominican.

When a religious assumed the papacy, he inevitably brought with him the customs and attitudes of his vocation. Sixtus' spirit of obedience and particular spirituality would present a challenge to the more worldly Roman court, and he had come from a humble background. In addition, few Popes had been in obscurity—and even disgrace—for fourteen years prior to their election.

Sixtus V has been overshadowed by the more famous Popes, Julius II and Pius V. We know of contemporary biographies, which appear to be official versions of his life, and of the biography by Baron Hübner in the nineteenth century, but there has been only one recent life—in Italian—by Italo de Feo, published in 1987. Modern references to Sixtus tend to draw on the colourful record of Gregory Leti, who was writing in the seventeenth century.[1] He relates for instance that, one night, the Pope disguised himself as a hermit and carrying a large bottle of wine under his cloak, walked to the Colosseum. He encountered a group of bandits and asked them to let him spend the night there. They were roasting meat on a camp fire and he offered them his flask of wine. But the wine was drugged, so one after the other the bandits fell asleep. Sixtus left the Colosseum and signalled to guards waiting outside. The next day, the bandit chief was hanging from a scaffold. It strains credulity that a Pope would walk about Rome in disguise and without a bodyguard, and brings to mind the legends of the Arabian Nights and the secret visits of Sultans to their unsuspecting subjects.

There is no record that Sixtus was ever a swineherd[2] or that his parents came from the Balkans, but one feature of the story rings true, for such were his laws against brigands in the first year of his pontificate that "there were more heads on the Castel Sant'Angelo than melons for sale in the market".[3] His policy spoke, even if he did not actually say the words, "While I live, every criminal must die". This contrasts with Sixtus' fairly relaxed theological attitude (from a former Inquisitor) to heretical opinions.

Legends are, however, seductive. They appeal to the mind far more than the truth—like fairy tales. Sixtus was not colourful in the manner of Julius II. He was not notorious, like Alexander VI. He was not outstandingly holy like Pius V, who, it is said, never spent more than six *giulii* on his meals. Nor was he responsible for the Sistine Chapel, the Sistine Choir or the Ponte Sisto (we must thank Sixtus IV for all these). But as W. T. Selley shows, Sixtus V *was* outstanding in his creation of Renaissance Rome, only fifty years after it had been sacked. He was outstanding, from the point of view of good civic policy and he greatly facilitated the path of pilgrims visiting the churches of Rome.

Sixtus was abstemious and devout, living quietly with his widowed sister and earning the nickname of the Hermit of Villa Montalto. He was also very intelligent in his diplomacy, not allowing the papacy to be over-involved in the expedition of the Armada and playing a waiting game in the matter of Henry III's succession in France, which ultimately curbed Spanish expansionist ambitions. He also reorganized the papal curia, departmentalizing the structure into Congregations and instituting regular *ad limina* visits to Rome (which included visits to the Congregations) by all diocesan bishops.

Selley traces the origins of Sixtus' career and his steady climb to his coming to the notice of powerful figures in the Church. He portrays the Conclave in detail, with particular attention to the individual Cardinals and their loyalties. He also describes the actual ceremonial, the subsequent papal coronation and the procession to St John Lateran. W. T. Selley was very familiar with Roman landmarks and had a feel for the great work of building and restoration which Sixtus set himself. He visited himself all the places in Rome, Venice, Naples and the surrounding countryside associated with Sixtus V. Unfortunately Selley died before he was able to finish his work. This book keeps largely to his text, but some details that have come to light since his death have been added.

Sixtus V was no villain, and perhaps no hero either, but in his five years as Pope he accomplished what few Popes before or since have been able to manage. Like Pope John XXIII, who became Pope at an advanced age, and was also to reign for just five years, he wanted to achieve as much as he could. The result puts Sixtus in the first rank of great reforming Renaissance Popes. It is sad that so many modern references emphasise his shortcomings and pay scant attention to his achievements. Samuel Johnson's words come to mind: "Be kind, ye judges, or at least be just".[4] Sixtus' contribution to papal administration survived virtually intact into our own time. That in itself is remarkable. But you only need to look at so many of the monuments of Rome, the obelisks and fountains, the frescoes and Church façades, to get an awareness of the measure of this Pope. With Sixtus as with Christopher Wren, the architect of St Paul's Cathedral in London, it can be said *Si monumentum requires, circumspice*—if you seek a memorial, look around you.

## Notes

1. G. Leti, *Vita di Sisto V* (Lausanne: 1669), 2 volumes.
2. This is repeated in the *Larousse Encylopaedia of Modern History* (London: Paul Hamlyn, 1964). The *NCE* 13, p. 273 calls his father a field labourer. Some now maintain that the family originally came from Bjelske Kruševice, a village near Bijela (Бијела) in the Bay of Kotor in Montenegro.
3. E. Duffy, *Saints and Sinners. A History of the Popes* (New Haven & London: Yale University Press, 2006), p. 219.
4. S. Johnson, Prologue to H. Kelly, *The Comedy of A Word to the Wise*.

# CHAPTER 1

### Fra Felice

*He was baptized on 26 December 1521 with the name Felice (happy or fortunate). His father liked the sound of the name which would console him for the loss of his own fortune and bring happiness to the whole family.*

Franco Tagliaventi, *Sisto V Papa e Principe* (1969)

MANY ILLUSTRIOUS MEN in history were born to greatness, of distinguished lineages and trod well-documented paths to power. Others were born to obscurity and spent large spans of their lives without note, rising to fame and influence after much of the evidence of their earlier activities was lost in uncertainty. Sixtus V was of the latter kind.

A number of biographies of this Pope were written during his lifetime or shortly after his death, two of them being supposedly corrected by the Pope's own hand. Written by members of the Papal Court or based on information supplied by them, these were often partisan. They described the Pope's achievements without establishing with precision the details of his earlier life. Even these early biographies make mention of his detractor, and somewhat more than seventy years after his death a renegade Calvinist nephew of an Italian Bishop wrote a new life of Sixtus V. Written originally in Italian but published in Switzerland it enjoyed a wide circulation and was subsequently translated into other languages. The author's lively imagination embroidered many of the incidents of the Pope's life with shameless invention and presented him in a critical and often damagingly disparaging light. The centenary of Sixtus' reign, coinciding with a fresh crisis for Protestantism in Europe, produced other attacks on his character and political pretensions, particularly in English. In the middle of the eighteenth century two new biographers searched the evidence then available with conspicuous diligence and re-established Sixtus V's reputation as one of the outstanding statesmen of the sixteenth century. In the nineteenth century the great German historian, von Ranke, was given access to the Papal records and wrote a fresh and judicious account of Sixtus's reign. Some forty years later, at the time when the Papal States were being embodied in the new Kingdom of Italy, an Austrian ambassador in Paris wrote yet another biography of Sixtus based on records available in Rome, with an emphasis on the diplomatic history of his reign. Almost simultaneously, Ludwig von Pastor was compiling his magnificently documented History of the Popes and devoted his attention to Sixtus' reign with great skill. In the 1920's new excursions into the records of Sixtus V's native country, stimulated by the fourth centenary of his birth, threw fresh light on his career, especially on his early years.

This wealth of material notwithstanding, the historian must content himself so far as the Pope's earlier career is concerned, with a limited number of authenticated facts scattered among considerable amounts of ignorance or uncertainty, punctuated by claims and counterclaims. Moreover, he is left substantially dependent on the contemporary writings of Sixtus' admirers who, influenced by hindsight and dazzled by his brilliant reign, were prepared to give literary currency to legends, which the present day finds unacceptable. Thus the date and place of Sixtus' birth, even the family name, are alike open to dispute; many of his family connections are uncertain, and the detail of incidents in his early life confused. The temptation to speculate beyond the authorised fact has firmly to be resisted.

*Fra Felice*

It is now generally, but not unanimously, agreed, that the future Sixtus V, Felice Peretti, was born on December 13th, 1521 at Grottamare. Grottamare was a small port of declining importance at the mouth of the Tesino, one of several rivers traversing the Marches from the foothills of the Apennines to the Adriatic coast of Italy. The town lay at the head of fertile fields on a small plateau, from which steep cliffs fell into the coastal valley below, and steadily climbing, ill-maintained roads led to the hills to the west. Transport by water was easier and cheaper than by road and when commercial dealings were on a small scale and boats were tiny, even the facilities of old-fashioned ports were valuable. Grottamare probably had a few hundred inhabitants and was a closely-knit community, largely self-managing—governing would be too pretentious a term. On the site of the cottage where Felice was born his sister later erected the church of Santa Lucia with the authority of one of his successors. It still stands, but nowadays is the venue for music recitals and said to have an excellent acoustic.

At the time of Felice's birth the Marches were the richest region of the Papal States, in some senses the Italian Cotswolds, a prosperous agricultural territory with compact, well-organised towns dotted on the summits of the hills. It was a region of peasant smallholders, holding their land by a variety of tenures, often by *mezzadria*, a system by which the landlord provided not only the land, but often stock and seed, taking annually in return a proportion of the yield. The capital of the region was Ancona, one of the leading ports of Adriatic Italy, and the equal in trade of Livorno on the Mediterranean. It had a substantial entrepot trade between Florence in the West and Ragusa in the East, from which connections were made with well-established land routes to Central Europe and the Middle East respectively. A city of perhaps 20,000 people with highly developed port facilities, impressive communal buildings, and churches of note and distinction, it was able to compete on a limited scale with the mighty Venetian Republic. The prosperity of Ancona provided a sustained outlet for the products of its hinterland. Ascoli, 60 or 70 miles or so to the south, was one of the leading industrial centres; Fabriana to the south-west was famous throughout Italy for its paper manufacture. Recanati twenty miles or so the south, had a fair of widespread fame which lasted for 15 days in each year. In times of prosperity a brisk trade existed at the markets of a number of these foothill towns. The wealthy had extensive lands and well furnished but modest palazzi; towns were closely integrated with the surrounding country. Grain was grown extensively on hill and in the plain; the ubiquitous vine was complemented by the olive tree, and cattle, pigs and sheep were kept extensively. Fields on the top of the steep-sided slopes were fertile and responded well to intensive cultivation, but rock was rarely far from the surface, and good crops were dependent on satisfactory spring rains and the preservation of the soil from erosion when mountain streams frequently reached torrential force. An expanding population exerted strong pressure on land and produced an eternal temptation to sub-divide the holdings until they ceased to be economic, a process which tended to widen the gap between rich and poor, leaving the latter increasingly depressed and dispirited. Periodically, pestilences decimated the villages, whilst the ravages of predatory bandits—often in the pay of distant nobles—were perpetual hazards. Prosperity and poverty succeeded each other with alarming rapidity. Although wealthy merchants existed in this rich countryside, many of the inhabitants were engaged in a relentless struggle for subsistence and had little capital to accumulate from one generation to the next.

Felice's father, Piergentile di Giacomo, and his family belonged to Montalto, a larger edition of Grottamare, a walled town, some thirty miles inland from Grottamare and high in the Apennine foothills. The supposition that the family had migrated from the Eastern Adriatic before the Turkish invaders in the middle of the fifteenth century rests on a Papal Bull which cannot now be found, and on Sixtus' interest in the rebuilding of the Church of San Girolamo degli Schiavoni in Rome, facing the port of Ripetta, which lay alongside the present

Ponte Cavour. It is more probable that the family had been settled at Montalto for at least a century. Certainly Felice's grandfather and great-grandfather had been men of substance and reputation there, the former being a stone-mason whom hard times reduced to a jobbing labourer, and who nevertheless became head of the local magistracy a year before Felice's birth. For some unidentified reason Felice's father, Peretti, left the ancestral homeland and after wandering for some time in the upland countryside, settled at Camerino, some fifty miles to the north-west where he married Mariana probably in the early years of the sixteenth century. Camerino was a small but important Apennine town with an established reputation for its shoe manufacture, well situated on a tributary of the Chienti, and on the land route from the Adriatic coast to Foligono and Perugia, key points in the mountain area of central Italy, from which the road led on to Rome. Along this route flocked traders, couriers and hundreds of pilgrims making their journey to Rome from the sanctuary of Loreto, fifteen miles south of Ancona. Though a later rumour tried to establish an association with the Ricci family, one of the very famous and powerful families of Italy, the social position of Mariana's family was, in fact, comparable with her husband's. One of Sixtus' contemporary biographers relates that fortified by his wife's dowry, Peretti recovered his self esteem, returned to his family territory and settled at Grottamare. There he cultivated land leased from Ludovico Vecchio da Fermo, for whom he may also have worked as a labourer, and Mariana was engaged in domestic service to Ludovico's daughter-in-law, Diana.

In 1517, four years before Felice's birth, as a result of Pope Leo X trying to deprive Francesco Maria della Rovere of the Duchy of Urbino over which he had ruled for nine years, the Marches were extensively ravaged. Montalto was sacked, the town walls destroyed, the streets devastated and many houses pillaged. The trail of destruction reached almost to the gates of Ancona. How far Peretti's slender fortunes suffered cannot be known, but it is certain that at the time of Felice's birth he was in serous straits, probably in debt. He already had three children, a son and two daughters; the elder daughter died "at a tender age" and the younger, Camilla, was two years senior to Felice.[1] Subsequently Mariana da Frontillo bore Peretti three more children, all sons. One of the sons named Prospero—whether senior or junior to Felice is unknown, survived to manhood and became one of the mainstays of the family. Of the other sons one died in infancy, and nothing is known of the other. Infant mortality in Italy as elsewhere in Europe was very high; living conditions of the poor in the Marches were primitive, sanitation was elementary and medical services exceedingly sparse, midwifery being generally practised by good natured and experienced housewives. It would not therefore be surprising that Peretti's family should produce only 3 children to live to adulthood, of whom one died in his early forties. Camilla proved to be long-lived, dying in 1605 at the age of eighty-six. Felice therefore, knew well the pangs of poverty and realised how easily even large families were decimated by infant deaths and the ravages of disease. Biographers writing whilst Sixtus reigned as Pope record that his father was forewarned by providence of his second son's future greatness and was instructed accordingly to call him Felice; this he faithfully observed, insisting on this name at the baptismal ceremony against the protestations of the friends present. The biographers relate how the child was miraculously saved from death by burning when his busy mother left a lighted candle near his cradle, which started a blaze from which he was rescued in the nick of time. Later he was almost drowned in a pond and was saved a second time.

The Pope himself made no secret later of the humble circumstances in which he grew up nor of his parents' poverty. His father toiled on the land and it is not improbable that his small son, like his elders, helped with such tasks as they could master, but the Pope vehemently denied that his father had ever been a swineherd by profession.

Very early in his career, he developed a keen appetite for learning and taught himself the rudiments from primers borrowed from children returning from school across the fields. His father was unable to pay even the modest fee demanded by the local schoolmaster, so he approached the boy's uncle, Fra Salvatore, *guardiano* (warden) of the Franciscan friary a mile or so outside the town of Montalto. Argument and counter-argument have failed to establish convincingly whether Fra Salvatore was brother to Peretti or to Mariana. Fra Salvatore agreed to pay the fee and Felice attended school. Soon, however, according to one of the contemporary biographers the schoolmaster found himself devoting so much time and attention to this willing pupil that others were neglected. Thereupon Fra Salvatore took the boy then aged nine to live in the friary so that his education could proceed. The friary, standing on a spur of the mountains a mile to the west of the town, overlooked the valley of the Aso, and was founded during the lifetime of St Francis in 1215. Fra Salvatore is likely to have entered it at an early age, for he celebrated his first Mass in 1517. By the time he took Felice under his charge he was guardiano, having charge and direction of the friary whose members are unlikely to have exceeded a dozen, three or four would appear much more probable.

Thus Felice returned to the ancestral township where lived three of his aunts, all of whom later married into Montalto families of the lesser grade, and which his father never quite deserted for he was in the township in 1510, in 1516, in 1528 and in 1531.

Montalto was a compact town situated on a hill, 1,700 feet high, with steep craggy sides, and surrounded by lofty stone walls pierced by two gateways; the administrative centre of an area with dependent villages in the river valleys below. Its houses were small and closely packed, with few inhabitants; a township of limited wealth and resources (the present population is only 2,345) with few churches and fewer palazzi of distinction. But it preserved a large measure of independence, electing its chief magistrate (or Potestà), and its senior administrator (or Sindaco), annually. The few rich families possessed great reputations and influence in the locality; the majority of the citizens were small freeholders, or lived by cultivating land of restricted size but notable fertility, held on lease, either on the hill or in the valley below where they grew grapes, olives, nuts and grain. It was a closely-knit community, wholly dependent on the land, whose people shared an intimacy spiced with rivalry or dissension, and the common misfortunes of pestilence and famine. Felice developed a deep and enduring affection for the town, taking its name when he was appointed Cardinal and raising it to the status of a city when Pope and throughout his life he retained close contact with his many relatives, guaranteeing their property transactions, attending their weddings, providing their dowries.

In 1533 Felice began his novitiate in the Franciscan order and a year later aged thirteen took his vows. At this time, on the evidence of a statement prepared by Felice himself in 1564, his "father was banished, his goods were confiscated". The cause of that situation is not known, though it is conceivably connected with the transfer of the administration of Ancona to direct papal control. The ceremony of the taking of vows—of chastity, of obedience to the Superiors of the Order, and of poverty—would be held in the chapel of the convent; the ceremony without any prescribed form might be conducted by the Provincial General or some representative of his, perhaps by the guardiano. In a friary as small as that at Montalto, the admission of new members would be sufficiently rare to cause a stir and probably to justify the attendance of brethren from other houses in the vicinity. It would be attended by Felice's relatives and family friends, and would be impressive in its austere simplicity and its resounding finality, for this would be the boy's last opportunity to withdraw from the Order, its tenets and principles, without disgrace or reproof except with the Minister General's special authority.

It seems unlikely that his father could have attended this ceremony if he was outlawed, yet Sixtus' biographer records that he insisted on the use of Felice as the boy's name and from then on he was known as Fra Felice. As a mark of respect for Felice's father and relatives, and because of his devotion to the Catholic faith and his esteem for the Franciscan order the grey robe of a friar was provided for the boy by Rogatus Rosatius, a member of Montalto's chief family with considerable possessions in the neighbouring country and beyond.

Fra Salvatore is portrayed by the Pope's biographer as an old man, though probably he was not yet forty. He is described as a jealous priest of wise and long established habits, a man of few words and of a severe nature; he was exacting in his demands on Felice, who became his attendant, and made little allowance for his youth and frailty. A cuff on the ears was punishment for spilling his uncle's food at table or failing to bring him sufficient. But such discipline in no way embittered relations between the two, for Felice retained a high regard for Salvatore and in later life entrusted many of his personal affairs to him.

Felice now gave himself readily to unremitting study; twice a day he was sent to the local school in Montalto, where he met masters no less severe and demanding than Salvatore. First, under Vicenzo Ferneto da Montedinove, then under Napulio Filarete da S. Vittoria, and finally under Pio Ottaviano Umili da Patrignone, he mastered the elements of Latin grammar and proceeded to study philosophy and theology. He learned "with incredible speed" as willing pupils often do from skilful teachers, and quickly acquired a facility in using the precepts of Cicero, Quintillian and Demosthenes to develop his oratory. Thus this eager boy in his teens grew up in a tiny earnest community, moving easily and gracefully in and out of the small hill town where his relatives lived as well-respected and reputable citizens. But even the modest prosperity they knew was liable to continued threats and sharp changes of fortune.

As a novice Felice was probably adequately fed but not well clothed; certainly he was clever, sharp-witted, quick to learn and closely-wedded to his books, perhaps too pre-occupied to be mischievous. Accustomed to austerity and chastened by a stern discipline not devoid of affection, he may have been introspective and detached.

Felice was now bound for his lifetime to religion and the Franciscan order by the strictest possible vows. This may seem to have had a daunting if not terrifying finality for a boy so young. The practice was however not unusual at that date, and thirty years were to pass before the Council of Trent dealt with this abuse. In any event, the Peretti family were already associated with the Order and there is nowhere in his life any suggestion that Felice subsequently had the slightest misgiving about his admission.

Assisi was only some seventy miles from Montalto and the whole region of the Marches had fallen under the personal influence of St Francis during his lifetime. This had been largely maintained throughout the centuries that had followed. Recent events had re-kindled the energies of the friars in the area, and an atmosphere of spiritual ferment was abroad. Felice thus joined the Franciscan Order at a time of intense and turbulent spiritual ferment.

Firstly, humanism had been present throughout Italy for something like a century, on the one hand enriching the study of Biblical texts, and the works of the Church Fathers, on the other engendering a rationalistic scepticism, a disposition to doubt many of the dogmas held sacred for centuries. Spreading from the Universities of Bologna and Padua, from the schools of dozens of towns the teaching of humanist scholars was disseminated far and wide. Many of their audiences were disillusioned by controversies with which they were intellectually incapable of wrestling. Probably nothing was more surely calculated to undermine the faith of simple folk than ambiguity and wavering uncertainty amongst their betters. Within the Church there were a number of Catholic evangelicals who were regarded by many of the orthodox as little better than heretics. The Franciscan Conventuals were widely suspected of abetting these deviants, and Carafa, a former Archbishop of Brindisi and one of the founders of the Theatines, a newly established Order, who would become Pope Paul IV and a powerful figure in the reform movement would have welcomed their suppression.

Secondly, the Catholic Church of the thirties faced the most serious schism in its history. The Lutheran Reformation challenged the authority of the Roman Catholic Church in fundamentals and by 1534, compared with previous heretical movements it had at least in Germany an unprecedented appearance of permanence, stability and acceptability. Calvin in France and Zwingli in Switzerland had begun to accentuate the Lutheran undermining of established ecclesiastical authority and were gathering congregations of enthusiastic followers. Basically the Reformers championed the authority of the individual conscience and personal spiritual experience against established tradition and the prerogative of the priesthood. Salvation came by faith through God-given grace. More immediately the doubt cast on the Real Presence, the ministration of Holy Communion in two kinds and the reduction of the sacraments to two all tended to diminish the status of the priest. To the regular Orders the demand for marriage of clergy was a particular and fundamental challenge.

In addition, however, the Franciscan Order had controversies of its own. During the past two centuries there had been almost continuous and often bitter public strife between the followers of St Francis. In particular there were disputes about the interpretation of the oath of poverty. These who wished to follow their Founder strictly condemned the ownership of possessions not merely by individual members, but by the Order corporately. Others, as conscientiously believed that ownership could be justified by the purposes it sustained and were disposed to take a less rigid and formal judgment of conduct generally (Conventuals numbered 25,000 in 1517 and 20,000 in 1600). Many whose devotion to the Order had waned, found refuge and convenient justification behind the contentions of the less inflexible members of their Order. In sheer despair of an amicable settlement of these issues Pope Leo X as recently as 1517 had recognised the stricter section of the Order as a separate and independent family by the Bull *Ite et vos in vineam meam* to be known as the Observants with a General, a discipline and habit of their own.

Even this failed to satisfy the more extreme members of the Observants. Fra Bonaventura, after some years at the head of a dissident faction within the Observant house of St Francesco della Vigna in Venice was allowed to set up a separate house and Matteo di Bassi of Urbino, another Observant, in 1525 founded groups of his followers as a new Order which the Pope recognised three years later. The severity of the Capuchins, as they were known and their punctilious observance of the rule of St Francis rapidly attracted large numbers of convents mainly from the Observants. The new Order flourished, creating a spiritual stir and some animosity within the whole Franciscan family. By 1534 they had six or seven hundred members in all quarters of the Italian peninsula and were organised in twelve provinces.

However, all Friars combined contemplation in private with determined action in the world. Temptations were to be met not avoided, doubts to be resolved not stifled. They were realists not escapists. The basis of their activities was strict, prolonged and fundamental training, both spiritual and intellectual, so that piety should be matched with deep thinking and unflinching mental scrutiny.

The young Felice, therefore, entered the Order when the interpretation of the wishes of St Francis was much in debate and when the dangers of schism and fragmentation were inescapable matters of discussion, highly confusing and provocative to a boy so young and inexperienced.

Leaving Montalto, therefore, in 1537 (at the same period as friaries of his own Order were being suppressed by Henry VIII in England), Felice was committed to ten years of severe and exacting religious and academic training—a sort of extended sandwich course in which the practice of the faith was combined inextricably with the firm discipline of scholastic rigour. There is again some doubt of where he spent the next three years. Tempesti states that he went to Pesaro for a year and then to Iesi for two: other writers say this period was spent at Fermo. In 1540 he proceeded to the University of Ferrara where he remained three years before going to the University of Bologna for a year and a half. Relations between Universities and the Religious Orders at this time were fluid. The former had established a large measure of independence not only of the bishops, but of the Papacy also. They were guilds comprising masters and students with the former having duties of teaching and of sitting as assessors for the granting of degrees. Teaching was a highly personal interchange of information, intellectual technique and scholastic judgment between the master and small groups of pupils, often as small as five. The activities of the master were supplemented by a kind of journeyman with a bachelor's degree who, having no permission to teach, repeated in the afternoon the substance of the lecture delivered by the master in the morning, a great deal of this being committed to memory. Men in Orders were debarred from Faculties of Arts in Universities, but having concluded studies in their own schools, were able to proceed to the faculties of divinity or law. There were large numbers of schools providing the *studia generale*, either as preparation for the higher faculties of the University or as autonomous studies pursued for their own interest. The Franciscans maintained a high standard of scholarship with a lector (a graduate at the master's level) in every friary of size, and it was usual for each custody (group of houses) to recognise a particular house as a school for brothers who displayed special promise. Latin was the basis of all study in the arts, for it was the language not only of religious services, but also of the courts, judicial, administrative and diplomatic, and therefore the criterion of promotion in all the professions. Felice would pursue his studies in the seven liberal arts—grammar, rhetoric and logic constituting the *trivium*; the more scientific subjects—arithmetic, geometry, astronomy, together with music constituting the *quadrivium*. There were set books in each subject and a number of summaries and compendia had been published to assist the student. There were also weekly disputations to attend when masters engaged in verbal duels with each other, the students listening and perhaps making their own interventions. At Ferrara University he was promoted to the faculty of theology, Master Bartolomeo Golfi da Pergola, subsequently famed as a theologian at the Council of Trent, being regent of studies in the Franciscan Convent of that town. At Bologna University he made a special study of metaphysics under the direction of Giovanni da Correggio, an eminent Franciscan Professor of Metaphysics of considerable repute, subsequently Minister of the Province of Bologna and theologian at the Council of Trent. Felice was a diligent and methodical student, for later he used his own example to encourage others by recalling how he used to study at night by the dim light of the cloister, and finally by the light of the sanctuary lamp burning perpetually before the Eucharist.

He was then sent as a conventual bachelor to the Franciscan friary at Rimini, and after three years there he went in a similar capacity to Siena, assisting the Master, Alessandro da Montefalco, and serving as tutor to the Master's pupils in those studies through which he himself had already passed.

In 1548 he proceeded to the degrees of both Master and Doctor within four days. Felice was now twenty-seven, perhaps somewhat older than the average age, having concluded eleven years of systematic and rigorous study. The ceremony of entering on his master's degree took place in the Franciscan Church at Fermo, a place for which he retained a permanent regard. Presumably having received the cap and ring after Mass, he was required to engage in a disputation with a number of masters in front of a large audience—a testing ordeal calculated to stretch a friar's mettle to the limit. One of his biographers records that "having explained with lucidity and subtlety [some] very difficult questions which had been put forward he was made a master of theology with the warm approval of all." The ceremony of advancing to the doctor's degree four days later was no doubt similar but presumably still more exacting and difficult:his performance must have been equally successful, for the vote to promote him was unanimous. Doctor's degrees in Divinity were obtained by only a small minority. Felice was now a fully-fledged teacher, highly qualified and very well experienced. He must have had fluency and command in Latin, a critical knowledge of the Fathers and of the current theological conflicts, and a deep attachment to his Order and the principles of its founder. In the full flush of manhood he was equipped scholastically for his career in the Order.

This period of his life was crowded with incident—Ferrara was one of the most distinguished cities of Italy noted for its lavish and highly cultured court, the performances at its ducal theatre, its famous school and University, and its open door to thinkers of all shades of opinion. Its duchess, Renée of France, patronised the arts and protected writers generally regarded as heretical, even accommodating Calvin himself only three years before Felice's arrival there. Its intellectual and cultural atmosphere was electric, and the city deeply suspected by the Papal authorities. Bologna also encouraged progressive thinking and was well known as a centre of humanist activity. No cities could have been chosen to challenge more thoroughly the convictions and personal integrity of the young friar. The challenge was accentuated by the effects of the apostasy in 1542 of Bernardino of Ochino, the Vicar-General of the Capuchin branch of the Franciscan Order. Ochino, who had been described as the most renowned preacher of his time,[2] was a scholar and administrator in the new Order devoted to the revival of the Franciscan ideals in their severest austerity and had been elected Vicar-General for a second term only the previous year. He was suspected of heretical views, had been summoned to Rome for examination. He promptly fled to Switzerland, where he was welcomed by Calvin. He travelled to England in 1547 during the regency of Edward VI. There he wrote a play in which the Pope appears as the Antichrist. He eventually joined the Moravian Brethren in Germany and died in 1564.

This was a scandal without parallel, which left its mark upon the whole future of the Catholic reformation in Italy. For the Capuchin branch of the Franciscan Order it was a disaster; its return to the original austerity of St Francis was discredited and the support it had won from the Pope was undermined. The whole Franciscan Order was smitten with a deep sense of shame and failure and the downfall of so eminent and devout a leader placed others under grave suspicion and spread uneasiness and alarm in the Order. The dissolution of the Capuchins seemed imminent, but the skill and diplomacy of the Protector of the Franciscan Order, Cardinal Carpi, enabled it to weather the storm and indeed to recover its former vitality and prestige. Since Capuchins were largely drawn from the ranks of the Observants, it is unlikely that a friar so earnestly engaged in the search for truth as Felice could escape the perplexity to which this astonishing event gave rise.

Shortly after Felice reached Bologna the city was visited by Pope Paul III who was returning from Busseto where he had been negotiating with the Emperor Charles V in an attempt to withdraw the Papal States from involvement in Franco-Imperial rivalries. The Pope was accompanied by an immense mule train carrying a substantial retinue of church officials, the papal kitchen, dining room, and personal quarters for the Pope and his attendants. A member of the noble and powerful Farnese family, the Pope now aged seventy-five, favoured ecclesiastical reform and was a warm promoter of the development of the religious Orders. Only the previous year he had established the Congregation of the Holy Office and endowed it with wide powers to hunt heresy and control the printing presses. A papal visit must inevitably have created a great stir for both the University and the Franciscan friary, one of the great centres of the Province of Bologna. Unfortunately no diary of Felice has survived and there is no record of his impressions of the visit though it can almost be assumed that he saw the Pope.[3]

Meanwhile, his sister Camilla, to whom he was always deeply attached, had married Giovanni Battista Mignura, a well-known citizen of Montalto. Felice's father was joined by his uncle, Fra Salvatore, in providing Camilla's dowry, the final payment being made in 1543—evidence that Peretti, Felice's father, whatever his social situation twenty years earlier, was now re-established.

For Franciscans scholarship and learning were no cloistered virtues but preparation for activity in the world at large. Even though preaching never achieved amongst the Franciscans quite the supremacy given it by the Dominicans, and though distinguished preaching was even more characteristic of the Observants than of the Conventuals nevertheless Felice's branch of the Order could boast some very eminent exponents of the preachers' art such as Fra Giuseppe da Fermo and Fra Cherubino da Maria, his contemporaries who were making for themselves a great reputation over large areas.

Franciscan establishments were planted in the towns where audiences were readily gathered, their churches were designed to accommodate a vast congregation, and a lively preacher would almost unfailingly attract his audience from many miles afield. Once launched in the pulpit, they could stimulate the naturally responsive instincts of people living near the soil, give assurance in the light of human destiny, bring comfort in the hour of trial and death, encourage integrity in human conduct and probity in social dealings. Preachers could exercise influence, mould opinion and shape action. So Felice made his debut in the pulpit whilst still a student in the friary of Fermo and before he had said his first Mass, as one of the contemporary biographers records. He preached first at Montepagano little more than an Apennine village, a hundred miles to the south of his friary; he doubtless tramped his way on foot, calling at Franciscan houses or other religious establishments en route. Whilst a student at Ferrara and Bologna he preached in neighbouring centres and then whilst engaged as Conventual bachelor at the Rimini friary he preached the festival sermons in his own friary and then at Macerata—a larger and more important township and site of a diocese, and at Ascoli Piceno, the social centre of his native country, one of the leading towns of the Marches which possessed one of the larger Franciscan houses.

One of the decisive events of Felice's career took place in 1549. The General Chapter of the Conventual branch of the Order was held every third year, when the Minister-General of the Order was elected for a three-year period, the state of the Order reviewed, and problems discussed and resolved. Each of the thirty provinces would be represented and the chief officers—Protector, Minister-General, Procurator, Provincial Generals—were expected to attend. This particular General Chapter was held at Assisi, the mother church and friary of the Order and its spiritual home, meeting there for the twenty-fourth time in almost two and a half centuries. Felice, then Regent of Studies at Siena, in the Franciscan province of Tuscany, attended. The position of Regent was an important one with status within the Order equivalent to that of Professor in a University. It entailed directing the studies of intellectually able and promising members of the Order drawn from families within a considerable area so that the best of them would in turn advance to degrees as bachelors, masters or even doctors. Great emphasis was laid on intellect, scholarship and rigour of thought in the Franciscan Order and a high standard of systematic and ordered training in learning was demanded.

A certain Persico of Calabria whose reputation was widespread in neighbouring Perugia as a progressive thinker and follower of Telesio was at the Chapter. The latter was outspokenly critical of Aristotelian philosophy, generally accepted at the time, and a strong supporter of empirical observation. His writings were subsequently placed on the Index. The importance of the occasion was fully recognised. The Protector of the Order, Cardinal Carpi, wrote to Bonaventura Pio Fauni da Costacciaro, the Minister-General, recommending him to select carefully from the most well-tried, those who should defend the faith and to choose someone with "fluency of language and agility of mind" to oppose Persico. The Minister-General chose Felice for this exacting task. Felice held the orthodox position, overcame his opponent with some distinction and was admired by all the spectators. He attracted the attention of the Protector of the Order, Cardinal

Carpi, who became his firm and consistent supporter. The biographer of Sixtus records that Carpi recommended Felice to the Minister-General as a character "to be nourished and favoured" and gave the young friar his personal encouragement to pursue his studies diligently and with assurance of a distinguished future. Carpi, a most distinguished and scholarly Bishop and Cardinal, who had served successive Popes as skilful diplomat and Nuncio, a man with an international political fame, had been Protector of the whole Franciscan Order for eight years. He had taken a vigorous but statesmanlike attitude to Ochino's apostasy and was respected for his high principle, probity of conduct and zeal for the Church. That so eminent a Catholic statesman should take notice of a young scholastic tutor in the Order, aged only twenty-eight, suggests not only that Felice already had outstanding qualities but also that the leaders of the Church were observant, sympathetic and helpful to young men who seemed capable of contributing to the revival of religion.

Felice was appointed Regent at the Franciscan friary at Fermo where he had spent so much time as a student, and he may have taken up this appointment perhaps on a temporary or short-term basis. Carpi took the initiative to have him appointed Regent of Studies at the important friary of Macerato in the custody of Camerino, his mother's native township.

Already, however, Felice's rapid progress and reputation were resisted by envious members, perhaps by conservative traditionalists in the Order. The General of the Province, the Marches, opposed the appointment with such force that Felice did not take it up, bearing this disappointment with equanimity. However, when this slight to his protégé came to the Protector's ears, he recommended the General of the Order, Iohannes Iacobus Passeni, to provide some compensation to the injured friar, and Felice was appointed Disputator and Regent of Studies at Siena where he had already served as a Conventual-bachelor before obtaining his degrees. The office of Conventual-bachelor was a half-way stage to that of Regent and gave no authority to teach but only to supervise. A young man, twenty-nine years of age, was appointed to a very senior and important academic post in circumstances which could easily prove damaging to him. The Protector of the whole Order, a man of very great distinction, skill and integrity, secured Felice's promotion by direct intervention with the General of the Order. Although, the Provincial General of the Marches had succeeded in excluding this young, promising friar from his own province, that triumph was considerably dimmed by this appointment to a post of at least equal importance, though at a considerable distance and in another state.

Siena was the spiritual home of St Bernardine, one of the most famous of fifteenth-century preachers, to whom a commemorative Oratory had been built, not far from the Basilica of St Francis. Even though St Bernardine had belonged to the Observant branch of the Franciscan Order, his example and influence would inevitably make an impression on Felice, the conventual friary was a house of considerable size in a University town, so for the erudite friar, scholastic responsibility and opportunity were well matched. He now had charge of the most promising friars in a large and important province and was able to direct their intellectual and spiritual development. Siena was politically a notably unstable city whose radical adherence to autonomy produced recurring agitation and discontent. Recognised by the Emperor, Charles V, as a free city in 1522, its relations with Tuscany were continuously embittered (as Siena always suspected its neighbour of designing to annexe it) and Siena was constantly accused of harbouring exiles from Florence. In 1549 Spanish soldiers from Naples, in collaboration with Cosimo Duke of Tuscany, occupied Siena and one of the contemporary biographers of Felice states that on that account he left the city. He appears to have returned, however, and to have lived through recurring conflicts, for as he finished his three-year assignment there, the Spaniards were expelled. Perhaps this was his introduction to the frustrating entanglements of Italian politics and the sense of relief with which he left the city may have continued and become more important in later life. Whilst Regent at Siena he received a special invitation from the Bishop of Camerino to preach the Lenten sermons in his Cathedral and was received with great acclaim. Friars were in any event forbidden to preach in churches within diocesan control without the Bishop's consent, but the incident is recorded in Felice's notebook as if it were a particular direct invitation extended to him on the Bishop's initiative. He also preached in Belforte, and his fame quickly spread through the whole of the Marches. By this time, possibly considerably earlier, Felice's father and mother had returned from Grottamare to Montalto, but they were still plagued by poverty and his father's name appears in a list of debtors to the commune authority.

At this time Felice was entrusted by the Provincial Minister of the Marches with administrative duties of increasing importance. He was commissioned to free a member of the Order from the Vice-Legate's (the representative of the Pope's civil powers) prison in Fermo and presumably was engaged in one of those disputes with the civil authority, which so frequently punctuated the history of the Orders. He was authorised to inspect the friaries in the whole distinct of Ascoli, to reinstate brothers at two houses and to examine the accounts of one of them. These duties he must have discharged satisfactorily for, whilst still in office at Siena, he was empowered to carry out visitations through Montefeltre, Caglia and Urbino. He was also commissioned by Cardinal Carpi, Protector of the Order, to settle a dispute between the guardian or head of one of the friaries with his kitchen superintendent.[4] Felice was establishing a reputation as a friar of determination, decision and firmness of judgement, who could be entrusted with important and difficult tasks where impartiality and integrity were needed. These duties and his preaching engagements were carrying him far afield and as he probably covered many of these journeys on foot, his powers of physical endurance were rapidly tested and developed.

At this time also the General Council, which was engaged in a thorough on-going revision of the Church's doctrine, discipline and organisation, was re-convened and met at Trent, a secluded city state tucked away in the shadow of the Dolomites on the borders of Austria and the Republic of Venice. Felice had such a reputation for scholarship and dialectical skill that he was one of six conventual Franciscans appointed as Theologian to the Council, serving with the Vicar-General of the Order, the Bishop of Monopoli, the Regent of Milan and other notables, though there is some doubt that he actually attended at Trent.

Personal reward for Felice's scholarship came in 1552—a landmark in his career. He was invited by the Cardinal Protector to preach the Lenten sermons in Santi Apostoli—the headquarters of the Order—in Rome. The journey from Siena to Rome—220 miles—led him through the city of Viterbo by one of the great highways of Western Italy. At intervals he would pass staging posts for the regular couriers and find himself mingling with crowds of travellers. If his impatience to reach his destination did not deter him, there were numerous Franciscan houses within easy range of his route where he would be welcome. Passing the Vatican Palace and St Peter's, crossing the Tiber by the Ponte S. Angelo, he would arrive in the Piazza Santi Apostoli, almost unnoticed. This journey he made on a horse which he obtained by the support of Cardinal Carpi and against the wishes of Giulio Magnani, the Vicar-General of the Order, himself a distinguished preacher and a theologian at the Council of Trent, who had been appointed Vicar-General on the death of the Minister General, whilst serving as Procurator-General. Following his two years as Vicar-General, he served two terms as Minister General, six years in all, subsequently becoming a Bishop.

Only recently Magnani had bowed to Carpi's influence by appointing Felice to the post of Regent at Siena after the Provincial Minister of the Marches had resisted his appointment to the Regency at Macerata. In his view Felice was not the man to succeed in Rome and

*Fra Felice*

in any event there were more senior friars to be considered. However, the Protector of the Order was unmoved and his secretary advised the Vicar-General of the Cardinal's views and the former "made a virtue of necessity". Two things are clear: Carpi's support for Felice was unreserved and at this stage decisive; secondly, some elements in the Order were unprepared for the rapid advancement of so young a man, brilliant scholar and preacher though he might be. However justified Felice's promotion, and however commendable Carpi's faith in him, the accusation of favouritism was hard to escape.

## Notes

[1] F. Pistolesi in *Sisto V e Montalto da documenti inediti* (Montalto:1920), p. 36 gives the date of Camilla's birth with some reservations as 1523, so making her two years younger than Sixtus but his *La Prima Biografia Auteutrea di Papa Sisto Quinto* (Montalto:1925), p. 8), is categoric in making both Peretti's daughters senior to Felice and all Peretti's younger children males. Tempesti also states that Camilla was two years older than Felice; see C. L. Tempesti, *Storia della vita e geste di Sisto Quinto* (2 vols.) (Roma: a spese di Remondini di Venezia, 1754).

[2] Pastor 21, p. 486–487.

[3] M. L. Ambrosini & M. Willis, *Secret Archives of the Vatican* (New York: Little Brown, 1996), pp. 117–118.

[4] Cugnoni, p. 124.

# CHAPTER 2

### Called to Rome

*Already in 1289, when they had first accepted a representative of the Holy Inquisition on Venetian territory, they had done so only on the understanding that his duties should be those of an examining magistrate rather than of a judge, and that his findings should always be subject to the secular authority.*

John Julius Norwich, *A History of Venice*

WITH A POPULATION estimated at between 40,000 and 50,000, Rome was one of the largest cities in Europe.[1] In Italy it was surpassed by Naples, Venice and Milan but growing at a quite exceptional rate. It was the focal point of Italian communications, linking Naples in the south with Florence, Genoa and Milan in the north, whence arterial land routes led into Central Europe, to Amsterdam, to France, and even to Spain. Roads crossed from Rome over the Apennines to the Adriatic, to Bologna and Venice, and there met sea routes to the East. It had its own Mediterranean port at Civitavecchia, and Ancona served as its port on the Adriatic. Though its population was predominantly Italian, it was a cosmopolitan city in which bankers and merchants were drawn from families belonging to all the major cities of the peninsula. The Papal Court enlisted the resources of large numbers of lay and clerical officials, lawyers and administrators. Near to the Tiber many Italian nobles had raised magnificent palaces such as the Farnese where often immensely valuable classical antiquities and records were collected. But more important still, Rome was a city remarkably popular with visitors from all parts of Europe and with pilgrims, so that the native population is estimated to have been inflated by as much as 30,000 per year. There was little industry either in the city itself or in the neighbouring countryside, though a group of linen workers had their workshops and their residences in the Coliseum. Large numbers of workers were engaged in the food trades as bakers, wine merchants, and many depended on the tourists for their livelihood in hotels and taverns. Tailors, glove-makers and leather workers were also numerous. The city also contained large numbers of workmen in the various building trades, and Renaissance initiatives created a great and continuing demand for skilled labour. But if there was ample evidence of opulence in the city, very many citizens of Rome were extremely poor and its streets were constantly invaded by the irresponsible rabble, and miscreants to be found in any large city of those days. The city was expanding rapidly as people flocked to it from the surrounding countryside and whenever the supply of grain ran thin and famine threatened, acute distress became rapidly widespread. Narrow streets, overhanging gables and crowded conditions added greatly to the hazards of malaria in the low-lying areas where the concentration of population was constantly increasing. Elsewhere in the city there were considerable, handsome parks and areas largely uninhabited, especially in the south and east. The population of the city was most unevenly distributed, and opulence and pitiful penury were never far removed from each other. Above all Rome was a city of churches with the developing St Peter's, on which Michelangelo was heavily engaged, pre-eminent. The fascination of this Christian capital was unconquerable and in the Holy Year, which Peretti had narrowly missed, the number of pilgrims and visitors was estimated at 60–70,000.

The church of Santi Apostoli faced the Piazza Santi Apostoli, one of the large open squares, which were the glory of Rome and essential breathing spaces for its crowded population. It lay close to the heart of the City, a magnificent building dating from the sixth century, and Headquarters of the Franciscan Order, the church being in the direct jurisdiction of the Minister General. Next to it stood the Palace of the Colonna family, one of the most powerful and distinguished amongst the Roman nobility, who over the centuries had maintained a close connection with the church. Within a stone's throw was the Palazzo Venezia, where the Pope was often resident, and a little farther away was the church of Santa Maria sopra Minerva, the Headquarters of the Dominican Order. The church was the largest in Rome apart from the four great basilicas and, with the exception of the apse at the east end, had been wholly rebuilt only seventy years previously. Only a decade after it had been transferred to the Franciscan Order, because of lack of financial resources, the reconstruction had been effected under the direction of the Colonna family and with the support and encouragement of Sixtus IV, the second Franciscan to be elevated to the Papacy and the originator of the Sistine Chapel and Sistine Bridge. It therefore served the parish and was a focal point in the life of the whole area. A striking arcaded portico gave access from the square and opened immediately on to an impressive area almost 200 feet long and nearly 170 feet wide. The chancel was dominated by the baldacchino of Lorenzo di Toledo with four columns of porphyry at each corner and a rich colonnaded canopy, whilst three pairs of granite columns separated nave from aisles. The simplicity of design, the openness of the central space and the impression of loftiness of the nave gave it an unmistakably handsome dignity and an austere magnificence. The preacher would be conscious, as in theatre in the round, of a vast crowd closely packed around him, expectant and responsive. There was always the possibility of controversy ending in violence, and it is said that on the occasion of Felice's visit, guards were placed in the portico ready to deal with any emergency, which might arise.

    The Lenten sermons preceding the greatest of the church's festivals (Easter) were of outstanding importance, and to be invited to give them was a notable honour, outstandingly so for a friar as young as Peretti. The congregation was likely to have been as cosmopolitan as the city itself: doubtless there would be present clerics from a variety of religious Orders, but there would be many lay people too. Some would be there because attendance at Lenten sermons, and particularly those in a church as popular and central as Santi Apostoli was fashionable; others came out of sheer curiosity to listen to this young friar from the Marches whose reputation as a preacher there had already been established; others may have been there simply to watch the spectacle of a large congregation fascinated by the skilled oratorical, perhaps histrionic, technique of a preacher in the best Franciscan tradition; yet others must have been there out of genuine interest, and reverence for religious scholarship. The motives of congregations would be as diverse and variegated as in any other century. It is possible that at some time in the sermon series Michelangelo was found in the congregation. At the time, though he had his workshop in the Baths of Caracalla, he lived within the Santi Apostoli parish. One of the contemporary biographers of Sixtus V records that "Felice seemed greater than was expected to such an extent indeed that although the church of Santi Apostoli was spacious it could not hold the crowd which flocked together so that platforms were built all round from which he might be heard." The sermons were of such length that they were divided into two sessions with an interval between them. There is no record of the subject or substance, except that the contentious topic of predestination was included, though it is recorded that Peretti "scattered the axioms of the Catholic faith in their appropriate context." On the basis of records of other sermons he delivered, however, there is no doubt that he followed strictly orthodox lines, and it is reasonable to assume that he drew heavily on his intimate and extensive knowledge of the Christian fathers and condemned the corruption, laxity and depravity of the times. The emphasis of his sermons was probably on the importance of the Church in man's salvation; individual conscience of itself was capable of distortion, individual interpretation of Scripture was not wholly reliable; man's conduct could not safely be left to direct divine inspiration. Man needed the Church—its teaching, its guidance, its canons, above all the Sacraments, which only the priesthood could administer, and a respect for its divinely recognised authority and a submissiveness to its directions as the expression of the divine will. These sermons were very well received and congregations continued to flood the Church so that it can safely be deduced that Peretti's delivery was compelling, his subject-matter arresting.

One incident which is recorded in the biographies had a considerable significance for Peretti's future career. He had already preached his fortieth sermon and was taking the usual interval in which he sorted notes passed up from members of the congregation requesting special reference to some point or other or to some particular person in distress. One of these notes when opened proved quite exceptional, for someone in the congregation had tabulated a series of points Peretti had made in his various sermons, and against each had written the comment "Thou liest". Taken by surprise Felice, greatly embarrassed and disconcerted, had difficulty in finishing the second part of his sermon and drew it to a premature conclusion.

Felice retired to his cell in the adjoining friary. Accounts of his ensuing actions vary in detail. One states that he sent the friend who had brought the note to him, to Antonio Ghislieri, the Commissioner-General of the Holy Office, the Roman Inquisitor, the future Pius V.[2] A second records that he gave it to the Prior of the Friary who in turn passed it to Cardinal Carpi, the Protector of the Order, another that Felice himself passed it to Cardinal Carpi. All are in agreement that the incident was referred to Ghislieri. Some of these accounts credit Ghislieri with calling on Felice at his room, others say that Felice was summoned to Ghislieri's office. There is general emphasis on the promptness of Ghislieri's action and it is indicated that the interview took place "the same day". On the threshold of his career as a preacher the young Franciscan friar, aged thirty, faced the Dominican Inquisitor-General, seventeen years his senior. Both were children of humble parents, both had joined their respective Orders whilst still tender in years—Felice at the age of twelve, Ghislieri when he was two years older; both had submitted unquestioningly to the most rigid and inflexible discipline, both nursed a consuming passion against heresy. Ghislieri was a fiery, intimidating martinet with knitted eyebrows, deep set eyes and prominent nose and voice, which could strike terror into those he confronted. Even, when fourteen years later he became Pope his life was so strict that he continued to wear a friar's shirt and sandals, fasted regularly and heard Mass daily.[3] He had been Lector (Regional Director of Studies) at Pavia before being appointed Commissioner of the Holy Office in the dioceses of Pavia, Como and Bergamo. There he persecuted the numerous heretics who had invaded the area from Switzerland and Germany with bitter and righteous hatred and dogged persistence and in return moved around in perpetual danger of his life, being shadowed and hunted and on more than one occasion brutally attacked. The close friend and loyal supporter of Cardinal Carafa, the future Pope Paul IV, he was now Commissioner of the Holy Office with responsibility for directing the crusade against heresy throughout the whole of Italy. In Rome his very name was heard with awe or stunning panic as men, even friars, suspected of unorthodoxy were hounded before the inquisitional tribunals and the obdurate were sentenced to do public penance in the church of S. Maria sopra Minerva before being sent to their death. In the cold starkness of Ghislieri's own room, Felice was closely, extensively and relentlessly questioned, but the more incisive the probing the more he was able not only to establish his innocence of any suspicion of unorthodoxy, but also to convince the terrifying Commissioner of his genuine zeal for the faith.

At the end of the interview Ghislieri embraced the young preacher, kissed him profusely and assured him of his confidence. The incident shows how sensitive Felice was of suspicion of unorthodoxy; his immediate recognition of the danger of being watched by the Holy Office, and his intense desire to clear his name, are reminiscent of modern police states. It also highlights his courage and positive preparedness for challenge.

Felice was making his mark in the most influential quarters. His biographers record that he was entertained by three Cardinals and these are thought to have been della Corgna, the nephew of the reigning Pope, Julius III, Carpi the Protector of the Franciscan Order, and Dandini, Protector of the Arch-Confraternity of Santi Apostoli. Such was Felice's success at Santi Apostoli that he was given a pension by the Pope, Julius III (1550–1555), and retained "in the office of public preaching" for a full year. During that time he "read the epistle of St Paul to the Romans three days in every week." This must have brought him to the heart of the Lutheran controversy and the examination of the part played by grace and by works in man's justification. Unfortunately, whereas Luther's Wittenberg lectures were printed very early and the basic theology he set out was elaborated in large number of books and pamphlets published in the subsequent years, Felice published nothing so far as the records show. These gaps in the evidence excite conjecture, but it would be likely that he adhered very strictly to the accepted teaching of the Church.

Religious circles in Rome at this time were dominated by the Holy Office of which Cardinal Carafa was the leading spirit. Ten years earlier Paul III had appointed six Cardinals as Inquisitors-General and assigned to them the direction of efforts to discover and examine heretics whatever rank they held, and to exert the most strenuous efforts to persuade them to abandon their heresy. If they, or their subordinate officers, succeeded, it was still necessary for the Pope to accept the recantation. If they failed, they were empowered to imprison the offenders and to confiscate their goods. They were particularly authorised to act independently of the diocesan authorities, even in cases where the Bishop was competent to take action. The six Cardinal Inquisitors in Rome were empowered to dispose of all appeals from decisions of their subordinates. The newly-organised Holy Office set a premium on energy and incisive initiative. Primarily it was to concentrate on halting and repulsing the advance of heresy in Italy, particularly in the northern cities such as Lucca, Bologna and Ferrara, but it was in no sense restricted to these areas, and quickly it began to push forward its attempts at reconquest far and wide, especially in Central Europe. Cardinal Carafa, now seventy-six, a man of vast experience and powers of decision and action wholly unimpaired by his years, had converted a house into the Head-quarters of the Holy Office at his own expense. He had been a noted and insistent reformer since he was first appointed to a bishopric at the age of twenty-nine: he had been Nuncio in England and Spain, a member of the Oratory of Divine Love and one of the founders of the Theatine Order—both intended to effect the reform of the Church by concentrating on simplicity and austerity of life and by a strict observance of poverty. Purity of conduct, personal piety, absence of extravagance, were beacons in a city like Rome. Nevertheless, these virtues were of themselves insufficient; conviction of belief, unquestioning submission to the Church's teaching, regular and evident attendances at its rites were expected. Carafa was a man of single-mindedness, to whom the objectives were clear, to stem the tide of heresy and then to turn it back. Personally unblemished, he was possessed of a fierce determination which could make him relentless and uncompromising. Meetings of the Holy Office were held at least once in every week, and it is said that on one occasion a large conference attended by the Cardinals of the Holy Office, the generals of the various Orders and many Prelates was held to consider the circumstances in which a Minorite church in the Marches was destroyed by fire, but the host remained unaffected. When the conference found itself puzzled and defeated, Cardinal Carpi insisted on taking Felice so that his opinion should be heard. The conference was convinced, it is said, by the young friar. Even if the detail of the incident might be disputed, its intention of proving the great regard in which Felice was held and the closeness of his relationship to Cardinal Carpi, are clear and likely to be justified.

In his turn Felice must have been impressed with the efforts of the Inquisitor to turn the heretic from his perverted beliefs to persuade him to recant and to save him from final doom. And yet as obstinate and relapsed heretics were led to S. Maria sopra Minerva, the Headquarters of the Dominicans, to be burned with their offending writings or to be executed, he doubtless subscribed to the doctrine of destroying the body to save the souls of the offenders and of many others who might be enhanced by their example.[4]

Modern minds find it difficult to comprehend the significance of preaching four hundred years ago. Despite outstanding figures like Savonarola, Bernardino Ochino and Luther, it remains hard to imagine churches all over the continent crowded to the doors by rich and poor, the politically influential and the insignificant. Oratory, histrionic devices, personal command alone cannot adequately explain; audiences contributed some measure of genuine interest and respect for the subject, a sense of vocation and a receptive atmosphere. Felice was known as a successful and popular preacher in Rome, as he already was throughout the Marches. What is equally difficult to appreciate, however, is that this success had carried him to the centre of Christendom—the Papal Court—and had won for him the support and friendship of its innermost circles. In an age of widespread corruption and venality, when the rich and the patricians had already stamped their image on Rome, religious circles were open without restraint to the humble, the scholarly, the conscientious who would offer the Church devotion, energy and leadership. The only questions left open were how much more had Felice to offer and how far the road would lead him.

During this year spent in Rome, he made contact with several movements, which were to shape the future Counter-Reformation. S. Maria della Strada, the church of the recently-founded Order of Jesuits, with the house of Ignatius Loyola adjacent to it, stood approximately a mere quarter of a mile from Santi Apostoli, and the newly-founded Collegio Romano rather less than half that distance.

The Jesuit Order, recognised by Papal Bull only twelve years earlier, had about 1,000 members, with colleges at Bologna, Messina and Palermo, seven colleges in Spain, one in France, and missions in India, the East Indies and Japan. At Catholic courts and especially amongst the Italian nobility, Jesuits had established themselves in positions of influence and power. Loyola's *Exercises* had become a spiritual training manual for its members and everywhere personal convictions were being integrated in a concentrated loyalty to the Church, to the Pope, to the Order, so that apostasy and apathy were sternly combated, and positive attachment to the established faith deepened. Loyola himself was a model; actuated by deep personal conviction and faith, maintained by rigorous daily meditation and discipline, he was in every sense the General of this militant, expanding Order, demanding not merely support for the faith in areas uninfected by Protestant heresy, but its repudiation in areas still wavering. They were the willing crusaders of the sixteenth century. Their ideals and their success must have appealed to Peretti, and it appears that he and the influential Loyola met each other and shared a common interest in the activities of the Holy Office. Indeed, Peretti was responsible for the foundation of the Confraternity of the Blessed Sacrament, which was later amalgamated with a similar institution founded by Loyola.

Somewhat further away, more down-town, near the arching banks of the Tiber, was another religious coterie of a very different kind, with which Peretti also made contact: Philip Neri, the Florentine mystic, one-time tutor to the two children of the Florentine head of the Customs service. Newly-admitted to the priesthood, Neri was established in a tiny upper-storey chamber of a house adjoining San Girolamo della Carità in the Via dei Pellegrini, with a peaceful view across the Tiber to the Janiculum. Philip was an unusual combination of the pietist, the scholar and the philanthropist. Around him had gathered in the previous decade a group of ardent men drawn from all sections of Roman society. They formed a Confraternity with no intention of founding a new Order, for which they saw no need because of their close connection with the Dominicans whose church, S. Maria sopra Minerva, they frequently attended. They took no special vows, but evolved an ethos by personal example and community of spirit. Philip and his followers laid emphasis on sustained meditation in private, close study of the Scriptures and the Fathers as the basis of personal integrity and devotion. The Oratory itself was an informal study group held in the afternoon, when a book or a piece of ecclesiastical history was systematically studied under the leadership of one of the members. Personal piety inspired charitable work for the poor, especially for pilgrims, hundreds of whom were to be found hungry and footsore in the foyers of the various basilicas, and also promoted relief visits to prisons and hospitals. Philip himself served as a priest in the adjoining church of San Girolamo della Carità and as Superintendent of his followers who served San Giovanni dei Fiorentini a little farther down the Via Giulia and nearer the River Tiber and the Ponte Sant'Angelo. Great pride was taken in promoting pilgrimages to the seven basilicas where crowds frequently followed the Oratorians in going to confession, listening to the sermon of some preacher of repute and receiving communion. The mammoth Sunday service held once in each month was often attended by great crowds of all ranks. The simplicity, informality and friendliness of the Oratorians made a considerable impression in this city of extravagant pomp, vice and corruption. It was easy for Felice to show interest and to develop contact with this body, especially as San Girolamo was a Franciscan church, and though no close friendship developed with Neri their common desire to promote elevation of conduct and sustained discipline created a firm bond of interest and understanding. Both were acutely conscious that many of the Roman populace were seriously disturbed at the immorality and sensuality of the city, and remained inherently attached to the peace and sense of security, which could be derived from the traditional faith. Both Neri and

Felice, neither yet great figures in Rome, were activated by personal initiative and conviction.

During this year spent in Rome, Felice was a frequent visitor to the Palazzo Colonna and tutored Marcantonio, Archbishop of Taranto. His year in the limelight came to an end; he left Rome with his reputation as a scholar and preacher vastly enhanced, with many new and influential friends impressed with his vivacity and his devotion. His own feelings on leaving the capital are not known, for though he kept a notebook to record the main events of his life this was in no sense a personal diary. There can, however, be little doubt that his sense of mission had been re-doubled and that he was increasingly confident of his own powers and perhaps now had a growing conviction of his own destiny. In 1553 he attended the General Chapter of the Conventuals held at Genoa where his critic, Giulio Magnani, the reigning Vicar-General, was elected Minister-General. Felice preached in the city and was appointed Regent of the friary at Naples.

The journey to Naples was long—470 miles—and led through Tuscany and Siena and the Papal states. It lay along arterial roads—the Via Tiberina and the Via Casilina frequented by regular couriers, state postal services, and crowded with hundreds of earnest pilgrims and hordes of merchants. The kingdom of Naples, an extensive and varied territory including the rich grain fields of Apulia as well as the wild mountains of Calabria, salt, iron and silver mining areas and ports like Naples, Bari and Taranto, belonged to the Emperor Charles V. The power of the feudal nobility had never been broken and their virtually independent judicial courts and their vast rights of property enabled them to live in splendid luxury on their extortions from the ordinary people. The administration of royal justice was corrupt, inefficient and oppressive: that of the feudatories was worse. Legal rights were difficult to establish and were often overridden by superior force or lost in the confusion of contending jurisdictions. Royal taxation increased by the frauds and malpractices of the tax-farmers and collectors was extremely heavy and increasingly vexatious: feudal levies reduced the peasantry to penury. To protect the coasts from the perpetual ravages of Turks and pirates, large numbers of soldiers and a growing fleet of galleys were employed, and vast and costly works of fortification undertaken. But trade, much of it in the hands of foreigners, Florentines, Genoese, Luccans, Ragusans, was slowly growing. Population was growing too, and had almost doubled since 1501 to almost 2,130,000—partly due to natural growth, partly to immigration to meet increasing commercial opportunities. In this country dominated by the Southern Appenines, communications were totally inadequate and in years of failing harvests, the concentration of population in cities imperilled the lives of thousands and gave rise to serious political unrest. Felice was to spend three years here.

The whole kingdom was dominated by the city of Naples. For a period it was the largest city in Europe except for Constantinople and Paris. Its cosmopolitan population exceeded 200,000 and a further 12,000 lived in adjacent hamlets. The city was heavily fortified and considerations of defence were pre-eminent in public policy. A range of high walls, punctuated by formidable bastions, ran from Castello del Carmine at its eastern extremities in a great half circle to re-join the sea near Castel Nuovo, gaps in these man-made fortifications being allowed only where material defences—sheer cliffs and almost unclimbable crags—already provided adequate protection. These walls and their subsidiary defences had been continuously maintained, strengthened and frequently extended. Building outside the walls and in a prescribed area within them had been forbidden as recently as 1534. The focus of this whole defence system was the Castel Nuovo, designed as a gigantic fortress protected by a moat overlooking the harbour and the bay. The enemies against which these defences had been raised were Corsairs raiding from the sea, rebellious barons from the east and south of the kingdom and less formidably from disaffected factions within the city. Directly connected with the Castel Nuovo was the Palace of the Viceroy, built as recently as 1540 and surrounded by an array of formal gardens. Don Pedro di Toledo, Viceroy from 1532, had ruled the kingdom with skill and some success; he had supplemented the natural magnetism of the capital by encouraging the nobility to settle in the city. The Via Toledo, now the Via Roma, was developed as one of the main areas of the city and along its flanks the immigrant nobility and members of the Spanish ruling class quickly built magnificent and costly palaces. In their new residences these noble families lived in prosperous opulence, attending jousts and tournaments sponsoring fashionable salons and competing with each other for the patronage of the arts. The city streets were simultaneously embellished with a series of sparkling fountains, the drainage system and water supply were improved and dangers to public health removed.

The cost of these improvements was that heavy and fresh salt taxes (*gabelle*) had to be imposed on the populace. They also entailed the dispossession of considerable sectors of the populace from their properties and a very substantial invasion of gardens and copses, which had been a notable feature of the city. As its population continued to expand these encroachments increased and discontent was enhanced.

The commercial activities of the city were restricted and precarious, the most part still being handled by foreigners. The mercantile interests of the city received little encouragement or assistance from the authorities, shops and banks remained scattered without control. The dockyards were struggling and ship-building was almost at a standstill until the establishment of an arsenal after 1570 and was further impeded as urban development quickened, by the depletion of supplies of timber from the hills behind the city. The market, increasingly confined in a quite inadequate and ill-equipped square on the eastern extremity of the city, benefited not at all by developments in the city and business interests remained subordinate to those of defence and the elaborate provision for a rapidly expanding landed nobility. The city accommodated some industry, particularly textiles and leather, and there were a number of hand craftsmen operating in its eastern quarters. Nevertheless growth was of small significance and considerations of public health tended to augment the restrictions under which industry operated. The height of new buildings increased often to four storeys, many streets became overshadowed, oppressive and stifling; overcrowding in the popular quarters reached a desperate dimension.

The task of Viceroy was onerous indeed. To keep the city of Naples at peace, to maintain the powers of feudal nobles within check, to ameliorate the conditions of the poor, to defend the kingdom from the Turks and at the same time to supply the king with funds and loans, were daunting tasks which only men of great capacity could discharge. The splendour of much of the city to which Don Pedro di Toledo had added significantly was matched by the incredible squalor and overcrowding of large sections of the down-town streets. Beggars, prostitutes, unemployed dock workers, aged domestics of all sorts in the most bedraggled and tattered clothes were always to be seen.

Since 1549 Cardinal Carafa, with whom Felice appears to have recently formed a fairly close acquaintance in Rome, had been Archbishop of the City. His appointment was sternly resisted by Charles V, and his induction was delayed for a considerable time by the King's refusal to issue the writ *exequatur*. Felice was in a position of some difficulty: on the one hand he sincerely admired Carafa for his reforming zeal and singleness of purpose and stood to benefit from their acquaintance; on the other, the hostility between the Archbishop and the King and his Viceroy could involve Felice in political entanglements in which he saw no reason to take sides, especially as other friends from his days in Rome, the Colonna, were firmly attached to the King's cause. Moreover, five years earlier at Carafa's initiative, an attempt had been made to introduce the Holy Office into the city. This had led to a violent outcry culminating in bitter riots in which whole streets were burnt down, the viceroy's officials were attacked and driven from his residence where he himself was beleaguered. The viceroy drove his Spanish soldiers to enforce a regime of repression, and noble families left the city in terror. After three months peace was restored on the basis that the rising was aimed at the Inquisition, not the King. Charles V offered pardon to the rebels and fined the city 100,000 ducats. With the quelling of this anti-Spanish and anti-royal outburst, the Holy Office did in fact begin to operate in the city with little resistance, and the first public burning of a heretic took place in front of the Cathedral shortly after Felice arrived in the city. The kingdom's isolation had often made it the refuge of some of the followers of Valdès including Bernardino Ochino, one-time Capuchin leader, and heresy-hunters had little difficulty in finding prey, especially in the remote regions.

Felice's appointment in 1553 took him to the friary attached to San Lorenzo. Even by Neapolitan standards, this was no ordinary church. It was built by the Franciscans at the end of the thirteenth century on the site of a church dating from the sixth century, and it was here that Boccaccio, then a writer and verse-composer in the city, first saw his love, Fiammetta,[5] and the poet Petrarch (1304–1374) also lived here for a while. At the time of Felice's arrival there existed a close connection between the friary and the civic authorities, for the meetings took place of the six *eletti* who were largely responsible for the administration of the city. The church itself, centrally situated, was spacious and the generous and efficient charitable services of the friars attracted large numbers of all classes. Here Felice spent three eventful years, directing the studies of the most able and earnest Franciscan scholars of the area, and here he preached regularly to critical and discerning congregations. He delivered a series of lectures on the Gospel of St John in which his exposition and his convincing orthodoxy attracted special note. His rising fame as a scholar created a demand for his sermons to be printed and when the Neapolitan press began to publish them his learning extended to wider audiences. As regent in the Convent he made close contact with the University, then a well-endowed, vigorous and progressive institution. Such was his reputation that when the Minister-General of the Order understood the Minister of the Province of Calabria had died, he appointed Felice to the vacancy. Unfortunately for Felice, the General's information was incorrect. Such an appointment would have been a singular honour. Evidently Felice was by this time completely acceptable to his Minister-General in spite of his earlier disapproval.

In 1554 Charles V surrendered the kingdom of Naples to his son, the future Philip II of Spain. The installation of the new King took place in the refectory of Felice's own church with magnificent ceremony, the King being represented by Francesco Ferdinando d'Avalos, Marquis of Pescara, and the Viceroy receiving acts of fealty from the Secretary of the Kingdom, the electors of the city and the feudatories of the kingdom. In that year Felice returned to Montalto to settle some family differences between his father and Santone Mignucci, an uncle by marriage of his brother and sister. He bought a small plot of land from this Santone, probably spent the winter in the town and went on in the spring 1555 to Perugia where he preached the Lent sermons in the Cathedral at the request of Cardinal Carpi. Those journeys were often, perhaps usually, made on foot.[6]

Moreover, it is clear that his rising fortunes did not diminish his interest in either his own folk or his native land. With good grace he did what a son should for his relatives, sharing their burdens and calming their feelings. There can be little doubt that his three-year stay in Naples had provided Felice, still in his thirties, with invaluable experience. Apart from his own duties at the Friary, he had watched a great and expanding city in social tension; he had lived in a Spanish dominion and felt the weight of its antagonism to the prerogatives of the Pope; he had seen a regime of repression in operation and must have reflected on the bases of social order and political stability.

At the end of 1555, or very early in 1556, he was called by Pope Paul IV to Rome. The Pope had established a Reform Commission comprising sixty-two members (including twenty cardinals and a number of bishops) to forward the work of the Council of Trent whose sessions had been suspended in 1552 and would not resume till 1562. After the Commission had been lectured by Paul IV, about two hundred theologians and clerical lawyers were added to the Commission, which was then divided into three classes each presided over by a Cardinal, and addressed by the Pope. This Commission was to advise the Pope on intricate and disputable points of doctrine and ecclesiastical practice, but the Pope who, at the age of eighty, was predominantly a man of action, grew tired of interminable debates, and meetings ceased at the end of March.

At this time, Felice lived with Cardinal Carpi's secretary, Sigismondo Botio, in the Cardinal's house in the city, having maintained a close friendship with both during his regency in Naples. At Carpi's house, he renewed his friendship with Ghislieri, now engaged at the Headquarters of the Holy Office on the Ripetta and a close associate of Pope Paul IV by whom he was made Cardinal in 1557.

The strain of long journeys, the demands of his duties, more particularly the jealousy and opposition of his rivals in the Franciscan Order, were beginning to tell on Felice. The responsibilities of Regent were heavy but the Regent himself, outside the circle of his students, could be somewhat isolated and lonely. His appointment was normally limited to a period of three years and he was unlikely to share fully the companionship of his fellow brothers nor be able to participate completely in the life of the house. He became very seriously depressed, even suggesting to the Cardinal Protector that he should withdraw from the Order with the Cardinal's consent. Wiser and more experienced, the latter brushed aside Felice's dispiritedness, "exhorting him to be patient and forbearing because he trusted in God that in due time he would give him the opportunity to do great things." It is likely that it was out of regard for his health that Felice was allowed to use a horse borrowed from an acquaintance in the Marches to go to the General Chapter held at Brescia in 1556. There he was appointed Regent at the friary in Venice. Thus he escaped the war which broke out between the Pope and Kingdom of Naples, when the newly appointed Viceroy, the Duke of Alba, occupied part of the Papal states, and advanced to within sight of the capital.

A journey of 120 miles led Felice through some of Italy's most beautiful country with the Alps towering majestically into blue skies as the road crossed mountain defiles until he reached the immensely fertile region, which constitutes the northern flank of the valley of the Po. So, for the first time, Felice arrived at the city of islands and lagoons. Though posterity, handsomely endowed with hindsight, judges her to have been past her zenith, the Venetian Republic which Felice traversed from west to east was extremely wealthy. Maize, introduced earlier in the century, had become the staple diet of the poor; other grains supplied the needs of the rich and met the major part of the country's requirements. Wine and oil were extensively grown and the Republic was at least self-sufficient in many primary products except grain. A splendid climate, a fertile soil, natural assets of great importance, were supported by substantial and increasing investments of capital and a growing willingness to adopt the most sophisticated methods of cultivation then known. The Republic was equally rich in manufacturers; it had a notable production of textile fabrics, its glassware of all sorts had an international reputation beyond dispute, the ship-building on the waterfront by the standards of the day was advanced and extensive.[7]

Above all its commerce, largely undertaken by its own ships, was outstandingly lucrative. Venice was the supreme entrepot of the Adriatic, carrying goods between the whole of northern and central Italy on the one side, and the Turkish Empire and the Far East on the other. In spite of the competition of Spain and Portugal using the Cape route, her share in the spice trade of the Far East, was considerable and probably increasing. Only in pepper was Portuguese competition serious.[8]

The Brenner gave it access to Central Europe, the Rhine, and thence even to the Low Countries. Venice was the principal carrier of salt and still had important trade centres in the islands of the

Adriatic. Such was the prosperity of the Republic that it was able to invest extensively and to lend its credit to many financial ventures, which brought it great profit.

The Republic's economic prosperity was matched by its political power. It was consistently jealous of its autonomy and because of its wealth was able to play a significant part in the Franco-Imperial rivalries of the century. Her wealth and stable income supported a large and effective soldiery with a considerable element of hired *condottieri* as well as a fleet of great renown. She was Europe's chief protagonist against the Turks and effectively policed the Adriatic against numerous corsairs.

The stability of her government and the absence of serious discontent were the envy of Europe. The Doge, Lorenzo Priuli (1556–59) the Republic's titular head, was responsible for the co-ordination of the various organs of government and presided over the Pien Collegio or Cabinet comprising six ducal councillors, the three heads of the supreme judiciary and sixteen other members, five of whom were of a quite subordinate character. The burden of legislative and many executive functions was carried by the Senate, a body of some 200 members, whilst the Council of Ten acted as a kind of Committee of Public Safety charged with the maintenance of public order. Final political authority was vested in the Great Council comprising some 2000 members drawn from no more than 150 noble families.

Venetian Society was rigidly stratified. The Avogadori maintained a golden register of the nobility containing only between 1600–2500 names and scarcely any new families had been added since the end of the fourteenth century.[9] Only nobles whose names were registered were eligible for the Great Council, which elected office-holders and confirmed new laws. A Venetian noble was reluctant to engage in industry and could not exercise a mechanical trade though nobles were not debarred from managing such enterprises or from engaging in commerce.[10] Indeed trade with the Levant was confined to Venetian nobles or to citizens who had qualified by a period of twenty-five year's residence.[11] Many noble families were heavily in debt but their superior rank was unaffected whilst the bourgeoisie, though immensely rich, were excluded from political power. But governmental offices were occupied in rotation and there were severe limitations on their being filled simultaneously by members of the same family. On the other hand, nobles and other classes shared responsibilities in non-political organisations, particularly in the *Scuole Grandi*,[12] and the numerous charitable associations existing in the city. Many citizens including many of those employed at the Arsenal were in the service of the state. The impecunious were dependent on employment provided by the state or their superiors and in times of famine, sickness or economic distress, were rescued from disaster by various means of public assistance. Dangerous social tensions were therefore diminished and antagonism to public order rarely reached explosive force. "A relatively open system of government";[13] and a strong community spirit made Venice an example to less well organised states and the "symbol of peace, moderation and good sense".[14] Such a society had become a close knit community unreceptive to outsiders, proud of the purity of its stock, boastful of its traditions and its heritage, bitterly hostile to the intervention of strangers and unwilling to accept any form of dictation.

The City of Venice was the administrative centre and commercial power house of the Republic. A very densely populated city by sixteenth century standards (its population probably exceeded 160,000 at that date),[15] the second largest in Italy, larger than Rome, smaller than Naples, its wealth was regarded as phenomenal. The immense prosperity of the previous century and the profound inspiration of the Renaissance schools were reflected architecturally not only in the area around the Doge's Palace but also in almost all the narrow streets which flanked the canals, and socially in very high rents and a high rate of crime.[16]

Perhaps in no other European State was the church so completely part of the establishment. The Patriarch of Venice was directly appointed by the Doge. When the Patriarchate of Aquileia became vacant the Republic, since 1552, was able to submit four names from which the new Patriarch would be chosen. There were sixteen bishoprics on the Italian mainland and thirteen in Dalmatia, the Adriatic Islands and other outlying territories. A small number of the Venetian noble families had a virtual monopoly of the major sees, especially on the Italian mainland with annual revenues up to 10,000 ducats. Such were Aquileia, Padua, Bergamo, Treviso, Ceneda and Verona. Moreover often these noble bishops appointed coadjutors with right of succession and in this way as well as by normal election a number of the most important sees became almost hereditary fiefs. The Grimani family had an almost permanent hold on the Patriarchate of Aquileia and the Cornei-Pisani family on the Archbishopric of Padua. The Church had shared fully in the prosperity of the Republic and now possessed immense wealth in far reaching, fertile lands, in revenues from investments of many kinds, in artistic, architectural and scholastic treasures of immeasurable value acquired from the magnificent splendour of the Venetian Renaissance.

The Republic was richly endowed also with establishments of the Regular Orders. In the city of Venice and on its neighbouring islands there were some forty religious houses for men, ancient establishments of the Benedictine, Cistercian, Carthusian and Carmelite Orders, friaries of almost every description and houses of the more recent foundations such as the Servites, the Theatines and the Jesuits. There were more than fifty houses belonging to the Conventuals in the mainland territories of the Republic. In all these Orders Venetians predominated or had a virtual monopoly; very many of their members were drawn from the nobility or were socially well-connected and a number of bishops, especially of the lesser and more remote dioceses were recruited from the Orders. [17] Their houses had often extensive financial resources and considerable annual revenues and generally they were independent of Episcopal jurisdiction. Amongst the Orders were many well-qualified and well-trained theologians, distinguished scholars and writers of eminence. Standards of moral conduct naturally varied greatly and scandals in the houses in the remoter parts of the Republic were sufficiently frequent to discredit many of them.[18] The standard of the secular clergy was much less satisfactory; frequently they were young men elevated from the ranks of vergers and acolytes, often of mediocre intellectual calibre and ordained after inadequate training. Serving in an affluent society still living opulently on prosperity accumulated in former decades, the insidious temptation to worldliness was ubiquitous. Yet Venice had been notable for its efforts at reform and its continuing outbursts of ecclesiastical vitality.

Nunneries of which there were fifty in the city and lagoons, half Augustinian or Benedictine, were much more discredited. There were twice as many nuns as regular clergy, of whom two-thirds were Venetian noblewomen, for the nunnery had become the refuge of these society wallflowers, relegated by their families to escape the immensely costly dowries which noble marriages entailed. A place in a nunnery was often obtained as a reward for a gift or by influence and maintained by a regular subscription. The task of an abbess was unenviable; the *clausura* was difficult to enforce; study and devotion fought a wavering battle with sloth and a retinue of vices. So frequent were scandals that the Republic was obliged to appoint a *Magistratura sopra i Monasteri* comprised of some of the most experienced magistrates who were specially concerned with breaches of the *clausura*.

Yet the Republic was by no means indifferent to affairs of religion; it had nothing to gain by conflict with the Church which was consistently regarded as a bulwark of the State and whose decline or collapse would inevitably damage the whole social order. The State was generally diligent and often quite vigorous and determined in hunting down heretics and bringing them to trial. Yet its cosmopolitan population, its far flung commercial enterprises and its wide financial interests obliged it to tend towards much religious tolerance. This in turn occasioned misunderstanding of its intentions and some acid criticism of its policy. It was sensitive of the need to safeguard the interest of religious minorities; especially of those who were willing to give undertakings to refrain from religious propaganda and to cause no trouble. It was particularly favourable towards the Jews; and in the University of Padua students from all over Europe, especially Germans, were allowed to study without undergoing religious tests and to take degrees without being required to subscribe to the Catholic faith.[19]

On the whole the Republic's relations with Rome had been harmonious. Popes raised no problems about clerical appointments being monopolised by Venetians and rarely used the power of veto. On the other side, the State did not impede heresy trials to the point of conflict with the spiritual arm. It allowed the annual publication of the bull *In Coena Domini*, which allowed the papacy to censure secular rulers. Nevertheless there was only a delicate balance between the Republic and its Church on the one side and Rome on the other. The Republic closely restricted alienation of real property to the Church, it excluded close relatives of ecclesiastics from the major Councils of State when affairs with Rome or religious matters were under discussion and clerks were excluded from many offices of state. It was particularly watchful of any attempts by the Inquisition to establish an independent jurisdiction, of claims to have Venetians extradited so that they might be tried for religious misdemeanours and of efforts by non-Venetian ecclesiastics to carry out the visitation of Venetian dioceses. The Republic insisted that representatives of the lay power should be present at all inquisitorial proceedings; it forbade Venetian subjects to be tried outside the state and on occasions, with the connivance of the secular authorities, Venetians ignored or evaded summonses to Rome for trial. There was particular dispute about both the bishoprics of Bergamo and Brescia which, though part of the Republic, were subject to the Metropolitan of Milan. When these and other dioceses were to be inspected, the Republic attempted to control the appointment of the Visitors and to exclude nunneries, hospitals and charitable institutions from their scrutiny. Venice was also extremely sensitive about the censorship and control of the press for the Republic possessed a most thriving printing industry with an immense international reputation and was apprehensive that a Papal censorship might curtail it and damage one of the Republic's sources of prosperity. During the course of the sixteenth century there evolved within the Republic a growing rivalry between the established nobility and the commercial classes which developed into conflict between the *Giovani* and the *Vecchi*, the former striving to break the political dominance of the ennobled families, the latter resisting their attacks. Church and nobility being so closely integrated, assaults on the entrenched position of the latter inevitably produced increasing resistance to the Papacy.[20]

Felice took up residence as Regent at the Frari. The *La Grande*, as the Frari was normally described, flanked one of those innumerable small, intimate squares with which Venice is so richly adorned, perhaps 250 yards to the west of the Grand Canal. The Rialto, Venice's commercial centre, was half a mile distant and the Campo dei Frari enjoyed a large measure of peaceful detachment. Across the Campo stood the Scuola Grande, the building being owned by the Friars and leased to the Scuola, an important charitable foundation caring for members and non-members, tending them in sickness, making loans to them in times of distress, educating their children, ministering to their spiritual needs and ensuring a dignified burial.[21] Here the newly-arrived Regent could watch Christian philanthropy at work and as ships were lost and sailors drowned, as food supplies dwindled or as winter winds swept in from the mountains of the North, he could listen and observe.

The Friary was large and the Friars numerous for they were drawn from a wide area of the Republic; the Friary being the centre of one of the largest custodies in Northern or Central Italy. At various periods, but not at the time when Felice arrived, the Provincial General of the Order was a Venetian and then he normally resided with the Provincial Secretary and the Provincial staff, such as it was, at the Frari.[22] But the La Grande had already established a reputation for indiscipline, resistance to authority and a narrowly isolationist attitude;[23] a non-Venetian was unlikely to enjoy his residence there and the Regent's students could be relied on to produce trouble with little provocation. They were of notable ability and had been carefully selected for their scholarship and intellectual capacity. Felice faced a testing and exacting situation.

The church attached to the Friary had been completed less than a century before; its campanile was one of the landmarks of the city (as it still is) and its spacious rectangular nave accommodated very large congregations.

Arriving at the City on 30th June, 1556,[24] he settled quickly and with a will to his task. His duties as Regent were onerous; there were three Franciscan houses in the city, a further seven or eight in the districts immediately surrounding it, and approximately forty in the province. The Republic's University was at Padua, almost thirty miles away. With two colleagues Felice was authorised to promote masters' degrees.[25] In his first year eight of his pupils were not admitted to the doctorate by the Minister-General of the Order, Master Giulio da Piacenza, a most learned and distinguished member of the Order, now in his second term in that office, who had previously served as Procurator-General and Vicar-General.[26] It was he who earlier had been critical of Felice's rapid promotion, and it may be significant that at this time those eight students were promoted to the doctor's degree, but not admitted by the General: subsequently they were admitted to the doctor's degree by Felice himself. Obviously he and his Minister-General were in close personal contact, and the latter doubtless made a careful assessment of the scholarship and judgement of his subordinate. Felice was also committed to a heavy programme of public preaching. He himself recorded his engagement for three sermons each week at St Catherine's, and later he preached there four times each week as well as at Santi Apostoli. He does not record preaching in his own church of S. Maria dei Frari.[27] Santi Apostoli was a popular church not far from the Rialto, one of the leading commercial quarters of the city, and not far from the house where Titian lived, now at the peak of his prowess. S. Caterina was situated rather further from the densely populated centre of the city (near to the church of the Jesuits.) Neither church where Felice preached belonged to the Franciscan Order so, presumably, he had the agreement of the Patriarch. It is curious that his major preaching commitment was not in his own church though large and centrally situated. Santi Apostoli was near the German quarter,[28] where almost a thousand Germans lived, with its business centre at the Fondaco near the Rialto on the Grand Canal; S. Caterina could be described as near to dockland, and it may be supposed that Felice deliberately sought a platform where heresy or disbelief was likely to be most prolific.

The design of Santi Apostoli was simple, even its central columns having the minimum of ornamentation and its austerity contrasted sharply with the City's ostentation. The friars had for a number of decades breathed the Renaissance atmosphere of the city with zest and the church could boast two of Titian's masterpieces—the Assumption and the Madonna of Pesaro completed in 1518 and 1526 respectively and also an altar piece by Bellini. They had collected a number of remarkable statues including two of St John. Unfortunately, Felice's notebook records no impressions of the city, nor whether he approached it with elation or apprehension. In fact he was about to face one of the major crises of his career. It is probable that he sensed the atmosphere of religious crisis as he entered the city. The possibility of overthrowing Protestantism lay in the balance. England had been reconciled to Rome. Mary Tudor had married Philip of Spain and although her hope of a son had been disappointed, hope for a Catholic future lived still; the Marian martyrs were on their way to the stake. If England were restored permanently to the Catholic fold was it impossible that the Reformation breach in Western Christendom should be healed? But Felice's experience in Naples had taught him how sharply national independence and dynastic ambition could conflict with the religious objectives of the Church. A Spanish England might not accept Papal control or Roman policy and the restoration of church unity at the price of establishing Spanish domination in Western Europe might be too costly a transaction. Cardinal Pole, the Papal Legate who had played so eminent a part in the restoration of England to the Roman Catholic church, had proved himself too pro-Spanish and when Paul IV and Philip II were in conflict, he was deprived of his office, recalled to Rome and even accused of heresy before the Holy Office. Papal authority recognised no national limitations yet its claims were wholly dependent on political support from the civic powers and papal officials who became involved in politics could not avoid living dangerously. Felice's political education, begun in Naples was to be greatly extended and deepened in Venice.

For the sermon was regarded as one of the most effective antidotes against infidelity.[29] Taking the fight to the enemy was consonant with his known character. His regular preaching engagement led him past the *Fondaco dei Tedeschi* through the area in which many of the German inhabitants worked, past the famously ornate Ca' d'Oro and over the Rialto Bridge, the only bridge spanning the Grand Canal at that time. Thence a brief walk behind the magnificent Balbi palace would bring him to the large open Campo dei Santi Apostoli (and the church where he frequently preached). When his engagement was at S. Caterina he would walk into what is now known as the Campo dei Gesuiti (the Gesuiti church was not then built) where he turned westwards to his destination. The journey from the Frari to S. Caterina was substantially more than a mile. Week by week the Regent's knowledge of the city and his acquaintance with its inhabitants, some rich, many poor, some purely Venetian, others of foreign extraction extended until he had acquired an intimate understanding of Venetian society, its aspirations, its fears and its habits and attitudes. At first in his regular preaching Felice was well received[30] by the Fathers of the Friary where Cornelio Divo, the future Provincial Minister of Venice, was Guardiano, and by the Papal Nuncio himself, and he resumed his friendly and intimate correspondence with Cardinal Carpi's Secretary.[31]

Soon, however, "a very great persecution sprang up".[32] Only three months after his arrival he was in Rovigo, more than fifty miles from Venice, and from there he went on to Ferrara the capital of an independent Duchy, ruled by the d'Este family where as a student, he had spent many happier days. Indeed, he wrote to Cardinal Carpi's Secretary asking to be allowed to return to Rome, and the Secretary wrote to the Minister-General. Everyone did their utmost to stiffen Felice's resolve. The Minister-General promised to do his utmost for him, but assured him Cardinal Carpi was most unlikely to allow him to leave his appointment because he believed Felice had "great powers and knowledge."[33] The efforts of the Minister-General and the Protector appear to have been temporarily successful, and Felice returned to his post.

On 17th January 1557, he was appointed Inquisitor for the whole dominion of Venice with very wide powers to search for heretics, to persuade them to recant their heresies or to bring them to trial.[34] In this capacity his responsibility was to the Holy Office at Rome, where his friend Ghislieri was in command. The mainland of the Republic covered an area considerably larger than Wales, extending approximately 200 miles from West to East, and about 100 miles from North to South. It bordered Switzerland and the Hapsburg territory on the North and the Turkish domain on the East. In the northwest, Bergamo and Brescia, which were subject to the jurisdiction of the Archbishop of Milan, were notable for their reception of heretics and the readiness of their indigenous population to embrace the new heresies; in the East the Udinese and Capodistria were equally celebrated for their heterodoxy. From the Turkish Empire as well as from her commercial contacts with the Middle and Far East, the Republic faced the threat of infection by a militant Islam.

In the City, a number of Jews lived in the Ghetto, patrolled and locked in at night,[35] and about the middle of the century operated a press near the Rialto, which published the Rabbinic Bible and the Talmud, a large number of copies being seized by the Inquisition and burnt in 1568.[36] The University of Padua, with its world famous law school, welcomed students from all quarters without any serious distinction of creed or any attempt at repression,[37] and the whole Republic was pervaded by a liberal but pragmatic tolerance of a wide diversity of opinions. The English ambassador was allowed to hold a Protestant service in his private chapel and to introduce whatever books he wished.[38] The representation of the Church in the Republic had long been undermined by the non-residence, moral laxity, greed and worldliness of its clergy, the political opportunism of the higher echelons of its hierarchy and the misconduct, corruption and social indifference of its Regular Orders.[39] The populace was subjected to the exploitation and deception of the 'sfratati'—members of Orders who had left their monasteries and neglected their vows whilst continuing to extract alms and to administer the sacraments, particularly confessions, without authority.[40] Especially in the isolated valleys of Northern and Eastern Venice, the regulars lived almost without supervision or direction, often returning year after year, during the summer, to their families. The numerous houses of nuns were celebrated for their vice—neglect of the clausura, open and welcome fraternisation with the secular world, unruliness and high living.[41] The spread of heresy was therefore facilitated by the weakness and low esteem of the Catholic Church.

The task of the Venetian Inquisition was therefore immeasurably difficult. Complete success would only be attained if Central Europe returned to the Catholic fold and when the Catholic Church had met the intellectual challenge of the Reformation and restored its pristine standards of personal and corporate conduct. In the short term the frontier with Protestantism had to be stabilised and the spiritual life of Catholicism revived.

A great part of the work of inquisitors, patriarchs, or rather—of their spiritual vicars—must consist in improving ecclesiastical standards, in putting the brake on scandalous licence, in stopping the rot which facilitated the spread of new religious ideas.[42]

The difficulty of the Inquisition's tasks, immense as it was, was aggravated by the complex and uneasy relationship, which existed between the Republic and external authorities. The Inquisition was responsible to the Pope, who regularly attended in person the meetings of a group of Cardinals whose office was on the Ripetta in Rome; this group determined its policy, received its reports and gave it direction and impetus. Although the Republic had no sympathy with heresy and was generally ready to take rigorous measures to root it out, it believed the jurisdiction of the Inquisition challenged the autonomy of the state: it resisted the claim to initiate proceedings which might infringe the rights of a bishop as an unacceptable intervention in the powers of the established clerical hierarchy and its rigorous pursuit of heretical beliefs, prohibited books and misconduct as an invasion of the sanctity of the individual Venetian citizen. There was a considerable and troublesome history of open friction between the Republic and the Papacy, and whenever the latter endeavoured to have trials removed to Rome, hostility was engendered comparable with that raised by the British attempt to deport American political offenders before the outbreak of the Revolution.[43] Because of its suspicions the Republic had insisted on having representatives of the secular authority as members of Inquisitorial tribunals, and these frequently obstructed proceedings and prolonged business so that sentences of important citizens were difficult to obtain.

The administration of ecclesiastical justice in the Republic defied every canon of modern management theory. There was widespread and provocative overlapping of jurisdiction since the state, the Church and the Inquisition were each capable of acting independently, often in conflict with each other. Heresy and clerical misconduct could concern all three. The Senate appointed three Venetian nobles to deal with heresy, and shortly before Felice's arrival in Venice they had begun to sit each day;[44] the Council of Ten also had jurisdiction in cases of clerical misconduct and the Senate controlled the establishment of new monasteries;[45] the state used internal disorders in monasteries as occasions for comprehensive investigations into their administration, particularly with a view to extending their taxable liabilities; disputes between Church and secular citizens similarly provided opportunities for the state authorities to bring Church administration within their powers. Excuses could be found for the dismissal and replacement of monastic heads, and on occasions they were prevented from taking possession of their official property.[46] The bishops and their subordinates had an extensive system of tribunals to which the clergy were subject but in which seculars also could seek redress for a great variety of grievances. Heresies, irregularity in Church offices, prohibited books, were their particular concern. Often when non-resident bishops were negligent in their duties and their vicars became dilatory, appeals to rival jurisdictions multiplied. The absence of a single authoritative list of forbidden books until the compilation of the Index in 1559 left prosecutions dependent on the whims of a diversity of authorities. The Papal Nuncio also had wide powers of intervention, sometimes in association with the clerical administration, often independently and under direct instructions from the Pope. For example, he appointed an Auditor with the sole duty of hunting for prohibited books and controlling the press.[47]

Through this labyrinth of disputes the powers of the Inquisition ran with independent initiatives, spurred on by Rome and the ruthlessness of Cardinals like Carafa and Ghislieri.[48] It could sentence offenders to life imprisonment, and (until 1558) to service in the galleys, to drowning or strangling; it could deprive them of their possessions, but death sentences had to be carried out by the civil authority and possessions seized from offenders could be bequeathed to their heirs. Paul III (1534-49) had consented to the secular courts dealing with criminal cases involving ecclesiastics, and these courts had called cases affecting the Inquisition, and the latter found great difficulty in disposing of cases where sentences could be passed in the Republic. Friction was particularly rife in the Patriarchate of Aquileia and the diocese of Ceneda.[49] Cases within the Inquisition's authority were so numerous that it needed to meet three days per week though it had not yet acquired a permanent office.[50]

There was an immediate outcry against Felice's appointment, which appeared to have been made arbitrarily and without consultation with the Minister-General, and representations were made presumably by his brother friars, to Carpi as Protector of the Order. Responsibility for the Inquisition had rested with the Franciscans since 1289 and it was intolerable that so important an appointment should be given to a non-Venetian, particularly to one who had already made himself immensely unpopular and who in 1556 had charged a brother friar from Brescia with Lutheran beliefs before the Inquisition.[51] Naturally, their representations had no success.

Felice inherited a considerable list of outstanding cases and unresolved disputes. Eighteen cases had been launched the previous year. Encouraged by his success in having a heretic brought to Rome for trial and sentence (he was burnt publicly in Piazza Navona on 22nd August, 1556), the Pope was unsuccessfully demanding the surrender of another notable heretic, Aurelio Vergerio, nephew of the famous Pier Paolo, the apostate Bishop of Capodistria, whose example had infected many. Papal authorities were also pressing for the surrender of a heretic who had been before the Inquisition at Brescia,[52] and Felice found himself committed without preparation or respite to numerous important and tantalising disputes. He was taken ill in April but was able to preach the Lenten sermons at Cotigoro in the neighbouring Ferrarese where he repeatedly found refuge. Later in the year when a vacancy arose for a Provincial Master of the Marches, Carpi canvassed the election of Felice but the opposition was too strong, the attempt failed, and Tommaso Marconi da Penzola (Pesaro) was elected. This great disappointment Felice bore with equanimity, the more surprisingly because this was his native province in which he had spent the whole of his early life and in which he had built up an immense reputation as a preacher. Hard work is often the antidote to despair. Three full days of each week were spent in the Court of Inquisition, and numerous cases were subjected to searching and meticulous scrutiny, many suspects being convinced of their errors, others being placed under continued observation, yet others remaining obdurate had to be handed over to ecclesiastical or civil authorities for punishment. At this time he was able to enlist the understanding of the Republican authorities and apparently, on its own authority, the Inquisition in June 1557 forbade the sale of Erasmus's *Colloquies* and Valdès's *Mercurio et Caronte*; Felice must have been personally familiar with both of these works.[53] Such were the demands on Felice by his appointment as Inquisitor that his preaching had to be curtailed somewhat. At the same time he was given administrative investigations to undertake by the General of the Province.[54] He was engaged also on work on St Matthew's gospel and was preparing for publication an annotated edition of the works of St Bonaventure, the great Franciscan theologian and preacher of the thirteenth century. Overwork may well account for his illness in April.[55] He recovered his equilibrium and at the end of September 1557 he wrote to Carpi that "by the grace of God things had quietened down, the uproars had ceased, even the affairs of the Inquisitor were prospering", and he received an encouraging and contented reply from the Cardinal.[56] Fourteen new cases were initiated during the year,[57] and the Holy Office at Rome was pressing for action in the case of one, Luigi Cavallo, and others held "in the hands of secular notaries".[58] Difficulty was experienced in effecting action against Alessandro Caravia in spite of his being cited to appear before the Tribunal,[59] but Aurelio Vergerio made his public recantation in the

Cathedral of Capodistria, his heretic uncle's diocesan church, and commenced a year's penance.[60]

Ghislieri was promoted Cardinal in 1557 (Cardinal Alessandrino), and made Grand Inquisitor next year; Felice could count on his full support for energetic measures against heretics and recalcitrant dissidents. He appointed a number of Commissioners each serving an individual diocese so that a considerable proportion of the Republic was covered and it was clearly intended that these Commissioners should work closely with the Bishops and officers of their courts. Preaching, hunting heretics, converting the disaffected, occupied his time and energy.[61] His Commissioners met political opposition and their jurisdiction was questioned and resisted.[62]

Inquisitorial activities reached a peak in 1558, forty-six new cases being opened, including twenty-eight involving charges of Lutheranism, three of other heresies and seven of the possession of prohibited books. The influence of the Grand Inquisitor was clearly felt, for he personally pressed the Venetian ambassador to persuade his Government to send two suspected heretics, Francesco Stella and Fra Bartolomeo Fonzio, a Conventual friar, to Rome for examination. He also wrote to the Patriarch of Aquileia asking him to send to Rome for verification the bulls by which a Jew, Giulio Marcello, turned Christian, was selling indulgences, and followed this with a request for his assistance in effecting the surrender of yet another heretic, Agostino Sereni da Capodistria, to the Roman authorities.[63] Early in the year Pier Paolo Vergerio, the apostate Bishop of Capodistria, who had been in Poland, made a fleeting excursion across Venetian territory from Pontebba, almost on the Carinthian border, to Duino a dozen miles from Trieste, distributing heretical books as he went. But the Inquisition failed to arrest him and by April he was safely back at Tübingen.[64] Nevertheless the understanding between the Inquisition and the Republican authorities continued unabated. In February of that year the Holy Office ordered all importers of books to deposit an inventory of their books with the tribunal before they cleared customs. It also questioned bookmen who had failed to submit books before publication for scrutiny in accordance with a decree of the Heads of Council of Ten—fines were imposed on some. Then in August of that year fifty-seven booksellers were summoned before the Inquisition and reminded of the prohibition of the printing of the Bible in the vernacular.[65]

In 1559 the Generalship of the Province of San Antonio, comprising the custodies of Padua, Venice, Verona and Friuli, fell vacant and Cardinal Carpi made vigorous efforts to have Felice appointed. Although he was made Commissioner and charged with making arrangements for the Provincial Council held at Bassano,[66] Carpi's plan did not succeed, and in May of that year the Venetian, Cornelio Divo, Guardiano of the Frari, one of Felice's own inquisitorial deputies in the diocese of Rovigo and a fellow Franciscan, was elected.[67]

Provincial Councils comprised representatives of all the houses in the Province, some forty in total, and whilst the Protector of the Order had considerable influence, he was not able to override the wishes of the electors. In any event, a Regent was a transitory figure who, however respected for his scholarship, lacked local connections. Felice had no Venetian ancestry or associations, he was not yet well known in the provinces generally, and he had made a number of enemies by his religious zeal and disregard for popularity, and by his forthrightness as an Inquisitor. However, when the whole Order met in General Council in May of the same year at Assisi, he was re-appointed for a second period of three years as Regent and Inquisitor in Venice, and returned, probably conscious that the most serious problems lay in front of him.[68]

For centuries, Bishops had been empowered to approve books for publication and authorised to forbid the people of their diocese to read books they considered heretical or detrimental to the faith. The religious orders had always supported efforts to identify irregularities in books published, to discover those who read illicit literature and to bring the intransigent to trial. In 1557 Pope Paul IV ordered the preparation of an Index of prohibited books classified in three categories—authors whose entire works were prohibited, secondly books written anonymously, and lastly authors some of whose works were prescribed even though others were permitted.

The new Index was severe and often indiscriminate: for the first time it included books which though not heretical were anti-clerical, immoral or obscene. It prohibited all the works of Erasmus, Aretino, Machiavelli and Rabelais, the poems of Francesco Berni and Giovanni della Casa, the *Facetiae* of Poggio Bracciolini, and the *Decameron* might only be read in expurgated editions. In addition, all translations of the Bible into vernacular languages were prohibited and the printing or possession of any such Bibles was forbidden, except with permission. The Talmud and all works based on it were prohibited. Nearly sixty editions of the Bible were not to be sold, harboured or read. More severe still was the enactment that some sixty publishers (most of whom were German or Swiss) were completely forbidden to publish, but one Italian (a Venetian) fell under the same ban.[69] This new Index gave particular offence to the Republic because it was promulgated unilaterally by the Papacy in its capacity as spiritual leader of Catholic Christendom. Paul IV did not invite the bookmen of Venice or elsewhere to comment on his Index but demanded immediate implementation and enforcement.[70] The Republic was outraged by this intervention in a sector of its domestic affairs and one in which a considerable measure of harmony had been preserved in recent times. The powerful Venetian book industry sensed immediately the dire threat to its livelihood. Battle with the Inquisition was inevitable.

This index was published at the Vatican in 1559. As Grand Inquisitor, Cardinal Ghislieri sent a copy of the new Index in manuscript to Felice with instructions that it should be published and that the bookmen should submit inventories of books in their possession which were listed on the new Index. Meanwhile sale of all prohibited books was forbidden pending correction and confessors were forbidden to grant absolution to those who held them.[71] Felice seized on this as a most important duty of utmost urgency. Since publication required the co-operation of the Civil Authority, he acted with the greatest speed; surprisingly he succeeded in obtaining the sanction of the Senate, had it printed and set out prominently in the Republic. Within the Catholic church itself, the first Index was widely criticised for its lack of discrimination, was subjected to serious examination by the Council of Trent when it re-convened in 1562 and quickly revised.

Even the faithful had serious misgivings, but Venetian agitators also represented it as a fresh attempt by the Pope to intervene in the domestic affairs of the Republic and in the personal privacy of its citizens and the Authorities were apprehensive that a papal censorship might curtail the profits of their flourishing printing presses.[72]

In the Frari, trouble, already smouldering now burst into flames. The leader was the new Guardiano (or head), a certain Andrea di Micheli da Bergamo, who had replaced Cornelio Divo when he was elected Provincial Minister—Bergamo was noted somewhat earlier for the number of its heretics, and Ghislieri himself had twice been Inquisitor there and experienced fierce hostility. With him were four ringleaders, one described by the Provincial Minister General as "an old established heretic"[73] who had taken his master's degree and was therefore well qualified in theology, and clearly an inveterate rebel against authority; another called by one of Sixtus' biographers "a man of a wild nature"; the third already suspected of heresy; and the fourth "a man without capability in any other art who trailed after the other three".[74] It appears probably that within the friary itself there was consistent and bitter resistance to the efforts of the Inquisitor to enquire closely into the opinions held by the friars and undetected or unpunished misconduct or heretical views would be thought to discredit the Guardiano. Almost immediately after Andrea's appointment the Procurator of the Order wrote to the newly-elected Provincial Minister about him.[75] Felice had one firm supporter in the friary, Fra Antonio Posio da Montalcino, a young man in his late twenties, a former pupil of his at Siena, who had taken his master's degree in

1556 during the General Council held at Brescia, which had first appointed Felice to his post in Venice. This internal conflict within the friary had immediate political repercussions in the City. The brothers quickly began to harass Felice with incessant accusations before the senators.[76] Still jealously resenting the intrusion of a foreigner, they made their case more plausible by adding accusations of "excessive severity" and of his publishing the Index in Venice merely to win the favour of the Papal Court.[77]

Simultaneously, the bookmen's guild took resolute and spirited action, refusing as a body to obey the Inquisition's instructions or to print the new Index. Attack was met by counter-attack. The guild was summoned twice to appear before the Inquisition and Ghislieri involved himself personally in the dispute, sending Felice five copies of the Index, instructing Confessors to deny absolution of every holder of a prohibited book and demanding the names of disobedient bookmen. In this acrimonious atmosphere the Senate tried, by following a policy strictly in accordance with past traditions and practices, to preserve its neutrality. It refused to ask for the withdrawal of the Index but it would not take steps to coerce the bookmen to comply with the orders of the Inquisition. It was disinclined to become involved in this affair which could be regarded as lying outside its responsibility. The Collegio however (a small cabinet responsible for preparing the Senate's agenda) was more belligerent. It ruled that the bookmen might sell all their books, prohibited or not, that if the Inquisition wished to burn books it must first buy them and any which had been published in Venice within privileges granted by the government were exempt from condemnation. Challenged in this way within the Republic, the Papacy retaliated by seizing Venetian books in bookshops owned by Venetians within the Papal States and by prohibiting Venetians from attending book fairs within the Papal States.[78] In any event a desperate famine[79] followed by an outbreak of plague drove many of the residents away from town and the death of the Doge occupied their attention.

The city was reduced to desperate straits. Its trade was shattered and finally halted as Venetians retired to the mainland and foreigners ceased to visit. The roll of dead and dying grew longer day by day and the streets became empty and silent. Felice's journeys through the city became more and more fruitless and depressing as he watched the services of the Scuole being increasingly in demand, the Monte de Pieta under ever mounting pressure and hospitals crowded with patients many of them mortally sick. During those weeks he learned the frailty of man and woman smitten by natural pestilence and recognised with humility how human suffering could be mitigated by compassion and benevolence. Meanwhile he and the other faithful clergy continued to exhort their congregations to purge their libraries perhaps even depicting the pestilence as the hand of God against their sinfulness. Early in March the Inquisition had collected over 7,000 prohibited volumes and on the Sunday before Palm Sunday, a total exceeding 10,000 were publicly burnt.[80] Felice maintained his pressure with the greatest possible determination and in the Spring 1559 his efforts began to be rewarded. One bookman after another began to submit inventories of prohibited books and in July the Council of Ten finally accepted the Index and it was published by a Venetian printer. Moreover driven on by the indomitable Ghislieri, the Inquisition was able to impose penances on five of the bookmen and three days later, on August 14th eight more voluntarily presented inventories to the Tribunal together with twenty-one bales of books.[81] Nevertheless it is almost certain that under one pretext and another they contrived to maintain considerable numbers which the Inquisition might have claimed.

Felice with the relentless support of Ghisheri had won a notable victory. One of Venice's influential, though small, guilds had met the Inquisition in open battle because the issues at stake threatened its very existence. It had invoked the assistance of the Government at every possible point but in the end it had to acknowledge defeat. The right of the Papacy to impose a precise and systematic censorship of the press so as to keep religious opinion and doctrinal criticism under rigid control had been conceded and with that was established its authority to introduce inspection and limited powers of entry. Rome, and in particular the Congregation for the Index were triumphant. Felice's name was fêted.

Unfortunately his victory proved hollow—opinion in Italy generally had become severely critical of the Inquisition, on the one hand, questioning its ruthlessness and the rigidity of its methods, and on the other doubting the effectiveness of its efforts. Pope Paul IV, now in his eighties, was egocentric, frustrated and querulous, often in conflict with Cardinal Ghislieri personally and with the other Cardinals concerned with the Inquisition. In August 1559, Paul IV died, lamented by few, and there followed an unusually long interregnum during which popular hatred of the Inquisition led to the sack and total destruction of its office on the Ripetta in Rome. Felice's defender, Cardinal Carpi, Protector of the Order, who had recently suffered an illness which drove him to the depths of despair, was fully occupied with state affairs and the Conclave. Indeed, he himself was only prevented from succeeding to the Papal throne by the fierce opposition of the French to his election, and even so an attempt to proclaim him Pope by "adoration" narrowly failed. Not until December 26th were the Conclave proceedings concluded and Pius IV elected. Venetian affairs could only therefore receive a small part of Carpi's attention. During this interregnum the presentation of inventories to the Inquisition at Venice came to an end and it seems probable that Paul IV's Index was suppressed.[82]

For the Inquisition in Venice, therefore, the year 1559 was a period of ebb tide. Prosecutions fell drastically in number and in spite of the publication of the Index, only one case, involving prohibited books, seems to have been brought. In the face of continuing opposition and knowing that adequate support from Rome was unlikely, Felice left Venice shortly after the death of Paul IV and made the eighty mile journey to the safety of Ferrara, leaving Montalcino to attend to the duties of the Regency in his absence. From there, in accordance with established practice, he made representations to the Vicar-General, Giovanni Antonio Delfini,[83] and the Cardinal Protector, urging that some arbiter should be appointed to effect an agreement about the situation at the la Grande. It is said the Vicar-General readily agreed to this suggestion as many people believed that he should suspend the Guardiano from the Order whilst he himself effected control over the situation. Cardinal Carpi, however, ordered Felice back to his post and sharply reproved the General.[84] In fact, Felice now faced serious family troubles and journeyed on to his native homeland—Montalto. His mother, to whom he was very deeply attached, died, probably earlier that year, his sister's husband was seriously ill and died shortly afterwards. His only brother and cousin both married during the course of that year also, Felice and his brother providing the dowry of the cousin who had lived with his father since the death of her parents.[85] To a member of one of the regular Orders, perhaps particularly to a friar who lived according to his vows in the ordinary world, with neither wife or family, the understanding of a sympathetic mother, the companionship even if remote of a sister, were assets of magnitude. But to Felice the faith his parents always maintained in him and in his destiny made his natural affection for them immeasurable. There is little doubt that in the autumn of 1559 he was a deeply stricken, disconsolate man. In such circumstances, Montalto was always his refuge. This was his home. To return to the tranquillity of the foothills, to walk through the fields, along the Aso and Tesino valleys, and turn steeply towards the town walls, above all, to mingle day by day with the citizens of the town who treated him naturally and unostentatiously with affection, admiration and respect, healed his wounds, restored his peace of mind and his faith in mankind.

Meanwhile, Carpi's defence of Felice continued totally unabated. Indeed he was frustrated and angered by what he judged the lack of support given to Felice by the Vicar-General who had been appointed in July following the death of the General. Probably a connection of the Delfino, a notable Venetian patrician family,[86] Giovanni Delfini was a scholar and writer of great distinction with several theological works to his name and had taken a notable part in the two earlier sessions of the Council of Trent. He had already served as Provincial Minister of Bologna at the age of forty and had more recently become Professor of Metaphysics at Bologna University. He knew both the Venetian Republic and the Inquisition well, having been Regent in the Convents of both Padua and Venice and Inquisitor in Romagna.[87] Between him and Felice there evidently existed jealous rivalry and, on his part, perhaps disdain; the older and more experienced friar saw more fully the political complications of Felice's position in the Republic, and almost certainly the Vicar-General felt little sympathy for the determined stand he had taken. Carpi had his Secretary write somewhat testily to the Vicar-General, expressing confidence in Felice and indicating that he expected him to be given a suitable post where his talents would have proper scope.[88]

Carpi also instructed the Procurator, or Deputy General, of the Order, Antonio Sapienti d'Augusta, a former Professor of Theology in the University of Pavia, who in 1536 had saved his native city of Aosta from apostasy and rebellion against the Duke of Savoy, to let the Franciscans in Venice know the outcome of their hostility to Felice and to urge them to retain him as Regent and Inquisitor. Sapienti was authorised to inform them that if Felice was displaced as Inquisitor, no other Franciscan would succeed him, but "the office would be transferred to the Dominicans".[89] This was Carpi's method of dealing with "the greed of a few", who were motivated by ambition and the prospect of succeeding to this important office. This was a matter of the greatest importance, not merely for the City but for the whole of the Republic, since the Franciscans had for centuries been responsible for the administration of the Holy Office throughout the whole Republic. Moreover, the Dominicans were well known for their stern repression of heresy, and in these circumstances it was highly unlikely that Felice's replacement would bring any relaxation of treatment to Franciscan houses in the area. About the same time Francesco Stella was imprisoned by Bishop Michele di Ceneda, one of the suffragan bishops in the Patriarchy of Aquileia, well-known for his reforming energies, and it was evident that a very determined prosecution of heretics was afoot.

Next Carpi summoned Felice to Rome so that consultations should take place with the Cardinals of the Holy Office, and in November 1559 Felice again took up residence at Santi Apostoli.[90] There he prepared a spirited memorandum to Cardinal Carpi bitterly attacking the public contempt the Guardiano had shown for letters of Pope Paul IV, of Cardinal Carpi, of Ghislieri and others, and urging that the Holy Office should not tolerate this insolence.[91]

Meanwhile in Venice, the conspirators were making fanatical efforts to hound Felice from his office. The Guardiano succeeded in making representations to the Council of Ten who were persuaded to ask the Venetian ambassador in Rome, Mocenigo, to prevent Felice's return to the Republic. The Council also instructed the Delegation which was being sent to convey the congratulations of the Republic on his election to demand Felice's dismissal. Events in Rome were running no less strongly in the opposite direction. To his fellow Cardinals of the Holy Office the indomitable Ghislieri, fully convinced of Felice's "courage, learning and knowledge", proposed that to confound his persecutors, he be re-instated in Venice with even fuller powers.[92] Convinced that opposition to Felice sprang only from jealousy, the Cardinals unanimously and enthusiastically accepted Ghislieri's proposals. By February 22nd, 1560, Felice was back in Venice as damp mists lay heavily over the lagoons and the chill wintry air drifted in from the North. He was now in the middle of a political tug-of-war.

Immediately on arrival Felice found himself not only spurned by the Guardiano and his fellow conspirators, but physically excluded from his rooms and left for three days "in deep need".[93] The Guardiano and his supporters renewed the attack on Felice before the powerful Council of Ten, submitting a memorandum and appearing in person before the Council, shrewdly maintaining that the Inquisitors' actions were inconsistent with the freedom of Venetians and the traditions of Venice. They made such an impression that the Council drew up a formal statement of charges against Felice and demanded from the Pope his recall.[94] Only a little imagination would be required to reconstruct the animated scene in the Sola del Consiglio dei Dieci in the Ducal Palace, a room of sinister shadows and tantalising echoes, as the gaily brocaded counsellors, the Doge himself probably presiding, listened to their solemnly tonsured informant, and avidly seized on his attacks on the Marchian Inquisitor, supplementing them with their own patriotic strictures on these hateful infringements of Venetians liberties. The remarkable ornate ceiling, with its brilliant gilded decoration surrounding Veronese's painting of Jupiter attacking the Vices and the vivid wall panels scarcely dry, must have provided a striking background for the tenseness of the meeting and the ebullience of the discussion it provoked. Meanwhile, they forbade him to operate as Inquisitor pending the hearing of their case in Rome.[95] The charges set out against him were firstly that he was too austere in his office, secondly that his severity was likely to produce violent outbreaks both in the city and in the rest of the Republic, thirdly that he had denied absolution to those who kept books included in the Index or who had failed to hand over heretics to the Inquisition, and that he had instructed all confessors to do likewise. Fourthly, that he had conducted irregular trials in holding "processi informative"—exploratory sessions to determine whether there was sufficient evidence to justify proceedings—without lay representation.[96] The Council also complained that Felice should not have extended his office as Inquisitor beyond one year—a novel and unsupported contention, born of bitter antagonism.[97] Quite undaunted, Felice made representations to both the Doge and the Senate, roundly accusing the Council of inflicting injustice on him.[98] So far as the refusal of absolution was concerned, he made it clear that this had been done on the authority of the General of the Order. The Provincial General vigorously defended Felice and wrote to Carpi's Secretary urging the Cardinal Protector to make strong representations to the Bishop of Velletri, the Papal Nuncio, who was expected in the Republic shortly, so that any application the Provincial might make for the punishment of the rebels should be properly considered "lest they should escape their deaths." At the same time, he prepared charges against the ringleader and sent a copy of them to the Protector's Secretary.[99] About the same time the Papal Secretary wrote to the Doge demanding that Francesco Stella should be handed over to the Papal Authorities at Ancona. In Rome the Pope presented to the Venetian ambassador a memorial from the Holy Office demanding that the magistrates of the Republic should give Felice, whom it described as "a good theologian", "every help and favour".[100] The Republic was following the rules of diplomatic propriety, and both sides were engaged in one of the recurring disputes between rival jurisdictions. The former carefully avoided condoning clerical misconduct but resisted stubbornly every attempt to subject Venetian subjects to Roman jurisdiction. The Pope, on the other hand, personally well-disposed to the Republic and anxious to escape every avoidable conflict with it, nevertheless was obliged to defend the claims which sprang from his authority as ruler of the Catholic church. He had recently curtailed the Inquisition's prerogatives, removing simony, blasphemy and sodomy from its jurisdiction.[101] He also announced his intention to moderate the Index of 1559 and soon a Commission was at work on this project.[102]

For several weeks this ugly situation continued unchanged so that at the end of March Felice told Carpi's Secretary that there could never be peace with the Guardiano. He was obliged to reduce his preaching engagements, abandoning Santi Apostoli and preaching only at S. Caterina, thereby perhaps escaping the more bitter controversies.[103] The Procurator of the Franciscan Order again wrote to the Convent ordering them to desist from their mutiny, and Felice was convinced of his loyal and active support.[104] But the Guardiano used

Called to Rome 71

even this to inflame the hostility of the Venetian people. The Pope who had recalled his Nuncio in April 1557 when the Republic refused to support his war again Spain, appointed a new Nuncio so that he might lend his weight to the Papal authority in Venice.[105] The Papal Secretary immediately briefed the new Nuncio, telling him of the Pope's demand for the surrender of Francesco Stella and asking him to lend his authority and assistance to Felice, whom he described as "our beloved son, a man exceedingly approved by us",[106] "so that he might be able to exercise the office committed to him by the Holy See freely and safely.[107]

Within a week the Nuncio arrived and immediately worked enthusiastically on Felice's behalf.[108] Only five days later the latter was able to record that "with the help of the Nuncio the difficulties of the Regency have been resolved and I am in my room and on Tuesday I began to read".[109] Heavy clouds still hung over the Inquisition, for the Patriarch himself set out to nullify the refusal to give absolution by demanding that these cases should be referred to him; his Vicar would then be able to authorise the retention of prohibited books "in cases of Conscience".[110] This had been the established practice but in the absence of understanding and co-operation could completely defeat the purposes of the Index. Felice was also accused of inflaming opinion at Rome by libelling the rulers of the Republic.

For some weeks more Felice had to suffer indignities and persecutions whilst the Provincial Minister gave him full support and consolation. By the end of May two of the rebels had been called before the Provincial Vicar to answer charges of sedition,[111] and about the same time the Guardiano was deprived of his office and called to Rome.[112] Felice himself was talking of the loss of Venice and asking the Protector's Secretary to do everything possible to let him remain at Rome after his recall for "already he was in such a state that he could not live in Venice." He complained bitterly that his situation was occasioned "not by his evil nature," but by the "persecutions of his superiors".[113] In letters to Carpi and his Secretary he explained that he had found "letters of the worst possible kind against his conduct at Venice and these brothers would never had done him so much ill if they had not had someone to incite them, and although some have retracted yet there are some who have not hesitated to incite the governors of the Republic to show to the Cardinal Protector a letter emanating from the hand of the Vicar-General of an evil kind against his conduct there".[114]

In Rome battles raged relentlessly with the Pope still committed to the conflict. On May 6th 1560, when the Venetian ambassador, Mocenigo, took his leave of Pius IV he very irritably expressed his great desire for the end of "this tiresome business".[115] A week later the four representatives of the Republic saw Carpi, and four days afterwards the Grand Inquisitor, but found both perfectly firm in their support of Felice. Carpi agreed that Felice should be recalled but not until an appropriate interval had elapsed "to restore honour to the friar and to let him exercise his office of the Inquisition for a little time" and insisted that his successor would not be "one of those who are in Venice because he knew their moods but he would be a well qualified person whom he himself would find".[116] On May 22nd, in a final audience with Mocenigo, the Pope again discussed the very serious infirmity of the Inquisition, recommended that its activities should be confined more narrowly to strictly religious offences, and the Ambassador stoutly defended the involvement of representatives of the secular authority in the Inquisition's proceedings. Similarly when Melchior Michael (an ambassador-extraordinary of the Republic to Rome) returned he reported to his Government on 8th June that the Pope commended the Holy Office and the nuncio with great zeal.[117]

Mula, who was replacing Mocenigo and rapidly establishing himself as one of the Pope's closet confidants, had an audience on 15th June, and was puzzled and worried about the Pope's intentions. When he sent his Secretary to obtain clarification, he discovered the Pope had prepared a brief authorising Felice to continue as Inquisitor. It needed further representations from Mula before the Pope agreed to cancel this brief but he insisted on sending a Dominican to replace him.

Even at this late hour the authorities in Rome were quite unwilling to change their position, and the decree to transfer the office of the Holy Office from the Franciscans to the Dominicans was published and despatched to Venice. This was so serious a blow to the Order that the Provincial Minister convened a meeting on the 7th June of the senior fathers who drafted a submissive memorandum to the Council of Ten advocating comprising to which "all the Franciscan fathers subscribed except the Guardiano". The latter maintained that the apparent change of attitude was effected under duress, the fathers being afraid of the Vicar-General's displeasure.[118] Felice also was critical of this attempt at compromise because the conspirators were able to go round recruiting supporters and were suggesting that the Provincial Minister had been coerced. Felice was offended that the Provincial Minister had taken his action "without consultation and without his agreement" and he doubted whether anything would come of it.[119] But by June 21st Felice had been recalled. He spent eight days with the Provincial General who wanted to give him "a little peace in harbour after so many troubles, threats and dangers in which they had been together in Venice".[120] Felice complained that the Venetian Government had "the mind of the Pope and that this was harmful".[121] The fact that Pope Pius IV had an unqualified respect for the Republic and maintained a friendship towards it which even rebuffs and insults did not break. Evidently the Republic now understood that the Inquisitor's policy was unlikely to have the Pope's support and his political position was therefore seriously damaged. Pius IV and Ghislieri, the Chief Inquisitor in Rome, were in deep disagreement. Popular hatred of the Inquisition continued, and Catholic opinion was deeply divided on this subject. Its methods and the success of its efforts were both under serious scrutiny. The time for a compromise peace was past. The Roman Inquisition did not wish to revoke the transfer to the Dominicans, and Felice himself was asking that when it was decided that he should not continue in office the Cardinal Protector should find him another appointment because he could not stay "without great danger".[122] In due course the Congregation of the Holy Office authorised his recall.[123]

Cardinal Carpi and the Provincial Minister for Venice stood firm in unwavering support for Felice. When the Venetian ambassador was taking leave of Carpi, the latter assured him that Felice would be found another post where he would "serve God and satisfy his honour because he is a virtuous man of good quality who has always had that reputation".[124] He also wrote to the Nuncio, urging him "to do his utmost to ensure that so long as Felice was in Venice no innovations should be introduced by the Patriarch or by anyone else lest they commit errors which cannot be amended".[125]

Before he left the Republic Felice took official leave of the Doge, protesting his innocence of responsibility for the conflict; the Doge in return assuring him that he personally, and the Senate, thought well of him, that what had happened had been to uphold the Orders of the Republic and that he hoped, with goodwill, to see him as Inquisitor again.[126] Felice finally left Venice on June 17th to the great regret of the Provincial Minster.[127] Any suspicion Felice entertained of the Minister's good faith must have been entirely transitory and wholly unjustified. Two days later a Dominican Bartolomeo de Luga, was appointed Inquisitor.[128] Meanwhile, the newly-appointed Regent, Felice's disciple, Antonio di Montalcino, had gone to Padua, and it was decided to leave him there as Regent because of the energy he had displayed, and to make a fresh appointment at Venice.[129] On18th July 1560, Carpi wrote to the Minister General recommending Marco Antonio da Luga as Regent for consideration on the grounds that religion needed young men and such an appointment would allow the city "to make amends for the unjust persecution which had been perpetrated or at least fermented by some of them".[130]

Felice retired whilst the battle was far from finished. He withdrew badly mauled in a political conflict of notable consequence for which, particularly at the age of thirty-eight, he was inadequately trained. It is perhaps significant that whilst the biography *Sixtus V, Pontifex Maximus*, written anonymously, records Felice's four years in Venice in great detail, the *Vita Sixti Quinti Ipsius manu emendata*, complied by Antonio Maria Graziani, and revised and corrected by the Pope himself, passes over this period with only the briefest reference. These were apparently four years the Pope did not choose to recall. Nevertheless, Felice had acquitted himself very creditably and his supporters admired his indomitableness and tenacity, his determination and singleness of purpose.

All the sovereign states, whether Catholic or otherwise, regarded the control of religion as essential to the preservation of the throne; the Venetian patrician families regarded possession of high ecclesiastical office as a national support for their political dominance, and the new generation rising to power in the Council of Ten was becoming belligerently hostile to papal claims to juridical authority within the Republic. The Republic itself, having suffered from papal territorial aggrandisement earlier in the century, now fought stubbornly to preserve the Church within the dominion from invasion or attack. Ambitions of the papacy or the regular Orders whose loyalty was focused outside the Republic, were inevitably in conflict with the autonomy of the State. Warfare waged over this territory was necessarily bitter, devastating and uncompromising: conflict continued for many months, and a year later Papal authorities were still demanding the surrender of the miscreants at Ancona. So jealous was the Republic of its control of clerical office that when the Pope wished to make Mula, one of the Venetian ambassadors in Rome, Bishop of Verona, the appointment was successfully resisted by the Republic and when Mula was promoted to the Cardinalate in February 1561, he was dismissed from his office as ambassador because he had not obtained the Republic's permission to accept the purple. Felice left behind him a high regard for his integrity and determination, so almost twenty years later Venice learned of his election to the papal throne with apprehension and misgiving. Government circles both in Venice and at the Vatican recognised that the battles of 1557 and 1560 involved fundamental issues of principle. The Republic remained sensitive of every intrusion on its prerogatives and even a year later it warned the Papal Nuncio against innovations.[131] Both sides had wounds to nurse and a renewal of open strife was to be avoided by a clear understanding of the respective positions of each.

Controversial figures often achieve publicity and receive obloquy beyond their deserts. The records show in fact that cases brought before the Venetian Holy Office under Felice's regime were not dissimilar in number or nature from those of other periods, preceding or subsequent. They were indeed fewer than for the previous quinquennium, though more numerous than in the succeeding one, and much fewer than those for the following decade. Defendants whose place of origin lay within the Republic always formed a large majority of the list, and of these a substantial proportion—about a third—were from the City itself. The proportion from the city during Felice's period of office was notably greater than before, though not significantly greater than in the succeeding decade, and considerably less than in the period 1571–1580. The proportion of accused drawn from outside Italy was naturally small and fluctuating: in a religious sense the Republic tended to be insular in-bred and exclusive, and in addition the civil government was consistently cautious about cases involving foreigners.

About three-quarters of the accusations refer to heretical opinions, more particularly to Lutheranism, though this term was often used imprecisely. Cases were also brought against Anabaptists, Huguenots, Agnostics, Jews, Greeks and Mohammedans. Proceedings were launched for "speaking against the Pope, for showing contempt of holy religion, for sacrilege," and other offences against the church. Sexual offences figure in a small number of cases before the Holy Office, and were approximately equal to those brought for witchcraft and similar offences. The pattern of charges in Felice's time was not in any significant way different from that of other periods. Heresy tended to grow throughout the period from 1547 to 1580 and prosecutions on that account were particularly numerous immediately after the establishment of the reconstituted Holy Office in the Republic and again in the latter part of that period. Felice's activities conform to the pattern of the intervening period of comparative quiescence. Even the storm which followed the publication of the Index roused only a minor ripple in the total flow of prosecutions, though the number of prosecutions for prohibited books at least doubled and exceeded the level of the next decade.

Just as a policeman's efficiency cannot be judged by the number of prosecutions he initiates, so an Inquisitor's energy cannot be estimated simply by enumerating proceedings before the Holy Office. Inquisitors were encouraged to reform the deviators rather than to destroy them, and voluntary renunciations of heretical opinions were readily accepted. Felice's known relentlessness, his determined pursuit of all forms of heterodoxy may itself have obstructed the flow of heresy into the Republic. Nevertheless, it seems likely that the hostility he aroused sprang as much from his alien extraction and from his unyielding, even provocative, manner as from his zeal and ardour. The conflict was indeed more political than religious; the sovereign rights of the Republic were made to appear as under attack and the claims of the Inquisition were seen as antagonistic to the historic chauvinistic traditions which the Republic had consistently established.

The personal bitterness engendered in the battle soon faded, leaving no lasting animosity behind. When, in April 1561, Cornelio Divo, the Provincial Minister, was nominated for what must have been his second term of office, Felice wrote to express his pleasure.[132] Nine years later Felice received an invitation to take part in the celebration of Christmas at the Frari and regretfully was unable to accept it.[133] A year later, when promoted to the Cardinalate, he received congratulations from the Venetian friars.[134] Yet the problems created by the operation of the Inquisition in the Republic remained unresolved, and the attitude of the civil Government remained unchanged or even stiffened. In 1578 the Papal Nuncio was involved in controversies precisely similar to those of Felice's time, and in his Report to the Papal Court at the end of his appointment he described the Inquisition as of the greatest importance, and commented that "it needed to be in continuous action". In 1607 this long and hostile feud between the Republic and the Papacy culminated in the imposition of the interdict. The causes of these controversies were so deep-rooted and fundamental that only a political initiative of exceptional imagination at the highest level could resolve them. The failure of a young, politically inexperienced Regent friar was no disgrace.

Such battles were unpalatable to the Vicar-General who doubtless regarded them as peripheral to the interests of the Order. Probably sceptical of Felice's rapid advance in the Order, irritated perhaps by the consistent support he received from the Protector, maybe regarding Felice as impatient, impetuous and ambitious, and being himself only newly appointed as Vicar-General and having therefore to prepare for the next election of a General, he felt unable to give Venetian affairs the priority that authorities in Rome expected. Moreover, it would be natural for the Franciscan Order to be apprehensive of the new and extensive powers vested in the Inquisition and of Ghislieri's fanatical belligerence. The incident leaves little doubt that Franciscan discipline in the Republic was undermined by politics, that men like the Guardiano were ready to dabble in political intrigue for their own purposes, and that the concentration of Franciscan houses on local recruitment made them vulnerable to local pressures. Even the loyalty of a Provincial General was tested by a situation which seemed to call for at least the suspension of one of the local governors. Within the Republic obviously it was the Council of Ten which inspired and maintained the bitterness of the conflict with Rome. For them the ejection of a foreign misfit and the repulse of extraneous attacks on their sovereignty were primary aims. Felice's stay in Venice had exposed the incompatibility of the new reforming agencies and spirit with existing political structures and developments.

His personal career, however, was undamaged, for within the Roman Church it was clearly the reformers, the zealots, the orthodox, who were taking possession of the future. But it was Carpi who was his rescuer. Indeed, he may have taken up residence again with Carpi's Secretary, Sigismondo Botius, who lived either in his master's palace in the Campo Marzio or in the villa he was building on the Quirinale. Within a month of his arrival, at Carpi's instigation and with Ghislieri's ready support, he was made Consulter to the Roman Inquisition where, Carpi said, "To his great honour he had been admitted with unqualified favour and the Holy Office does not fail to employ him and always with the highest respect." This office brought him a very necessary pension, for he was so short of money on leaving Venice that he was obliged to sell small plots of land he had previously purchased in Montalto. But the Roman Inquisition was passing through rough waters. Pope Pius IV was so heavily engaged in political diplomacy, and his compromises were so frequent and substantial, that he could almost be accused of time-serving opportunism. He was sincerely attached to the cause of reform and intent on re-convening the Council of Trent so that the Church might recover its unity and present an undivided front to Protestantism, but he wished to achieve these objectives by agreement with rulers even though this entailed some sacrifice of the Church's principles and some measure of surrender to their ambitions. The Pope had little sympathy with Ghislieri's singleness of purpose and found the inflexibility and fanaticism of the Holy Office inimical to his pursuit of peace with European rulers. Papal spinelessness was a great grief to all the Inquisitors and a serious wound to Ghislieri, Carpi and the other Cardinals of the Office.

Moreover, all was not well with the Franciscan Order. The bickering of the several branches of the family were virtually continuous, and a possible merger of the Conventuali with the Capuchins was rarely outside the realms of discussion, even after Paul IV had confirmed the separate existence of the Capuchins in 1559. Carpi began to press the Vicar-General of the Conventuali, Giovanni Antonio Delfini, to treat the reform of the houses with much greater urgency, urging on him the conversion of those who had lapsed from the faith and the establishment of better discipline in the friaries. Delfini, a scholar and writer of great distinction, and himself a former Inquisitor for six years in the Romagna, had played a notable part in the discussions during the earlier meetings of the Council of Trent. At this very time he was preparing a pamphlet ready for submission to the Council when it was re-convened: his learning and his literary skill earned him high respect in the Order, but he probably was not well fitted to deal with a situation calling for action and decision and leading to formidable resistance. He had had no previous experience of the highest offices in the Order, having been Professor of Metaphysics and Logic at the University of Bologna when he was appointed Vicar-General on the death of the General, Giovanni Antonio Muratori, after holding office for only two months. Sixtus' biographer records bitterly that at Delfini's death the need for reform was still "either neglected or postponed, certainly it was untouched".

The strain arising from this situation, the burden of thirty years of study, travel and controversy, above all the weariness which followed his persecution at Venice, took a heavy toll of both Felice's nervous and physical powers. He collapsed and was sent away to recuperate in the Marches. He spent seven months at Montalto where family affairs added to his sorrow. His uncle, Salvatore, to whom he owed his early education and initiation into the Order, and with whom he had shared responsibilities for the family for many years, died about this time. Then his only surviving brother, Prospero, married little more than a year previously, lost his infant child and shortly afterwards died himself. Only his sister, Camilla, now widowed, remained with Felice as the direct descendants of Peretto, and it was natural that he should seek solace with her and her two children, Francesco and Maria. His only other close relative was his cousin, Flora, recently married to a respected citizen of the town who eventually bore two daughters and a son; Felice formed a close affection for the latter.

Suddenly on 5th September 1561, Delfini, the Vicar-General died at Bologna. It was essential to appoint his successor without delay so that he would take office until the Chapter-General to be held the following year could choose a new General. The choice of the Vicar-General was critical, especially as six months later he could be expected to become General. The Procurator (regarded as Deputy to the Vicar-General), Antonio Sapienti, was also absent from Rome making preparations to resume duties as a theologian to the Council (he had served there in 1552) which was in the process of re-convening at Trent. Sapienti had repulsed the attempt of the Calvinists to occupy the town of Noyon and to detach it from the Duchy of Savoy; a man of military determination and courage, he was also a great scholar who after being Regent in two Franciscan houses had become Professor of Theology at the University of Pavia. Sixtus' biography records that he had nursed a long-standing but groundless animosity against Felice, but it would appear this had not yet led to open conflict. Carpi instructed his Secretary, Botius, to recall both Sapienti and Felice to Rome immediately. Sixtus' biographer records that the Secretary urged Carpi to appoint Felice as Vicar-General. Carpi, however, knew that this would be contrary to the traditions and practice of the Order, realized that it would sow strife at a time when unity was urgently required, and that, in any event, Sapienti's scholarship and reputation as well as his experience in the highest office then open to him in the Order, could not lightly be set aside. In the words of the papal biographer, the Cardinal Protector warned his Secretary that to make Felice Vicar-General would displease himself and would not profit Felice, and proposed to make an approach to both Sapienti and Felice simultaneously so that neither should take offence. Unfortunately, the conversation was overheard by a valet and in due course re-told to Sapienti who, perhaps not unnaturally, resented the attempt to supplant him. However, the Secretary pursued his proposal no further, and after Carpi had consulted appropriate people Sapienti was appointed Vicar-General and Felice succeeded him as Procurator. At the age of forty this earnest friar was almost at the head of the Order and in a position of great influence. He had thirty years' continuous experience in the Order, he was an extremely able scholar who had had major administrative responsibilities, had been involved in political complications of a delicate and educative character in several Italian states, and needed only the final training of major office to be ripe for command of the Order. In this situation, if the animosity with the Vicar-General was bitterly wounding, Felice enjoyed a close and greatly valued friendship with Gaspare de Crispi, the vice Procurator, appointed to serve Sapienti as Procurator following the death of the Procurator Oltramontani.[135]

Unfortunately, this personal enmity between Vicar-General and Procurator was exacerbated by Felice's ebullience. Delfini had left a substantial estate which, in the ordinary course of events, would have passed to his successor, Sapienti. Felice, however, persuaded Carpi to allow this to be spent on improvements to the building and furnishing of the friary at Santi Apostoli, and these were carried out very successfully, as a result of which the Vicar-General developed an "implacable hatred of Felice". Nevertheless, the latter was surprisingly capable of showing the other cheek, and when the General Chapter met at Milan in 1562 he took the initiative in bringing about the election of Sapienti as General—a task which probably would have been difficult to avoid. At the same time Felice was elected Procurator.

Sapienti returned to Trent as a theologian and took an active part in its deliberations, though when the decrees of the Council were completed, unlike the heads of all other Orders taking part in the Council, he did not sign "manu propria". Meanwhile, Carpi was urging him to proceed with spirit and vigour to the reform of ill-conducted houses in the Order, and when the General paid little attention to the Protector's representations, Carpi withdrew his protection from those houses with which he was seriously dissatisfied one after the other. This form of discipline was highly unpopular: it revealed the inaction and lack of diligence of the General with regard to the whole Church, it flashed a stark light on those houses which had failed to reform, but at the same time it awakened a sense of guilt throughout the Order which some tried to assuage by accusing the Protector of ostracising those who needed his assistance most. Much of the consequent dissatisfaction fell back on Felice whom Sapienti regarded as the author of those troubles and who he was convinced was actuated by jealousy and unreasoning ambition.

One profound sorrow Protector and Procurator shared together. On 18th February 1564 the incomparable architect, sculptor, engineer and artist, Michelangelo, who had been working in Rome for the past twenty-seven years, died. His body was carried by the Confraternity of San Giovanni Decollato, a guild to which Michelangelo had belonged for more than half a century, in a vast procession from his studio in via Macel dei Corvi, near Trajan's forum, to the Basilica of Santi Apostoli. It is inconceivable that Cardinal Carpi or Felice, Procurator of the Franciscan Order and therefore resident in Santi Apostoli, should have failed to pay their respects to the Master. Carpi, as a Cardinal member of the Papal commission responsible for the rebuilding of St Peter's had resisted with unwavering pertinacity the attempts led by Michaelangelo's great enemy, detractor and rival Nanni Bigio, to have him removed from his appointment as architect of St Peters. In lower but intimate tones Felice must have admired the Protector's friend and his own distinguished and aging parishioner. Michelangelo had always wanted to be buried in his native Florence and his nephew, knowing and respecting his wishes, surreptitiously removed the body disguised as merchandise and within three weeks brought it safely to Santa Croce in Florence, where it was buried. In many senses Michelangelo's death marked the end of an era in the Roman calendar. The loss of his inspiration and dominant direction may have been appreciated and understood to a special degree by Carpi, the greatest patron of the arts and letters and by Felice, whose order had been pledged from the outset to the dedication of all human gifts to religion and to the cultivation of the beauties of simplicity. Neither could have dreamt of the part the younger of the two would play in marrying the skills of the Renaissance artist to the devotion and scholarship of the Reformer.[136] For Rome also, the death of Michelangelo closed a long chapter of history. It was almost seventy years since he had first come to the city; he had lived and worked there almost continuously for the past forty years. His artistic skill, his dexterity, his mastery of many of the arts, his fecund imagination and his eye for the magnificent and the imposing had stamped his impression on the century. His death was followed by a disputed succession to his position at St Peter's; there was rivalry amongst lesser men cast in a different mould. Much more than half a century was to pass before Bernini, less dominantly and more temporarily set his seal on the artistic life of the City.

Tragedy then overtook Felice. In May 1564, Carpi died in the Curia itself. For sixteen years he had been Felice's staunchest supporter and firmest friend. Descended from a noble and wealthy family, a doctor of the University of Pavia, he stood as Secretary beside Clement VII at the Sack of Rome and witnessed the dreaded price of papal involvement in Franco-Imperial politics. Subsequently he was Papal Nuncio in France in two separate periods (1530–1537 and again in 1551); he was also responsible for negotiations with the Emperor and the King of France in 1538, and on two occasions was named as Papal Legate in Rome when the Pope left the city. He proved himself a diplomat of great skill, complete loyalty and strong determination. He became Bishop of Faenza at the age of twenty-eight, and after renouncing that in favour of his brother was installed as Bishop of Agrigento in Sicily, never taking up residence in either diocese. At the age of thirty-six he was nominated Cardinal and from then onwards held great influence in the Curia. Carpi was Protector of the whole Franciscan family for twenty-three years, and he was responsible for dealing with the apostasy of Bernardino Ochino, the Minister-General of the Capuchin Order, and for preventing at that time its collapse or dissolution. He was also the first and only Protector of the Jesuit Order and a leader of the Roman Inquisition with the full understanding of Ghislieri, the Inquisitor-General. Only the most determined opposition of the French prevented him from becoming Pope in 1559. He never feared to espouse unpopular causes when his own conscience or judgement were at variance with current opinion. He was the only Cardinal not to oppose the introduction of the Spanish Inquisition under Royal control into Milan; he opposed the vendetta against the Carafa after Paul IV's death because he saw this as a distraction from the cause of Reform and believed it would increase bitterness and widen divisions to the detriment of the Church. He owned a palazzo in the city and built a new villa with large attractive gardens in the Quirinale; in his palazzo he gathered a collection of valuable small bronzes, terra-cottas, vases, antique furniture and books, manuscripts and pictures. His gardens with their beautiful trees and olive groves were the envy of Rome and in them Carpi arranged an immense collection of classical and Renaissance statues which was second only to that of Cardinal Ippolito d'Este (the owner and architect of Tivoli) and drew visitors from all quarters of Europe. He was a member of the Fabbrica, a Papal committee responsible for the re-building of St Peter's, and had a close friendship with Michelangelo.

It was Carpi who, impressed by the reputation of a young preacher friar in the Marches, recognised the quality and potential greatness of Felice, then aged only twenty-eight and a fledgling doctor. To this rich and influential Cardinal poverty and humble background were no impediments. From the day when he heard him dispute with Persico at Assisi, he was convinced of Felice's capacity and stood by him with unwavering faith. He was responsible for bringing him to Rome as Lenten preacher at Santi Apostoli, and for ensuring his appointment as Inquisitor. Three times he had taken steps to have him elected as a Provincial General. It was he who had supported him in every possible way during the Venetian crisis. More than once he had had to save him from collapse, even withdrawal from the Order. In his closing years Carpi recognised the strong opposition amongst the Conventuals to the advancement of this young scholar and preacher, and was content to see him installed with the full agreement of the Order as Procurator so that he should advance by the traditional route to be Minister-General. The Conventual hierarchy tended to be dominated by tradition and its emphasis on scholarship and learning produced a deep preoccupation, almost an obsession, with dialectics. It was probably no accident that many Ministers-General had been Regents in large friaries or Professors in Universities. Moreover, even in Italy, the organisation of the Order into provinces together with a severe control of monastic mobility, often created an unhealthy dependence on the state. Carpi saw learning as a tool by which the authority of the Church could be stamped on its members, as an inspiration to action, not a decorative talent, and whilst he respected the discipline of the Order, he regarded the Order itself as a servant of the Church, having responsibility through the Curia to the Pope. However initiatives might ebb and flow as one Pope succeeded another, the Papacy was evolving a consistent policy for the re-establishment of the spiritual direction of Christendom. Young men were needed with vision and drive and with loyalty through their superiors, however remote from Christian capital, to the Pope and his court.

Recognising the Renaissance Arts as allies, not enemies, of the Church, and uninhibited by his own non-residence in his dioceses, Carpi was fully committed to the reform of the church and the repulse of Protestant heresies. He saw the dangers of political entanglements outside Italy and set the spiritual responsibilities of the Pope far above those of his temporal sovereignty. As an untiring Cardinal of the Roman Inquisition he accepted the need to achieve theological orthodoxy with as much conviction as was possible; as a member of the Papal Commission for the reform of morals he recognised the damage inflicted on religion by laxity and indiscipline and personally followed the highest possible standards of conduct; he saw clearly the importance of the Council of Trent, celebrating High Mass in S. Maria sopra Minerva (the Dominican church in Rome) when the Bull reconvening the Council was published in November 1560. As Protector of the Franciscans he was deeply convinced of the part scholarship, the training of the regular and secular clergy and the education of the populace by impressive and forceful preaching would play in the restoration of the Catholic church. To him, Felice was one of the young men to whom the future belonged, whose learning combined with religious conviction to make their preaching effective in both religious and secular circles, and whose determination and indomitable purpose made them face unpalatable tasks with initiative and ruthless pertinacity. Carpi's faith in Felice had not only saved the young friar at moments of crisis but had matured his determination and ripened his judgement with wisdom and experience. A deep understanding had developed between the two and on Felice's side, at least, admiration and discipleship. How would he survive the master's departure?

## Notes

[1] P. Pecchiai, *Roma nel Cinquecento* (Bologna: Capelli, 1948), p. 447. *CEHE* 4, pp. 81–82.
[2] Delumeau1, p. 276.
[3] Ranke, p. 281.
[4] Pastor 13, p. 451.
[5] Fiammetta was Maria, King Robert's daughter. The date was Easter Eve 1341.
[6] Cugnoni, p. 124.
[7] B. Pullan, "Crisis and change in Venetian economy" in *Economic History Review* (22 August 1969), p. 368.
[8] D. S. Chambers, *Popes, Cardinals and War: The Military Church in Renaissance and Early Modern Europe* (London: I. B. Taurus, 2006), p. 39.

9   Archivio di Stato di Venezia, *Speculum Venetae nobilitatis, 1263 - 1654*. Serial number: IT ASVe 0325 009. See also F. D. Logan, *Excommunication and the Secular Arm in Medieval England: A Study in Legal Procedure from the Thirteenth to the Sixteenth Century* (Toronto: Pontifical Institute of Medieval Studies, 1968), p. 32.

10  B. Pullan, "Service to the Venetian State: Aspects of Myth and Reality in the Early Seventeenth Century" in *Studi secenteschi* 5 (1964), pp. 110–112.

11  *Ibid.*, p. 96

12  These were comparable in many senses to the medieval guilds: they had frequently a strongly religious character, accepted responsibility in life and death for their members and did much to raise their moral standards and their submission to state direction and supervision. See B. Pullan, *Rich and Poor in Renaissance Venice. The Social Institutions of a Catholic State to 1620* (Oxford: Basil Blackwell, 1971).

13  B. Pullan, "Service to the Venetian State", p. 145.

14  *Ibid.*, p. 101.

15  Logan, *Excommunication and the Secular Arm*, p. 32

16  Pullan, p. 150 Chambers, *Popes, Cardinals and War*, p. 128

17  Logan, *Excommunication and the Secular Arm*, p. 32

18  See *ibid.*, p. 21.

19  See *ibid.*, p. 20.

20  This section is largely based on Logan particularly to the intervention of the Nuncio who claimed extensive rights to supervise the Venetian church and clergy. Disputes about ecclesiastical jurisdictions multiplied and relations with Rome affecting ecclesiastical matters within the Republic deteriorated.

21  J. J. Norwich, *A History of Venice* (London: Penguin, 2003), pp. 194, 196.

22  A. Santori, *La Provincia del Santa dei frati Minori Conventuali* (Padua: 1958).

23  Archivio di Stato (Cat. 257), pp. 21, 45.

24  See I. L. Gatti, "Chiesa e Stato a Venezia nel Cinquecento in alcune lettere private dell'inquisitore fra Felice Peretti" in *Il Santo* 2-3/49 (2009), pp. 427-473.

25  Cugnoni, p. 125

26  *Album generale*, p. 329 and F. F. Benoffi, *Spirito della Regola de' Frati Minori commentata dalle Sacre Costituzioni Urbane de' Minori Conventuali* (Fano: Presso Giovanni Lana, 1841), p. 24

27  Cugnoni, p. 123.

28  D. Stella, *Eximii Vergi Divini Concionatoris* in *Sacrosanctum Jesu Christi Domini*

*Nostri Evangelium Secundum Lucam Enarrationum* (Antwerp: 1622), p. 278.

29  Some twenty years later, in 1583, when the Papal Nuncio was concerned about the faith in Venice, his tactic was to arrange a preaching mission—with disappointing results. (Stella, *Eximii Vergi Divini Concionatoris*, p.59).

30  Cugnoni, "Documenti Chigiani", p.123.

31  I. L. Gatti, "Chiesa e Stato a Venezia".

32  *Ibid.*

33  *Ibid.*

34  Cugnoni, p.122.

35  Chambers, *Popes, Cardinals and War*, p.134

36  P. Paschini, *Venezia e l'Inquisizione romana da Giulio III a Pio IV* (Padova: Editrice Antenore, 1959), pp. 108, 111.

37  In 1565 a Papal Bull ordered degrees to be restricted to professed Catholics (Paschini, p. 144). It was said that 4,000 German and English heretics lived there and corrupted the scholars. (P. Paschini, *Venezia e l'Inquisizione*, pp. 118–140).

38  Brown, p. 385.

39  In 1565 the Patriarch of Venice had to issue a decree to forbid clergy to carry arms.

40  Stella, *Eximii Vergi Divini Concionatoris*, p. 117.

41  In 1551 evidence was that "In the Udine of Friuli there are many Lutherans, including some in the monastery of Santa Chiara di Udine". The abbess was in touch with the heretical Bishop of Capodistria whose sister and niece were members of the monastery. (P. Paschini, *Eresia e riforma cattolica al confine orientale d'Italia* (Romae: Facultas Pontificii Athenaei Lateranensis, 1951), p. 85).

42  A. Battistella, *Brevi note del S. Officio e sulla Riforma religiosi in Friuli* (Atti dell'Accademia di Udine: 1903).

43  Paschini, *Venezia e l'Inquisizione*, pp. 104–105.

44  Paschini, *Eresia e riforma* , p. 47

45  G. Cecchetti, *Giovanni Vergara* (Boston: Twane, 1978), p. 197.

46  Stella, *Eximii Vergi Divini Concionatoris*, pp. 109, 110 and 124

47  Paschini, *Eresia e riforma*, p. 36

48  In 1560, Holy Office matters were delegated to Cardinals Ghislieri, Carpi, Madruzzo and Truchsess (Pastor 16, p. 309)

49  Stella, *Eximii Vergi Divini Concionatoris*, p. 49

50 *Ibid.*, pp. 290 and 293
51 Archivio di Stato, *Indice cronologico dei Processi del Sant'Ufficio* under year 1556.
52 P. F. Grendler, *The Roman Inquisition and the Venetian Press, 1540–1605* (Princeton University Press: Princeton NJ, 1977), p. 206.
53 *Ibid.*, p. 122.
54 I. L. Gatti, "Chiesa e Stato a Venezia".
55 Cugnoni, p. 23.
56 I. L. Gatti, "Chiesa e Stato a Venezia".
57 Archivio di Stato, *Indice cronologico dei Processi del Sant'Ufficio* under year 1557.
58 Paschini, *Venezia e l'Inquisizione*, p. 124.
59 *Ibid.*, p. 125, n. 2.
60 *Ibid.*, p. 124.
61 Some twenty years later, in 1583, when the Papal Nuncio was concerned about the faith in Venice, his tactic was to arrange a preaching mission—with disappointing results (Stella, *Eximii Vergi Divini Concionatoris*, p.59).
62 D. Sparacio, *Storia di San Francesco d'Assisi a ricordo del VII Centenario* (Assisi: Cefa, 1928), p. 34.
63 Paschini, *Venezia e l'Inquisizione*, pp. 123, 125; P. Paschini, *Due episodi della Contro-Riforma in Italia*, (Roma: Rivista Societa Romana di Storia Patria, 1927), pp. 324–325. Fonzio was drowned for his heresy and died impenitent and Sereni abjured two years later.
64 EC, Article on "Vergerio".
65 Cf. Grendler, *The Roman Inquisition*, p. 206.
66 Archivio di Stato (Cat. 257), p. 48.
67 I. L. Gatti, "Chiesa e Stato a Venezia".
68 Paschini, *Due episodi*, p.314.
69 Grendler, *The Roman Inquisition*, pp. 207–208..
70 *Ibid.*, p. 208.
71 *Ibid.*, pp. 208–209.
72 J. Hale, *The Civilization of Europe in the Renaissance* (London: HarperCollins, 1993), pp. 473–474; H. F. Brown, *The Venetian Printing Press* (London: John C. Nimmo, 1891).
73 *Pont. Max.*, p. 68. Andrea himself was not heretical.

74 Archivio di Stato (Cat. 257), p. 49.
75 Letter of Cornelio Divo, 20th February 1560, I. L. Gatti, "Chiesa e Stato a Venezia".
76 *Pont. Max.*, p. 68.
77 *Ibid.*, p. 65.
78 Grendler, *The Roman Inquisition*, p. 210.
79 *Ibid.*, p. 212.
80 *Ibid.*, p. 211.
81 *Ibid.*, p. 214.
82 *Ibid.*, p. 218.
83 The chronology of Sixtus V is somewhat imprecise. Muratori died on 24 July, and Giovanni Antonio Delfini was subsequently appointed Vicar General: the exact date of Felice's arrival in Ferrara is uncertain. Cf. *Album Generale*, p. 32.
84 *Pont. Max.*, p. 65.
85 Pistolesi, *Sisto V e Montalto da documenti inediti*, pp. 62–64.
86 Logan, *Excommunication and the Secular Arm*, p. 257.
87 G. Odoardi, "Serie completa dei Padri e Teologi Francescani Minori Conventuali al Concilio di Trento (1545–1563)" in *Miscellanea Francescana* 47(1947).
88 I. L. Gatti, "Chiesa e Stato a Venezia"; *Pont. Max.*, p. 67.
89 *Pont. Max.*, p. 66.
90 *Pont. Max.*, p. 67; I. L. Gatti, "Chiesa e Stato a Venezia".
91 I. L. Gatti, "Chiesa e Stato a Venezia".
92 *Ibid.*
93 *Ibid.*
94 *Ibid.*
95 *Pont. Max.*, p. 69.
96 Grendler, *The Roman Inquisition*, p. 219.
97 The Bishop Michele della Torre was an unusually energetic ecclesiastical reformer.
98 *Pont. Max.*, p. 69.
99 I. L. Gatti, "Chiesa e Stato a Venezia".
100 Paschini, *Venezia e l'Inquisizione*, p. 127.
101 Pastor 16, p. 305.
102 Grendler, *The Roman Inquisition*, p. 218.

103 *Memorie autografe di Papa Sisto V*, as quote in Ranke, p. 218.
104 I. L. Gatti, "Chiesa e Stato a Venezia".
105 Grendler, *The Roman Inquisition*, p. 256.
106 Pastor 16, p. 305.
107 *Ibid.*
108 I. L. Gatti, "Chiesa e Stato a Venezia".
109 Letter of 11 April 1560 as quoted in I. L. Gatti, "Chiesa e Stato a Venezia".
110 *Pont. Max.*, p. 69; I. L. Gatti, "Chiesa e Stato a Venezia".
111 I. L. Gatti, "Chiesa e Stato a Venezia".
112 Paschini, *Due episodi*, p. 320.
113 I. L. Gatti, "Chiesa e Stato a Venezia".
114 *Ibid.*
115 Paschini, *Venezia e l'Inquisizione*, p. 127.
116 Paschini, *Due episodi*, p.315.
117 Cecchetti, *Giovanni Vergara*, p. 332.
118 I. L. Gatti, "Chiesa e Stato a Venezia"; *Pont. Max.*, p. 70.
119 I. L. Gatti, "Chiesa e Stato a Venezia".
120 *Ibid.*
121 *Ibid.*
122 *Ibid.*
123 The Republic firmly resisted the demand for Andrea's surrender and long negotiations followed between Mula and Cardinal Carpi, Finally, Andrea having gone to Rome, Felice himself obtained his pardon from the Pope and he was restored to favour. Cf. Paschini, *Venezia e l'Inquisizione*, p. 129.
124 I. L. Gatti, "Chiesa e Stato a Venezia".
125 *Ibid.*
126 *Pont. Max.*, p. 70; I. L. Gatti, "Chiesa e Stato a Venezia".
127 I. L. Gatti, "Chiesa e Stato a Venezia".
128 Bartolomeo's departure for Venice was postponed so that "more effective and express instructions about this office" should be given (Paschini, *Due episodi*, p. 319) and in the event he apparently did not take up the appointment. Tommaso da Vicenza was the first Dominican Inquisitor from July 13th (Cecchetti, *Giovanni Vergara*, vol. 2, p. 10 and Pastor 16, p. 342n.).
129 I. L. Gatti, "Chiesa e Stato a Venezia".
130 *Ibid.*

[131] Grendler, *The Roman Inquisition*, p. 219.
[132] Archivio di Stato (Cat. 257), p. 51.
[133] Archivio di Stato (Cat. 257), p. 52.
[134] *Ibid.*
[135] Named Baldassare in *Sixtus V, Pontifex Maximus*.
[136] Pastor 13, p. 454

# CHAPTER 3

## The Hermit of Villa Montalto

*He could be stubborn, downright troublesome and persistent to the point of intense annoyance in order to get what he believed to be right. He did not like to be proved wrong on the albeit few occasions that he was. What he didn't want to hear, he ignored. He listened to criticism but he did not necessarily act on it.*

Martin Booth, *Carpet Sahib: A Life of Jim Corbett*, 1986

FELICE WAS NOW in a position of great difficulty. His unfailing patron, who for fifteen years had guided, encouraged and defended him, was dead. For Carpi, Felice had deep gratitude and great admiration, but the social gap between them was wide. Felice possessed the attraction of immense devotion to the faith, of unquenchable energy and relentless determination, but in their correspondence there is almost no sign of intimate attachment or personal affection. To Felice therefore the death of Carpi may have been a material rather than a personal loss. He now faced the bitterness and searing hatred of the Minister General of his own Order. As Procurator, Felice lived in Rome almost shoulder to shoulder with the Minister, and the depth of their antagonism became harder and harder to conceal. Regrettably Sapienti, like so many other great men in the Regular Orders, is little more than a name to history: whether the cause of the controversy with Felice was personal antipathy, or a genuine difference of religious conviction, cannot be discovered. That Sapienti was passionately orthodox in his beliefs is beyond doubt: almost thirty years earlier he had prevented the city of Noyon being overrun by the Calvinists and detached from the Duchy of Savoy. He had been Regent in the convents of Brescia, a city notable for its reception of heretics, and at Milan, and a Professor of Theology at the University of Pavia. He had attended the Council of Trent both during the period 1551–1552 and again in 1562–1563. Clearly a very able and distinguished leader of the Order, obviously much senior to Felice, and a formidable adversary. Felice must have been conscious too that even if his difference with the General was personal, there were deep and pervasive rifts in the Order. The Inspiration of the Founder was dimmed, inevitably the worldliness of an affluent and ostentatious Italy cast tempting allurements before the friars whose duties brought them into close contact with the secular world. Moreover, political pressure on the Order existed in the independent states like Venice, Milan and Genoa, which those who lived in the Papal States did not readily understand. The feud between the Minister and his deputy was particularly damaging because a large body of opinion was bitterly hostile to the religious Orders in general and particularly critical of the divisions between the three branches of the Franciscan family.

It was no doubt inevitable that Felice should be regarded by many as having achieved advancement beyond his age and merits, that he should be accused of inordinate ambition and that his success should be attributed enviously and maliciously to favour in high places. His close connection with the Holy Office (the Roman Inquisition) would do nothing to enhance his reputation in the Order. Challenge to the established order breeds sharp divisions of policy based as much on genuine differences of philosophy as on calculating opportunism. For many the relentlessness, rigidity and obsessive bigotry of the Inquisition were regarded as mistaken and of transient effect: its independence and arbitrary powers were sullenly resented. But Felice's new defender was the Commissary-General of the Holy Office, Ghislieri, whom Carpi had strongly recommended to his friends. Since they first met in Rome in 1552 when Felice had pleaded his orthodoxy and devotion after preaching in Santi Apostoli and when he was struck with terror by Ghislieri's penetrating eyes, a long association had developed. During his duel in Venice no-one could have been a more able and tenacious support. The Cardinal now had a profound admiration of Felice's resilience, endurance and determination. Ghislieri was a man after Felice's own heart. Seventeen years his senior, the son of poor parents in Alessandria in the Duchy of Savoy, a Dominican distinguished in an Order noteworthy for crusading energy, he was described by Delumeau as a "great fighter". An eminent scholar, highly qualified in philosophy and theology, he had fought heresy with unflagging pertinacity in several of the vulnerable cities of northern Italy such as Como and Bergamo. His talents and virtue had been generously recognised, for he had been Bishop of Sutri and Neri and then of Mondovi, and Cardinal since 1557, yet he continued a modest, abstemious man who insisted on travelling everywhere on foot and whose habit and table were rigorously frugal. Till his death a philistine in art, he remained shocked by the nudity of Renaissance statues. He had endured the misunderstanding of Paul IV, his friend of many years, and the compromises and lack of support of the current Pope, Pius IV: he was coldly indifferent to popularity and followed his own spiritual convictions with undeviating firmness. Attached to the Dominican Church of Santa Maria sopra Minerva less than a mile from the Franciscan Santi Apostoli, and sharing common interests and duties at the Holy Office, the two must have been in frequent contact.

Pius IV was openly critical of the work of the Roman Inquisition, but the suspicion that he wished to abolish it was unjust. He regarded the conversion of the heretic and his reconciliation with the Church as the Inquisition's main task. Sentences of death he regarded as an admission of failure to be imposed only when the heretic was obstinate in his heresy and dangerous to others. The Pope particularly wished to avoid conflict with the secular authorities. So long as this policy and the circumscription of their functions were accepted, he was prepared to confirm and even extend the powers vested in the Inquisition. It was to act against heresy (Protestanism, anabaptism and apostasy) and against witchcraft if it were heretical. Its jurisdiction extended even over bishops, cardinals, and royalty, though in these cases the right to sentence was reserved to the Pope himself. In 1564 the Roman Inquisition, now directed by eight Cardinals, was ordered to meet at least once per week either at the palace of the senior member or of some other Cardinal, for the number of cases pending was very large. In particular, the Inquisition was encouraged to hear abjurations in private so that heretics might be reconciled to the Church without the scandal of their heresy being publicly revealed and so that they might return to their offices without loss of reputation except that, even after abjuration, priests were debarred from hearing confessions. Felice had already been appointed as one of the Consulters on whose assistance any of the Cardinal Inquisitors could call and who were expected to assist in the close questioning of suspects, in the elucidation of controversial points of theology, and in the persuasion of the accused to accept orthodox interpretations of dogma so that they might be restored to its communion. In 1565 Felice, then Procurator or Deputy General of his Order and resident at Santi Apostoli, was given fresh duties. He was to serve as a member of a Tribunal, all of whose members were Franciscans, specifically charged with hearing abjurations in secret. All the proceedings of this tribunal were reported to the Cardinal Inquisitors. In this work his skill in debate and his power of persuasion would be given full scope, whilst his own integrity and personal conviction would guarantee that abjuration in private would not be a cloak for continued heresy, nor recantation an easy path to restoration of office. On the contrary, it was intended that removal of the disgrace of abjuration in public should encourage those whose lapse into heresy sprang from genuine frailty.

Felice was also a member of the Commission of theologians enquiring into the suspected heresy of Grimani, from whom Papal recognition as Patriarch of Aquileia (in Venetian territory) was being withheld and whose promotion to the Cardinalate was being firmly resisted by the Pope, even though it was vigorously advocated by the Republic and by Cardinal Mula, its former ambassador.[1] The allegations of heresy were based on a letter written by Grimani in 1549 and subsequently published and widely circulated. This was a most important case involving one of the premier Venetian ecclesiastics whose recognition and promotion were involved. The Pope particularly wished to avoid conflict with the Republic, potentially his most powerful ally against the Turks. Great theological skill and ability to unravel differences of interpretation were needed: Felice's merits had been recognised and to these he could add valuable experience in the Republic.[2]

Felice's campaign in Venice was well-known also to the Pope himself and he may have had contact with the Papal Curia through Pius IV's *Assistente* and domestic Prelate, Cornelio Musso da Piacenza. Musso was one of the most eminent theologians of the Conventuals who had occupied the Chair of Philosophy at the Universities of Padua, Pavia and Bologna, and who had been successively Bishop of Bertinoro (in the Romagna) and of Bitonto, and who had attended all the phases of the Council of Trent. He had an outstanding reputation as a preacher and delivered the sermon at the death of Federico Borromeo, the nephew of Pope Pius IV, in 1562. He too attended the sittings of the Holy Office and seems to have preferred the Papal Curia to the highest offices of the Franciscan Order, for he was never Procurator or Minister. Felice was still then not without the support of powerful friends from whom he derived the strongest possible inducement to be faithful to his convictions.

The new Protector of the Order was the Pope's nephew and counsellor, Cardinal Charles Borromeo, since 1560 Archbishop of Milan, a most fervent supporter of Church Reform, who was about to take up residence in his Archbishopric. There he was to prove himself a powerful hunter of heretics, a zealous Reformer, and the most devoted friend of the poor and infirm the city had ever known.³ It is said the Pope's choice of Borromeo as Protector was at the General's request and it is perhaps understandable that whilst the Observants also remained under Borromeo's protection, the Capuchins were allowed for the first time since their establishment to have a separate Protector, Giulio della Rovere. Whilst some form of amalgamation of the several branches of the Franciscan family was under almost continuous consideration, the Capuchins, who enjoyed Pius IV's particular favour, were taking steps to preserve their independence. Whatever the precise truth of this confused situation it is certain that the Protector's mind stood far above internecine rivalries and that he had too much regard for Felice's skill and reformist fervour to support any attempt to persecute him. In any event, Borromeo was busily engaged in completing his tasks at the Papal court so that he might take up those of his Archbishopric. In these circumstances the Protectorship of the Order was effectively undertaken by Borromeo's trusted colleague and friend, Cardinal Francesco Alciati, another faithful adherent of the cause of reform who subsequently took an active part in the reform of religious orders in general.

Inevitably distracted by these family and personal squabbles, Felice continued to follow his own convictions. The conclusion of the Council of Trent at the end of 1563 marked a watershed in the history of the Catholic Church. Doctrines were defined with a minimum of compromise. Misconduct, in particular clerical non-residence, was rigorously and in detail proscribed; steps were taken to produce an elevated standard of learning and teaching and the Papal power was immensely strengthened. Accepting, at least for the time being, the secession of Protestant countries, the unity of the Church was emphasized and the flow towards heresy was identified. Discipline in the regular Orders was to be enforced with determination. Specially important for the Conventuals was the Council's insistence on a strict observance of the vows, and the attempt to reconcile the authority of the Order with the jurisdiction of the bishops, the complete proscription of private property and misappropriation of communal possessions. Felice accepted these new demands with contentment. If the Tridentine decrees were to be obeyed by the Order (more than sixty Conventuals had assisted in the Council) it was essential that its leaders should set the example for the more lowly brethren to follow. In any event, the position of the Procurator General, the deputy of the Order, was too vulnerable for risks to be taken; surrounded by volumes of ill-will, the slightest breath of scandal could easily wreck his career. For reasons of honest conviction or of prudence in November, 1564, Felice "of his own free will" surrendered all the rights he then held in his personal property to the Vicar-General as the head of the Order, the use of which he had enjoyed by orders of previous Generals "for the necessities of life". The instrument of renunciation records that he had no hereditary property, for anything which might have been bequeathed to him on the death of his brother was given with the consent of the General of the Order at that time to his niece. What he surrendered to the Order therefore were goods "acquired by honest labours of teaching and preaching". These included a plot of land in Montalto, certain monies owing to him by the Order in respect of sums he had expended as Procurator, against which he offset "many" debts he owed to others, a library of 740 books, a small amount of silver, a few items of clothing and two chests. Various other debts were outstanding, particularly for hay and straw and the daily expenses of the mule he kept. The most valuable property surrendered to the Order was undoubtedly Felice's library. Many of the books had been bequeathed to him nine years earlier whilst he was Regent in Naples by Marmilio Adamantino da Monte Lupone, others had been bought in Naples from Brianzo and others in Rome.[4] Almost two-thirds of his books were works of theology, philosophy or jurisprudence. The precision with which Felice's possessions are recorded for solemn surrender seems somewhat pedantic, for in aggregate they were no more than his clerical position would warrant, and were no distracting luxury. Equally, it has to be said that the surrender entailed little sacrifice and seems almost self-righteous. However, it was important that the Tridentine decrees should be strictly observed, it was necessary for the leaders of the Orders to set the brethren an unequivocal example, to Felice it was imperative that his character should be completely beyond reproach. Nothing is known of any similar act of renunciation by the General.

The feud between General and Procurator was bitter and unconcealed when the Chapter-General met at Florence in 1565. The Chapter grievously wounded Felice. Sapienti was re-elected General for a second triennium, a clear sign of confidence the Order as a whole reposed in him. Moreover, he produced a new Constitution for the Order framed in the spirit of the Council of Trent and this was received with overwhelming acclaim by the Chapter and the friars throughout the Order. History has acknowledged this as a work of great merit from which the Order derived considerable benefit. This same Council resolved to bring to an end the arrangement by which the Order had two Procurators and Tommaso Origoni da Varese was elected to the post: Felice no longer held any office or responsibility in the Order and the future must have seemed most unpromising. Felice was at the Chapter so that he might deal with any matters concerning his Office, but the General gave him no opportunity to contribute to the proceedings and showed how grudgingly his presence was permitted. As his forbearance wore thin Felice returned to Rome, outraged, and complained to the Pope, to the Protector, Cardinal Borromeo, and to his friend Cardinal Ghislieri. Reconciliation was impossible, the removal of the General was not to be contemplated, and in any event, would have been impracticable so soon after his re-election. It would appear that Felice had understanding and support in the Roman curia, for in the latter part of the same year Pope Pius IV, on Ghislieri's recommendation, named him as theologian to the Commission being sent to Spain to deal with the case of Archbishop Carranza of Toledo. The Commission comprised Cardinal Boncompagni as Legate, Castagna, Archbishop of Rossano as Nuncio, Aldobrandini as Auditor to the Legate, and Felice as theologian—a quartet of future Popes said to be unique in history: Gregory XIII (1572–1585), Urban VII (1590), Clement VIII (1592–1605) and Sixtus V (1585–1590).

The Archbishop, one of the foremost ecclesiastics in Spain, had been accused of heresy, and Philip II, notwithstanding the Archbishop's faithful service to the Crown, allowed him to be imprisoned, hoping in this way to re-emphasise royal power over the Church. The king insisted, however, that the Archbishop be tried in Spain and Pius IV had finally been persuaded to send this Commission to Spain to examine the Archbishop on the understanding that sentence would be passed in Rome. When in November the Commission arrived, it found its members would merely sit alongside the Spanish members of the Inquisition, and the King was quite unwilling that sentence should be the prerogative of the Pope. Pius IV died on December 9th, and when the news reached Spain, Boncompagni immediately set off for Rome so that he might take part in the Conclave. Proceedings against Carranza were therefore again suspended. To have been appointed theologian to so important a Commission was a great honour for Felice, clear recognition of his scholarship, and a tribute to his experience with the Holy Office and skill in the intricacies of theology. The enterprise took Felice to Spain for the first time in his life, and re-introduced him to the world of political machination.

For Felice, however, this undertaking was a further disappointment. Boncompagni studiously slighted his theologian. He was made to go short of food, and not having been assigned a mule for his own use was obliged to travel in the baggage train. Whatever the cause of their disagreement, the antipathy appears to have been personal, for there is no evidence of disagreement with other members of the Commission. Boncompagni was almost twenty years Felice's senior and may have resented his theologian's confidence and assertiveness. The Cardinal was a very distinguished lawyer and Felice may have found his precision and exactitude irksome: in the absence of any strong feeling of regard for his theologian the Legate may have paid less regard to Felice than he should. On the other hand, it is hard to avoid entirely the suspicion that Felice may have been excessively sensitive, prone to suffer injury where none was intended, though it must be added that Sixtus's Biographer credits him with "long-standing patience" and outstanding equanimity in bearing misfortunes. Certainly Felice had lived through nine testing years since he was sent to Venice; he was impatient for reform, though on this count he could have no complaint against Boncompagni who had played a quite notable part in the Council of Trent and who later as Pope forwarded the cause of the Counter-Reformation with every possible diligence. It is certainly curious that an association of a mere two months left so bitter an antipathy that it was revived when Boncompagni was Pope. It was probably a dejected Felice who made his way back to Italy nursing a sense of frustration and injustice.

Suddenly and with no warning, Felice's fortune changed. The Conventual General who had undertaken the long journey to visit his brethren in Spain, collapsed at Milan and died on 6th January 1566. His body was carried to Rome, and buried in Santi Apostoli where a notable monument was subsequently raised in his memory. Three days after Sapienti's death, Ghislieri, Felice's friend and supporter, was elected Pope. Nothing could have been more opportune for Felice. The Procurator, Tommaso da Varese, taking advantage of Felice's absence, immediately claimed the office of Vicar-General, producing letters from Pope Pius IV nominating him to that position in the event of the Minister's death, and petitioning both the Pope and the Protector, Cardinal Borromeo, on this basis. This contention was unacceptable to the newly-elected Pope for "mindful of his old companion he replied that he knew that that office belonged by the established rules of that Order to the Procurator-General but because Felice had been overthrown unjustly by violence and faction at the chapter in Florence it was proper that as a man who had been wrongfully harassed he should recover his rights." The leaders of the

Order were convened at Milan where the protector, Cardinal Borromeo, was Archbishop, and after the Pope's wishes had been conveyed to them by Cardinal Borromeo and Varese, Felice was unanimously chosen as Vicar-General. The Pope expressed his satisfaction with their decision and the appointment dated from 14th January. The news of his elevation reached Felice on March 1st when he arrived at Asti. Little more than a fortnight later the great and little seals of the Order were presented to him in the Mother church at Assisi and he was provided with two mules and a horse. Three months later on June 21st he presented himself to the Pope and received his blessing as Vicar-General. This must have been a memorable meeting of old friends; the Pope, confident that at the head of one of the largest religious Orders there was now installed a man of immense religious devotion and conformity, unbounded energy and zeal; the friar knowing how much he owed the Pope and how entirely united were their sympathies and propensities.

According to the *Vita Sixti V, ipsius manu emendata*, soon after his election to the Vicar-Generalate (*nec multo post*, not much later) "he set out with the authority of Pope Pius V for an inspection of Franciscan affairs in Spain and brought back from there a reputation for bringing friends together and for restoring established discipline by his diligence." It is impossible to give any greater precision to the phrase *nec multo post* and the record of the Vicar-General's activities in the Registers preserved in the archives of Santi Apostoli in Rome makes it difficult to specify in 1566 when such a visitation could have taken place. Visits by a General of the Order and by his Vicar-General only shortly afterwards indicate the transaction of highly important business. There were thirty-seven Conventual monasteries in Aragon, forty-two in Castile, the same number in Portugal, virtually all founded within a century of the death of St Francis.[5] Very many of these houses were small, supervision was difficult and conditions and conduct had deteriorated. King Philip urged on by Bernardus de Fremeda of the Observants and Bishop Concleusis had been pressing for reform and amalgamation of the Conventuals with the Observants, a reorganisation which had been attempted almost half a century earlier by Cardinal Ximénes. It would be reasonable to suppose therefore that these two visits were in some way related to the changes being contemplated. Friction between the two branches of the Franciscan family was to be prevented by every possible measure. In December of the same year whilst Felice was in Southern Italy, the transfer of all these Conventual houses to the jurisdiction of the Observants was approved by Pius V, apparently without friction.[6] The Annals of the Order record that "although the greater houses of the Conventuals were transferred to the Observants, the total transfer was not completed on account of the distances from one house to another and of the smaller number of the Observants in relation to the number of the friaries to be occupied." Curiously enough there is no reference to this very drastic amputation[7] in the registers of the Vicar-General.[8] Nevertheless the event must have made an ineradicable impression on his mind and made him permanently sensitive to the designs even of Catholic monarchs to establish control over every part of their realm. He may however have been disposed to accept the decision because it was approved by the newly elected Pope Pius V, his personal friend or it is likely that he judged the transfer to be in the interests of the Franciscan family and of the church as a whole. If so he proved himself a realist whose appreciation of broad religious interests outweighed any partisanship he may have had—information on this curious affair is frustratingly incomplete.

Later in the same year, on 15th November, Pius appointed Felice Bishop of Sant'Agata dei Goti, a suffragan bishopric within the jurisdiction of the Archbishop of Benevento instructing him, however, to continue in office as Vicar-General of his Order. On January 12th 1567, Felice was consecrated at a ceremony of great pomp in the Cathedral of San Lorenzo in Naples by the Bishop of Castellammare, a suffragan of the diocese of Taranto, the Archbishop of Naples and a number of other bishops attending.

At the age of forty-five, in the very prime of life, the up-country boy, born in penury, arrived to direct the Order he had served for thirty-six years. Under his command were twenty-eight provinces and four vicariates covering the major part of Europe, the Holy Land, Trebizond and Tartary: he had responsibility for more than 1,300 houses, accommodating perhaps 20,000 brethren. Even though the charge of some of these provinces was little more than titular, in the peninsula of Italy alone there were fourteen provinces (Sardinia and Corsica were also Franciscan provinces) with 561 houses and perhaps 15,000 friars. He was a man of no more than medium build, but of remarkable vitality and powers of endurance; he was now the sole survivor of his father's five sons. His devotion to his Order was intense and unwavering. In a century noted for learning he was remarkable for his scholarship. He was well skilled in Latin with a thorough knowledge of classical texts in that language: he knew some Greek and was patient and painstaking in searching for precision in theological sources. He had a keen memory and an acute sense of relevance and context. Nevertheless, he was never credited with great originality of thought, he was analytical rather than creative and his study of the Fathers, especially of St Ambrose and St Augustine, never tempted him, as they had tempted Luther, to question established opinions. He knew well that the line between orthodoxy and heresy could be like one syllable and its neighbour. His experience had taught him to respect his masters and authority, rather than rely on individual initiatives. He therefore enjoyed an outstanding reputation for skill in disputation. He had a talent for marshalling argument, for countering claims with rebuttals based on proof; he had an eye for the advantage in dispute and an alert capacity for making an impression. Always a formidable opponent in theological debates at a high intellectual level, he could be merciless in the demolition of questionable prepositions.

His reputation in the Order was first established by his preaching. As a young friar in his twenties he had begun to attract large congregations in the Marches and his drawing power had brought him preaching commissions in Cathedrals and the capital church of the Order as well as in numerous towns from Venice to Naples. His sermons were not distinguished by originality of subject matter nor, so far as can be judged from such records as remain, by strikingly logical development of reasoning or felicity of phrase. His subjects were generally doctrinal and his method dialectical; he concerned himself with fine points of belief; subtle distinctions and accurate definitions. His appeal was to the intellect which he stimulated with frequent quotations from the Fathers, he was erudite and analytical, rarely creative or emotive. The success of his preaching derived, it seems, from his personal magnetism, the flash of his eyes, the force of his words, the attraction of his personality and outspokenness. He was listened to with awe, his argument was followed with eager respect and enthusiasm; crowds thronged to his pulpit to enjoy the vigour of his delivery. His appeal was personal, immediate, and perhaps ephemeral. It is true that 400 copies of Felice's work on St Matthew were printed at Naples, that a publisher there bought some of his books and a hundred of his sermons, and that his sermons—reprinted at least twice—passed into a third edition during his Papacy, and were finally translated into Latin,[9] but in an era when printing presses were avid for material this is not particularly remarkable.[10] For example, his fellow Franciscan, Cornelio Musso, had eight volumes of sermons published at Venice and Turin between 1554 and 1590, with a striking burst of publications in 1575 following his death. His sermons were translated into Latin, French and Spanish.[11]

Felice's experience in the Order was impressively extensive and varied. He had travelled some thousands of miles throughout Italy, generally on foot but on occasions, to the irritation of the purists in the Order, on horse. He knew intimately almost all parts of the Papal States. He had taught in the Duchy of Tuscany, the Kingdom of Naples and the Republic of Venice: he had spent some time recently in Spain. In those countries he had seen the political influences which weighed on the Church and from which the mendicant Orders were by no means exempt, and he knew that political entanglements could not be evaded. For many years he had been associated with the Roman Holy Office, and it was through this that he won the support of his three champions, Cardinals Carpi, Carafa and Ghislieri. These three had shaped his career, given him scope for the display of his talents, encouraged and sustained his religious enterprise and advanced his interests. Few men of correspondingly humble origin have enjoyed such continuous and undeviating support and to them was largely due his advancement. Through them he enjoyed many contacts with the Roman Curia and was able to maintain a close understanding of the tide of Catholic opinion and policy. With such powerful favour he could neglect the widespread antagonism his exceptional fortune promoted within the Order. Crusaders make many enemies and fewer permanent friends. The new Vicar-General indeed was already notorious for his obsessive preoccupation with church reform, his hostility to all forms of laxity, particularly amongst clerics, and his implacable and relentless campaign against heterodoxy. To him the successful conclusion of the Council of Trent inaugurated a new era in which the Catholic faith was to be restored and re-vitalised.

For two and a half years he now had the opportunity to show how his religious Order could join with crusading fervour in the campaign to re-establish the unity of Christendom under the leadership of the Papacy. From the outset he tackled the task with complete clarity of vision, an immediate recognition of priorities and an unequivocal determination firmly directed towards certain identifiable objectives. The central organisation was minute for so large and diffuse an Order comprising a large number of houses, mostly quite small, each with a substantial measure of autonomy: this pattern of organisation gave scope for local initiatives but it also carried the dangers of lack of direction, variable and fluctuating standards of conduct, and loss of vitality. Felice recognised the Provincial Generals as the guardians of the Order's good health; he therefore withdrew the powers of General Commissioners who had, on occasions, invaded the rights of Provincial Ministers, weakened their authority and created duality of supervision. Having restored the control of the Provinces, he immediately recognised the critical importance of a wise choice of Provincial Ministers and of consistently exercising the centralised influence of the Order over them. Every three years they were elected by representatives of all the houses in their respective provinces: in practice certainly, the Minister General had no veto over this choice which was, however, subject to his approval. During the two and a half years of Felice's vicariate, elections were held in all the Italian provinces and in eight European provinces outside Italy. The Vicar-General appointed Commissioners to supervise these elections, except that in the Province of Naples (perhaps a significant exception); they were charged with making electoral arrangements, perhaps choosing the town where the provincial assembly should meet. In accordance with a decree of the Council of Trent, elections would be held in secret. Possibly these Commissioners mobilised opinion in favour of candidates known to and favoured by the Vicar-General—not unnaturally, there is no proof in existing documents, though it is known that at least one Protector-General of the Order had sought to influence provincial elections; it should be added, without success. During this period (1566–68) one Provincial-General was deprived—for unspecified reasons; for the rest, they were men of learning, long experience in the Order and, where we have information, they were men in sympathy with reformist elements in the Church.

    Felice was conscious of the far-reaching influence which an alert and active Vicar-General could exercise. From his quarters in the convent of Santi Apostoli at Rome he was able to meet regularly with his Procurator (a kind of ambassador for the Order at the Roman Curia), the General Secretary who was also Provincial Minister for the Marches of Ancona, the Provincial Minister of the Province of Rome and his personal Secretary. From this secure base he was able to make extended tours of inspection. In July 1566 he set out on a tour through the Province of Umbria, conducting official business at a number of Franciscan houses and spending a month at Assisi, the acknowledged spiritual home of the Order. From 23rd September 1566 until February 1567 he toured the Provinces of Rome and Naples, and took possession of his bishopric during the course of this visitation. This visit coincided with a determined but difficult attempt by the Pope to initiate an apostolic visitation of the Kingdom of Naples by the Bishop of Strongoli which the Viceroy bitterly resisted. Whether the two met is unknown, but since both were nominees of Pius V selected for their burning concern for the reform of the church, it may be presumed that each knew and approved of the other's mission. Returning to Rome for a fortnight Felice then spent three months in Tuscany, the Republic of Venice and the Marches of Ancona. During this tour he transacted business at forty places and spent three days at Florence, almost a week at Bologna, two days at Ravenna and a week at Venice. Almost certainly these journeys were made on horse or mule; they covered probably more than 2,000 miles and would have taxed the endurance of lesser men. Wherever he went we may suppose the Vicar-General brought encouragement and an example of drive to those he met, administering reproof and condemnation where he found it necessary. Perhaps he preached at least to his fellow friars, though the Registers do not record this. Certainly he must have conveyed his high expectations, zest and fervour, and demanded good standards of conduct and learning. Here was a Vicar-General satisfied with nothing less than undivided energy in the service of the Church, singleness of purpose and unquestioning attachment to the Order.

Felice hated misconduct, particularly because he knew there were many critics of the religious Orders who would seize every occasion to attach lurid scandal to them. He appointed a Visitor in each of the Italian Provinces, men of long experience and proven learning and ability. In co-operation with the Provincial Ministers they visited the friaries, praising achievements, criticising deficiencies, remedying inefficient administrations and reporting, it may be assumed, to both Provincial Ministers and the Vicar-General. In the middle of 1567 Felice appointed his Procurator, Tommaso Origoni da Varese, as Visitor and reformer of the whole Order. Wherever the Vicar-General went or when he resided in Rome, offenders were brought to him, or punishments imposed by Provincial Ministers were referred to him for confirmation. He recognised that the quality of the people was more important than the pattern of organisation. He took a close and personal interest in the elections of the heads of friaries and was careful to ensure that they were properly organised and faithfully administered so as to remove any possibility of corruption or mismanagement. The guardian of all but the three largest houses—Santi Apostoli at Rome, Assisi and Naples—were to be elected annually, though apparently they were eligible for re-election, this being intended to prevent them "becoming reckless and fractious". Here and there direction of a friary was so inefficient or conduct so lax that there was no alternative to the deprivation and replacement of its head. Consciousness of a concerted effort to return to the piety and virtue of the Founder must have spread contagiously from convent to convent; the lax and the perverse knew they were out of favour and faced discovery and disgrace. It is perhaps significant that the Vicar-General's registers record only one instance of his having to be concerned with heterodoxy of belief, a brother being accused "of publishing opinions contrary to the Council of Trent".

Standards of conduct were raised, discipline was tightened, and insubordination was severely punished; taking women into a friary, filthy conversation, violent attacks, murder and sedition, were some of the crimes recorded. Offenders were deprived of office, banished from their native provinces, bound in irons, beaten, or condemned to the galleys for up to fifteen years. One was ordered to be handed over to the Inquisition. Conduct in monasteries of the Poor Clares (the second order of the Franciscans in which women were enrolled) was a particular concern, and many such houses were closely examined, abbesses being deprived of their offices in some instances, young entrants being sent away and those who failed to take their vows and to become full members of the Order being dismissed. As years of subjection to the Rule wore on, the itch to return to the normal world would become unbearable for some, and the lure of the ordinary life may have been particularly strong amongst friars whose duties necessarily brought them frequently into contact with the cities and villages in which they laboured, ministering to the sick, teaching the young, helping the needy and the handicapped. Absence from the friary had therefore to be licensed, particularly if it entailed entry into another province. Authorisation was rarely withheld, it would appear, when adequate reason was provided, but in Felice's time applications to live outside a friary were closely scrutinised. During his period he issued a hundred such licences—relatively a quite small number—to enable friars to serve particular religious communities, to assist a bishop, to take up office as organists in churches, to superintend particular pieces of family business or simply to return to their native land. Transfers to other Orders were specially supervised, and in accordance with the decrees of the Council of Trent, this was only permitted in the case of an Order whose Rule was of equal severity.

But tight-reined discipline and rigorous punishment for dereliction from strict rules were not ends in themselves, but the means by which the Order was enabled to be efficient in its work. Religious Orders existed under the direct authority of the Pope, to assist the Church in a scrupulous maintenance of the faith and the pursuit of high moral and ethical objectives. As Vicar-General, Felice did all in his power to ensure that only those for whom religion had become, or was likely to become a vocation, were admitted to the Order, that novices were properly instructed in the consequences of taking their vows, that the friaries concentrated on genuine religious duties and spiritual preparation for them. Preachers, especially those undertaking duty at the great Church festivals or in churches outside their Order, were specifically licensed; elevation to the priesthood, which carried the right to administer the sacraments, was rigorously controlled so that unworthy candidates were not advanced; the right to hear confessions was tightly controlled, for abuses of the confessional were a frequent cause of scandal. Special emphasis was laid on scholarship. The intellectually able in the Order were encouraged to undertake rigorous study leading to the Bachelor's degree and then to proceed to the Master's or Doctor's degree, so acquiring the right to teach. Facilities for these studies were concentrated in certain of the larger friaries, often closely associated with the Universities. Master's and Doctor's degrees were conferred by the Vicar-General himself, the candidates being presented by one of the Provincial Ministers or by the Director of Studies at one of the large friaries. Standards of learning in the Order were high, and emphasis laid on attempts to rebut the contentions of the heretic and to support the beliefs and religious practices of the faithful.

The Order's temporal affairs were brought into conformity with the decrees of the Council of Trent. Friars who held private property, contrary to their vows of poverty, were obliged to submit to tribunals and to convey their possessions to the Order, having henceforth no claim to ownership or to use as of right. Guardians, Abbesses, Provincial Ministers, were all made aware of their responsibilities for the Order's communal properties, and applications to apply funds to particular purposes were closely scrutinised. At the same time, the Vicar-General ensured that funds were made available to assist particular friaries which were in need.

Friction between the regular Orders and the diocesan authorities had been frequent throughout the centuries and had brought much discredit on Christendom. Felice was meticulous in trying to obviate causes of such squabbles and to promote a closer understanding. The powers of the Order's visitors were carefully defined to remove conflict with Bishops and special commissioners were appointed to assist the Vicar-General in dealing with disputes.

Felice's years as Vicar-General were notable and he himself made an outstanding contribution to the tightening of discipline and the raising of standards of scholarship and activity in the Order. There is no evidence on which can be judged the extent or permanence of his influence; there is ground to suspect that, like his preaching, it rested largely on his personal energy and his own integrity and example. Only a succession of similarly motivated successors in the direction of the Order could guarantee the continuity of progress. When the General Chapter met at Rome in 1568, there was no move to elect him Minister. One Vicar-General had already been elected Minister that century and another would be similarly elected three years later; two had died before completing their period of office as Vicar-Generals. Reforming leaders possessing Felice's energy and forthrightness do not expect acclaim, particularly within the ranks they have commanded with such decision. Doubtless sighs of relief were breathed in some, perhaps many, quarters, that the reign of severity was ended: even if the new General were cast in the same mould he would need a little time to take up the reins, and even a temporary respite would be welcome. In the event, Felice's successor was Giovanni Tancredi from Colle Val d'Elsa, a Tuscan, who appears never to have held any senior office in the central organisation of the order; he died only four months later—a severe challenge to the Order's spirit and vitality. Felice perhaps had to learn as Churchill had to learn four centuries later, that monumental achievements bring no assurance of lasting affection, or even guarantees against unwanted retirement. To have attained supreme office in maturity of middle age must have been warmly exhilarating and a tribute both to his personal qualities and the judgement of his electors. But when his reign came abruptly to an end, like any other holder of an office of fixed duration, he faced the dilemma of choosing between alternative occupations of equal distinction and rigour, or sliding, either passively or disconsolately, into retirement and unwanted oblivion. With disappointment or good grace, Felice left Rome to return to his Bishopric of S. Agata, but even this high office must have seemed something of an anti-climax, especially as the prospect of further promotion must have seemed remote. The kingdom of Naples was a Spanish possession where suspicion of papal claims and a determined adherence to its natural independence were firmly established traditions. Ordinarily four days' journey from Rome[12] the capital breathed a detached, often hostile atmosphere, where Vatican appointments were distrusted and their loyalty to the kingdom closely scrutinised. Felice had known it more than a dozen years previously and had visited it as Vicar-General; to him, therefore, the problems and pitfalls of his new office must have been clear.

S. Agata lay some thirty miles northeast of Naples and about twenty miles from Benevento, to whose Archbishop Felice was responsible. Felice's ecclesiastical situation was particularly difficult and susceptible to quite remarkable political complications. Benevento was an island of papal authority surrounded by Neapolitan territory, and was frequently accused of harbouring refugees from the kingdom. How far the Bishop of S. Agata, suffragan to the Archbishop, was subject to the jurisdiction of the King must always have been problematical.[13] Situated in a fold of mountains, on a tributary of the Volturno, it enjoyed a picturesque detachment and a measure of substantial prosperity, with the city of Naples an open market for its surplus produce. Felice possessed too strong an energy and too powerful a spirit of unsatisfied restlessness to succumb to the temptations of gentility and ease. Pastoral responsibility for the diocese was a difficult and unpromising assignment. Felice's predecessor, a Sicilian from Palermo, Giovanni Beroaldi, was greatly skilled in civil and canon law and a most distinguished preacher who had been engaged in many tasks at the Papal Court and had preached at many ceremonial occasions there. Promotion to the bishopric in 1557 had been his reward, but from 1560 he was occupied at the final session of the Council of Trent, taking a leading part in its proceedings, delivering the oration at the opening of Session XIX, claiming to disclose the views of the Pope on a number of theological points and strongly resisting attempts to prolong the Council so that Lutheran representatives might be persuaded to attend. Neither the strictness of his orthodoxy nor his loyalty to the papacy were ever in doubt, but the exalted importance he attached to the Council brought him under suspicion of attributing to it authority greater than the Pope's. When he returned to a diocese to which he must have been almost a stranger, accusations were made and a Commission appointed to investigate his crime.[14] His favour with the Pope had been further compromised by an abortive attempt to have his relative, Alessandro, succeed him in the bishopric. Following his death in 1565 or 1566[15] there was a considerable delay in nominating his successor, and then a further delay whilst Felice was occupied in accordance with the Pope's instructions with the Vicar-Generalship. In effect, the bishop's throne had scarcely been occupied for a number of years, and this neglect was hard to remedy because of the many preoccupations of the Archbishop of Benevento, one of the most extensive archdioceses in Southern Italy, with no fewer than twelve suffragan bishops.[16]

Felice quickly began to reform the diocese, tightening clerical discipline, eliminating abuses, setting an example of punctilious attention to his religious duties. Had he remained there long he might have repeated the turmoil of his stay in Venice, for the Spanish Kingdom was as jealous of its autonomy as the Republic, the nobility wedded to extravagance, the clergy consumed with worldliness. Even after recent determined attempts to exterminate the Waldenses, the threat of Waldensian heresy and of rationalism had never been totally eliminated, and Felice could easily have stumbled into some hornet's nest. Instead he returned at an early date to Rome. The Council of Trent had condemned non-residence in the most unequivocal terms, ordering any bishop who was absent from his diocese for a continuous period of six months without lawful impediment or just and reasonable cause to forfeit a quarter of his revenues, and if absent for a further six months he was required to surrender a further quarter. Thereafter his absence was to be denounced by his metropolitan to the Pope. Even authorised absence was to be limited in any year to two months, or three at most, and the absentee bishop was required to appoint a qualified vicar to whom he was obliged to give a suitable portion of his revenues. He was forbidden to be absent from his Cathedral church in Advent, Christmas, Lent, Easter, Pentecost or Corpus Christi.[17]

Felice fully subscribed to the Tridentine decrees and so far as available evidence shows, set out to fulfil them. He was fully aware of the Pope's unwavering insistence on bishops being resident in their dioceses, but realised that the needs of the Papal Court and the Inquisition and the requirements of the Pope himself demanded his presence in the city. He therefore appointed in succession during the five years of his bishopric three distinguished and zealous Vicars,[18] and probably he adjusted his income from the bishopric so that proper provision was made for the care of the diocese. S. Agata could be reached from Rome in three or four days, and it is probable that Felice was able to visit his See at least occasionally, perhaps more frequently. Provincial Synods were held at Benevento in 1567 and in 1571, and as one of the archbishop's suffragans he is likely to have attended.[19] The Pope's agreement to Felice's transfer in 1571 to the bishopric of Fermo seems sufficient indication that his duties at S. Agata had been properly discharged.

In Rome, the Bishop lived modestly and without pretension with his widowed sister and her two children, a daughter and a son, probably both in their early twenties. The former, Maria Felice, married Fabio Damasceni, a Roman gentleman, probably in 1568 or 1569,[20] and the Bishop provided a handsome dowry of 3,000 scudi, and the bride was so comfortably placed that she was able to renounce lands in Montalto which she had received from her uncle at her majority in favour of her younger brother.[21] Subsequently Maria Felice bore four children, two boys and two girls, of whom Felice became extremely fond, Maria Felice and her family continuing to live with Camilla and the Bishop. It is said the Bishop lived in Via Papale which ran from Campo dei Fiori towards Piazza San Pantaleo;[22] in 1570 he was residing at number 22, via dei Banchi Vecchi.[23] Both were near the heart of the medieval city on a low-lying basin behind the main loop of the river Tiber between Ponte S. Angelo and Ponte Sisto. Streets in that area were dark and narrow, the houses cramped and overhanging in spite of Sixtus IV's edict forbidding projections[24] and Pius IV's recent effort to demolish them; the water supply was drawn from the dank and polluted river which was in perpetual danger of flooding; malaria was prevalent and would be instrumental in Sixtus's own death. This was the Parione, the most densely populated quarter of the city where almost an eighth of the inhabitants lived in little more than a hundredth of the city's area.[25] It was an aristocratic area where lived the well-to-do, the officials of the Curia, booksellers, shops-keepers and merchants. But this was also the thriving centre of the artisans' trades where busy workshops lay behind many street doors or in the gardens beyond. In 1527 the Parione had a greater number of artisans than any other quarter except Ponte: it had a disproportionately large number of tailors and leather tanners and almost half the total of workers in precious stones and metals in the City. The Florentine quarter was situated to the North-West of it, the Spanish quarter to the North-East, the Bishop thus living on a cosmopolitan axis of the city. The Vatican and the Papal Chancellery were within easy reach; the office of the Inquisition somewhat more distant; Santi Apostoli, the Bishop's spiritual home and the neighbouring Palace of the Colonna towering more than a mile to the East at the foot of the Quirinale hill. Felice was now a fully-fledged Roman citizen; his sister sold her house in Montalto for 300 scudi, so proclaiming as permanent the family's transfer to the capital.[26]

Camilla was an attractive and accomplished woman, a careful household manager, resourceful and modest. In her company Felice became relaxed and content. But the City and the Papal court were full of whispers. There were recurring muffled accusations of wealth acquired and maintained contrary to his Franciscan vows, and Cardinal Bonelli, the Pope's nephew, is said to have encouraged Felice's detractors.[27] Whilst still Vicar-General, it was reported that the Pope himself visited his rooms at Santi Apostoli to remove from his mind doubts of his protégé's extravagance, but as a result of the visit Felice was completely exonerated. He was accused of unwarranted ambition in a Report to Cardinal Farnese, and the *Avviso* of May 12th 1568, reported that he was in disgrace because the Pope had discovered he had two daughters in a Tuscan convent—the only accusation of immorality ever recorded by history against Felice and one for which there exists not the slightest shred of evidence.[28] Then on May 17th, 1570, Pius V created him a Cardinal and attaching to the appointment a gift of 500 gold scudi, two copes, a silver mace and a pension of 1,200 scudi per year,[29] though he remained one of the poorest of the Cardinals.[30] Then the Pope appointed him to the Congregation of the Index and to that concerned with Bishops and regular clergy.

The fact was that Felice was deep in Pope Pius V's confidence and entrusted by him with tasks of greatest importance. After Carranza, Archbishop of Toledo, had finally been brought to Rome in May, 1567, a tribunal comprising four Cardinal Inquisitors was established and assessors appointed to assist them. Felice was appointed one of these assessors, and when the Pope called for the minutes of the trial to examine them before pronouncing sentence, he employed Felice along with Aldobrandini, one of the Pope's intimate friends, an able lawyer and an important official at the Papal Court, to assist him.[31] Under Pius V's inspiration the Inquisition was extremely active in the city, tracking down heretics with relentless energy and tireless effort, persuading them to abandon their beliefs, bringing the obdurate and the relapsed to heel and dealing severely with those who remained obstinate in their heresy. Four, seven, ten, even twenty-five heretics at a time were herded into S. Maria sopra Minerva, the Dominican church just off the Corso, to abjure in public before twenty, even twenty-five Cardinals and an immense crowd of onlookers. Some were imprisoned, many were sentenced to the galleys for varying periods or for life, some were beaten, the worst were handed over to the secular authority represented by the Governor of the City, who was often present, to be burned alive or to be hanged on the bridge of Sant'Angelo—the bodies being subsequently burned. Some of Felice's fellow friars of his own Order were amongst the condemned.[32] These occasions were calculated to publicise the Pope's determination that heresy should be eliminated from the City, to strike terror into the citizenry and the immense numbers of visitors and to arouse a feeling of righteousness in the hearts of the faithful. Felice was so deeply involved in the affairs of the Inquisition that he must have been a willing and active participant. He continued to assist the Pope in the case of the Archbishop of Toledo, was one of the four Cardinals to whom rumour whispered that the Pope would commit responsibility for all temporal affairs, and in 1571 joined the Commission of six which was charged with the examination and refutation of the confession of Augsburg.[33] Henceforth he was in a position of very great ecclesiastical influence. His promotion gave great satisfaction to his home town of Montalto which presented him with a mule specially selected by two men of the town who were commissioned to undertake a six-day tour in search of the best animal available.[34]

Next year the Pope allowed him to exchange the bishopric of S. Agata for that of Fermo. From this he would receive an increased revenue, amounting, the Venetian ambassador reported, to approximately 8,000 crowns per annum,[35] but in addition it entailed his official return to the Marches, his native land for which he retained throughout his life a deep and genuine affection. He did not, however, take possession of his new bishopric until 1574 when he stayed there for three months.[36] At Rome he was preoccupied with a study of the works of St Ambrose, a task entrusted to him by Pius IV and Pius V, which had been interrupted by his other commitments.[37] St Ambrose, Bishop of Milan in the latter part of the fourth century, described as "one of the most unbending men even known ..."[38] had played a great part in the conversion of St Augustine. Strictly orthodox in his theology, he was a most distinguished preacher and hymn-writer, probably the author of the Athanasian creed, and accepted as one of the four Doctors of the Latin Church. A fierce upholder of the autonomy of the church against the civil power, he had excommunicated an Emperor. None of the Fathers would have provided a more acceptable study for Felice, and few could be considered more relevant to the Counter-Reformation. His extremely extensive works, chief among them the *De Officiis Ministrorum*, had been published at Venice at the end of the previous century but a new edition with an authoritative commentary, particularly in the context of the Lutheran doctrinal controversies, was urgently required. So important a commission is unimpeachable tribute to Felice's scholarship and impeccable orthodoxy. The work was his prime commitment for the next ten years.

In 1571 also, Felice shared with the Pope, the city of Rome and the whole Church the celebration of the Battle of Lepanto, at which the threat of Turkish advance was turned aside and the Turkish fleet comprehensively defeated. Even if subsequently the triumph seemed more qualified than it appeared initially, largely because the extent of this success discouraged Venice from further efforts and made her less ready to be involved in similar entanglements, yet resounding victory it undoubtedly was. The hero of the hour was Marc Antonio Colonna, relative of the Marcantonio with whom Felice had had frequent discussions, who returned to St Peter's to be received in triumph by the Pope.[39] The city which had lived under the threat of Turkish attack for more than half a century gave the victor a triumph such as had not been seen since imperial days.[40] Permanent recognition of his exploit was effected in the provision of a magnificent new ceiling for the church of Santa Maria in Aracoeli and the creation of a fund out of which 73 spinsters clothed in red received 40 crowns each in that church.⁴¹ When Felice was Pope he nourished an insatiable thirst for the final overthrow of the Turkish enemy.

At this period Felice moved in a circle of well-respected ecclesiastics. Philip Neri was his neighbour: Cornelio Musso, Bishop of Bitonto, one of the foremost theologians at the Council of Trent and the most outstanding preacher in the Franciscan Order, was an intimate friend until his death in 1574.

Unhappily, jubilation was short-lived. Six months later on May 1st, 1572, Pope Pius V died and Cardinal Felice was present at his death, and no doubt at his funeral eleven days later. To Felice, Pius V's pontificate was an abiding example and inspiration. The stark austerity of the Dominican's personal life, his rigorous self-denial, the frugality of his household, his abandonment of every form of comfort or luxury, his complete and unqualified dedication to God, the Church and his fellow believers made an indelible impression on his Franciscan admirer and devotee. The relationship between them was that of master and humble pupil sharing the same singleness of purpose, the same abomination of heresy and infidelity, and the same faith in the final victory of the Church over its enemies. Pius V's determination to implement the Tridentine decrees, his insistence on the residence of the secular clergy, especially Bishops, and his undeviating opposition to the Turks were injected into the pupil's character. For six years Felice had lived at the Papal Court, sharing personal confidences with the Pope himself, imbibing from him attitudes of devotion and dedication, admiring his severity and resolution. Now that warm friendship was ended, the period of active employment in tasks of the highest importance was terminated. Felice stood alone. The Conclave which followed lasted only a single day, and elected without dissension Felice's one-time enemy, Cardinal Boncompagni, as Gregory XIII.⁴² This was in fact Felice's only experience of a Conclave other than that at which he himself was elected thirteen years later. Those years have often been described as a period of disgrace, virtual banishment and official inactivity for the Cardinal.⁴³ It is possible that this 'exile' gave him the sobriquet 'The Hermit of Montalto'. It is certainly true that he did not enjoy the Pope's personal confidence or favour, that he took a less prominent part in Curial proceedings, that he surrendered his bishopric in 1575 following some disagreement with the Pope,[44] though he continued to employ an administrator for at least certain of the Bishopric affairs, and claimed to retain the right of re-entry,[45] and that finally in 1581 the Pope deprived him of his pension on the grounds that he was no longer poor.[46]

His criticism of the Pope was open and unmistakable; he disapproved of Gregory's ineffectual administration, of his policy towards Spain, of his alienation of Venice and of his reform of the calendar; it was said in 1585 that the Pope's nephews and their adherents would have preferred any other candidate than Felice as Gregory's successor.[47] On the other hand, the Pope maintained a high regard for his theological erudition, his scholarship and his critical judgement. From 1571 till his election to the pontificate fourteen years later, Felice was a member of the Congregation of the Council, a very important Papal Commission established to direct the implementation of the Tridentine decrees continuously. Nor was he a merely titular member of the Congregation for as late as 1581 he took a significant part in the discussion of a controversial matter referred to the Congregation by his friend Charles Borromeo, the Archbishop of Milan.[48] The Pope consulted him freely about the case of Carranza, Archbishop of Toledo, whom Pius V had succeeded in bringing from Spain to Rome in 1567, and whose case was still running its course because of Philip II's opposition to a verdict being given by the Pope. In 1575/6 Felice was one of the Cardinal Inquisitors who concluded the Archbishop's examination and proclaimed judgement.[49] He was a member of the Congregation of the Council throughout Gregory's long reign and took an active part in its proceedings. For example he was one of the foremost members in response to an enquiry by Charles Borromeo to urge that the Holy Knights of Jerusalem, a quasi-military organisation in Milan, be subject to the jurisdiction of the Ordinary and be punished by him.[50] He was also a member of the Congregation of the Index, and was given wide powers in connection with the revision of the Index.[51] He was to examine Cardinal Charles Borromeo's request for confirmation of his fourth provincial council[52] and St Teresa's application to the Congregation for Bishops and Regular Clergy for the division of the Carmelite Order into two sections and the recognition of two Provinces each subject to the same Protector.[53] He was appointed in 1577 to consecrate the Bishop of Martirano in remote Calabria.[54] He had no difficulty in obtaining audience of the Pope.[55] In 1574 and again the following year he sought the Pope's assistance towards the cost incurred by the Priors of Tolentino, a town in the Marches near to Felice's birthplace, in repairing the walls of the town and in strengthening the banks of the River Chienti, and succeeded in inducing the Pope to order firstly the Legate of the Marches and then the Governor to attend to this business.[56] He made representations to the Pope about the establishment of a printing-press in Rome and the publication of works of the Church Fathers.[57] In 1578 he was a member of the Commission appointed to deal with the petition of John III, King of Sweden for certain ecclesiastical concessions, including the authorisation of Mass in the vernacular and permission for the marriage of clergy.[58] In the same year he was chosen by the Pope to hear complaints lodged by the civil authority in Milan against its Archbishop, Charles Borromeo.[59] Four years later, in 1579, he was appointed first Protector of the *Confraternita della Pietà dei Carcerati*, a newly-founded association in which the Pope was personally interested and involved. This was concerned with obtaining the release of prisoners, especially of those imprisoned for debt, and with their rehabilitation.[60] These duties obviously involved the Cardinal in responsible work in the Papal Curia and made it quite evident that his talents were not neglected, even though he was no longer in the inner circle of the Pope's confidants and was recognised as a determined critic of the Pope's administration.[61]

He played a prominent part in the celebration of the third Jubilee Year of the century in 1575. Fortunately, the inauguration of the Festival was not marred by an interregnum, as it had been on the previous occasion in 1550 when the Jubilee began during vacancy and the opening ceremony, which should have taken place on Christmas Eve, had to be performed by Pope Julius III after his election.[62] Pope Gregory XIII made himself responsible for the preparation for the Jubilee, held a special consistory to urge the Cardinals to enter with enthusiasm and determination into the celebrations and to warn them of the importance of the impression left on the participants. The celebrations had the fervour and moving atmosphere of a Crusade and were designed to reinforce the faith of the faithful and to awaken genuine repentance in the apathetic and the sceptical. The city is estimated to have received a total of 400,000 visitors, the crush being particularly heavy at Easter, in the month of May and during the Christmas season. A majority of the pilgrims came from various parts of the Italian peninsula, but large numbers came from almost every European country, particularly from Germany. Special indulgences were offered to those who made the pilgrimage, and special arrangements were made for their accommodation by the Confraternity of Santissima Trinità dei Pellegrini so that they were not left to the mercies of the professional hoteliers or to tramp the streets. Groups were formed so that they might undertake their religious solemnities in an orderly fashion. Cardinal Charles Borromeo, Archbishop of Milan, made the journey of more than 200 miles on horseback, specifically to join the celebrations. The Pope himself, now seventy-three years old, completed the pilgrimage of the Seven Basilicas with great pertinacity, and none was more devotedly prominent in these pilgrimages than the saintly Philip Neri, the re-building of whose church of S. Maria in Vallicella was just beginning. Cardinal Felice joined in these celebrations with enthusiasm, including the Pilgrimage of the Seven Churches, often with Philip Neri; possibly preaching some of the sermons. He is likely to have experienced great satisfaction in leading groups of visitors around the sites of religious significance and in conversing with the visitors.[63]

Meanwhile, he concentrated on the publication of the works of St Ambrose and his commentary on them. By 1577 much of the material was ready for printing and it was decided that this should be undertaken at Rome. Felice had the blessing, encouragement and help of the Archbishop of Milan in this task, from whom he received notes made after verifying the works of the Father, two sermons which had not been printed with his other works, and a portrait. The proofs were regularly sent in batches of five pages from Rome to the Archbishop for scrutiny, and by 1581 five volumes were completed and were highly praised by Borromeo.[64] The completed work was dedicated to the Pope.[65]

In 1573 his nephew, Francesco, married Vittoria Accoramboni, sixteen years old but already a notable Roman beauty, whose family hailed from Gubbio, and whose loose living had already opened the mouths of the gossips.[66] The marriage took place in the church of S. Maria della Corte (demolished 1594). On this occasion the Cardinal made his nephew a gift of 5,000 scudi.[67] Soon after the marriage Vittoria was receiving advances from Paolo Giordano Orsini, Duke of Bracciano, a member of an ancient Italian family of great distinction, and now a commander of bandits, notorious for harbouring assassins and brigands in his castles. He was suspected of having murdered his first wife, Isabella de Medici. The Cardinal and his sister tried to combat the influence of the Roman underworld by providing Vittoria with a little luxury and making her abundantly welcome in the household, whilst the Cardinal continued to pay Francesco a subsidy. Their efforts were unrewarded for soon she was grossly extravagant and spendthrift, and at odds with her mother-in-law, who dreaded her profligacy and wantonness. She was not on speaking terms with her husband, whose seniority made him an abrasive partner, in a marriage which, not surprisingly, was childless, and patently jealous of her sister-in-law's domestic equability.[68] As Maria

Felice's family increased, pressures on the Peretti household were intensified, especially as the Cardinal had accepted responsibility for his cousin's younger daughter. The elder daughter had been placed in the monastery of S. Giuliano at Fermo, the Cardinal providing her with a dowry of 300 scudi.[69] Subsequently he brought the son of his cousin's second marriage also to Rome, the child's mother having died as he was born.[70] To relieve the tension in February 1574 the Cardinal bought a house in Camilla's name in the Via dei Leutari, a street in the same neighbourhood, for 2,500 scudi.[71] This house he renovated and extended.[72] He also acquired several houses nearby, and five other houses all within the city area and for the most part purchased in his sister's name.[73]

Soon, however, Felice's secular activities grew to a scale which aroused critical comment. By 1578 he had acquired another house on Via Giulia[74] and in 1576 he had purchased a *vigna* on the Esquiline[75] and had engaged Domenico Fontana, an architect and engineer from Como, as his mason to build a villa there for him. At one time thirty builders were engaged in propping up the site on the slope of Santa Maria Maggiore, and Felice had to make payments to a number of workmen.[76] The Cardinal himself began to plant trees and to take a great personal interest in the development of the gardens. These would be one of Rome's largest and most beautiful estates. It was this new villa, still under construction in 1581, which attracted the notice of the Pope during his visit to the church of Santa Maria Maggiore nearby. This led Pope Gregory to withdraw the Cardinal's pension, allegedly with the caustic but understandable comment "Poor Cardinals do not build palaces".[77]

At the fifth-century basilica of Santa Maria Maggiore, Felice had already erected a monument to Nicholas IV, an eminent Franciscan, elevated to the Papacy at the close of the thirteenth century, who had built the apse in this church and made great improvements to the Lateran Palace.[78] Now he commissioned Fontana to build a chapel on the northern side of the basilica and to this the remains of Pius V were to be transferred and later his own remains were similarly to be re-interred there.[79] Such major undertakings in one of the four most notable basilicas in the city must have entailed consent of the authorities and inevitably became widely noted. When Felice's pension was removed, Fontana continued the work at his own expense, hoping that at some time Felice would again be in a position to repay him.[80] In fact, the Grand Duke of Tuscany recompensed the Cardinal for his lost pension[81] and made him other gifts,[82] including a payment of 1,000 crowns in 1583,[83] so that it would appear that the Cardinal and his family continued to live comfortably though in modest circumstances.

The purchase of properties in his sister's name and the conveyance of others to her ownership were devices too transparent to deceive any but the gullible, and suggest that the Cardinal recognised the vulnerability of his position, if not his guilt, in these transactions. But his sister had never had more than slender means,[84] was diligent in the care of her Cardinal brother and was acknowledged to have kept house frugally and entirely without ostentation. Was a Franciscan friar, sworn permanently to poverty, justified in using income, honestly acquired, for personal and family maintenance? His integrity was at best equivocal and not surprisingly he was suspected of being crafty.[85]

In the days of his prosperity, Felice was notably generous to his homeland. In 1578 he gave 1,000 scudi to provide a grammar school master for the township and neighbouring villages, together with houses as residences for the master and the scholars, supported by a further 300 scudi to be invested to maintain them. The following year he donated 1,000 scudi to the Commune to pay a Doctor to meet "the needs of the poor in sickness".[86] He also used his influence to forward the interests of Tolentino, some twenty miles from Camerino, his mother's birthplace, with whose Priors he maintained a correspondence extending over a decade.[87] Success in the capital never made Felice forget his humble beginnings or his country homeland.

However completely he became a citizen of Rome, he remained at heart a countryman, enjoying simple pleasures and cultivating natural tastes. Bitterness and ostentation were foreign to his character.

Suddenly and without warning in April 1581, the Cardinal's family hit the headlines. On the night of the 16th, Francesco, deaf to his mother's warnings,[88] was lured by his brother-in-law, Marcello Accoramboni, from the Peretti establishment into the darkness of the streets beyond. In the Sforza gardens at Magnanapoli, at the foot of the Quirinale, he was ambushed and murdered. Next morning his body was discovered on the street nearby, his head pierced by bullets and his body slashed by the swords of the assassins. There is some doubt that Vittoria was so depraved as to be an accomplice in this dastardly and brutal murder, though the fact that she was later carried off and married Paolo in spite of a Papal annulment and prohibition lent colour to her complicity, and Pastor states that she was privy to it.[89] In spite of the desolation of the Peretti household, the Cardinal attended the Consistory next day where his stoical fortitude was seen with astonishment. After suppressing his emotion during the discussion, he had a private audience with the Pope where he gave vent to his grief, though it is said he dissuaded the Pope from action against the Orsini for fear of causing armed conflict. An enquiry was launched but no effective action was taken. A criminal named Pallenrieri was put up to confess to the crime, claiming he had acted in self-defence; one of Francesco's servants was arrested as an accomplice. Meanwhile, Paolo and Vittoria were married, though a year later she was arrested and imprisoned in Castel Sant'Angelo for disobeying a papal order confining her to her father's house. She was subsequently released and exiled to Gubbio. After a re-marriage to Paolo she was allowed to return to Rome and the pair lived peaceably till the Cardinal succeeded to the Papal throne.[90] The incident demonstrated beyond all doubt the complete defencelessness of the Pope against lawless noble families supported by paid armed forces, defiant of all restraints of law and order. Gregorian Rome had its own Mafia. When he became Pope, Felice was to tell Orsini, "I voluntarily pardoned all you did against Cardinal di Montalto, but I shall not pardon what you may attempt against Sixtus". It is known that Orsini retired from public life.

Cardinal Felice withdrew from Court activities, living in the seclusion of his new Villa on the Esquiline, his sister his only companion. Her daughter Flavia died in 1582,[91] leaving her responsible for four young children, the eldest aged twelve, who were brought up in the household of Lucrezia Salviata, wife of Latino Orsini.[92] Felice, now in his early sixties, became a complete enigma. His former forthright outspokenness contrasted with the new morose taciturnity; the friar of fiery energy and distinctive vigour was now almost a recluse who appeared even physically frail and exhausted. The brittleness of his spirit, which had been evidenced so clearly during the Venetian episode, now seemed to have re-appeared with acute intensity. An air of mystery developed from his isolation; it was incredible that his ambition had evaporated, and consequently he was suspected of manoeuvring, of avoiding abortive conflicts, so that he might be prepared for a veritable onslaught when a propitious moment should arise. His talents were regarded as undiminished by papal disfavour; his support was still reckoned valuable; he was still reckoned "papabile"—a possible candidate for the succession. At the Papal Court he had few friends, but some of these had decisive influence; foremost among these was Cardinal Rusticucci, a middle-aged, able and energetic fellow-countryman from the Marches, promoted to the Cardinalate at the same time as Felice, a defender of the religious Orders and Protector of the Cistercians, who had been a Secretary of State under Pius V, and who—like Felice—suffered neglect and relegation under Gregory XIII. Perhaps Felice's most powerful friend at the Papal Court was Cardinal Farnese, immensely rich with expensive artistic tastes, his neighbour in the Parione, a certain candidate for the Papacy at the next election, to whom Felice had already pledged his vote,[93] and for whom he did, in fact, vote at the final scrutiny, after he himself had been elected by "adoration".[94] Farnese had been a close friend and energetic supporter of Felice's former patron, Cardinal Carpi, and had worked most strenuously in the Conclave of 1559 to have Carpi elected to the Papal throne. In fact, he came within an ace of success; Felice was unlikely ever to lack gratitude to such a man.

How far had thirteen years in the shadows damaged Felice personally or discredited him in the Curia? Much of Gregory XIII's policy deserved his support; Gregory energetically continued and extended Pius V's measures for the reform of the church and the implementation of the Tridentine decrees; he was determined in his attempts to unite Christian Europe against the Turks and had, therefore, a share in the victory at Lepanto: he showed great enthusiasm for the re-shaping of Rome; building roads, bringing in a fresh water supply, encouraging the restoration of old churches and the building of new. He contributed generously to these projects. Why, then, was Felice so strenuously hostile to the Pope and his entourage, until in the last years of Gregory's reign he virtually withdrew from the Court? Firstly, experience on the Commission to Spain in 1565 had shown the gulf which lay between their personalities[95] and the bitterness this engendered. Secondly, Felice nursed an acute sense of mission and a deep conviction of destiny and having outgrown fulfilment within the Franciscan Order felt exasperatingly frustrated by the neglect, even hostility, he experienced in the Papal Curia. Though by common consent a man of great fortitude and incredible forbearance, he was sensitive and easily wounded: perhaps family responsibilities and personal dependence on Camilla increased his vulnerability. Not notably egotistic, not ambitious in the accepted sense, and unskilled in scheming manoeuvres, he nevertheless regarded obstacles as unjust and disparagement as myopic. In his nature there was perhaps some element of puritanical self-righteousness. Men of action frequently find inertia galling, wounding, and finally intolerable. Thirdly, in the Curia there was critical resistance to Gregory XIII's advancement and enrichment of his two nephews, Cardinal Boncompagni and Cardinal Guastavillani, and outspoken opposition to his vaunted recognition of his twice legitimised natural son, Giacomo, and to the Pope's continuous attempts to endow him.[96] Felice was the more ready to support this opposition because another of the Pope's nephews, Cristoforo, was appointed Governor of Ancona where he was authorised to accept 'danegeld' from the bandits who had long scourged the region, and because Giacomo was appointed Governor of Fermo whilst Felice was still its Bishop and was actively supported by the Pope in his exactions on the district. Fourthly, Pope Gregory was deeply critical of older established religious Orders, though he gave generous support and favour to the Jesuits. In a period when antagonism to the Orders was widespread and sustained and after the powerful defence lent them by Pius V, this attitude on the part of the Pope himself was irritating and disturbing. Gregory's increasing dependence on Spain, even though it promoted continued resistance to the Turks, seemed to Felice imprudent and supine and potentially debilitating to Papal influence in foreign affairs. But above all, Felice was antagonised by Gregory's timid and inept failure to curb the bandits and maintain law and order, especially during the latter years of his reign when advancing years and ill-health sapped his physical strength and his will. The Francesco affair had understandably made Felice desperately contemptuous of a Government which could not ensure that its own dictates were obeyed and which was clearly powerless against a lawless and mutinous nobility. Felice was a man of authority, who believed just laws should be supported by effective sanctions, and was convinced that without civil order religion was weakened. Finally, perhaps posterity would be most critical of Felice's opposition to Gregory's reform of the calendar for this has been regarded as one of the Pope's great achievements and the reformed calendar as a most ingenious and beneficial measure of whose merits the whole of Western Europe was in due course convinced. It has to be remembered, however, that although Gregory employed the best mathematical skill available and consulted universities on a wide basis in search of a solution to the problems of the calendar, there emerged no clear balance of argument in favour of any particular scheme, opinion in the most learned circles of the day was deeply divided and the reform ultimately adopted was decided by the initiative of the Papal Court itself. Felice was therefore by no means alone in his condemnation of the new calendar. Moreover, he perhaps foresaw that this would be a fresh cause of division between the Churches of Rome and Constantinople. Though it is improbable that his family was of Slavonic origin, he was genuinely sympathetic to the Slav sector of the Roman populace in whom he took a great personal interest, and he may well have been apprehensive of the immediate opposition to the new calendar put up by Greeks, Russians, Serbs, Bulgarians, Rumanians, Armenians, Georgians and Copts,[97] particularly as Gregory's attempt to negotiate with the Patriarch of Constantinople completely failed before the Inquisition at Brescia,[98] and Felice found himself committed without preparation or respite to numerous important and tantalising disputes.

## Notes

[1] See P. Paschini, "Giovanni Grimani accusato d'eresia" in *Lateranum* 23 (1957), pp. 153ff.
[2] See Pastor 16, Chapter 9.
[3] He tended the sick during the plague of 1567–78 with complete disregard for his personal safety: his attempts to reform the Umiliati provoked an attempt to assassinate him.
[4] *Codice Vaticano Latino* 8656, III p. 595.
[5] R. B. Brooke, *Early Franciscan Government. Elias to Bonaventure* Cambridge Studies in Medieval Life and Thought, VII (Cambridge: CUP, 1959), p. 292.
[6] Edict, 12 December 1566.
[7] It involved the loss of almost ten per cent of its friaries to the Conventuals.
[8] *AM* 20, pp. 69–70.
[9] Narducci, p. 6.

10 Cugnoni, pp. 25, 29.
11 Pastor 17, p. 252.
12 Delumeau 1 p. 50.
13 See Pastor 16, pp. 373 and 17, p. 346.
14 Eubel, p. 215.
15 DBI.
16 Alire, Araino, Ascoli, Cerignola, Avellino, Boiano, Bovino, Larino, Lucera, San Severo & Sant'Agata de' Goti, Telese, Termoli.
17 H. J. Schroeder, *Disciplinary decrees of the General Councils* (St. Louis: Herder, 1957), pp. 28,165.
18 Information kindly supplied by the office of the Bishop of St. Agatha. The three vicars were: 1. Giovanni Battista di Picco: a doctor of law. 2. Andrea Lollo: a deacon of the cathedral. 3. Paolo Pagano: a doctor of law.
19 Pastor 17, p. 215n.
20 Pastor dates the marriage in 1572 (p. 43) but her son Alessandro was probably born in 1570 (Pastor gives his age as 15 when he was made Cardinal in 1585 (Pastor 21, p. 62). C. L. Tempesti, in his *Storia della vita e geste di Sisto Quinto* (Roma: a spese di Remondini di Venezia, 1754), gives it as 17 (p. xv); J. A. F. Orbaan in *Sixtine Rome* (New York: Baker and Taylor, 1911), p. 34, states that Alessandro was 13
21 Pistolesi, *Sisto V e Montalto da documenti inediti*, p. 76.
22 Hübner p. 22n.
23 Cugnoni, p. 7.
24 Delumeau 1, p. 240.
25 *Ibid.*, p. 225.
26 Galli, p. 58. Pistolesi suggests that the sale may have been to meet expenses expected to arise from the marriage of Camilla's son, Francesco.
27 Pastor 21, p. 38. Any animosity against Bonelli was short-lived, for Sixtus V made him Vicar-General of Rome and the Papal States very shortly after his election (See *EC*).
28 Pastor 21, p. 39.
29 Tempesti, *Storia della vita e geste di Sisto Quinto*, p. 77.
30 Delumeau 1, p. 453.
31 Pastor 17, p. 345.
32 Pastor 17, pp. 400–404.

33 Pastor 17, pp. 110, n4 and 129.
34 Pistolesi, *Sisto V e Montalto da documenti inediti*, p. 74.
35 Hübner 1, p. 223.
36 Tempesti, *Storia della vita e geste di Sisto Quinto*, p. 77.
37 Pastor 19, p. 41.
38 A. M. Renwick & A. M. Harman, *The story of the church* (Leicester: Inter-Varsity,1998)., p. 56.
39 See P. Paschini, *I Colonna* (Roma: Istituto di Studi Romani,1955).
40 Pecchiai, *Roma nel Cinquecento*, p. 133
41 Delumeau 1, pp. 263 , 431.
42 See pp. 102–104 above.
43 The author of the contemporary biography of the Pope, *Vita Sixti V ipsius manu emendata,* and the later writer Platina (1626) omit all reference to Gregory's reign.
44 Pastor , p. 40.
45 G. Beneducci, *Della signoria di Francesco Sforza nella Marca* (Turi: 1892), p. 23.
46 Pastor , p. 41.
47 Hübner 1, p. 203.
48 See *La Sacra Congregazione del Concilio 1564–1964*, pp. 254, 326.
49 The Archbishop was declared not guilty of heresy but was instructed to retract certain propositions he had published and was suspended from his Archbishopric for two years. He accepted this sentence but died almost immediately. See Pastor 19, pp. 297–320, and *EC*.
50 *La Sacra Congregazione del Concilio 1564–1964*, p. 254.
51 *Ibid.,* p. 262
52 Pastor 19, p. 99 n.1.
53 *Ibid.,* p. 158.
54 Cardella, p. 303
55 *Ibid.*
56 Beneducci, *Della signoria di Francesco Sforza nella Marca,* pp. 11 and 13.
57 Tempesti, *Storia della vita e geste di Sisto Quinto,* p. 86.
58 Pastor 20, p. 429.
59 Pastor 19, p. 99.
60 Delumeau 1, p. 499.

*The Hermit of Villa Montalto* 137

61 Hübner 1, p. 203.
62 See Pastor 19, p.203; Pecchiai, *Roma nel Cinquecento*, pp. 368–371; Delumeau 1, pp. 170–172.
63 Pastor 13, p. 27.
64 Cugnoni, pp. 136–146.
65 Pastor 21, p. 41.
66 Hübner 1, p. 232.
67 Pastor 21, p. 44.
68 The date of Francesco's birth has not been ascertained with precision. His parents were married in 1542, his father died in 1559 or 1560 (see Pistolesi, pp. 36 and 64), his sister was his senior. Placing his birth in 1546 seems reasonable; on that basis he was eleven years older than Vittoria.
69 Pistolesi, p. 77.
70 Galli, p. 71.
71 Cugnoni, "Documenti Chigiani", p. 7n1.
72 Hübner 1, p. 223.
73 Pecchiai, *Roma nel Cinquecento*, p. 151.
74 Cugnoni, "Documenti Chigiani", p. 127.
75 Pastor 21, p. 44.
76 *Ibid.*, p. 128.
77 Hübner 1, p. 224.
78 *Ibid.*, p. 225.
79 *Ibid.*
80 *Ibid.*, p. 226.
81 Pastor 21, p. 45.
82 Hübner 1, p. 225.
83 Hübner 1, p. 453.
84 See Pistolesi, pp. 76–77. She sold a house she owned in Montalto for 300 scudi in 1573, perhaps to contribute to the expenses of Francesco's wedding.
85 Ranke, p. 353.
86 Galli, pp. 98–99.
87 Beneducci, *Della signoria di Francesco Sforza nella Marca*, pp. 11–24.
88 Francesco and Vittoria lent the *Vigna* for 2 years, but Camilla had warned against going out (Hübner).

[89] Pastor 20, p. 536.

[90] Paolo died in November, 1585, possibly poisoned by a relative of his first wife, and Vittoria was murdered at Padua a month later by cut-throats hired by the protector of her husband's son by his first marriage.

[91] Pastor 21, p. 43.

[92] *Ibid.*

[93] Tempesti, *Storia della vita e geste di Sisto Quinto*, p. 145.

[94] Pastor 21, p. 22.

[95] See p. 102–104 above.

[96] During the celebration of Jubilee Year, Giacomo was sent away from Rome, much against the Pope's wishes.

[97] *EC*, article on "Calendario". In 1593, the four Byzantine Patriarchs and many bishops met in the Synod of Constantinople to launch an anathema against the calendar as contrary to the deliberations at Nicaea.

[98] *Ibid.*, p. 122.

# CHAPTER 4

### The Conclave of Sixtus V

*One of the most important who have worn the tiara, gifted with great singleness of purpose he proved himself a man of both genius and greatness in all his undertakings and in all his far-reaching designs.*

Baron Ludwig von Pastor (1854–1928)

ON WEDNESDAY, APRIL 10th, 1585, Gregory died, at the age of eighty-four, having held a Consistory only two days previously. Next day his body was carried in procession by the Jesuits, as penitentiaries of St Peter's, from the Pauline Chapel in the Vatican Palace to St Peter's, and there for three days it lay in state in the newly constructed Gregorian Chapel on which he had lavished so much care and expense. Then after the final obsequies at which a Jesuit, Stefano Tucci, preached the funeral oration, he was buried in a simple tomb.[1] Holy Week followed: the Cardinals resident in Rome began to assemble and those in more distant places were summoned. On Easter Day the Mass of the Holy Spirit was said in St Peter's and Marc'Antonio Muret, an eminent French scholar distinguished in Latin and Greek studies and a song-writer of considerable ability, whom Gregory XIII had called to Rome, delivered the oration *De elegendis* in which he emphasised the need to choose an able and eminent Cardinal for the Papal throne. Muret was credited with a masterpiece. Then a procession of thirty-nine Cardinals[2] fully robed in scarlet and singing the *Veni Creator*, threaded its way between two rows of onlookers up the grand staircase into the Sala Regia.

For many the death of a Pope was a calamity. Papal offices, many of them purchased or obtained by influence, came to an end like leases expired with no firm options. Debts contracted in the former Pope's name had now to be redeemed or contracted for afresh; often a new Pope gave his business to fresh bankers, brought fresh friends and advisers to court, followed new canons of administration and adopted novel or unfamiliar practices. Public business came to a halt and in many departments the shutters went up or transactions were deferred for unknown periods and officials were reluctant to engage in duties for which they no longer had their customary authority. Responsibility was so concentrated in the hands of the Pope or delegated specifically from him that a serious hiatus inevitably followed his death. Only the Papal Camerlengo, or Chamberlain, and a few senior Cardinals gathered around him could take decisions, and understandably even they were disposed to confine their activities to the minimum. The city authorities were so dependent on Papal administrators that political uncertainty, indecision, even confusion and chaos descended. The Pope's death was the signal for old feuds to be revived, old scores to be settled, for brigands and vandals to break loose. An atmosphere of carefree irresponsibility developed; everyone was apprehensive waiting to be plundered or assaulted. Protracted Conclaves were disastrous, as the continued preservation of law and order became increasingly difficult and the city authorities frequently had to petition Conclave to expedite its proceedings to save the city from ruin.

During the vacancy of 1585 disturbances in the city had been fewer and less serious than usual. Some prisoners escaped, including 36 due for execution before Easter,[3] and irregular troops, some under the command of Prosper Colonna, appeared in the streets. Cardinal Guastavillani, one of Gregory XIII's nephews, Cardinal Colonna and Cardinal Medici, were specially deputed to prevent bandits from raiding the City, and Giacomo Boncompagni, Duke of Sora, was allowed to take charge of 2,000 infantry and four companies of light cavalry, all armed and ready for action, whilst Monsignor Ghislieri had another 1,200 infantry to guard the Borgo (the district lying between St Peter's and the Castel Sant'Angelo). Whilst the Conclave was in session this firm control was maintained so that the election was able to proceed uninterrupted. The Camerlengo maintained a guard over all the rooms from within the Conclave and the marshal of the conclave (a hereditary office in the Savelli family) was responsible for guarding them from without.[4] Nevertheless the Interregnum was a period of intrigue, of lobbying, of endless negotiations, of half promises and speculative predictions. Rome was a city of shadows and whispers.

During the ten short days which, by a bull of Pius IV[5] were required to elapse between the death of a Pope and the commencement of the Conclave a small sector of the Vatican Palace in the vicinity of the Sistine Chapel had been prepared with feverish speed. The whole of the Conclave area was walled off from the remainder of the Palace and each of the entrances from outside was heavily guarded by *sbirri* (or constables) so as to prevent any possibility of outsiders obtaining access either to the Cardinals or their servants. Both were forbidden, under pain of excommunication, to disclose any of the proceedings of the Conclave, and information which from time to time leaked out was shadowy and unreliable.

The Sala Regia and the Pauline Chapel constituted the Conclave's working centre. The Sistine Chapel led off the Sala Regia but eight cells had been erected at its eastern end adjacent to the Sala Regia and occupied about one-third of the area of the Chapel. The grandeur of its High Altar and Michelangelo's *Last Judgement* were obscured but their beauty could still be seen over the ceiling line of the cells, for the Chapel was almost seventy feet in height and one hundred and twenty feet long. Cardinals were familiar with the spiritual inspiration of the Chapel, its brilliant vault which Michelangelo had so skilfully decorated, and the superb paintings of Botticelli, Perugino and Pinturicchio on its walls. They passed between their cells to meditate, to hear Mass, or to say their devotions before the altar. They were charged to elect Christ's Vicar on earth. It was the Pauline Chapel which was at once their temple and their studio. It was a modest Chapel, leading off the Sala Regia, the crossroads of the Conclave, and lying adjacent to the atrium of St Peter's Basilica. It was approximately 80 feet long and fifty feet wide and had been built for Paul III less than a half century previously. It retained the Renaissance richness and beauty of detail of that Farnese Pope, he being at once the original convenor of the reforming Council of Trent and the Machiavellian intriguer in European rivalries. Altars were specially erected in the Chapel for the Conclave so that Cardinals might not only hear Mass and receive daily communion at the hands of the Senior Cardinal Deacon—a younger Farnese—but also so that they might undertake their personal devotions there. Here bulls were read, oaths were sworn and ballots taken. Small thrones had been erected against the walls of the chapel in an egg-shaped formation and were allocated in order of rank (Cardinal: Bishop, Priest and Deacon) and by seniority within each rank. When ballots were taken or newly elected Popes saluted, each Cardinal took his place by rank and seniority. This was the heart of Conclave proceedings.

The Sala Regia was an immense and imposing building, fifty feet wide and almost eighty feet long: it had a majestic height and its loftiness gave it an air of spaciousness where Cardinals could breathe in comfort. Its walls bore a large number of coats-of-arms and inscriptions recording events in the history of its decorations and a galaxy of paintings commemorating gifts made by princes to the Papacy and events in its relationship with the Emperor. Many of these pictures had been commissioned by the late Pope and displayed in dazzling colours the skills and tastes of the late Renaissance. The Sala was a bright, warmly attractive ceremonial hall where foreign ambassadors were received by the Pope and festive celebrations were held.

In the Sala the Cardinals regularly congregated in groups for serious discussion, in pairs and trios for more discreet conversation or gentle relaxation. Every movement was carefully noted, every whisper attentively listened to; the meaning of a look or a gesture was thoroughly analysed and the result transmitted to the heads of the groups.[6]

Dining accommodation was provided in a remote and isolated location at the southern boundary of the Conclave premises so that it was readily accessible to the *conclavisti* (or attendants) who received their Cardinals' food daily from servants who naturally were not allowed under any circumstances to enter the Conclave premises. No provision appears to have been made for the cooking of the food and eating and drinking generally were relegated to positions of little importance.

Sixty cells were ranged for the most part round the Cortile Borgia; eighty rooms remained vacant. Accommodation was therefore available for every living Cardinal whether he attended the Conclave or not. Cells were arranged in groups and allocated to particular Cardinals by lot, this procedure being intended to prevent factions from taking possession of blocks of cells. There were three groups with eight cells in each, two with four, two with three and two with two cells each, and there were groups of seven, six and five cells each. The drawing of lots did in fact ensure that those created Cardinal by particular Popes were effectively scattered. Though there was a large measure of privacy within the cell groups, the development of cliques was made difficult and negotiations had therefore to be carried on mainly in the Sala Regia or the Pauline Chapel. There was necessarily a good deal of quiet tramping to and from the cells and this accentuated the sense of uneasiness and apprehension; Cardinals and *conclavisti* alike must have felt themselves under close observation and must equally have kept diligent watch on their colleagues and their *conclavisiti*. Montalto was allocated number 50, one of four cells situated in the second sala of the Borgia apartments which formed part of the northern wing of the Conclave. The cells were formed by wooden partitions and consisted of one or two rooms, the second being occupied by the Cardinals' *conclavisiti*, but Cardinals frequently effected extensions to their cramped and temporary accommodation or took over cells allocated to Cardinals who did not attend.[7] Cardinals were forbidden to go out of their cells after the fifth hour of the evening (about 11.00 p.m.) and were in any case debarred from returning to the outside world until the Conclave was concluded. Their attendants, limited to three, ate and slept in their masters' cells.[8]

Special consideration was given to the needs of the aged and infirm Cardinals at a Conclave, but in that of 1585 it would appear that Cardinal Riario was the only Cardinal needing special care; though he was only forty-two and had been a Cardinal only seven years, he was described as "feeble on his feet and restless in spirit";[9] in fact, he was only three months from death. Nor does any special consideration appear in the allocation of his cell (number 26) which was at the south-eastern extremity of the Conclave.

The cells were small, sometimes irregular in shape conforming to the existing lay-out of the palace, but generally were about sixteen feet by twelve feet.[10] They were mostly ill-lit, airless and stuffy, for windows had been bricked up and only small panels could be opened and would have appeared drab and lugubrious if the Cardinals had not been expected to have walls and ceilings draped with lavish coverings. The quarters of the Gregorians (Cardinals created by Gregory XIII) were coloured purple, all the rest were green: floor coverings were of the same colours. Each Cardinal provided a substantial proportion of his furnishings at his own expense, and these were emblazoned with his heraldic arms. In an Italy famous for its sumptuous materials and rich colours and at a time when rivalry between the foremost Cardinals was keen and sustained, the interior of the Conclave was a dignified and handsome sight worthy of one of the richest courts in Europe. Each Cardinal needed a writing table at which to work and a bed in which to sleep: these were often elaborate in style and exquisite in workmanship and were similarly draped in the appropriate colour, either green or purple, and bore the heraldic arms of the Cardinal. Some of the lesser paraphernalia of the Cardinal's quarters, such as bedspreads and clocks, as well as some of the soft furnishings, were drawn from the palace dispensary. Much of the bed linen and certain vestments were taken from the official wardrobe. There would be a rich display of silver candlesticks, snuffers and caskets, ink-pots and trays, much of it brought from the Cardinal's personal treasure. Provision had similarly to be made for the *conclavisti* who were important and perhaps rather sophisticated officials.[11] Passing from one cell to another, rich and poor, ostentatious and frugal, were easily distinguished. Conclaves were occasions of outstanding importance and no pains were spared to ensure that they were staged in surroundings of unexceptionable dignity and grandeur.[12] It was generally expected that this particular Conclave would last a long time, perhaps several weeks, and that it would raise formidable difficulties since there was an unusual number of Cardinals suited to the Papal throne and competition was expected to be fierce.[13]

Sunday evening, April 21st, was spent in social visits, exchanges of compliments between the Cardinals and conversations with the ambassadors and palace officials. The Cardinals assembled in the Pauline Chapel where the Papal bulls regarding elections were read and an oath taken to observe them.[14] An anticipatory oath was drafted which every cardinal swore to accept, binding the new Pope to restore peace amongst the princes, to carry on war against the Turks, to continue the reform of the church, to preserve its liberties and to complete the Basilica of St Peter's. Then, at hourly intervals between ten and midnight, three successive bells announced the closure of the Conclave and the Cardinals retired to their cells.[15]

The Camerlengo and three Cardinals then inspected the whole of the Conclave premises to ensure that no unauthorised persons had been concealed or allowed to remain, and as a further precaution on the following morning all the *conclavisti* were obliged to parade before them.[16] Already suspicion was abroad and Boncompagni and Farnese anticipated a coup d'état, and fearing that Medici, assisted by Cardinals Alessandrino and Altemps might seek to elect Cardinal Cesi by adoration,[17] refused to take dinner and spent much of the night awake.[18]

*Conclavisti* were also required to take an oath before the Camerlengo binding them to act in accordance with papal electoral decrees and requirements and to maintain secrecy regarding proceedings. The Master of the Camera and the Marshall took similar oaths individually, and every possible measure was taken to ensure the inviolability of the Conclave.

Instructions from Philip II of Spain who was probably able to exercise the strongest influence on the Conclave did not reach his ambassador, Olivares, until the day on which the new Pope was elected. Cardinal Medici, who expected to watch over Spanish interests in the Conclave, found this responsibility had in fact been assigned to Cardinal Madruzzo who did not reach the Conclave until two full days after the Conclave had closed.[19] Nor did Philip wish to exercise political influence in the Conclave; the outcome of papal elections was notoriously unpredictable and attempts to place a particular candidate on the throne were remarkably hazardous and often totally unrewarding. Deza, a Castilian aristocrat remote from court negotiations, was the only Spanish Cardinal present in the Conclave; Cardinal Granvelle, Cardinal Quiroga, Cardinal Tagliavia and Cardinal Rodrigo de Castro being absent. The Emperor, Rudolph II, observed a similar neutrality. Nor had the French king any organised party in the Conclave, the divided and strife-ridden state of the country being matched by Cardinal d'Este's support of the King, and Cardinal Pellevé's adherence to the newly formed Catholic League. Cardinal de Joyeuse, Cardinal Bourbon and Cardinal d'Armagnac, were all absent in spite of being summoned to the Conclave by Cardinal d'Este on the very day of Gregory's death, and the French ambassador himself arrived in the City only three days before the Conclave began. No strong political pressures emanated overtly from the Italian princes though most of them took a keen interest in developments; Tuscan interests were served by Cardinal de Medici, Venice did not wish to involve herself in Papal affairs. The Cardinals in the Conclave welcomed this uninhibited freedom and endeavoured to set the interests of the Church above all other considerations.

This was virtually an Italian Conclave; Cardinal Rambouillet was Bishop of Le Mans, Cardinal Pellevé was Archbishop of Rheims, Cardinal Altemps was Austrian by birth but had been Italianised for a quarter of a century, Cardinal Madruzzo had been Bishop of Trent, where he was born, but had recently served at the Imperial court, Cardinal Andrew of Austria, son of Ferdinand of Austria, was an Imperial subject; Cardinal Deza already mentioned was Spanish. Responsibility for Polish affairs prevented Cardinal Radziwill and Cardinal Bathóry from attending the Conclave and Cardinal Bolognetti who, as Papal Nuncio, had only recently returned to Poland, had nevertheless set out for Rome intending to take part in the Conclave but had been taken ill en route and, in fact, died a fortnight after the new Pope had been elected. In consequence, within the Conclave, control of the stage by Italian Cardinals was undisputed. All parts of the Italian peninsula were represented; from the north came a Milanese, a Genoan, a Savoyan, a Cremonese, a Brescian, a Bergamese, and a Florentine. Gregory XIII's promotion of personal friends as well as relatives gave a notable influence to men from Bologna amongst whom distinction in the law was characteristic but their aloofness and haughty manner made them subject to much suspicion. From Central Italy came several Romans, two from the Marches and an Umbrian; from the south were drawn several Neapolitans and one Calabrian.

The age range of the Cardinals was wide. Five were septuagenarians—Albani, Avalos, Santacroce, Savelli and Sirleto; Riario and Sirleto were frail, but the others were in good health and all were mentally alert. The youngest was Cardinal Sforza, aged twenty-three; Andrew of Austria was twenty-seven; the two Cardinal-nephews of the late Pope and Cardinal de Medici were in their thirties; the forty and fifty year olds each numbered nine; fourteen were in their sixties. Age therefore predominated; the average was fifty-five. Almost half the Cardinals in the Conclave were aged sixty or more. The Dean of the Sacred College was Cardinal Farnese, now sixty-five; more than half a century had elapsed since he was elevated to the Cardinalate at the age of fourteen. Savelli had served forty-six years as Cardinal, Simoncelli thirty-one. Four Cardinals had been promoted little more than one year previously, six had served for only two years, thirteen had been Cardinals for more than ten but less than twenty years, and a dozen had served more than twenty years.

More than a quarter of all the Conclave sprang from distinguished families in the Italian nobility, so that even those who believed a Pope should be elected from one of the princely families of Italy had adequate choice. Most of the Cardinals were well connected and probably only Bonelli and Montalto had truly humble antecedents. The majority of the Cardinals were immensely rich, Farnese, Madruzzo and Altemps in particular deriving vast incomes from their ecclesiastical appointments.[20]

Cardinal Facchinetti was Patriarch of Jerusalem, a majority of his colleagues had held bishoprics, and six of the Cardinals were or had been Archbishops. A considerable proportion of the Conclave had been Papal legates or Nuncios or had had charge of Papal missions. Cardinal Albani and Cardinal Sforza had had military experience. Scholarship in law, in theology, in classics, were represented by Cardinals held in the highest regard, and having contributed by published works of note to the spread of learning. Amongst the scholars Cardinal Carafa was outstanding. Though there were time-servers like Avalos and though many had had advancement by influence as well as merit, generally they were men sincerely and genuinely attached to the reform of the Church. The cumulative effect of the policy of Pius V and Gregory XIII was now clearly felt: since 1566 men of disreputable personal life had been largely excluded from promotion to the Cardinalate, political appointments had been curtailed and preference given to men of scholarship and ecclesiastical distinction. Even the relatives and favourites chosen by Gregory XIII did not disgrace the purple. A considerable number had taken active part in the Council of Trent where Cardinals Altemps and Gàmbara had served as legates. Cardinals Bonelli, Colonna, Deza, Facchinetti, Gàmbara and Montalto had held high responsibilities in the Inquisition. Of the Cardinals present, however, only Avalos, Bonelli and Montalto were members of religious Orders. If nobility of birth, social eminence, long experience of politics or diplomacy, high ecclesiastical office, attachment to the cause of reform, proven versatility, could guarantee a satisfactory selection of a new Pope, a successful outcome to this Conclave was assured. The wealth of talent and merit within the Conclave was remarkable; unworthy men were almost wholly absent and the opportunities for corruption almost totally removed. No one was suspected of serious venality.[21] The Pope who emerged from this election should be a man of outstanding character and great achievement, destined—if years were granted him—to contribute notably to the temporal and ecclesiastical reputation of the Papacy.

There being no Spanish, French or Imperial parties such as had greatly extended and embittered the conclave by which Pius IV had been elected twenty-six years previously, the most significant groups were those formed by the creations of particular former Popes. Farnese and Savelli were survivals from Paul III's elevations (1534/50), Simoncelli the sole survivor from Julius III's reign (1550/55). There were no representatives of Paul IV's pontificate (1555/59). From Pius IV's elevations (1559/66) there were fourteen Cardinals present; from Pius V's (1566/72) nine including Montalto, and from Gregory XIII's reign (1572/85) sixteen. The recognised leaders of these last three groups were d'Este, Bonelli and Filippo Boncompagni (San Sisto) respectively. Had all the eighteen absentees been present they would have added three to the representatives of Paul III's creations, one to Pius IV's and fourteen to Gregory XIII's.

Absence, due to engagements in distant countries and political complications in France therefore weakened the Gregorian group much more than the others, but an election from among the followers of the deceased Pope would in any event have been quite unexpected. These groups, however, were not permanent or indivisible, and anything like party homogeneity was absent; in particular, family connections and personal associations frequently broke through this largely arbitrary structure, and one of the main functions of the election managers was to take advantage of these factors to weaken loyalties within the groups. Experience in Conclave manipulations developed remarkable skills in these manoeuvres. The election of a Pope required a two-thirds majority, as laid down by Alexander III in 1179. It followed that the Gregorian Cardinals present were the only group strong enough when acting alone to exclude a candidate to whom they were opposed, and then only if they were completely united. Two dissidents from the group could invalidate this power of veto. No group was strong enough to carry an election on its own resources; indeed, even an unbroken coalition of all the members of the two largest groups (the Cardinals elevated by Pius IV and Gregory XIII) would have succeeded in carrying the election by only a slender margin. Agreement involving substantial proportions of three groups would be needed, therefore, to elect a Pope. Consequently, the scope for manoeuvre was very considerable. In fact, the Gregorians were particularly vulnerable for the leadership of Boncompagni was weak and though he regarded himself as authorised to speak for his group, there existed a strong and long-standing rivalry between him and the other Cardinal nephew of Gregory's reign, Cardinal Guastavillani, and Boncompagni's decisions, often taken without adequate consultation with his followers, frequently provoked disastrous challenges. Even before the Conclave proceedings began coalitions based on a general understanding of their respective interests had emerged between Medici (elevated to the Cardinalate by Pius IV) and Bonelli (leader of those created of Pius V) on the one hand, and between

Altemps (a creation of Pius IV) and Boncompagni (leader of the Gregorians) on the other.

The crucial and decisive factor in this Conclave, however, was the bitter and sustained opposition of Cardinal Ferdinando de' Medici[22] to the ambitions of Farnese, Dean of the Sacred College since 1578. Farnese, tall, handsome, dignified, with a commanding presence, is described by Pastor as the most brilliant of the Sacred College.[23] He was also the richest of the Cardinals with an annual income of 120,000 scudi,[24] and a great patron of the arts with an impeccable taste in painting, sculpture and classical antiquities. He had paid for the building of the Jesuit church, the Gesù, one of the most elaborate churches in Rome (it had been completed only the previous year). He had built the Farnese palace, finished in 1579, acquired the Farnesina from the Chigi family, developed the Farnese gardens on the Palatine described as among the earliest botanical gardens in Europe,[25] constructed a sumptuous castle at Caprarola near Viterbo in magnificent hilly country (some eighty miles north of Rome), and established a magnificent villa at Capodimonte near Lake Bolseno thirty miles further north. Having a court of 277 people,[26] he entertained with regal splendour, and yet was greatly respected for his generosity:[27] in the city he enjoyed immense popularity. He had the distinction of being given the right to a personal bodyguard armed with arquebuses, and though without great political influence he enjoyed much of Pope Gregory's personal confidence. His father had been legitimised by Pope Julius II and he himself was elevated to the cardinalate by his uncle, Paul III, when he was only fourteen. While his uncle reigned, he lived very near the centre of the Papal Court and in spite of his youth had been given considerable responsibilities, particularly in Spanish affairs, showing skill and a genuine capacity for foreign affairs. He had taken part in six Conclaves, acting as Pope-maker on these occasions and celebrating the Mass of the Holy Spirit before the Conclave which elected Paul IV. He had been a candidate for the papacy when Pius IV was chosen, but was never seriously in the hunt.[28] Almost at the end of a very long Conclave he needed only two more votes for success but the opportunity passed never to return, and, in agreement with the pious Cardinal Borromeo, he was responsible for the election of Cardinal Ghislieri, Montalto's friend and patron, as Pius V. When Gregory XIII was elected exceptionally quickly by "adoration", Farnese had been warned beforehand by Cardinal Granvelle who spoke with all the authority of the Spanish supporters that he must give up all hope of being elected. Now, if ever, he was to succeed, he would have to spare no effort. He himself was reported to have said, "This is my last Conclave. Whether it is prolonged or not I am resolved to succeed".[29] Even before the Conclave began he had made a number of probing forays, but everywhere he was disappointed. His opponent, Cardinal Medici, was so hostile that nothing would reconcile him to Farnese's election, and when the Conclave opened for business he knew the odds were heavily against him;[30] opinion in the city was that he had almost no chance of success. His only hope lay in a protracted Conclave in which his colleagues might be driven by attrition to vote for him, but against an opponent as vigorous and vigilant as Medici even a sudden manoeuvre was unlikely to succeed.

An inflexible opponent, Cardinal Medici was cast in a different mould. Tall but stout, with a high forehead and fierce eyes, he was formidable in appearance and in character; a man of great vigour and determination, painstaking and incredibly persistent. The son of the first and former Grand Duke of Tuscany, Cosimo I, and the younger brother of the reigning Grand Duke, he nursed an almost fanatical attachment to the interests of his house. In particular, the Medici resented the growing power of the Farnese in the Duchy of Parma,[31] and suspected them of working for the restoration of Piacenza to the Duchy, of negotiating for an alliance with the Duke of Savoy, and of aspiring to the re-establishment of the Kingdom of Lombardy. Cardinal Medici was therefore bitterly exasperated by Philip's refusal to exclude Farnese from election. The Medici were sensitive also of

Spanish assistance to Siena now incorporated in the Grand Duchy and were constantly vigilant against attempts to restore independence to that city. Vulnerable therefore to encroachments on the north, and on the south they pursued an inevitably defensive policy with justifiable apprehension. To the Medici, therefore, the election of a favourable Pope was of the greatest possible importance, the exclusion of a rival or an enemy an absolute necessity. Stronger, more vigorous and intellectually more penetrating than his brother, the Grand Duke, the Cardinal was deeply involved in the politics of Northern Italy, and saw with complete lucidity their relevance to the Papacy. Two years later he was to surrender his Cardinalate to marry and raise an heir to the family fortunes and unexpectedly he succeeded his brother in the middle of Sixtus V's reign. Promoted at the age of fourteen to the Cardinalate after the death of Cardinal Giovanni, his brother, Cardinal Ferdinando de' Medici had lived in Rome since 1571 acquiring six years later the Palazzo Fiorentino, an impressive building of the first half of the century overlooking the Tiber, but somewhat towards the northern boundary of the city. His great riches, derived in large part from sources other than his benefices[32] enabled him to live in magnificent splendour. In 1570 he purchased the Villa Medici which he transformed into a magnificent private museum to which he attached a menagerie with bears, lions and ostriches. He drove round the city in a most unusual carriage, drawn by four horses and equipped with a kitchen and a furnace for baking bread. A notorious gambler, he bore his losses with cheerful equanimity[33]—only a year earlier the Grand Duke had given him 100,000 scudi to meet his creditors' demands.[34] This man of the world was well known for his dislike of common people, his tactless manner and his forthrightness.[35] Medici himself did not aspire to the throne, but the campaign he initiated against Farnese was conducted with the relentless determination of a warrior committed to a life-or-death contest. He had taken part in two Conclaves; in 1572 he had been a candidate but had polled few votes and was prevented by illness from making any serious bid for election; he therefore lacked the long experience which was one of Farnese's assets, and had to offset this deficiency by his resourcefulness.

It was impossible to forecast the length of a Conclave: Gregory XIII had been elected after a single day, but the Conclave which elected Julius III lasted nearly three months (from 29th November 1549 to 8th February 1550);[36] that which elected Pius IV in 1559 lasted three months and twenty-one days;[37] and that which elected his successor, Pius V, lasted from 19th December 1565 until 7th January 1556. It was therefore essential that at least the leaders of the various groups should watch trends in the daily elections with the acutest vigilance and be ready to counter any stratagems their opponents might devise. In an atmosphere of perpetual intrigue, alliances and counter-alliances, insubstantial as bubbles, were born and died with incredible rapidity, and rumour, innuendo and accusation circulated freely, and the intervals between one ballot and the next were particularly hazardous. Vigilance could never be relaxed, and protracted Conclaves were therefore exhausting for the Cardinals as well as unsettling to the world outside. As recently as 1550 the Conclave had debated whether voting should be by secret ballot, but since the Council of Trent had prescribed the secret ballot in ecclesiastical elections this would apply *a fortiori* to the election of a Pope.

On Monday 22nd April, the Conclave set to work in earnest but the day was spent in tentative and somewhat desultory negotiations, though two scrutinies, or ballots, were taken. Communion was received, as it was each day, in the Pauline Chapel, administered by Farnese as Dean of the Sacred College.

After Mass, the first scrutiny, was taken—a tantalising but highly formalised and carefully regulated ceremony. Each Cardinal was provided with a printed voting paper, ingeniously designed, on which he recorded his own name and that of the Cardinal he wished to nominate. He then folded the paper in the correct place to ensure that the printed ornamentation covered the two names, so that even if held up to the light neither could be read. Any Cardinal was permitted to complete and seal the paper in his cell if he wished, and this permitted him to have the service of one of his conclavists which was a convenience to the elderly and the frail. On a table in front of the altar of the Pauline Chapel was placed a golden chalice covered by a paten, and into this each Cardinal in turn placed his voting paper, raising his hand, kneeling, and saying a brief prayer as he did so. Often Cardinals would vote as a kind of compliment for a colleague they had no intention of electing, and, at least in the early scrutinies, this made it more difficult to obtain the requisite two-thirds majority—26 votes on the first day of the Conclave and (because of late arrivals) 28 later. When all Cardinals had voted, one of three Cardinal scrutators emptied all the voting papers from the chalice on to the table and then examined each individually before whispering the name of the Cardinal voted for to the second scrutator who, again in a whisper, repeated the proposition to the third scrutator. The latter then announced the nomination to the assembled Cardinals. Each of these had been provided with a list of the names of all Cardinals on which to record the number of votes cast for each. As, at this first scrutiny, no candidate attained the necessary majority, the voting cards were then set on a pile of straw and carried to be burned in a corner of the Sistine Chapel so that black smoke could escape up a chimney and inform people in St Peter's Square that the scrutiny was ended. Records of the ballot were thus destroyed, and Cardinals were in any event forbidden to disclose Conclave proceedings. Yet the *Avvisi* or daily news-sheets of the time often gave information about the voting and subsequently even the results of individual scrutinies were published,[38] but these are generally difficult to reconcile with each other and are subject to reservation or mistrust. In general, there is little reliable information about the detailed proceedings of the Conclave of 1585. The afternoon was spent, as normally, largely in deliberations in the Pauline Chapel.

Sirleto was one of the oldest members of the Conclave, having served as Cardinal for twenty-four years and having sat in two previous Conclaves. A Calabrian of distinguished birth, he was a scholar of outstanding ability, reputation and achievement. After studying at Naples, he came to Rome to study in the Vatican library where he acquired an exceptional mastery of the classics and the Fathers as well as profound and skilful knowledge of Greek. Perhaps more important, he made the acquaintance of Seripando, later Cardinal, already well known for his remarkable understanding of the works of St Augustine. Sirleto also formed an intimate and lasting friendship with Cardinal Cervini (later elected Pope Marcellus II), a man of great personal piety and immense reforming enthusiasm. Sirleto attended early sessions of the Council of Trent, where his erudition was used to great advantage; he assisted Cervini in the preparation of a critical text of the Vulgate, and he himself prepared for publication an edition of several of the Church Fathers. Pope Paul IV appointed him Apostolic Protonotary and sent him to join Cardinal Seripando in the final and decisive stages of the Council of Trent. Warmly recommended by Cardinal Borromeo—the powerful spearhead of the Counter Reformation—he was made Cardinal by Pius IV. When he was appointed successively Bishop of S. Marco and then Bishop of Squillace, both Calabrian dioceses, he grieved that the wishes of the Pope and duties at the Papal Court and the Congregation of the Index prevented him from taking up residence in either See and, after five years, he transferred the latter bishopric to his nephew. If learning, intellectual energy, personal integrity, unremitting adherence to church reform and administrative skill, were qualifications of a Pope, Sirleto was a most formidable candidate—and this Conclave took full account of such qualities. But perhaps his colleagues foresaw that his days were numbered (he died six months later), and recalled how his close friend Cervini had died after a pontificate of a mere twenty-two days. In any event, Neapolitans were not popular in a Conclave where representatives of North Central Italy preponderated so notably, and Sirleto's candidature was vigorously opposed by d'Este whose leanings were towards the French, and who refused to entertain "a Spanish Chaplain who would be guarded by Galli, Cardinal of Como".[39]

Furthermore, in this Conclave Altemps carried little weight. His early life had been given to earthly pleasures, and even after promotion to the Cardinalate and his appointment as Bishop of Costanza he consorted with a woman of Genoa who bore him a son who was later legitimised. Altemps' conversion to the cause of Church reform under the influence of Cardinal Borromeo happened too late to re-establish his reputation. His intellectual ability was not of the highest, and in manner he had become retiring and taciturn. Though he was wealthy and had the splendid villa of Mondragone built and lavishly furnished for his son, Roberto, whom he handsomely endowed with other possessions in the Papal States, he had little place amongst the Roman nobility and yet was regarded as too pretentious to win general support. With such questionable and ineffectual support, Sirleto's candidature went no further.

When the first ballot was taken, Albani topped the poll, but with only thirteen votes: half the number needed for election. Albani, now aged seventy-four, was highly respected. Born of a noble family of Bergamo he was a very distinguished lawyer of the Paduan school, who had been Vice-Commander of the military forces of Venice. His wife, who died when he was only thirty, bore him four sons and three daughters, and before being appointed Cardinal he had been arrested in Venice for complicity in the assassination of a family enemy in the Church of St Mary Major in Rome. Two of his sons were responsible for hiring the assassins, but their father could not establish his innocence and he was tried, condemned to five years' confinement on an Adriatic island and banished from the Republics. Advancement and changes of fortune came when Ghislieri was elected Pope in 1566: some sixteen years earlier Albani had saved him from Bergamese heretics who were hunting him. As Cardinal Albani's personal life was blameless, his juridical skill was extensively used by Gregory XIII and he has been described as "one of the most authoritative members of the Sacred College".[40] It was expected that Boncompagni, nephew of Gregory XIII and Albani's patron, would press his claims energetically and that he might carry the Gregorians with him, but the stains on Albani's character were ingrained too deeply and the Conclave refused to support his candidature. To most of the Conclave, Boncompagni seemed to have displayed a complete lack of spirit and leadership, and his indecision began to undermine the confidence of his group and to render them incapable of concerted action. Cardinal Andrew of Austria, son of Ferdinand, Duke of Tyrol, one of the Gregorians, arrived during the day after the Conclave had begun, having travelled from Innsbruck in six days.[41] This introduced a distraction into the proceedings since Farnese and Boncompagni urged that he be excluded from voting on the grounds that he had not received deacon's orders. He was able to cite the dispensing bull granted to him by Gregory XIII at his election and with the assistance of Bonelli and Medici succeeded in establishing his right to vote. Farnese was piqued at suffering another wound inflicted by Medici, and Boncompagni was aggrieved by his failure.

During the later hours of the day the names of Castagna (the future Urban VII), Torre and Santoro were canvassed. It was Boncompagni, the leader of the Gregorians, who began to canvass for Castagna, one of his group. Born of a noble family of Genoa, he had become an eminent lawyer after studying at Perugia, Padua and Bologna. He had been a skilful diplomat in Spain and Venice and a trusted administrator in the Marches, Umbria and Bologna. He had taken part in the Council of Trent and had been Consultor of the Inquisition, but he was particularly respected for him energetic attempts to forward preparations against the Turks. Whilst his ability led to his election seven years later, he had at this date been Cardinal for only two years and he was attending his first Conclave. Moreover, his backer, Boncompagni, was now deeply suspected by influential sections of the Conclave and it was feared that long diplomatic service at Madrid had left him seriously under the influence of Spain.

Cardinal Torre, another of Gregory XIII's elevations had played no part in Curial affairs and had not arrived at the Conclave. He died a year later. He had support from Farnese, d'Este and the Gregorians, but was forcefully resisted by Medici and was never able to amass any general support.[42] His candidature was described as a joke which had to be taken seriously.[43]

Santoro, a middle-aged Neapolitan, was originally a lawyer but had taken orders, had served as Vicar-General to the Archbishop of Naples and subsequently became Archbishop of San Severina in Calabria. He was greatly respected for his learning and skill in ecclesiastical affairs, and could count fifteen years as Cardinal. His candidature was said to be supported by Farnese but his youth (he was fifty-three) and Southern associations stood against him and Boncompagni spoke against him.[44]

Cardinal d'Este, meanwhile, set about a determined canvass for Cardinal Savelli, the most senior member of the Conclave after Farnese, with whom he was very friendly. Although some support was likely from the Gregorians, the attempt was totally fruitless and left d'Este frustrated. Such were the characteristics of the early stages of a Conclave.

Three hours before sunset a second scrutiny was held, but no Cardinal obtaining the necessary majority, voters were given the opportunity of transferring their votes to an alternative candidate.[45] Sometimes the number of these "accessi" was sufficient to allow one of the candidates to attain the needed majority, but in 1585 at the second scrutiny of the first day, no Cardinal obtained more than eleven votes[46]—less than half the votes required. That night rumour ran through the City that Farnese had been elected, excitement and pleasure rose high, for the Dean of the Sacred College was both respected and popular. Soon, however, it was realised that this news was false.

At the end of the first day, therefore, an election seemed remote and the expectations of a protracted Conclave with all its consequences increased. Medici had successfully thwarted Farnese's attempts to have one of his protégés elected; worthy candidates who could be expected to succeed as Pope abounded, but none with general support had yet appeared. Sparring and in-fighting continued. Medici, therefore, saw clearly that if this deadlock was to be broken, firstly he must cement the association of those created by Pius IV with those of Pius V to establish a coalition commanding twenty-three votes. Only one dissentient amongst Pius IV's creations had to be reckoned with—Galli. A notorious supporter of Spanish interests, who had exercised great influence as Secretary of State during Gregory XIII's reign, he remained openly hostile to Montalto; convinced that Montalto's election would bring him summary and irrevocable doom. During Pius V's pontificate, he had been removed from his post as Secretary of State and replaced by Rusticucci, Montalto's friend, and he recognised clearly that his fortunes lay with the Gregorians. Secondly, he must expose the disunity of the Gregorians and detach a sufficient number of them from Boncompagni to produce the necessary majority. The plan was simple but there were many drawbacks. pitfalls. Every vote had to be garnered with the utmost care; neither he nor his colleagues could afford to alienate anyone.

Giacomo Boncompagni, Gregory XIII's nephew, had worked on Guastavillani's discontent and on the general resentment of Filippo Boncompagni's inept and clumsy leadership amongst the Gregorians. He also worked on Altemps' antipathy to Torre whose suggested candidature Altemps regarded as outrageous, and then made approaches to Bonelli and, using Cardinal Gesualdo as an intermediary, succeeded in detaching him from Boncampagni. Meanwhile Montalto lay quietly and circumspectly in the background. He was in no position to organise support for himself, had nothing to gain by disclosing whatever ambition he nursed, and remained entirely dependent on initiatives which other Cardinals might promote. He was sufficiently unimportant amongst an array of politically more commanding colleagues to avoid entanglement in the Medici–Farnese feud, especially as neither of these was as yet organising any campaign for his own election. On account of the financial assistance which the Grand Duke had given to Montalto, Medici might expect his support. Montalto was pledged, no doubt secretly, to Farnese , but what might have become an embarrassing situation never developed, but no doubt it strengthened Montalto's resolve to keep an iron grip on himself, to be cautious and taciturn and to avoid becoming openly committed to any particular group. His concealment was assisted by the distance which separated his cell from the main centre of electoral proceedings—the Pauline Chapel and the Sala Regia—and the fact that Medici was accommodated in the Sistine Chapel itself. His own cell in the second sala of the Borgia apartments was almost adjacent to Farnese 's and opposite Guastavillani's; his inactivity was therefore certain to be noticed and this encouraged belief in his detachment and perhaps deluded his two colleagues into neglecting his intentions. It was comparatively easy for him to escape suspicion: he was not the object of any particular design.

Tuesday, the 23rd April, the second day of the Conclave, was the crucial day. Medici made a bold bid for the support of Cardinal d'Este, one of the Cardinals created by Pius IV. Cardinal d'Este was born on Christmas Day, 1538, was now aged forty-seven, and but for serious ill health which was to bring him to a premature death a year later, would have been in the prime of life. The son of Duke Ercole II of Ferrara and a princess of France,[47] he was brought up in a strongly humanist atmosphere at Court where his mother's Calvinistic leanings necessitated her being under close surveillance and caused her ultimate return to France after her husband's death. Appointed Archbishop of Ferrara and elevated to the Cardinalate by Pius IV in 1561, d'Este maintained close contacts with the French court and over a long period enjoyed the confidence of Henry III, whose interests he now represented in Rome. He had a cordial friendship with Torquato Tasso, the famous Italian poet and playwright whom he introduced to the Duke of Ferrara. Very rich and handsomely endowed by his brother, the Duke,[48] he was notoriously generous and an open-handed patron of the arts. A man of fine character, unquestioned integrity and eminent scholarship, he was well known in Rome, living in considerable splendour in a villa recently constructed on the Quirinale where his French wines were greatly respected. There he collected a considerable entourage of rowdy boisterous servants who caused so many commotions for which they claimed immunity that in 1580 the Pope expelled him from the Papal States and only rescinded the ban when the King of France made strong representations on the Cardinal's behalf. Because the Pope disliked the Vatican particularly in summer, d'Este had repeatedly entertained Gregory in his villa and had leased to him land on which the Pope built the Quirinale Palace. When the Palace was finally nearing completion and Gregory lived in it for short periods, the Cardinal and the Pope engaged in frequent quarrels and only a year before Gregory's death was d'Este restored to favour. The Pope tried to make some compensation for his recurring displeasure by letting it be known that he intended to bequeath the new Palace which was too small for court purposes to d'Este at his death. Like Montalto, therefore, d'Este had ample and bitter experience of Gregory's mercurial temperament. Cardinal for almost a quarter of a century and representing all the interests of the French court, d'Este was now in a position to act decisively.

Medici approached d'Este to formulate an agreement to put forward a candidate who would enlist widespread support, selecting either Albani or Montalto. D'Este stipulated, however, that no final choice should be made before the views of Cardinal Madruzzo, whose arrival was imminent, had been ascertained. Madruzzo arrived the same evening. He would have preferred Sirleto, but on finding that the latter had met considerable opposition and that d'Este was completely opposed to him, Madruzzo gave his support to Montalto in preference to Albani. Medici, having ascertained from Madruzzo as the protector of Spanish interests, that Montalto would be acceptable to Philip II, obtained Madruzzo's promise of support. The Cardinals elevated by Pius IV and Pius V were now united and it would be possible to bring the Conclave to an early conclusion. Nevertheless, no further progress was made at that late hour and Montalto was strongly urged by his sponsors to behave very discreetly, avoiding all attentions and taking advantage of the obscurity of his cell. The situation called for caution and concealment; many candidates in the past had been within an ace of success only to find the tiara wrested from their grasp. Early revelation of intentions did nothing but stimulate opposition. One of Paul III's maxims was that Cardinals must wait for the Papacy, not go to meet it.[49] The opposition must be discovered and taken by surprise. Confused and tantalising whispers continued through the night as puzzled and apprehensive Cardinals shuffled hither and thither through the half-light of the corridors hoping for genuine news.

Next day, Wednesday 24th April, the third day of the Conclave, Cardinal Ferrero arrived,[50] and he and Madruzzo went together to the Pauline Chapel to hear the election bulls read before they took oaths to observe them. Medici had been up before dawn finalising the details of his plans and taking every possible precaution to prevent the frustration of his intentions. Whilst the bulls were being read to Madruzzo and Ferrero, d'Este and Bonelli called Boncompagni from the Pauline Chapel to acquaint him with the fact that they now had the requisite majority to proceed to Montalto's election and that they were resolved to do so without further delay. According to contemporary accounts d'Este contended that Montalto's election was being promoted by the Holy Spirit and resistance was therefore completely fruitless.[51] To delay merely gave others the opportunity to take the initiative in offering him the crown whereas if Boncompagni accepted the situation he should have this honour for himself and his followers.

When a strong determined man faces one who is vacillating and procrastinating, and when the former presents to the latter a variety of arguments, some plausible, some flattering, others threatening, the outcome is almost certain. Boncompagni insisted in consulting his followers but could do no other than urge them to accept what had been represented to him as a *fait accompli*; Gonzaga was already committed to support Montalto; Guastavillani was ready to follow Medici's lead; Riario, a Bolognese, noted for his piety, his skill in the practice of canon law and a former Legate to Spain, agreed that the day was already lost; only Facchinetti spoke with bitter sarcasm against Montalto, the other Gregorians remaining passive and discomfited. Facchinetti's opposition to Montalto's precipitate election was significant and might have been decisive. Though a Cardinal of only two years' standing, he has been described as "one of the most notable prelates of his day".[52] Two years older than Montalto, he had been Bishop of Nicastro (Reggio Calabria) for fifteen years and subsequently Patriarch of Jerusalem. He had served Gregory XIII as Papal Nuncio in Venice for nine years and had taken a leading part in organising the Crusade against the Turks which culminated at Lepanto. He had attended the Council of Trent and had been an energetic and forceful Inquisitor. Six years after Sixtus V's death, with the support of the Spanish party, he was himself elected Pope as Innocent IX. He argued strongly that Montalto was too young for the papal throne. Had the Gregorians not completely collapsed as an electoral group, Facchinetti might have gained a following, but they were utterly discomfited by the suddenness with which Montalto emerged as a serious candidate for election. Montalto's sponsors took full and immediate advantage of this situation. No time was left for tortuous negotiations or protracted deliberations, and Gonzaga was despatched to inform d'Este of the Gregorians' agreement to Montalto's election. The Cardinals who had assembled in the Sala Regia were then summoned to the adjoining Pauline Chapel for a ballot. When they arrived, and whilst Madruzzo and Ferrero were still waiting to take their oaths, d'Este is said to have exclaimed, "There is no longer time to read bulls! The Pope is made: let us proceed at once to the 'adoration'." Thereupon Boncompagni and the Gregorians rushed into the Pauline Chapel and crowded round Montalto to name him as the new Pope and to offer him their allegiance and congratulations; immediately all the other Cardinals, some intuitively, others directed by d'Este or Medici, did likewise. Even Farnese was swept along in this movement after making some very brief but bitter remarks about Boncompagni's treachery. Thereupon Montalto was invested with the Papal vestments—the white cassock, the surplice, the white cap and shoes embroidered with a golden cross—and installed on the Papal throne erected in the centre of the Chapel before the altar. Each Cardinal in turn by seniority within his Order —Deacon, Priest or Bishop—then rose to cast their open, oral votes. Farnese, as Senior Deacon, was first to recite the ritualistic words, "I, Alessandro Cardinal Farnese, elect as Pope my Reverend Deacon of Montalto" and the rest followed suit, each in turn kissing the newly-elected Pope's foot and right hand and receiving from him the kiss of peace on the cheek. The appearance of a new Pope clothed in the official papal robes and bearing for the first time the authority of election was always impressive. The vacancy was ended, a new Pope reigned. Yet is seemed that morning that many of the Cardinals must have been still stupefied by the suddenness with which the election had concluded. Although Montalto had been a candidate to be reckoned with, his precipitate election by adoration so early in the proceedings was as startling as a meteor in the heavens.[53] The ballot taken next day was a formality, Montalto himself generously voting for Farnese.

It has been said that Farnese failed to act to prevent Montalto's election as he remained convinced that Medici would never allow Montalto's election because the new Pope would revenge himself for Francesco Peretti's death on Paolo Giordano Orsini, a relative of the Medici family by his first marriage. Whilst this may be true, it underestimates Farnese's vigilance, it disregards the Medici family's open opposition of Paolo's association with Vittoria and it neglects Farnese's regard for Montalto's ability and his personal friendliness to him. It is perhaps more reasonable to assume that when Farnese realised that his own election was impracticable and that his friend Sirleto had been firmly rejected, a Cardinal as well disposed as Montalto became acceptable to him. Moves to promote Montalto were widely recognised within the Conclave and there is no adequate ground to suppose that Farnese was taken unawares.

Following the election, Montalto was carried into St Peter's where the Cardinals renewed the act of 'adoration' and kissed his foot. The the tell-tale white smoke from the Sistine chapel informed the world that a Pope had been elected. His election was proclaimed by Cardinal Farnese as Senior Deacon of the Sacred College from the Loggia della Benedizione.

A salute was fired by the canon of Castel Sant'Angelo. Quickly the news of Montalto's election was carried to all the palazzi, banks and shops of the city, into all the hotels and taverns, the churches and the convents. Soon the princes of Italy and the monarchs of Europe were informed by their ambassadors and agents. The election of a new Pope was headline news; that of a friar was staggering, even frightening. Outside Rome and scholarly and ecclesiastical circles elsewhere, not a great deal was known of the new Holy Father, and to many he was an enigma, born in obscurity and recently living in seclusion.

He took the name of Sixtus V in honour of the previous Sixtus, another Franciscan who had added so must lustre to the Papacy and of Pius V, his own patron and defender and as a compliment to San Sisto (Boncompagni) whose help had facilitated his election so much. After blessing the people assembled in the Basilica and crowding the square beyond and having saluted the College of Cardinals gathered round him, Sixtus speedily made his way to the adjoining Palace to take possession of his official residence and to begin his official duties.

Wednesday 1st May was Coronation Day, a public holiday and a day of high ceremony. At noon precisely the Cavallieri di San Pietro gaily and splendidly clad in their traditional uniforms carried the Pope in the *sedia gestatoria* from the Vatican Palace to St Peter's, followed by a procession which included ambassadors from the courts of Europe and envoys of lesser states, the special envoy of the Grand Duke of Tuscany, the new Pope's colleagues of the Sacred College and distinguished prelates. Philip II's representative, the Spanish Duke of Olivares, was a notable absentee, stubbornly interpreting court etiquette as preventing him from yielding precedence to the representative of the King of France. But Japanese princes were present in their oriental splendour, and one of them, Don Marzio, was chosen to present to the Pope the water in which he washed his hands before celebrating Mass.[54] Cardinal Farnese had a place of honour and carried the linen towel with which he wiped them whilst the Pope's chaplains bore the papal tiara in their arms. A vast throng of distinguished guests filled the new St Peter's, still far from completion, crowding together to form a magnificent array of continuous splendour. The Pope then said Mass with great dignity, assisted by members of the Sacred College and other prelates, and works by Palestrina, the *compositore della capella* to St Peter's, now at the height of his powers, were performed with great emotion. No coronation oath was required for he had been elected Vicar of Christ, and he was already bound by the oath which all the Cardinal electors had taken at the opening of the Conclave.[55] After he had taken his seat on the papal throne, the senior and second Cardinal Deacons placed the cope and mitre on him, kissed his foot and embraced him. Patriarchs, archbishops and a long retinue of prelates pressed forward to do him homage, after which he descended from the throne and resumed his place on the ceremonial chair, now covered by a brightly coloured canopy, to be carried to the Vatican balcony where the papal choristers sang several pieces. Farnese, as Dean of the Sacred College, preached the Coronation oration. The second Cardinal Deacon then removed the ceremonial mitre from the Pope's head—he would never wear it again—and the climax of the ceremony was reached as Cardinal Medici crowned him with the tiara.[56] Thereupon Sixtus rose to bless the people three times. Then whilst trumpeters sounded a fanfare, cannon from Castel S. Angelo fired salute after salute and clocks and bells burst into a musical panegyric, Sixtus was carried back to the Palace. Sixtus was only the third Franciscan to be crowned Pope.[57]

Only four days later on May 5th the final ceremony to inaugurate the Pope's reign was performed: he took official possession of the Papal Church of St John Lateran and made his ceremonial triumph in the city. An immense entourage of Italian nobles and Papal officials, comparable in splendour with a mediaeval tournament, assembled at the convent of S. Maria in Aracoeli at the foot of the Capitol. An advance guard of attendants, then a column of cardinals, ambassadors, princes and men at arms, all on magnificent horses of impeccable breeding, followed by twelve papal officials, eight in a noble red and four in striking white colours. After more court attendants came fourteen trumpeters drawn from the service of the fourteen quarters of the city, followed by forty Roman citizens and then by four marshals of the Roman people in vivid satins. The Senator, the three Conservatori and the Governor of Rome followed, proclaiming the full authority of the City and forming a distinct group as representing the city's pre-eminence in the Pope's domain. A sub-deacon carried a gigantic cross in front of hundreds of princes and knights on horseback, accompanied by their pages, their patrons' arms emblazoned on their tunics. Behind this formidable guard came the Pope riding a striking, well-groomed white horse. Self-composed and confident, his face solemn and strangely unmoved by the effusively loyal crowd. This was already a Pope whose monastic severity and stern immutability had made an impression in the City. Here he rode with command and dignity. Behind him were courtiers and three hundred Swiss guards carrying their halberds. A corps of soldiery clothed in brilliant costumes with red and yellow sleeves of exquisite velour, and bearing the arms of the Pope, brought up the rear of this vast cavalcade. Few, if any, of the colours of the spectrum were missing from the pageantry of that day; magnificent horses pranced with ceremonial harness glittering in the sun, every oriental finery was to be found in the costumes; an Italian sky above and a natural atmosphere of hilarity and carefree excitement made it a day of jubilant celebration.

The incomparable procession made its way up the hill to the Basilica of St John Lateran. All along the route the people of Rome crowded, colourful, excited, festive, not merely to salute their new Pope, they hoped also to collect the coins which were normally thrown to them on these occasions, but Sixtus refused to observe this custom and made donations instead to recognised organisations. Rome was on holiday. At the portico of the Basilica the Pope left his litter and was met by its Cardinal archpriest whom he saluted and embraced. The Pope was then installed on his throne, and the Cardinal Prelate of St John Lateran made the act of homage to the Holy Father and kissed his foot, delivered an oration in Latin in a picturesque ceremony, and presented two keys to the Pope. After blessing the church, Sixtus was carried to the Altar of Saints Peter and Paul, where he received the homage of the Cardinals who pledged obedience to him. Proclaiming the final benediction, the Pope withdrew to the adjoining Lateran Palace where he distributed commemorative medals. The premier cardinal removed the mitre and the second cardinal divested him of the tiara. This ceremony of the *Possessio* symbolised the installation of the Pope as Bishop of Rome and allowed the City authorities and the Roman populace to offer their allegiance to him and to express their joy at his elevation. It was a public occasion.[58] A banquet normally followed, but Sixtus, having blessed the people, refused to take part in this method of squandering money. The banquet was suppressed and the Pope withdrew unobtrusively to his own *vigna* near S. Maria Maggiore, where he enjoyed in quietness the company of his sister and her grandchildren.[59] Even after his election the enigma of Sixtus' character remained. He recognised the obligations to preserve tradition; he was prepared to act the leading role punctiliously and with great dignity when the occasion was ceremonial and the honour of the Papacy was to be upheld; yet secretly, even after almost twenty years' residence in the city, he remained a Montaltese in his simple, natural love of tranquillity and solitude, and a Franciscan in his understanding of austerity unadorned and in his desire for spiritual peace.

Sixtus V's election was immediately regarded as providential and his biographers quickly collected legends which emphasised the divine protection of the new Pope from his earliest days. He himself accepted election as the fulfilment of his destiny. Popes were not made without the favour of Divine Providence. How had success come Montalto's way? He had no personal following, he had little wealth and no political influence, his eminence in the Franciscan Order could have been a handicap rather than an asset. Since the reign of Paul IV, one of the founders of the Theatines, there was widespread fear of the unbending austerity and the secular inexperience associated with the religious Orders, and though the successful pontificate of the Dominican Pius V had reduced this apprehension, prejudice against the Orders was too deep rooted to be eliminated. That he was *papabile*—of stature appropriate to election—was recognised; indeed, in the City his chances of election were reckoned high, much higher than in the Conclave itself. His service as a Cardinal was shorter than that of eight of the preceding Popes of the century,[60] though longer than the remaining five. His talent in the pulpit and his scholarship had been proved beyond all reasonable doubt; although his experience was limited compared with many Cardinals who had been Legates, Nuncios or members of missions to foreign courts, it was of a major dimension and he had had command of one of the largest of the older Orders. His attachment to the circles of reform was unquestioned; he was of an acceptable age, though his detractors accused him of understating his age by four years; he was energetic and resourceful, though Bonelli is said to have supported him because he thought he would prove frail and in need of support. He had few enemies, and perhaps his retirement during at least the last years of Gregory XIII's reign saved him from controversy and animosity; in fact, he was respected for the dignity with which he had borne the snubs and personal bitterness of the late proud and aristocratic Pope. The dignified forbearance he had shown when his nephew Francesco had been assassinated had made a profound impression in Papal circles. The Gregorians who had most to fear from his election took comfort in the fact that they thought his (great) nephew too young to have any influence in the Curia.

Merits such as these could never guarantee elections; the majority of Cardinals could have provided an equally impressive list of achievements and virtues; very few could be genuinely disqualified. The fact was that the Conclave, though freed from dictation by the Great Powers, was riven by the feud between Farnese and Medici and was motivated by a profound prejudice against Southern Italians, Neapolitans and Calabrians. Petty Italian politics cast a long shadow over the electoral proceedings and the merits of candidates who stood apart from political entanglements were therefore enhanced. Moreover, within the Conclave there existed a great desire to avoid the protracted proceedings which on former occasions had proved so debilitating for the Papacy and so inconvenient and troublesome in the city. Most Cardinals were prepared for compromise if this facilitated an early election.

Nevertheless, one condition was paramount: the successful candidate must be of unimpeachable personal life, determined to govern, if elected, in the interests of the church and to restore its standing in the Western world. Montalto benefited from his neutrality and his detachment from political partisanship. He had the personal friendship of Farnese without ever being involved in his manoeuvres, and yet he was acceptable to Medici as a candidate likely to arouse a minimum of opposition and to command a considerable measure of support. The initiative of d'Este was decisive, and subsequently the new Pope acknowledged his indebtedness to him. Montalto was described picturesquely by the French ambassador as the one "furthest from the dish".[61] Montalto's own discretion, and his remarkable sense of discipline in avoiding the limelight in the final stages of the Conclave facilitated his success: indeed, commentators of the day began to accuse him of cunning and their cynical suspicions created the quite false and uncorroborated story which achieved widespread circulation of his lobbying round the Conclave supporting himself on a stick which he dramatically threw away immediately he had been elected. But perhaps the most significant single factor in his election was the disintegration of the Gregorians. An election could only be effected by a coalition which included members of all three main parties; Cardinals elevated by Pius V tended to stand firmly together; those elevated by Pius IV were united by the efforts of Altemps, Medici and d'Este. The Gregorians provided the "floating" vote, of which Medici and d'Este took full advantage.

What was the new Pope like in appearance and character? For the first time he began to be described and soon he was painted and sculpted. He was no more than average height; his figure was spare, lean and a little bent but he had a large head and dark chestnut hair; his face was long and his beard flowing, thick and rapidly turning grey; his shoulders broad and his arms sinewy—a muscular man, easily lost in a crowd but robust and vital. His face was bronzed; he had a high forehead, deeply wrinkled, and prominent cheek bones so that his features appeared long and angular. But his eyes were small, brown and shining, with contrastingly black pupils. Perhaps from his patron Pius V he had acquired the habit of looking closely and firmly at people as if even his glances penetrated deeply and sharply. He had a receptive memory and was credited with an exceptional ability to form almost instantaneously a picture of what he saw. His was a serious demeanour with only rare and almost reluctant smiles. He was never a man to be trifled with; formidable, perhaps forbidding, in appearance.

His health was good and he had great powers of endurance though his stamina could collapse suddenly and without warning; his nature was brittle and his temper unpredictable; he was highly strung and never spared himself. He slept little and would work all night if duty required it, observing a tight self-discipline; he ate and drank frugally and ordinarily dressed poorly, for he despised personal ostentation.

His morals were irreproachable and his personal life unblemished. Capable of deep and sustained affection, he was firmly attached to his sister Camilla, whose prayers he said had won him the Papacy, and he found immense satisfaction in the company of his relatives, particularly his two (great) nephews and (great) nieces. He never forgot his humble antecedents or tried to shun those who had helped him in earlier days: indeed, he was compassionate to the poor and mindful of their hardships and suffering. On the other hand, neither the poverty of his boyhood nor the jealousy of his Franciscan brethren during his rise to fame had seared his spirit; not even the hurtful wounds he had suffered under Gregory had made him bitter, spiteful or vindictive. Such petty defects of human nature he set firmly on one side. It was not that he had an equable temperament or a tolerant, forbearing easy-going disposition, but with an iron discipline on his emotions he was able to maintain an unerring sense of perspective, an unfailing estimate of priorities, refusing to be distracted by the irascibility of lesser men or the antagonism of opponents. On public occasions he was dignified, regal and commanding, and in appropriate places he was, as he had so often been in the pulpit, majestically eloquent, endowed with felicity of phrase and elegant quotation.

Sixtus was a man of profound piety and deep religious feeling, determined to serve with singleness of purpose the God who had chosen him for his incredible destiny to save the Church. He was rigorously painstaking, systematic and tenacious and immune to flattery. But he could brook no opposition, found idleness and lack of co-operation totally intolerable, and demanded immediate and unreserved acceptance of his own decisions. His demands could be terrifying and daunting, and his manner quite overwhelming. His contemporaries were struck by his fiery temper which always seemed to be on the point of bursting out, his hands trembling, his muscles twitching. Yet his anger could die as suddenly as it had been born, it was said; it rarely developed without adequate justification and when its purpose had been achieved the Pope could be magnanimous and forgiving; he was severe but not vindictive, exacting but not ungrateful.

Popes more than most elective rulers are liable to be inadequately prepared for the strangely diversified responsibilities of their office in which they are at once both the spiritual Father of a world-wide Church and the temporal ruler of territory comparable in size to the sixteenth-century kingdom of Scotland. How well did Sixtus measure up to the task? He was a Cardinal of fifteen years' standing and had substantial experience of high responsibility within the hierarchy of the Church, living in great favour under Pius V and in opposition under Gregory XIII. For a period of ten years he had the care of two bishoprics and for two years he had been the head of one of the large regular Orders: he knew intimately and well the problems of clerical administration. His scholarship was generally acknowledged and he was a painstaking and widely-read theologian whose judgement had been sought even by the critical Gregory XIII and used in highly important and controversial cases like that of Archbishop Carranza. Sixtus knew Italy well. He had lived in Rome for a quarter of a century with relatively short absences elsewhere. He had spent four years in Venice, three in Naples, three in Siena, shorter periods in Florence and Bologna; he was acquainted with Genoa, and must have known almost every hill and valley, town and hamlet of the Marches. Though his experience in Italy was predominantly clerical in character and though as Regent in his younger days he inevitably concentrated on scholastic duties, nevertheless as a friar he had had close contacts with the world outside his monastic quarters. As a preacher he had met the fashionable and the elegant, the noble, the bourgeois and the artisan; as a friar he knew the peasantry of the countryside and the city dweller

*The Conclave of Sixtus V* 175

of squalid slums. Possessed of genuine humanity, he knew from personal experience the problems and needs of the impoverished and had a genuine appreciation of the methods by which their conditions could be improved.

Clearly he lacked political experience and it is not surprising that the Venetian ambassador should describe him as "a novice in foreign policy".[62] He had almost no experience of diplomacy; he had never been given duties as Nuncio. He had visited Spain but only in a subordinate capacity. He had not travelled elsewhere in Europe, and so far as evidence shows he had no close or continuing contacts outside Italy. Nevertheless, his experience as Regent in Naples and then as Bishop of S. Agata had given him some acquaintance with Spanish administration of its satellite dominions in Italy, and his residence in Venice had made him watch attentively the operation of the Republic's complicated system of government. Never himself experienced in law, probably suspicious of lawyers and perhaps scornful of their tedious casuistry, he had been obliged to realise the importance of legal rights, the intricacies of rival jurisdictions and the widespread resistance to clerical and especially papal pretensions. The demands of his office as sovereign of the Papal States would test his skill to operate in a sphere of which he had little substantial experience and for which he had had no practical training.

The world awaited the new Pope's accession to the papal throne with curious expectation, some anxiety and many doubts.

## Notes

[1] Pastor 20, pp. 637–638.
[2] L. Rebaschi Carotti, *Il Conclave di Sisto V* (Mantova:1919), p. 21. This number is also given by F. Petruccelli della Gattina, *Historie Diplomatique des Conclaves* (Paris: A. Lacroix, Verboeckhoven et cie, 1865), Vol. II, p. 253. Rebaschi's list of Cardinals is difficult to reconcile fully with other records. Pastor gives 38, as also *Pont. Max.*, p. 85a, although he counts 42 Cardinals at the Conclave with only three late arrivals. P. Alaleone ("Vita e diario di Paolo Alaleone di

Branca, maestro delle cerimonie pontificie (1582–1638)", in *Archivio della Reale Società romana di storia patria* 16 (1893), pp. 5–46) says that after the initial procession into the Conclave "some Cardinals remained in the Conclave and others returned to their own homes". Ehrle's Plan of the Conclave shows only 36 Cardinals present on 21st April and three late arrivals; see F. Ehrle und H. Egger, *Die Conclavepläne. Beiträge zu ihrer Entwicklungsgeschichte* (Vatican City: Studi e documenti per la storia del Palazzo Apostolico Vaticano, 5,1933).

[3] Petruccelli, *Historie Diplomatique des Conclaves*, p. 34.

[4] *Ibid.*

[5] Pastor 17, p. 5.

[6] *Ibid.* 17, p. 418 and 20, p. 650.

[7] *Ibid.* 13, p. 35.

[8] *Ibid.*

[9] *Pont. Max.*, p. 88.

[10] Pastor 9, p. 12

[11] In the Conclave of 1550, Cardinal Pole's conclavist was the exiled Bishop of St Asaph.

[12] These paragraphs are based on documents in the Vatican Library: *Codice Barberiniano Latino* 4675, ff. 234–238; *Codice Vaticano Latino* 12179, ff. 240–242; *Codice Urbinate Latino* 9728, f. 222; *Codice Vaticano Latino* 12285, ff. 44v–46. The first three are assigned by the Library Catalogue to the seventeenth century, the last to the sixteenth century. There is no reason to doubt that all describe conditions generally applicable to the Conclave of 1585.

[13] See *Pont. Max.*, Chapter XIII and A. M. Graziani, *Vita Sixti Quinti Ipsius manu emendata* (Romae: 1587).

[14] Pastor 17, p. 6.

[15] Pastor 17, pp. 15–16; Hübner 1, pp1 86–187; *EC* article on "Conclave".

[16] Petruccelli, *Historie Diplomatique des Conclaves*, p. 35.

[17] Namely by a spontaneous and unanimous vote.

[18] Petruccelli, *Historie Diplomatique des Conclaves*, p. 253.

[19] Closing the Conclave effectively means the opening of electoral business.

[20] Delumeau 1, p. 450.

[21] Cardinal Medici claimed to have given Cardinal Spinola 500 écus and accused Cardinal Farnese of offering to pay off debts amounting to 150,000 écus for

Boncompagni. (Petruccelli, *Historie Diplomatique des Conclaves* 2, p. 248).
22. There was a second Cardinal de Medici in the Conclave, Alessandro.
23. Pastor 19, p. 12.
24. *Ibid.* 21, p. 74.
25. G. Masson, *Italian Gardens* (London: Thames & Hudson, 1961), p. 79.
26. Pastor 19, p. 217.
27. He presented a cross and two candelabra worth 18,000 scudi to St. Peter's (Pastor 20, p. 574).
28. He never polled more than four votes; see Pastor 21, p. 81.
29. Pastor 21, p. 83.
30. There was less betting than usual in this election.
31. The Duke was Cardinal Farnese's brother.
32. Delumeau 1, pp. 452–453.
33. Pastor 20, p. 645.
34. *Ibid.*, pp. 278, 438, 444, 470.
35. *Ibid.* 21, p. 11 n.
36. *Ibid.* 13, p. 3.
37. *Ibid.* 15, p. 6.
38. Petruccelli, *Historie Diplomatique des Conclaves*, pp. 28–32. Pastor 15, p. 388; Pastor 17, p. 32.
39. Hübner 1, p. 196.
40. See article by G. Cremanchi in *EC*.
41. Pastor 21, p. 17.
42. Tempesti, *Storia della vita e geste di Sisto Quinto*, 1, p. 137.
43. Petruccelli, *Historie Diplomatique des Conclaves*, p. 254.
44. *Ibid.*, p. 139.
45. Pastor 13, p. 12.
46. See Tempesti, *Storia della vita e geste di Sisto Quinto*, 1, p. 99 for the evidence of the anonymous Conclavist.
47. Hübner 1, p167.
48. Delumeau pp. 452 and 470.
49. Petruccelli, *Historie Diplomatique des Conclaves*, p. 46.
50. He also arrived late for the 1566 Conclave.
51. Particularly Sixtus V, see *Pont. Max.*.

52. *Dizionario Biografico Nazionale* (under Innocent X).
53. I have followed the account given in Alaleone's Diary. He was Master of Ceremonies at the Conclave, see Petruccelli, *Historie Diplomatique des Conclaves*, pp. 338–339.
54. Marchese di Spinazzola see Pastor 21, p. 155. The Japanese princes were Anima and Omura.
55. "To observe the constitutions of the Conclave."
56. Hübner 1, p. 258.
57. The others were Nicholas IV (1288–1292) and Sixtus IV (1471–1484).
58. Pastor 21, p. 290.
59. *Ibid.*, p. 230, n. 3.
60. *Ibid.*, p. 230.
61. Hübner 1, p. 204.
62. Lorenzo Priuli in Ranke 7, p. 286.

# CHAPTER FIVE

### Master of his House

*He had a prejudice to the effect that the mystical word 'Yes' should be distinguished from the equally unfathomable expression 'No' ... the Pope never pretended to have an extraordinary intellect; but he professed to be right.*

G. K. Chesterton, *Illustrated London News* 1914

ELECTION TO THE papal throne came unexpectedly: there were no defined routes to it, almost no specified requirements, certainly no succession. Though restricted *de facto* since 1522 to Italians, many might hope to attain it, but although Cardinals were divided into these *papabile* and those *non-papabile*, none could forestall or avoid the final vagaries of the Conclave and consequently preparation for the event was impossible. The Papacy, like the Dogeship in Venice, was an elective monarchy though with vastly differing prerogatives: both (unlike the Presidency of most modern republics) were elections for life. Sixtus could have discovered that of his thirteen predecessors in his century, one had reigned for sixteen, one for thirteen years; three had lived after election for a single year or less; of the remainder the average reign lasted a little more than six years and a half. Nor did age and length of reign coincide, for two of the longest reigns belonged to Popes above the mean age at election and of the three who had the shortest reigns the youngest was fifty-four and the eldest ten years older. The eternal uncertainties of life only caused Sixtus to live with an unremitting sense of urgency, deeply conscious that time was short.

Election made him the richest, the most influential and the most independent of all the Italian princes. Though Venetian Doges succeeded when younger and reigned longer than Popes, they were little more than titular sovereigns with little political authority. The Kingdom of Naples and the Duchy of Milan were Spanish dependencies and the Republic of Genoa no longer of comparable standing. The lands over which Sixtus would rule were extensive, centrally situated in the peninsula and though not comparable with the valleys of the Po and its tributaries, nevertheless contained substantial areas of fertile and well-developed country. Though his domain included no commercial centre of the first rank, the Pope had considerable, often vulnerable, interests in the Adriatic as well as the Mediterranean. Yet the secular assets of the Papacy were as nothing compared to the rich treasury of its spiritual powers. To many in Western Christendom the Papacy seemed founded on the Roman hills. To the faithful, the words of the Pope were decisive, his commendation rich, his censure terrifying; his final power of excommunication still capable of striking terror into the marrow of Catholic king and subject alike. The right to speak in the name of the eternal, immutable Catholic Church gave him absolute authority which few would dispute though many might doubt the temporal claims of jurisdiction. To hear him speak, to kiss his foot, be received in audience, to be offered his ring, were spiritual privileges which still cast their aura over millions. And as the New World opened, the prospect of fresh converts and new mission fields added lustre to the papal throne. The son of a peasant, the learned, inspiring preacher, the Franciscan Vicar-General, the Inquisitor, was now elevated to the Papacy. He might have been forgiven if had he been overcome by the immensity of the honour and the gravity of the responsibility which now rested on his shoulders. Such a career was at once astonishing and intimidating. He would need a sense of direction.

Yet one of the many remarkable things about the new Pope was the speed with which he set to work. His mind was clear, his intentions were quickly formulated and implemented with a sense of urgency and a refusal to accept obstacles as excuses for lack of progress. It seemed he had been waiting for his predecessor's departure and had employed the interval to define his objectives and to elaborate not only precise plans but a time-table for their completion. There was no period of running in, no tentative outlines, no surveys of the landscape, no commissions of enquiry, no time-consuming searches for guidance. From the day of his election an undeviating course was charted and orders given for full throttle to be operated. Already Sixtus IV and Pius V were his heroes whose example he would accept and whose footsteps he would follow. He believed the future could be shaped by the historic past. The sense of destiny he had nourished from his earliest days now gave him optimism, assurance, determination and inexhaustible stamina.

Sixtus V's central objective was to develop Rome as the metropolis of Christendom.[1] Rome was unique. It had a splendid, incomparable fund of antiquities which fascinated scholars from all quarters of the cultural world, it perpetuated the traditions and preserved the relics of the vast Empire which for centuries had dominated history, and in the latter part of the sixteenth century it possessed artistic and scholarly treasures of the Renaissance probably surpassed only in Venice, and then only if both scale and quality are taken into account. But in addition to those immense riches, Rome was the established home of the Christian church, with the tomb of the Prince of the Apostles in its midst and the prison and burial place of the great Apostle to the Gentiles not far away. Intrinsically Rome had been elevated by history and Christian tradition to incontestable supremacy. If the Avignon captivity and the Great Schism had sullied its ancestry, diminished the Papal court and halved the city population,[2] if the Reformation had produced ugly chasms in the Papal domain, the fortunes of the church and the prestige of the Papacy were in the process of restoration. The time had arrived to celebrate their triumph, to proclaim the incomparable wealth of their resources and the certainty of their final victory over all opposition. An atmosphere of belligerent confidence prevailed and the dominating spirit of optimism and sufficient support to make it possible to register the Church's faith in permanent physical form. It was a quarter of a century since the Peace of Cateau-Cambrésis (1559) had actually established the 'Pax Hispanica' in Italy, and Popes could now turn their minds to the re-establishment of their spiritual leadership. The hour had come when the intellectual stimulation and artistic energy of the Renaissance could be married to the unchanging tradition and heritage of the Church. Building on the work of the Council of Trent and fortified by the new religious Orders, the Church would offset its losses in Europe by fresh expansion in the New World. Defeatism was swept away in an outburst of spontaneous crusading vitality. Rome was to be re-established as the Head of the One true and eternal Church.

Sixtus well understood that progress was totally impossible until respect for law and acceptance of public authority were restored. In almost every age some state reaches a stage when constitutional authority is challenged by physical force, when confidence in the capacity of the government to defend them destroys the will of the citizens to support or defend their governors; and courts are rendered powerless either because they too are intimidated or because public fear prevents cases being bought before them for redress. In effect, civil war breaks out, but for some time the situation goes unrecognised and powers adequate to impose authority on the lawbreakers are not taken. The issue relates not to the form of government or the legitimacy of its powers but to the sovereignty of law itself and the authority of government to impose order and maintain public discipline. In these situations, so destructive of civilisation, force has first to be overcome whatever its nature or constitution, even though government is accused of tyranny and violation of private rights. Only then can confidence in established authority be restored and arbitrary and dictatorial powers surrendered by government. Such was the state of Rome when Sixtus was elected Pope. The latter years of his predecessor's reign had shown how readily anarchy and complete defiance of accepted canons of conduct reduced government to chaos. Concern for human life, respect for sacred things and places, deference for rank or virtue had disappeared. Cardinal Savelli's brother was set upon even in the supposed safety of his coach in broad daylight and killed just outside the city gates, almost within earshot of its main street,[3] houses were pillaged, travellers held to ransom, property stolen by force of arms; life and goods stood in perpetual peril. Outside the city regular postal couriers were ambushed by well-organised bands and transfers of money had often to be despatched under armed guard. Sixtus himself, as Cardinal, had found himself embroiled in a fracas between the Orsini family and a constable who had attempted to carry off a notorious bandit from their palace. In the incident his personal servant was killed before his eyes and he himself had to take refuge in a neighbouring house. Straightaway the Orsini family fortified their several houses in the city and pursued an armed campaign against the authorities in the course of which men were wounded and even killed within the walls of the Vatican Palace.[4] Only four years previously Sixtus himself had watched the authorities stupefied and helpless after his great-nephew had been done to death within yards of one of the Papal palaces by ruffians assisted by the brother of the victim's wife, in a carefully designed plot hatched by one of Rome's leading families. He had seen its author defy the Pope's embargo on his marriage and was aware that this villain was peacefully in the City while the Conclave was in session.

Brigands expelled from one city appeared unchallenged in the next or crossed the border into a neighbouring state without scrutiny or hindrance. Rome lay in a corridor between North and South and on a highway between Mediterranean and Adriatic with traffic passing endlessly through its gates and along its streets, wretched and unconstructed as they were. Though Rome was in no real sense a port, ships sailed frequently from the mouth of the Tiber to Ripa Grande in the heart of the city and on to Ripetta somewhat further north. In Trastevere and in the Ripetta there were nomadic sailors living in temporary, often desperate, quarters, and in the less respectable taverns and lodging houses lived numerous members of the lower echelons of the mercantile community. The city itself was a cosmopolitan chessboard on which were marshalled groups of foreign settlers speaking their own languages, maintaining their own traditions, culture and customs, supporting their own churches, living a closely circumscribed life where attachment to their motherland was never allowed to die. The Florentines lived around the northern end of Via Giulia and maintained the newly-built and recently completed San Giovanni dei Fiorentini; the Spaniards congregated round the Piazza Navona where they supported San Giacomo degli Spagnoli; there was a French colony nearby who maintained San Luigi as their national church, and a smaller German settlement with their national church Santa Maria dell'Anima to the west of Piazza Navona. There was a settlement of Slavs near the Ripetta and their church was San Girolamo degli Schiavoni. Cohesion in such a background was difficult to establish, especially as individual Popes tended to allocate their business and to admit to their service nationals with whom they already had connections and amongst these foreign settlements there operated a sort of place system which accentuated the transitory character of their residence and its continuous ebb and flow.

Native Rome added its own divisions and rivalries to the maelstrom. From the so-called Guelph and Ghibelline factions of former centuries had descended a powerful Roman nobility. Now living in Renaissance luxury, but heavily encumbered with debt, fragmented by bitter internecine rivalry and long-standing feuds, divided into hostile family groups, such as the Orsini and the Colonna. Most were hostile to any authority which threatened to curb their independence or regiment their activities. Each had its own contacts and satellite establishments outside the city to which they could retreat in times of repression or ill-fortune and from which they could organise new onslaughts on authority when circumstances appeared favourable. The mere imposition of order in Rome only managed to limit anarchy: ensuring not conquest but a temporary truce. No Pope had evolved a Star Chamber capable of exterminating the outlaws, for it seems likely that no political court was as effective or as rigorous as the Inquisition. In Italy brigandage was both ubiquitous and perpetual. In banditry lingered the traditions of the fifteenth-century *condottieri* who found such ready employment in the Northern Italian states and from which sprang the more effectively organised mercenaries amongst whom the prowess of the Romagnoli was outstanding. In the lands around the City, the decline of arable farming and the dispossession of the peasantry created restless, discontented and rootless people, the most unscrupulous of whom were ready for employment as desperadoes. The immense accumulated riches of the city provided ready targets for brigands and the attractions of employment at the papal court served as a magnet for large numbers of learned, unpractical, often unsuspecting men, mostly celibate, physically unresourceful, vulnerable to threats and a ready prey for the unscrupulous blackmailer and the well-connected parasite. The city, like so many cities of pleasure with a fluid population, harboured a sinister underworld of its own whose citizens lived very well on their wits, forewarned of dangers, well-informed of advantageous and unprotected booty. The city itself seemed designed for their purpose; dark, narrow streets leading shadily from one corner to the next were an invitation to crime and an unobstructed escape for its perpetrator, and ready to hand—still within the city walls—the almost uninhabited hills whose open spaces offered no obstacle to the fugitive, and whose numerous woods and coppices offered him shelter and cover. So many penniless, homeless, desperate characters squatted in and around the Baths of Diocletian that the Pope's extension of his adjoining Villa had to be curtailed.

Undeterred by any of these discouraging circumstances, totally unmoved by the impending prospect of an appalling bloodbath, Sixtus resolved to clean up the city without delay and to his task he brought a cold, unflinching sense of Franciscan discipline and order. Taking to heart the advice of Rehoboam's young men, he determined to make his little finger thicker than his father's loins (1 Kings 12:10), to strike quickly and hard, and moreover, to strike fearlessly and deliberately at the tallest trees. Even before his coronation and in the face of the Cardinals' remonstrances, he had four youths who had been arrested for carrying arms sentenced and put to death as an indication of the severity with which he intended to punish breaches of the law.[5] Paolo Giordano Orsini, now husband of the widow of the Pope's great-nephew Vittoria (Accoramboni), sought an audience with Sixtus on the very day of his election. But though he was pardoned, his reception was cold; he was warned unequivocally to abandon banditry and to liquidate the band of brigands at his Castle at Bracciano some twenty miles away. Having complied with this instruction he again had an audience of the Pope and was driven to the conclusion that he could never feel secure so long as he could be found within the Pope's jurisdiction. He withdrew to Salò in Lake Garda, and in November died of poison.[6] Vittoria's brother, Marcello, one of the ruffians responsible for the murder of the Pope's nephew, was amongst the fugitives from Bracciano and joined Orsini at Salò; Marcello was subsequently tried for homicide, committed at Padua and sentenced to death by the Vatican authorities.[7] Ludovico Orsini, another of the criminal members of that distinguished family, was captured, tried for Vittoria's murder and strangled in a Republican prison, his accomplices being executed next day. Subsequently one of his accomplices in another murder, Captain Fossombre, was tortured and hanged.[8] Temporarily the Orsini banditry was decimated and scattered, its power broken. In other parts of the Papal territory, brigands were hounded with equally exemplary determination. Bologna, a rich city with a population of 60,000 or 70,000, was a particularly vulnerable hunting ground for the bandits. Venice employed special bands of Dalmatian troops to repel and round up the fierce outlaws and drove them off into neighbouring lands such as Bologna where one or other of the rival factions, the Pepoli and the Malvezza, could be relied on to have the gates opened for them.[9] Brigands were adept in discovering points of least resistance and exploiting their weaknesses. Sixtus chose Cardinal Salviati, one of the younger members of the Sacred College, full of initiative and energy, as Legate to Bologna and assured him of full support for whatever resolute measures he found necessary. Giovanni Pepoli, leader of one faction, was attacked for sheltering bandits, brought to trial and executed, which brought terrible fear to the minds of all the Bolognese. The head of the Malvezzi was accused of treason and he and his followers fled for their lives. Another notorious brigand from the city, Count Boschi, was executed, even though his crime was committed forty years previously.[10] Cardinal Colonna was appointed Legate in the Campagna and put in charge of the well-disciplined, paid papal troops. There the priest Guercino, a ruffian who had terrorised the area and styled himself King of the Campagna was caught and beheaded.[11]

These disconnected acts of retribution alone would never have put a stranglehold on these irrepressible bandits and Sixtus therefore approached the other Italian princes to enlist their aid in mounting a coordinated campaign. Venice welcomed the Pope's advances, Naples, where Juan de Zúñiga ruled as Viceroy, agreed to help, and the Dukes of Urbino and Ferrara pledged their support to the Pope's operation. The new arrangements were of particular value to Benevento, a small papal enclave within the Kingdom of Naples, where raiding bandits could easily assault the town and retreat unharmed into the neighbouring kingdom. A series of extradition conventions was formulated and agreements evolved by which the troops of one state were empowered to extend the pursuit of the bandits into their neighbour's territory. Curzietto dal Sambuco, a most notorious brigand who demanded entry into Rome almost as soon as the Pope had been elected, was driven off but was captured at Trieste almost 500 miles away and faced with being handed over to Sixtus, he preferred to drown himself in the sea.[12] Another robber chief, Giovanni Valenti, who demanded 10,000 scudi as the ransom of a merchant, was hunted down until he fell into the hands of Neapolitan troops: he was handed over, executed and his head exhibited on the Ponte Sant'Angelo.[13] Tuscany was the weak link in this chain of allied police authorities for the Grand Duke Francesco's government was weak, dilatory and apathetic. Yet even there the Pope's efforts were not unrewarded, for he was prepared even to waive clerical privilege and authorise the Grand Duke to imprison and prosecute priests of any rank or Order for assisting bandits so long as they were handed over to the nuncio for sentence.[14] When Lamberto Malatesta, one of the most feared and hated brigands in the whole Italian peninsula with his headquarters at Rimini, was pursued into Tuscan territory, though at first he was allowed to winter, re-victual and recruit there, eventually after Sixtus had followed his denunciations of him in the Papal consistory and his complaint of the Grand Duke's inaction, by threats of extreme measures, he was arrested and sent to Rome in chains. His trial lasted six weeks but he was duly sentenced to death and executed in June 1587.[15] When subsequently the infamous Piccolomini whose bands, assisted by the Orsini, had once defeated Gregory XIII's troops in pitched battle, took refuge in the Grand Duchy, he too was expelled and finally put to death, though not until 1591.[16]

Less violent criminals were hunted with equal vigour and treated with corresponding severity. Neither rank nor even clerical privilege was allowed to divert the course of justice. Ascanio Sforza and Marco Antonio Incoronate, were included amongst those arrested. Roberto d'Altemps, natural son of Cardinal Altemps was arrested, imprisoned in the Castel Sant'Angelo for four months, and charged with abduction and sentenced to death, though later released.[17] Cardinal Guastavillani himself was arrested for allegedly obstructing the course of justice, and when the influential Cardinal de' Medici protested the Pope was surprised at his tone and told him simply, "We intend to be obeyed."[18] On another occasion he boasted that "were the Emperor himself ever in Rome he would have to obey the laws of His Holiness."[19] In the same vein Sixtus ordered Cardinal Sforza on pain of imprisonment in the Castel Sant'Angelo to dismiss his followers because the quarrels of his grooms had led to bloodshed. Rome had seldom experienced such a fierce reign of terror: though the citizens welcomed the restoration of law and order, they were quelled and intimidated by the insensitive severity of the new regime, fearful of the informer and terrified of malicious accusations. Even at the Papal Court people lived in fear and many began to creep away into less tense surroundings: even the powerful Cardinal Farnese and Savelli, a Cardinal of almost a half-century's standing and a former Governor of Rome, disappeared from the city and took no part in public affairs. It was estimated that the 27,000 bandits outnumbered the soldiers in the papal army by 500 per cent.

To maintain pressure on the miscreants the Pope addressed personal exhortations to the Cardinals, the barons and the citizens in general. In Consistory he specially emphasised to the Cardinals the importance of re-establishing the rule of law. Laws against the carrying of arms, conspiring, assisting or harbouring criminals were re-published and the Government demonstrated its unqualified determination to enforce them in spite of all resistance. The administration of the City was in the hands of the Senator, three *Conservatori* and the General Council. The Council contained more than a hundred members (the majority city officials, and in no sense a popularly elected body) and met normally in secret session twice and in public session once per month, a quorum of thirty members being required for the transaction of ordinary business. The City was divided into thirteen *rioni* or wards each the responsibility of a *caporione* and each represented in the Council.[20] Theoretically one of the main duties of the *caporioni* was the raising of the city militia, comprising one member of each family—the normal medieval popular army. In fact, however, the militia was very rarely raised and even when it was formed it was led by the Gonfaloniere to the city walls and handed over to the command of Papal captains. There was a very considerable municipal bureaucracy comprising constables, marshalls, financial and legal officials, engineers and officers responsible for streets, bridges, gateways and waterworks. The main functions of this city administration was the preservation of public order, the management of city property, the maintenance of communications and public buildings, the raising and dispensing of public funds, the issue of licences permitting the carrying on of a variety of businesses in the city, and the close supervision of weights, measures, prices and trading practices. There was a series of municipal courts, both civil and criminal, staffed by law officers assisted by administrative assistants. This imposing but costly and cumbersome city administration was nevertheless hollow and unreal. Ceremonial forms and civic functions were meticulously observed, orders of precedence were hotly debated, the appearances of civic dignity were fully maintained but the reality of power had long departed. Its funds were slender arising largely from the *gabello dello studio*, a tax on wine not produced in Rome and the *quattrino della carne*, a tax on the retailing of meat, from dues levied on merchants and shopkeepers, and from fees and fines imposed by its judiciary. There was no rating system; its tax collectors were unpopular and the taxes subject to widespread evasion. Real power lay with the Papal curia: the Papal Treasury was responsible for supplementing the city resources and therefore controlled the development of city projects and at the same time compelled the authorities to contribute substantially to schemes initiated by the Papal administration.[21] There were frequent disputes between the city judiciary on the one hand and the Cardinal Camerlengo and the Papal courts on the other. The powers of the Pope's representatives, the Cardinal Governors, expanded continuously and their interventions in matters of everyday administration increased almost daily. In reality, Rome was governed from the Vatican Palace, though the forms of power continued to centre on the Campidoglio. Indeed civic office came to be regarded as a tiresome burden rather than a welcome distinction; the courts were charged to examine the reasons for refusing office and the replacement of obligatory service by a system of compounding was considered though not adopted. In Pecchiai's words, "Everyone could see the misfortunes of the Roman people who were in fact treated by the Holy See as a prodigal son to whom money was given to preserve the family dignity but to whom not even a farthing was entrusted without the strictest examination."[22]

The inherent weakness and supine conduct of the city administration and the resistance to his own attempts to accentuate the transfer of power from the municipality to the Curia added immensely to Sixtus's difficulty in effectively restoring order in the Papal capital. Instinctively he appreciated that success depended not on the structure of government but on the quality of the governors. San Giorgio was replaced as Governor by Mariano Pierbenedetti. Cardinal Colonna whose firmness had curbed disorder during the Interregnum was appointed Legate of the Province of Campagna and given command of the papal troops. A special Congregation was created including Cardinals Albani, Salviati and Carafa (all men of action), to deal with the problem of banditry.[23] Since in the later days of Gregory XIII's reign papal troops had become as uncontrolled and dangerous as the bandits themselves, these were, with the exception of 300 trusted men, disbanded and their leader the Duke of Sora (Gregory XIII's natural son), whom Sixtus had temporarily confirmed in his appointment, was dismissed; a deputy, Mario Sforza, was removed.[24]

Laws were not lacking nor sanctions insufficient. Only against the most powerful brigands with formidable bands of well-trained, strongly armed men, were exceptional measures required. What was needed, at least in the Pope's view, was a dynamic determination to round up the hordes of lawless men in the Papal States (the Cenci being the most infamous), to bring them to trial and to impose exemplary penalties. This was a friar's diagnosis and remedy. Moreover, banditry was so widespread, and speed of movement so exceptional that large cumbersome forces requiring time for assembly and preparation were unlikely to prove effective. This was guerrilla warfare not a classic campaign. Sixtus preferred to rely on the co-ordinated efforts of a variety of local initiatives whose individual resources, though limited, could be offset by their multiplicity and their ability to call upon assistance from a number of sources including the Papal court itself. All ranks of the nobility and every commune was ordered to free its territory of terrorists on pain of fines of 200 golden scudi for any defaulting commune, of 1,000 scudi for any university or 5,000 scudi for a nobleman. The approach of the bandits was to be announced by the sounding of the tocsin, whereupon everyone of whatever rank was to present himself for service, ready armed. Defaulters were to be fined 500 scudi.[25] By the Pope's orders extensive woods in the Campagna were felled in a miniature scorched earth policy designed to facilitate the discovery and pursuit of the brigands.

Sixtus believed that amongst bandits allegiance was transitory and venal. In a Bull promulgated in June 1585 he offered a pardon for any head of a bandit band and four of his companions who surrendered, a pardon was offered to any ordinary bandit for himself and two of his companions for a fee of merely 200 scudi; a prize of 300 scudi was offered for the head of a bandit or 600 scudi for delivering him alive. The surrender of the leader of their band was worth a pardon for eight of his followers, that of an ordinary bandit, dead or alive, was valued at 100 scudi. The same rewards were available to soldiers or justices who were responsible for such surrenders and all these rewards were to be granted immediately, freely and without question.[26] Shortly afterwards a free pardon was offered to any who had contact with the bandits or had helped them if they confessed their fault and undertook not to repeat their offences. Severity for the obdurate, clemency for the penitent; such was the papal prescription.

Unfortunately, the success of the Pope's repressive measures was limited. In July, 1585, thirty criminals surprised a captain of the Papal police with six officers within a stone's throw of the Pope's Villa Montalto,[27] and two months later the courier from Venice was attacked on the Ponte Molle, only somewhat more than a mile and a half from Piazza del Popolo.[28] In the following year Bernardino da Magnano, chief of one of the bandit bands, contrived a plot to murder the Pope and two of the Cardinals which fortunately was discovered.[29] In 1587 a new series of brigand groups appeared at Velletri and Corneto respectively, only twenty and fifty miles from the capital. The bad harvest of 1589 and the resulting discontent produced a calamitous resurgence of banditry in the closing months of Sixtus's pontificate which threatened to nullify all his efforts, and the archleader, Piccolomini again made temporary use of refuge in the Grand Duchy of Tuscany to launch fresh attacks. Brigandage in Italy was so firmly established that even a Pope as resolute and resourceful as Sixtus could effect merely a temporary suppression of its virulence. Only a succession of strong Popes, a sustained policy of co-operation between the Italian states and a substantial raising of the social standards and security (particularly from flood and famine) of the masses, and the provision of alternative objectives for the nobility would enable this plague of disorder to be eliminated.

Repression alone can never be a permanent basis of government. The authority of public order once established needs to be maintained by a general consensus of opinion in its favour and a willingness to support its dictates at least in general terms. Justice to the community as a whole must appear to be maintained by a system of administration in which regard for the common interest transcends the private will.

The fortunes of the construction industry and the artistic trades depended substantially on the policy of the Pope and his Court and the attitude of the churches and religious Orders which tended to follow his lead and to accept the fashion which his Court set. In Rome, therefore, whilst there was almost no proletariat, there were many living on the subsistence level and many more who from time to time were in desperate straits. The physical conditions of the city bred endemic diseases, epidemics struck the city at intervals, famines were frequent, a volatile economy produced recurring disasters. Any government which could offer a measure of security to the poor and was able to ride out the storms for the unfortunate was assured of widespread support. If over the years the State could make it evident that justice was practiced, that administration was efficient and designed to support public order, if it could develop the common interests for the community and if it could convince those with wealth and responsibility of their duty towards society in general, then its people would be in good social health and its dominion would prosper. These objectives were the foundations on which Sixtus built a clear and co-ordinated domestic policy.

It was not in the public interest that law-abiding elements of the Roman nobility should be destroyed or weakened, but rather that their interests should be attached to those of the government. To relieve them of their crippling indebtedness, Sixtus enabled the nobility to float long-term loans (*monti*), guaranteed by the papal authority, generally without stipulated redemption dates, at rates of interest generally below those ruling at that time and certainly below those at which they themselves could have borrowed on their own security. A very large loan of this kind was raised by the powerful Colonna family, another by the Savelli family and a third by the Cesarini family, whilst sums needed by others were accumulated into the Monte dei Batoni amounting in Sixtus' reign to 245,000 écus.[30] In this way a substantial sector of the nobility became dependent on the goodwill and financial prosperity of the government. One substantial cause of the indebtedness of the nobility was the need, established by tradition and contemporary fashion, to provide inflated dowries and the most lavish wedding banquets for such of their daughters as married. To deliver them from their own follies successive Popes had imposed statutory limitations on these dowries. Sixtus followed their example when in 1586 he restricted dowries to 5,000 écus and empowered the government to seize ten percent of any amount above that limit even though dowries of even ten times that amount had become current. Unfortunately, he revoked this decree two years later and himself endowed his two great-nieces with 100,000 écus.[31] In this way a substantial sector of the nobility became dependent on the goodwill and financial prosperity of the government. The Pope shrewdly wove the interests of two noble families into those of his own. His great-niece, Flavia, married the Duke of Bracciano, the son of Paolo Giordano Orsini, the author of the plot by which her uncle was killed, and her sister Ursula married Marco Antonio Colonna. Powerful and inter-related interest was enlisted to support the administration of the papal capital. It had become the practice of the century for successive Popes to endow their own families with considerable wealth and in this way a new nobility was created which rivalled the ancient aristocracy. The Farnese, the Bonelli and the Aldobrandisi and the Boncompagni were such. Sixtus' advancement of his family was therefore in accord with this tradition though perhaps in a minor key.[32] Cardinals and principal officials of the Papal Court were similarly able to advance the interests of their houses. Although it would be difficult to assess the extent and influence of corruption during Sixtus V's reign there is no doubt that powerful court interests were being developed.[33]

Throughout his pontificate Sixtus was concerned also that the causes of discontent among the poor in the city should be removed. The Tiber-bend of Rome was densely populated and the population was constantly increasing. The ready supply of labour and the absence of productive industries in the city or its vicinity made the populace wholly dependent on employment at the Court, in the service industries it supported, or the building and luxury trades it maintained. Poverty and riches lived and worked side by side with large numbers of people penniless from time to time, cowed, apprehensive and intimidated. The greatest danger to the populace was famine.

Sixtus therefore extended the Corn and Fresh Food Law system which his predecessors had developed, and instilled into its administration the driving force of his personal concern and conscience. The objective was to guarantee to the city an adequate supply of foodstuffs at controlled prices and this entailed the subordination of the short-term interests of the producer to those of the consumer whenever circumstances required it. Rome was dangerously dependent on the primary products of an extensive countryside around it, particularly of the Campagna to the south and east and of the *Patrimonium Petri* to the north, and as its population grew or whenever the regular influx of tourists and pilgrims increased this dependence became more and more hazardous. The situation was constantly aggravated as bankers and merchants bought or leased land in this countryside both from the Papal Court and the nobility and turned it over to the rearing of cattle and sheep, often depriving the peasantry of their rights and their occupation in the process. These displaced families then drifted into the city in search of a livelihood and inevitably accentuated the pressure on declining food supplies. The Government's interest in this development was ambivalent, for on the one hand it was embarrassed by the rising demand for supplies and the declining source of foodstuff, on the other it drew a very significant proportion of its revenues from rents arising from these leases. Indeed Gregory XIII had resuscitated papal rights, liquidated encroachments over large sectors of these areas and vigorously exercised the papal right of pre-emption whenever lands in this area were offered for sale. Within these zones cattle and sheep breeders were protected from interference by the local communes or by private developers in return for dues levied on the number of cattle grazed on these lands. These dues proved so profitable as to produce almost twice the proceeds of export duties on grain levied in the whole of the Papal States.[34] Even this expansion of cattle-breeding and sheep-raising did no more than match the rising demand for meat. Sixteenth-century Rome was a carnivorous city. Though the ever-lengthening list of church festivals accelerated the demand for fish and produced a phenomenal increase in the number of fish merchants, that for beef, lamb and pork never ceased to rise. Butchers were surpassed in numbers only by hoteliers and tavern keepers, and it was said that in a single year Rome consumed nearly 23,000 sheep and 73,000 lambs.[35]

Yet the staple item of the Roman diet was bread, particularly for the poor,[36] and a Pope who could ensure a supply of cheap bread of good quality was certain of fame and favour.[37] Previous Popes had attempted to limit the spread of pastoral graziers and to encourage farming by peasants. A century earlier Sixtus IV had authorised the occupation of uncultivated lands by tenants who paid a fixed proportion of their crops as rent and he had established courts to ensure that such tenants were not obstructed by recalcitrant owners or subjected to interference or excessive rents. Pius V had set up a court to protect such tenants' rights and to prevent their eviction. Clement VII had also set a limit of 125 to the number of cows an owner within a radius of ten miles of Rome might possess. The owners of land in the *agro romano* around Rome were ordered to devote all their lands to grain or vegetables. But against the wishes of the moneyed men and the land speculators all these efforts were doomed to failure and the area of arable land continued to decline. Sixtus found some amelioration of the situation by developing drainage schemes. The Renaissance had added considerably to the knowledge of hydraulics and Italy was a country where the opportunities for experiment in practical applications of that subject were boundless. Sixtus revived a scheme in which Leonardo da Vinci had taken some interest and of which a small portion had been executed, increased the scale of the project and enlisted the help of Ascanio Fenizi, an engineer from Urbino. A vast area perhaps 62,000 acres (almost 1,000 square miles) of the Pontine Marshes lying to the north-west of Terracina and running inland to the Lepini mountains was examined. Here Fenizi was empowered to take possession of lands needed for the scheme, on payment of very favourable rents to the owners. He then formed a syndicate which could provide the necessary funds and which included an influential Florentine merchant, the Pope's nephew a boy of sixteen, now a Cardinal, and another Cardinal of the Pope's creation. A canal which had been cut as part of the previous scheme and which had been allowed to decline to ruin was restored and a new, much larger, one, appropriately designated the Fosso Sisto, was excavated. Within four months more than 10,000 acres were ready for cultivation and work in hand would provide more than 30,000 acres of cultivated land in the course of a year. The Pope himself visited the project and declared himself content. The scheme, though subject to some criticism, was estimated to be capable of supplying one-eighth of Rome's needs. Unfortunately, central Italy suffered a calamitous winter in 1589–90 when torrential and incessant rains flooded large areas of land, inundated large sectors of the papal territory and wreaked havoc across the whole peninsula. Indeed, this was a disastrous winter for a substantial part of the whole Mediterranean area. Work was halted and the scheme itself delayed until resumed more than three centuries later. Sixtus also planned a scheme of draining the marches near Orvieto but this made little progress. The Pope's vision of a greatly enlarged area of arable land for the benefit of the capital was soundly conceived and energetically and skilfully carried into effect: misfortune prevented its full development and greatly reduced its usefulness. His successors did not resuscitate his plans. Nature denied the Pope his due.

Meanwhile the grain, vegetable and oil producing industry of the whole Papal States was brought under central control. Its immediate environs were forbidden to export elsewhere: throughout the Papal States producers of grain and vegetables were obliged to obtain export licences from the Papal Court. Whenever Rome needed their products they were prevented from selling in other markets even though their profit would have been larger. Only when supplies in Rome were already adequate did Sixtus permit export elsewhere, though he exercised these controls with moderation and good sense. Some trade in grain with Venice continued and the export of beans was allowed more readily than that of grain, but when the city of Ravenna sent ambassadors to Rome to obtain sanction to continue their exports to Venice and obtained support from the Papal Legate in the Romagna they failed to extract the permission they wanted. Strong opposition to the Pope's arbitrary and rigid policy was widespread in Umbria and the Marches but Sixtus refused to yield or modify his demands. On the other hand when in 1507 corn had been requisitioned in the Marches in excess of the city's needs the surplus was re-sold to the producers. In the summer of 1587 the whole of the Roman Campagna within a radius of 30 miles from the City was ordered to send its entire harvest of cereals, grain and vegetables except what was needed for the following year's sowing to the city markets within 15 days under pain of the confiscation of their crop and considerable fines. In the summer of 1590 after the disastrous floods to which reference has already been made, a census was taken of all stocks of grain, and owners within 20 miles of the capital were instructed to send all their crops into the city markets. Taking advantage of the enhanced value of licences to the producers, Sixtus trebled the duties levied.

To make his control of supplies more efficient and to enable him to make provision for the needs of the ensuing year, immediately after the harvest was garnered, Sixtus made the first estimates of the city's grain needs—150,000 rubbia in 1587 and 200,000 rubbia in 1590.[38] Within these estimates the Pope made it his duty to ensure that supplies within the city would match its needs. When deficiencies could not be met by imports from areas within Papal boundaries, with great reluctance Sixtus had to initiate purchases from elsewhere, more particularly from Sicily. Such occurrences were rare, for generally payment had to be made in gold.

Sixtus concerned himself also with the problems of distribution. In 1586 he obliged the Conservatori of the City to launch a loan of 100,000 écus with which he would purchase food supplies for distribution to the people, and when they demanded repayment he gave them a brusque reply; next year he planned to add 300,000 écus from his papal funds. In 1588 he actually applied 200,000 écus to this fund. The management of the purchasing transactions was entrusted to two Florentine merchants, Guglielmo and Leonardo Dei, who also organised the transport of grain between Rome and the Marches. The Pope established granaries in Romagna and the Marches where grain could be stored from one year to the next and from which supplies could be drawn and sent to Rome as the needs of the people developed. The entry of the Pope into the market enabled him to curb the power of monopolists, to control prices at source and to ensure that laws against selling otherwise than to Rome were not evaded. In fact the Pope's policy was bitterly resisted and ambassadors from Spoleto, Ravenna and other committees were sent to Rome to protest to the Pope and to demand the closure of the papal grain shops.

Within the city retail prices were tightly controlled by the Apostolic Camerlengo and when prices rose because of shortages he was ordered to reduce the price in the papal shops so that the people should not be exploited. At the same time laws were strictly enforced against merchants who tried to purchase grain outside the market, and particularly on routes into it.[39] Bakers operated under the closest possible supervision: the amount of grain they were allowed to purchase was limited and they were obliged to declare their stocks periodically; they were compelled to mark their bread and to maintain standards of quality. A baker who sold bread outside the City was publicly flogged on the Campo de' Fiori and a baker was hung for over-charging his customers. When other measures failed to control shortages of foodstuffs the Pope reduced the number of people employed at the Papal Court and ordered others to take up residence elsewhere.

The enforcement of laws so vigorously resisted by the producers and the grain merchants required an energetic administration with a strong attachment to the public interest, a sense of integrity which made corruption impossible and a genuine conviction of the justice of papal policy. Gregory XIII had already established a Prefecture of Supplies charged with this task; Sixtus added a Congregazione dell'Abbondanza (a Ministry of Supply) and appointed as President of the Department of Food Supplies the redoubtable Venetian, Cardinal Cornaro, who had extensive experience in the Republic of the regulation of food supplies.[40] He removed from the Conservatori all duties concerned with the distribution of supplies and forbade them to take any decisions on these matters except in consultation with the Prefect of Supplies. Control rested unequivocally in Papal hands. These measures doubtless secured for the citizens of the capital a more reliable flow of supplies and more stable prices than they would otherwise have had. Unfortunately, the consequences of the ruinous floods of 1589–90 were disastrous. Prices rose to such an extent that controls had to be greatly relaxed or the city would have starved. Even so the poorer people were driven to living on cooked acorns or on flour made from acorns. Merchants were allowed to sell at the prices of a free market but the Pope authorised the Papal Treasury to buy up supplies and to re-sell them to the populace at reduced rates. At the same time he released 500,000 écus to be loaned to other communes in the Papal States free of interest for one year.

One main solution to the problems of the poor in Rome could be the introduction of local workshops. Sixtus resumed efforts of his predecessors, notably Pius V, to introduce textiles industries, wool and silk, into the city. He commissioned two woollen merchants to develop the woollen industry in the city, offering them a free loan of 12,000 écus and a further 2,000 écus from his own funds with which to buy a ship and material. He also spent more than 1,000 écus on the establishment of a public cloth-fulling mill near the Trevi fountain. Sixtus also hoped to establish a woollen mill in the Coliseum, but no progress had been made when he died and the woollen industry in the town was still precarious.

Sixtus also granted a monopoly of mulberry rearing in the Papal States (except in Bologna, where one existed already) to a Tuscan,

Pietro Valentino, with authority to purchase land compulsorily where necessary. He also contracted with a Jew, Magino Gabrielli, for the establishment of silk factories, and the Pope himself had workshops constructed near the Baths of Diocletian, near to his Villa Montalto. He allowed Jews to practice crafts, build schools and synagogues and exempted them from distinctive badges. This exemption was not continued under subsequent Popes.

When these efforts made very slow progress, the Pope contracted with two other merchants, one from Genoa and the other from Lucca, to establish the silk industry in the city, offering them a loan, free of interest, of 50,000 écus and exemption from judicial proceedings for their work people. The aim was to produce 1,000 pieces a year. Sixtus hoped to have silk made in convents where foreign workmen would teach the nuns the skills of the industry. It was hoped that within twenty years the Roman industry would be able to meet the needs of the city, extensive though these were, and then subsequently that it would produce a surplus for export. Sixtus also projected initiating a scheme for the spinning, beating and refining of gold and silver but the necessary contract was still being negotiated when he died. He also established a small dockyard opposite the Ripa Grande, but this also enjoyed only limited success.

All these efforts seem to lack the Pope's customary enthusiasm or determination, and the amount of money actually expended was far too small to be effective or to have any chance of substantially changing the economic character of the city. Only a sustained and well-planned project could exercise real influence on the Roman labour market and Sixtus' successors did not continue his projects. His efforts were therefore doomed to failure. Employment for artisans was unattractive in a city where the service industries were prosperous and the demand for white-collar workers extensive. A city which had despised manufacture for centuries was reluctant to change its character or to face the social consequences of the change.[41]

There were, however, in Rome thousands of men, women and children for whom even a guaranteed food supply and an efficient price control were insufficient or irrelevant; a considerable part of its population lived below subsistence level. Rome, like other large cities with a fluid population, had a grave and perpetual poverty problem, which not even the most compassionate of the sixteenth-century had been able to solve. In fact, it has been described as "an international capital for the poor as much as for the rich".[42] The atmosphere of the city fostered a plague of idlers and sycophants and made begging endemic; laws forbidding begging on the streets and in churches were ineffective unless they could be enforced unhesitatingly from day to day. But besides the shiftless and the professional beggars there were the handicapped, the crippled, the sick, victims of unsanitary conditions and malnutrition; there were the elderly without family support, and the children, of whom many were illegitimate. In these circumstances diseases were prolific and the mortality rate high, and in times of recurring epidemics, especially malaria, the city was little more than a breeding ground of contagion. There were homeless, destitute peasants from the depopulated countryside in search of a livelihood in whatever quarter it could be won. Crowds of beggars, many of them well organised, in closely-knit bands, disgraced the streets, pestered visiting pilgrims, caused disorder, and not infrequently engaged in crime. There were in the city already fifteen homes and hospitals with permanent provision for some 1,500 people, some restricted to particular categories such as the incurable, the crippled, the lepers, the mentally infirm, orphan children, others for those in need of help generally. This permanent provision could readily be expanded, perhaps doubled in times of abnormal demand or crisis. Many of these had been founded as the result of a growing sense of public responsibility, influenced by the spiritual vigour and sensitive conscience of the Counter-Reformation and were established by St Philip Neri, and his followers, by Cardinal Borromeo and by the Jesuits. They were generally monuments to the Church's recognition of its duty to the helpless. Moreover, they were intended to be channels through which these unfortunates were kept in association with the church, receiving the sacraments, being tended by men in orders and supervised by secular helpers closely involved in the faith. Following his predecessor's abortive example, Sixtus V, with characteristic determination, resolved to establish a hospital sufficiently large and adequately financed to solve the remaining problem. For 15,000 écus he bought land and houses near the Ponte Sisto and, engaging Domenico Fontana as architect, had built an establishment capable of accommodating 2,000 inmates, and having "vast halls, a large number of rooms with separate provision for women, young girls, old people and children".[43] This new hospital for the poor cost approximately the same as work undertaken on the Pope's Palace in the Lateran. He gave this foundation exemption from import duties and customs dues and provided it with an annual revenue variously estimated at 6,000 to 15,000 écus per annum, this income being secured on a levy on the sale in the city of wood and playing cards. Young girls at the hospital were taught sewing; boys were taught and then sent out to follow a trade. The sick were cared for and encouraged to live with dignity and composure. Rome had more generous provision, probably more humanely maintained and more adequately endowed than that in England even after the Elizabethan Poor-Law. With this provision made, begging on the streets was absolutely forbidden, the clergy were discouraged from indulging in private alms and the *maestri delle strade* were urged to arrest offenders and bring them to trial. In fact these laws were enforced with vigour and obdurate beggars were severely punished or committed to the city gaols. The Pope's administration, like the Elizabethan system, combined severe treatment of vagabonds with systematic training for the able-bodied and institutional accommodation for the sick and elderly. Temporarily one of Rome's serious problems was solved not by the introduction of innovations but by an assiduous appraisal of its size and components, a consistent application of existing principles of treatment and above all by matching financial support to the recognition of public responsibility for the necessary provision. Only comprehensive measures sponsored by the State to supplement private charity could succeed in eliminating what had long become a running sore in the capital's life.

Deeply imbued with Franciscan tradition, and following closely in the footsteps of Pius V, Sixtus naturally took great interest in the affairs of the Monti di Pietà. These were large-scale officially sponsored pawnbroking institutions designed to meet the short-term needs of the impecunious and to deliver them from the oppression of usurers, especially Jews. He relaxed many restrictions placed on the Jews by his Brief *Christiana Pietas.* Under the influence of the Franciscan Order foundations had multiplied during the second half of the fifteenth century: the Roman Monte had been established in 1539. It made loans free of interest to the genuinely poor on the security of some valuable, worth at least twice the amount of the loan, which was not normally for more than six months, unredeemed pledges then being sold. Pius V and Gregory XIII had allocated funds to the Monte to enable it to continue this philanthropic work and Sixtus gave it his blessing and the number of loans it made increased during his reign by almost sixty per cent.[44]

Those who fell into debt were liable to be confined in debtors' prison where many lingered in horrible conditions until death overtook them. At the beginning of his pontificate Sixtus found the number of debtors in prison was approaching 6,000, at least 6% of the city's population at that date. He had been Protector of the Archconfraternity of San Girolamo della Carità (Philip Neri's Church), whilst Cardinal (a Society which existed to effect the release of debtors and their return to a settled way of life). As Pope, in 1590, he imposed a tax on an association dealing with money exchanges and contracts and from the proceeds of this tax he gave to the Confraternity an assured annual income of 2,050 écus so that its work of liberating genuine debtors could continue unabated.[45]

In these ways Sixtus showed that charity, sponsored and supported by government, was keenly aware of the needs of those who suffered misfortune and consequent financial difficulties. Whilst the state had a duty to deter the idle and the feckless and to refuse them help, it recognised equally an obligation to support those whose distress arose from circumstances beyond their own control and in spite of their own efforts to preserve their respectability. This was particularly important for cities like Rome which were under persistent pressure from a naturally increasing population and from immigration. In Sixtus V's provisions there was nothing new, but he utilised to the full the instruments already forged to meet these social problems and he used them with imagination and vigour. The consideration which the poor received from his government doubtless helped to attach them to the established regime.

Still there remained the problem of accommodating the pilgrim. It has been estimated that in a normal year Rome received 30,000 visitors: in a Jubilee year the number rose to a figure between 300,000 and 500,000.[46] Sixtus V's pontificate did not include a Jubilee, but during his reign the many distinctive developments in Rome at the time no doubt increased the number of visitors attracted to the city. Though the majority were Italian, some came from lands as distant as Russia, even Japan, as well as France, Germany and Poland in significant numbers. Moreover, the flow was unevenly distributed, pressure of numbers being particularly high during an Easter season which extended for several weeks before and after Holy Week, and at Christmas, and being notably light in the first two months of the calendar year and at the height of summer. Winter and high summer conditions made travelling difficult and reduced the appeal of the city and the attraction of Church festivities. Many of the visitors were rich or well-to-do and resided during their stay in the city in households of similar station, but large numbers were humble and poor. The majority came by horse or mule, the hire of a horse costing 2–5 giuli per station of perhaps eight miles: the traveller, however, had also to pay for the feeding and housing of the horse and for its return to the owner. Clothes and other baggage were packed into a case or wooden box carried on the horse. Other travellers, usually men but of whom perhaps as many as a quarter might be women, came by litters generally closed in by glass windows and warmed by heated balls in winter or by two wheeled carriages especially in summer. Those who came over the Alps needed guides and from the Alpine passes to Rome took fifteen days by horse or twenty days by coach. They came by well-established routes, generally in convoy as protection against bandits, robbers or other marauders, Bologna being a notable staging post at which travellers from the several Alpine passes converged before going on by way of Florence. All would arrive in Rome jaded and weary, for the roads were in appallingly poor condition; many would be apprehensive and dispirited for attacks in travellers were frequent. The poorer travellers came in hordes on foot and for them the journey from the Alps to the capital would last forty days. They would arrive desperately sore and exhausted, probably blistered and shoeless, dejected and forlorn. Where any considerable journey was involved a visit to Rome was an adventure not to be lightly undertaken. The problem of ensuring accommodation in the city for such large numbers of visitors who on average stayed for four days was formidable, but much more than that was needed.[47]

Rome was well endowed with a generous fund of hotels, inns, hostelries, taverns and lodging houses, ranging from reputable establishments like the Orso to a simple one-roomed apartment in a tiny house on the waterside at the Ripetta. There were between 100 and 120 establishments in operation, the majority concentrated in the densely populated wards of the city situated in the loop of the Tiber, some of these being mere retailers of food and drink. There was already an elaborate system of regulation for their trade, partly by rules of the Papal Court, partly by the city administration and most of all through the five guilds in which members of the trade were organised. This system of control was designed firstly to protect the visitor not only from attack en route but from exploitation by his hosts during his stay, secondly to maintain a system of registration so that visitors could be traced and order effectively maintained, and thirdly to prevent this large and powerful trade exercising undue pressure in the markets to the detriment of the city inhabitants. Charges for meals, drinks and lodging were regulated and standards of food and cooking were supervised by the guilds and alteration of prices without the consent of the guild was forbidden. Measures for the service of wine had to be stamped, and the price of local wine fixed. Strict sanitary controls were imposed and hotels and taverns were liable to inspection by the city authorities. Hoteliers were prevented from buying in the market before the expiration of a defined period when only the private consumer was allowed to purchase, they were also forbidden to buy wine until the demands of the Court and the papal administration had been met and they were prohibited from buying grain except in the open market. They were also prevented from developing their trade by retailing sweets, biscuits or cakes, and to forestall controversies with their clients the length of time for which they might provide accommodation or food on credit was limited to two months and three days respectively. Travellers were obliged to carry certificates of good character and health from their places of origin or to obtain them from a priest en route. Hoteliers were threaded into the network of controls with which both the city and the Papal Court were responsible. They were obliged to display the regulations applicable to travellers, and to open their registers to inspection by the city authorities to ensure the enforcement of laws against the carrying of arms, to refuse to house women of ill repute, to see that no prohibited meats were served on holy days or prohibited books brought into their establishments. When epidemics threatened they could be ordered to refuse admission to travellers from infected countries, and when contagious or infectious diseases actually broke out their premises could be closed. The hoteliers were expected to meet the spiritual as well as the temporal needs of their clients by providing images and other requisites for their devotions. Each guild maintained a patronal church and their members were intended to encourage their clients to use the services of the priests attached to these churches. Travellers who were taken ill whilst staying in the city were normally transferred to establishments maintained by their own nationals in Rome. Provision for poor pilgrims and travellers, of whom many arrived barefoot and threadbare and with no lodging better than the porch of one of the churches, was made largely through the Archconfraternity of Santissima Trinità dei Pellegrini founded almost forty years previously by St Philip Neri and one of his followers. Credited with 3,000 members (probably an exaggerated figure) the Archconfraternity was able to provide lodging with mattresses, sheets and blankets sufficient for a four-day stay. Separate refectories were established for men and women and bread, wine, soup, meat and salad were served. The services of a surgeon were available, and as perhaps 20% of the inmates came from countries outside Italy, interpreters were regularly at hand. In 1575, a Jubilee Year, the Archconfraternity was responsible for up to 2,000 pilgrims per day; during Sixtus' reign many fewer would be accommodated but this remained a thronging centre for faithful pilgrims of all nations—a veritable international fellowship. Sixtus V had little reason to introduce innovations into the organisation of amenities for the visitor in sixteenth-century Rome. Nevertheless, the oversight of this vast, floating population and of the necessary facilities provided for its accommodation was within the purview of his newly-created Congregazione dell' Abbondanza, the Prefect of Supplies, the Papal Court and the municipality. Wishing to establish the Capital of Christendom as an incomparable centre for both tourists and pilgrim, whence they should carry away into the crowded cities and remote villages of Italy and even into far off lands unforgettable memories of the Catholic church, Sixtus was personally concerned with the facilities available to them and with the impression which could be made upon them, and there can be no doubt that during his Pontificate the tourist industry was well aware that its importance was fully recognised at the Papal Court and that it was conscious of operating administration capable of ensuring the effective working of the system already developed. Travellers to Rome returned as emissaries of the Church into a hundred different lands, carrying with them the picture of a church earnest in its convictions, zealous in its pursuit of social justice, resolute in its defence of public order, and of a Pope personally devout, vigorous, severe and stern, but compassionate and especially concerned for the poor and the oppressed.

Two evils might shadow their impressions—the prevalence of prostitution on the streets and the flaunting of pomp and extravagance in public places. The parade of splendour along the way no longer chimed with reproof of heretics outside Santa Maria sopra Minerva or the adoration of Michelangelo's Pietà in St Peter's. Rome's population was predominantly male,[48] the Papal court was largely manned by celibates, the City had many opulent citizens and crowds of tourists—many of them far from their homes and families—for long periods. Moral standards still suffered the undermining influences of the Renaissance and the reforming vigour of the church had not yet re-established the high calling of virtue. In and out of the gates flowed the more adventurous of a countryside peasantry depressed and resourceless. Rome was a luxuriant garden for women of fortune and easy virtue, a sector of a society in which everything had its price. For the pest of prostitution neither Sixtus nor his predecessors knew any prophylactic, but at least they could drive them from the most frequented streets and perhaps confine them within prescribed zones. He wished to limit them to the Campo Marzio and the area round the Piazza del Popolo without access to any of the main streets: he met so much resistance, however, and the bank of the farmer of the city taxes was put under so much pressure by those who demanded withdrawal of their deposits, that he had to grant them freedom of residence, at the same time proscribing them access to the main streets, forbidding them the use of carriages and prohibiting them from being abroad after the Ave Maria.[49] Moreover, he imposed extreme penalties against adultery; the death penalty was imposed for incest and abortion; adulterers, mothers who allowed their daughters to be used for immoral purposes and married couples who separated without adequate reason could be whipped or fined. Every possible repressive measure was taken against sex offences.

Charities already existed to provide dowries for young girls so that they were encouraged to undertake honourable marriages and to one of these, the Pope's nephew, though a youth of sixteen, began to contribute. Provision was also made for wives whose marriages collapsed to be accommodated and cared for in religious houses set apart for that purpose. Similar provision existed for prostitutes who repented of their vice and wished to return to a normal life. By these means Sixtus hoped not merely to drive prostitution from the streets but to castigate it as a form of human degradation from which women and particularly young girls were to be safeguarded.

Meanwhile the charitable work of individual churches, foundations and Orders continued unimpaired, or indeed, extended. The Counter-Reformation fully recognised that purity of doctrine, punctiliousness of rite, correctitude of ceremony were no more essential than spiritual compassion, care for the poor, the sick and the handicapped, understanding of the destitute, the bitter and the cynical. There also were virtues unquestionably inherent in the teaching of a church which wished to be relevant to its generation. Sunday piety alone would not suffice.[50] Though it was absolutely necessary to discourage the idle and the feckless, and though organised charity was able to promote uniformity of treatment, personal philanthropy was not to be discouraged. The poor house and the Monti di Pietà were not intended as deterrents, as was the Elizabethan poor law system in England, and institutionalised provision was never intended by the Catholic Church to replace personal succour. Sixtus and his church authorities did their utmost to extol the Christian virtue of charity and many of his Cardinals, bishops and officials were shining examples of generous philanthropy. Moreover, the serious study of the Pauline epistles, the passionate preaching of the Gospel and the general atmosphere of serious concern for eternity reinforced the readiness to engage in social work. Saving others was seen as a means of personal salvation as well as of individual satisfaction.

Counter-Reformation Popes had also fought against the gaudy splendour and ostentatious exhibitionism by personal example and by publishing a series of sumptuary laws. Pius V, Sixtus' ex-hero and spiritual guide, had lived as a monk even when Pope, clad in a coarse shirt, travelling on foot, keeping regular fasts, hearing Mass daily.[51] But Rome remained a city of vanity, its miserable streets crowded with nearly 900 carriages, many of them elaborate, even gilded,[52] the rich collected their own retinues of servants numbering hundreds.[53] Their calendar opened with the Carnival, a season of festivity intended as an insurance against the restrictions of Lent, which was studded with magnificent banquets, spectacular jousts, mummers' plays often bawdy and licentious. Duels and the hunt filled in their moments of entertainment. Few cities could equal, and probably none could surpass the luxuriant hilarity and brazen festivity of Rome: it provided equally for the boisterous exuberance of youth, the insatiable appetite of maturing years and the sensuality of age. Sixtus, never forgetting the humbleness of his birth and the constricting poverty of his upbringing, lived frugally; content and without recrimination or resentment, maintaining a modest household and a restrained table, hearing Mass and attending an immense variety of religious festivals with evident devotion and genuine piety. Around him he gathered men of a similarly serious demeanour and personality and he moved in the company of those who cultivated the reform of conduct and manners. He decreed the wearing of the cassock (*vestis talaris*) for sacred and public functions. At his court frivolity was frowned upon, all forms of showy extravagance were discouraged and vice and dubious conduct proscribed. But example alone was insufficient. The festivities of the Carnival were placed under rigorous control and the rowdy outbursts and disorders which had become normal disappeared. Plays were admitted to the Papal Court with reluctance and misgiving and when in 1588 a company of actors appeared performances were allowed only in daylight and feminine parts had to be played by men. Gambling and dicing were placed under strict police supervision, a fine of 100 scudi being imposed for a first offence, 200 scudi for a second, 300 scudi for the third, with the alternative of flogging or service in the galleys.[54] Blasphemy was severely punished and the display of obscene inscriptions in public or of offensive pictures in taverns was forbidden. Blasphemers were tied up and exhibited in public for a day, had their tongues slit for a repetition of their offence, and were condemned to the galleys for a further conviction. Laws were published to enforce propriety in dress and to forbid immodesty and indecency; hoteliers were prohibited from arranging fish in elaborate fashions.[55] Rich and poor alike were obliged to conform to this code of conduct. The nephews of the Pope's Cardinal Secretary were executed for repeated misdemeanours; a defrauder and his accomplice who used the papal ring to forge a brief for the purchase of a house were sent to the galleys. Like so many reformers, Sixtus was suspicious of the pamphleteers for their speculation about political matters, for their criticism of the court and its policy, for their misrepresentation of facts. Information was therefore frequently withheld and authors pursued with vigour and diligence. The city lost its traditional atmosphere of gaiety and instead a puritanical sense of guilt pervaded its streets, people lived under the shadow of suspicion and the threat of false accusation. Respectability was obtained at a price but many years of sustained enforcement would be needed before the habits of conformity would become ingrained and permanent. Nevertheless, even under the austere governance of the devout, Rome needed never be dull and certainly could never be commonplace or undistinguished. Its hind-quarters might be drab or even squalid but these were hidden artlessly behind the splendours of magnificent *piazze*, handsome *palazzi*, and an incomparable array of churches, large and small, ornate and simple. Even the scars inflicted by the most recent desperate Sack of 1527 had been largely obliterated. Sixtus' Rome might repel the vandals and the iconoclasts, the rowdy and the lawless, but it offered to the serious, the contemplative and the spiritually resourceful, the inspiration of a unique heritage and a richly endowed and impeccably maintained tradition, both ancient and Christian. The Renaissance, which had given rise to so much probing of the standing and teaching of the Catholic Church, had merely enhanced the beauties of its capital and multiplied its Christian endowment and its own intellectual understanding of its origins and its philosophy. Twenty years' residence had made this Pope a son of the Eternal City at whose shrines he never tired of worshipping.

Meanwhile, in the city, Sixtus made improvements and fashioned plans. He contemplated the erection of a new Palace near the Piazza del Popolo to accommodate new cardinals, ambassadors and princes who might be entering the city.[56] In the Via Giulia he planned to complete the Courts of Justice for which Julius II had laid the foundations and to build a mint.[57] He considered the construction of another bridge across the Tiber at Santo Spirito to relieve pressure on Ponte Sant'Angelo and so to reduce congestion of traffic between the city and the Borgo and St Peter's.[58] In the very heart of the city he contemplated two new but short roads from the Chancellery to the new church of the Gesù and from the former to Santa Maria della Pace lying west of the Piazza Navona, and set aside 100,000 scudi to meet the expense.[59] These plans were never realized.

Sixtus himself extended the church of Santi Apostoli and undertook such thorough restoration of San Girolamo degli Schiavoni at the Ripetta as virtually to constitute rebuilding. His (great) nephew, Michele, became its patron. In both he had personal interest, for the former was the main Franciscan church and the headquarters of the Order, the latter was (and still is) the church of the Slavonic peoples. Indeed, it is likely that his association with the latter gave credence to the belief (which modern research has confounded) that he himself came from a family of Slavonic ancestry. He also restored the church of Santa Sabina on the Aventine[60] and built a façade at Santo Spirito in Sassia[61] and restored San Clemente and Santa Pudenziana[62]. Sixtus stimulated cardinals and nobles to follow his example, and Cardinals Colonna, Caetani, Azzolini, Joyeuse and Sittich all improved the churches with which they were associated. Just as the Building Code of 1574 encouraged large-scale residential development and tried to reduce small, derelict waste spaces, so the Pope made it plain at Court that churches merited sustained maintenance and a practical regard for their dignity. Derelict or decaying churches he regarded as a disgrace and he openly stimulated the rivalry of the new clerical Orders—Jesuits, Oratorians, and Theatines—for the improvement and enlargement of their buildings; in a Renaissance city, shabbiness was not a Christian virtue.

Sixtus also put pressure on the authorities to pave or re-pave the city streets, many of which were in a deplorable state. Much paving work was undertaken, fresh levies being raised on the owners of horses and carriages to provide the necessary finance.[63] The Pope also brought about a re-organisation of the city's administration of street maintenance by adding two to the *maestri delle strade* so that there should be one for each *Rione* and arranging that they should elect two of their number to co-ordinate their efforts and to undertake special responsibilities. Since these officials were responsible for the issue of building licences and the supervision of new building, the construction of new streets and the maintenance of the old as well as for the licensing of shopkeepers, their efficiency was of great importance to the city. Sixtus spared no pains to ensure that their duties were effectively discharged and made a practice of regularly inspecting his own building works early in the morning after having said Mass. Through his five years as Pope, city and curial officials concerned with building and street works were kept unusually alert.

## Notes

1. E. Gibbon, *The history of the decline and fall of the Roman Empire* (London: Methuen, 1925), vol. 6, chapter 69.
2. R. C. Fried, "Planning the Eternal City: Roman Politics and Planning since World War II" in *Western Political Quarterly* 27 (2 June 1974), p. 15. See also Idem, *Planning the Eternal City: Roman Politics and Planning since World War II* (New Haven: Yale University Press, 1973).
3. Hübner 1, p. 265.
4. *Ibid.*, p. 263. See also A. A. Bernardy, *La vita e l'opera di Vittoria Colonna* (Firenze: Felice Le Monnier, 1927).
5. Pastor 20, p. 74.
6. Tempesti, *Storia della vita e geste di Sisto Quinto*, 1, p. 248; Hübner 1, p. 314; Pastor 20, p. 73.
7. Hübner 1, p. 314.
8. *Ibid.*, p. 278.
9. F. Tagliaventi, *Sisto V Papa e principe* (Fermo, La Rapida, 1969), pp. 44–45.
10. Tempesti, *Storia della vita e geste di Sisto Quinto*, 1, p. 331.
11. Hübner 1, p. 278.
12. Pastor 20, pp. 77, 80; Hübner 1, p. 275.
13. Tempesti, *Storia della vita e geste di Sisto Quinto*, 1, p. 331.
14. Pastor 20, p. 84; Tempesti, *Storia della vita e geste di Sisto Quinto*, 2, p. 27.
15. Hübner 1, pp. 290–293; Pastor 20, p. 85.
16. *Ibid.*, pp. 271–273.
17. *Ibid.*, pp. 276–277.
18. *Ibid.*, pp. 277.
19. *Ibid.*, pp. 279.
20. The Borgo was administered independently of the City until December 1586 when Sixtus transformed it into the fourteenth Rione.
21. Pecchiai, *Roma nel Cinquecento*, pp. 291ff.
22. *Ibid.*, p. 264; see also Delumeau 1, pp. 751–752. At the end of 1596 the Pope ordered the salaries of municipal officials to be charged against the Cabella dello Studio under papal control. But this was so bitterly resisted by the Senate that he abandoned this measure fifteen months later.
23. Pastor 23, p. 74.

24 Hübner 1, p. 275.
25 Tempesti, *Storia della vita e geste di Sisto Quinto*, 1, p. 253.
26 *Ibid.*, p. 265.
27 Pastor 23, p. 81.
28 *Ibid.*, p. 83.
29 *Ibid.*, p. 81.
30 Delumeau 1, pp. 804, 807, 810, 811, 812, 819.
31 *Ibid.*, p. 447.
32 *Ibid.*, p. 458.
33 Sixtus' nepotism is discussed in Chapter 7.
34 Delumeau 1, pp. 572–577.
35 *Ibid.*, Table I, pp. 372–373, and pp. 375–377, 566.
36 Travellers accommodated by the Archconfraternity of SS Trinità dei Pellegrini were allowed a litre and a quarter per head for four days. See M. Romani, *Pellegrini e viaggiatori nell'economia di Roma dal XIV al XVII secolo* (Milano: Università del Sacro Cuore, 1948).
37 In four central wards of the city in 1526 there was one baker for every 68 households, a butcher for every 50. (Delumeau 1, p. 255 and Table I).
38 1 rubbia is equivalent to 223.79 kg, or approximately 5 cwt.
39 Romani, *Pellegrini e viaggiatori*, p. 218; Purchase direct from cattle dealers within 12 miles of the market was totally prohibited, see *ibid.*, p. 170.
40 Cardella 5, p. 234.
41 Delumeau 1, pp. 501–514.
42 *Ibid.*, p. 404.
43 For Domenico Fontana, see Delumeau 1, p. 414.
44 Delumeau 1, pp. 493–497.
45 *Ibid.*, pp. 499–501.
46 Romani, *Pellegrini e viaggiatori*, p. 100.
47 *Ibid.*, p. 206.
48 Delumeau 1, p. 427.
49 *Ibid.*, p. 431.
50 A phrase from L. Elliott, *I will be called John* (London: Fontana, 1973), p. 167.
51 Ranke, pp. 279, 281.
52 Delumeau 1, p. 444; Romani, *Pellegrini e viaggiatori*, p. 170.

[53] Delumeau 1, p. 436.
[54] Orbaan, *Sixtine Rome*, p. 188.
[55] Pastor 23, pp. 90–95.
[56] Delumeau 1, p. 308.
[57] Pastor 23, p. 290.
[58] *Ibid.*, p. 231, n. 7.
[59] *Ibid.*, p. 230.
[60] Orbaan, *Sixtine Rome*, p. 123.
[61] *Ibid.*, p. 212.
[62] *Ibid.*, p. 270.
[63] *Ibid.*, p. 111.

# CHAPTER 6

## A New Rome has Risen from the Ashes

*His great claim to celebrity, and an unquestionable one, was the bringing of the Aqua Felice to Rome. He spared no expense in the accomplishment of this important scheme, insisting on the aqueduct being built on the exact model of ancient Roman works. He conferred lasting benefit on the city by making its inhabitants independent of the insanitary water of the Tiber, and insuring an abundant and pure supply to all the beautiful fountains of Rome.*

Valérie Pirie, *The Triple Crown*, 1935

THE BASILICA OF ST PETER and the adjoining Vatican Palace undoubtedly formed the religious centre of the city. Geographically ill-sited and isolated, the detachment of this complex was accentuated by the absence of any bridge across the Tiber between the Ponte Sant'Angelo and the Ponte Milvio at one extremity, and the Ponte Sisto at the other. Access to the Vatican was unsatisfactory, and, in times of pressure, grossly inadequate, so much so that in the Jubilee Year of 1450, two hundred people were crushed to death on the Sant'Angelo bridge.[1] Sixtus V considered the construction of a new bridge near the Santo Spirito Hospital, but death overtook him before any progress was made with this project.[2] The isolation of the area was further emphasised by the independent administration of the Borgo until Sixtus integrated it within the City as the fourteenth ward in the 1580s,[3] emphasising the importance he attached to the linking of development on both sides of the river. The Basilica of St Peter, despite its unrivalled historic importance and the fact that it was "the largest of all churches in the world",[4] no longer made a striking impression on the city landscape. Early in the fourth century Constantine the Great, the first Christian Emperor, had erected the great basilica over the shrine of St Peter.[5] This immense rectangular structure with its nave separated by rows of 24 Corinthian columns in four aisles, rising just over 9 metres to a timbered architrave,[6] was largely hidden from view by a large atrium or courtyard. Only the eastern façade of the basilica showed above the eastern colonnade[7] of this atrium which formed the portico of the church. The façade was a "straightforward affair",[8] and lent little distinction to the church. The atrium, itself 61 metres long and 54.5 metres broad, was colonnaded on four sides and originally accommodated penitents who were excluded from the basilica. Later the entrance was disfigured by makeshift kiosks and stalls erected by traders. The eastern front of the atrium was an unimpressive two-storied portico of three arches, flanked since the middle of the fifteenth century by an equally undistinguished and distracting Loggia of the Benediction, whence Holy Thursday and Easter Day the Pope issued his message to the City and the World (*Urbi et Orbi*) and pronounced his blessing on the faithful.[9] A massive square campanile, surmounted originally by a steeple, but at this time by a small dome (the largest tower in Rome, and thought to have been erected in the eighth century) projected almost incongruously from behind the entrance to the atrium.[10] Access was by a platform paved with marble at the top of a broad flight of thirty-five steps rising from the Piazza below. On the south side houses pressed hard against the basilica, and on the north a mish-mash of piecemeal structures of the Vatican Palace. Age, inherent defects of design and structure, the onslaughts of the elements and neglect during the Avignon captivity and the Great Schism had all contributed to an advanced stage of decay.

Since the pontificate of Nicholas V (1447-55) plans for the construction of a new basilica and the patchwork repair of the old had gone on simultaneously. Bramante's four massive central piers erected at the beginning of the sixteenth century and linked with arches formed the centrepiece of the new structure and dictated the basic design of the remainder. To the west the apse and choir were now complete and vaulted, to the north and south, apsed transepts had been erected and the Gregorian chapel had been built and lavishly fitted, and over it a graceful cupola had been constructed. The drum on which the dome was to be built was complete but the whole of the central crossing was open to the elements. Whether the design of the basilica should be based on a Greek cross (a square within a circle), or on a Latin cross (with an extended rectangle forming the nave and aisles), had not yet been decided, and the precise shape of the dome had yet to be determined. Although the western portion of the basilica and its portico had been demolished, the eastern portion of the Constantinian basilica was still standing and a wall was constructed across the nave to separate the new construction from the old building and the atrium. A temporary structure, erected over the Gregorian shrine of St Peter, was in progress.[11]

Sixtus met this confused situation with characteristic decision and urgency. He confirmed Giacomo della Porta as Capomaestro of the Basilica and appointed Domenico Fontana as his assistant. Both were entrusted with the Pope's full confidence, provided with an adequate flow of funds and urged to proceed with all possible speed. Completion of the dome was their main objective and before the end of Sixtus' reign this had been achieved and the construction of the lantern was in hand,[12] controversies about its shape (which had hampered progress since Michelangelo's day) having been resolved. The erection of the cupola was an astonishing task which had daunted all Sixtus' predecessors: it required 800 workmen working continually and cost 10,000 écus,[13] being 120 metres high. Its completion was marked by the celebration of a solemn Mass in July 1590, scarcely a month before Sixtus died.[14] Almost twenty years elapsed before the decision to prolong the nave and to follow the design of a Latin cross was taken, but it was Maderno, Domenico Fontano's nephew and assistant, who was entrusted with the implementation. With Maderno's completion of the eastern façade and the portico, the present-day St Peter's emerged. It remained for Bernini to design and build the colonnades between 1657 and 1666 and to erect the baldacchino over the Apostles' tomb. Pope Nicholas V had said that "A proper faith, sustained only on doctrines will never be anything but feeble and vacillating," and had called for "something that appeals to the eye … to create solid and stable convictions in the minds of the uncultured masses."[15] Sixtus, who never made pretentious claims to aesthetic taste, had vigorously forwarded the fulfilment of his predecessor's ambitions. An inspiring view of the dome was to be had from any of Rome's seven hills, and it could be seen from the top of the masts of vessels entering the estuary of the Tiber.

The exquisite beauty of St Peter's remained hidden from view, but the imposing dome loomed majestically over the city where domes were as yet uncommon: a perpetual memorial to citizens and pilgrims of the martyrdom of their first Bishop. Knowing that many Popes would reign and die before the basilica could be completed, and realising the importance of an integrated space to a building, Sixtus decided to re-organise the piazza and to give it a relationship to the new basilica. Three principal highways ran between the Castel Sant'Angelo and the Piazza San Pietro, the Via Alessandrina named after Pope Alexander, the central one of the three, being the broadest and most distinguished. Flanked by the famous *passetto*, or fortified corridor, over a secret passageway leading from the Palace to the Castle[16]. All of these streets ended abruptly at the edge of the square and one was aligned with the axis of the basilica. Building work was taking place on the northern side of the *passetto* and the population of the Borgo was increasing,[17] while the piazza itself remained the largest in Rome but with no significant pattern and without any distinguishing feature. Even the Vatican Palace was a disorderly medley of dull and unimpressive buildings, which were almost shabbily unworthy of papal dignity and gave neither distinction nor charm to the square below.[18] The only fountain in the piazza, substantial but poorly designed, was placed haphazardly.[19] Franciscans had an habitual distaste for frivolity, they understood the grandeur of simplicity. Sixtus, then, recognised, either by intuition or as a result of discussion with his architect, Fontana, the importance of introducing order into this untidy, shapeless space. He saw how ultimately the beauty of the new basilica would be enhanced by a simple geometric re-organising of the surrounding background. Alongside the southwest corner of the basilica stood a gigantic obelisk, reduced to total insignificance by being crowded against the sacristy and cramped between the basilica and the buildings in the adjoining street. It stood 38 metres high, including its pedestal, and was formed from a single piece of stone weighing 450,000 kilos, and surmounted by a bronze globe (now in the Capitoline museum). It had been transported from Egypt on the orders of the Emperor Caligula, the predecessor of Nero, and erected here, or on a nearby site, in AD 37. Its removal to a more appropriate and impressive location had often been considered, but even Michelangelo himself thought it impossible.

Sixtus saw in this obelisk the key to the planning problem facing him, for, if it were properly sited within the square, its immense height and delicate proportions would make an effective foil to contrast with the basilica itself. It may be that he recalled how the great Basilica of St Mark dominated the Piazza San Marco in Venice, and how the Campanile co-ordinated the piazza and the piazzetta and provided a focal point and perhaps how the twin columns at the waterside concentrated attention on the piazzetta with the campanile and the Basilica at its head. The spatial relationships of St Peter's are strongly reminiscent of those of St Mark's. Both are founded on an aesthetic appreciation of solid dominating structures matched by open space, its area unobstructed but carefully framed at the perimeter and unified by vertical structures of considerable height. Both proclaim magnificence and handsome beauty. Sixtus personally determined the spot where the obelisk was to stand, ordered the construction of a full-scale model in wood and had it erected in the Square, and then invited the submission of schemes for the transfer of the obelisk to the selected location. The plan of Sixtus' friend and architect, Domenico Fontana (who had designed the tomb of Nicholas IV in 1547), was chosen and he was provided with 3,000 scudi and given authority to requisition whatever workmen he needed, and empowered to order the demolition of any houses standing in the way of his project, paying the owners proper compensation, and to import wood, iron and other materials from whatever sources he thought best. The Pope demanded the successful and early completion of the project. There is no need to tell in detail the story of this famous exploit.[20] It was a perfect example of the art of delegation: an army of 800 to 900 men was recruited, the obelisk was covered in straw mats and wooden planking covered in scaffolding, and then raised by thirty-five windlasses, each controlled by two horses and ten men. It was lowered to the ground, and in June it was moved on rollers to its new location where it lay horizontal through the blistering months of July and August. Then, on September 10th, 1586, it was hoisted into its new position.

The magnitude of this project and the fame of Fontana's technical triumph must not obscure two striking features of the new Vatican complex which derive directly from Sixtus' imaginative plans. Firstly, the obelisk's new site was chosen to align it with the axis of the basilica, so that it should dominate the square and form a commanding and unmistakable link with the new basilica of which the dome was the symbol. The piazza was not designed to open on to a distant view (such as that later provided by the Via della Conciliazione) for this would divert attention from St Peter's, but was intended to appear dramatically and unheralded as the visitor emerged, unsuspecting, from one of the streets leading from the Castle. An orderly space with clearly defined boundaries enabled the basilica to burst upon his attention as if to stun him with wonder. Maderno's lengthening of the nave and the building of the eastern portico and façade was dominated and brought into focus by Sixtus' obelisk. Bernini's colonnades provided a finishing contour totally in harmony with Sixtus' vision.

Secondly, the transfer of the obelisk was a religious occasion of immense historical and spiritual significance. As if superstition and faith were relatives, the obelisk was lowered and raised again on Wednesday, the day of the Pope's appointment as Bishop and Cardinal, the day of his election and enthronement. On April 30th when the obelisk was to be lowered and on September 10th when it was to be raised, every workman engaged on the project went to confession and hear Mass in the open before the labours of the day commenced. Entry into an area marked out and protected by fences was forbidden on pain of death so that the work should not be impeded, but outside that area the inhabitants of the city and hundreds of visitors crowded to watch proceedings. As the obelisk finally settled in a vertical position a spontaneous burst of uncontrolled shouting echoed to the seven hills and prayers of gratitude were said throughout the city. Feasting continued far into the night, bells pealed from churches in all quarters of the city, firework displays were arranged, canon were fired from Castel Sant' Angelo. Sixtus himself was not present for the possibility of failure never entered his mind. His faith in the Almighty was so unquestioning that he could await the arrival of the French ambassadors who had hurried directly from the Piazza del Popolo to St Peter's to witness the event on their way to the Palace. Before being raised in its new position, the obelisk was solemnly exorcised by a Bishop. On 26th September, Mass was celebrated in St Peter's by Bishop Ferratini, and after the Mass the Pope and the clergy of the Basilica went in procession to an altar raised in front of the obelisk where the Bishop blessed the great gilt cross which was to be hoisted to its top to replace the bronze ball which had formerly crowned it and which was reputed (erroneously) to contain the ashes of Caesar. Thus the city was perpetually reminded of the triumph of Christianity over paganism and of the technical skill of the Renaissance. The inscription at the base reads: "Here is the Cross of the Lord: Begone, infernal hosts." Fontana was created "Knight of the Obelisk" and received an annual pension of 2,000 ducats.

Sixtus had little affection for the Vatican as a place of residence, even though it was the largest palace in the world.[21] In summer it was hot and stifling, the danger of malaria was always present, the crush of people at the court—officials, penitents, pilgrims, suppliants, visitors—was unbearable. He rarely attended festivities and where the Pope was to be represented he delegated that duty to his sister, Camilla, or his nephew. He preferred, particularly in summer, the elevation of the Quirinale where gentle breezes lowered the temperature and sharpened the mind; best of all he liked the gardens and the solitude of Villa Montalto on the Esquiline. It reminded him of the Montalto hillsides: a contented citizen of Rome from sense of duty, he remained a countryman at heart. Alterations made to the papal apartments in the palace were therefore purely functional, in the main, to allow more air and light to penetrate them. He ordered Fontana to build a new structure around a courtyard on the eastern (or city) side of the Cortile di San Damaso in front of the old Palace to link up with the tower of Nicholas V. In this building, which faced south (namely towards St Peter's Square), natural lighting was greatly improved and it was possible to view the newly erected obelisk in the square. Fontana also built a new staircase between the Palace and the basilica.

His most important addition to the Vatican, however, was a new building intended to accommodate the library. The Papal apartments surrounding the Cortile San Damaso which had been developed in Clement VII's reign lay to the south-east of St Peter's and were connected with the Papal chapel. Running approximately at right angles to the axis of the basilica, an immense courtyard had been laid out, flanked on its east and west sides by long corridors linking the Belvedere Villa at its northern extremity—a detached palace built for Innocent VIII at the end of the previous century—to the main palace buildings. Across this courtyard running east and west, Sixtus had a new wing constructed dividing the courtyard into two separate courts, and this wing was to house the Papal Library to which, with true Franciscan respect for scholarship, he attached very great importance.

The development of the Vatican complex—basilica, piazza and palace—was an integral feature of a comprehensive scheme for the development of Rome as the unmistakably distinctive capital of Christendom. Sixtus was largely responsible for the current papal apartments. Tommaso Laurenti decorated the ceiling of the Sala di Constantino with a fresco *The Triumph of the Christian Faith* showing the god Mercury (representing Renaissance humanism) humbled.

In importance second only to the Vatican complex was that of St John Lateran. At the summit of the Caelian Hill, one of the less famous of Rome's seven hills, was the city's Cathedral Church, an imposing building of magnificent proportions built in the tenth century to replace a Constantinian basilica. Alongside it stood the famous Baptistery erected in the fifth century to replace one built by Constantine the Great and reputed (erroneously) to mark the site of his baptism by Pope Sylvester I. Both Basilica and Baptistery were prominent landmarks in the story of the recognition of Christianity as the religion of the Empire. Within the complex was also the Papal Palace, and until the Avignon captivity the official residence, with the private chapel and the Scala Santa. This was the ceremonial staircase, for five or six centuries identified by tradition with the stairs by which Christ ascended into Pontius Pilate's Palace and which Helena, Emperor Constantine's mother, had transported to Rome. The religious and historical significance of the complex was outstanding and it attracted legions of pilgrims and was a place of veneration. However, since the return of the Popes to Rome, the Vatican had replaced the Lateran and the Papal Palace had been grossly neglected. The surrounding area was only lightly inhabited and the Lateran complex seemed detached, isolated and not easy of access. It commanded magnificent views to the countryside in the south, over the neighbouring hills and the city. To Sixtus, always deeply conscious of historic traditions and of the awe owed to holy places, the Lateran's shabby state and disarray seemed wanton disrespect, and this he set out to remedy. In spite of resistance within the Court and the City, he had the Papal Palace demolished and re-built, the Scala Santa re-sited and the new Palace equipped as a summer residence. The tallest and oldest obelisk in Rome, which had been brought from Thebes in the middle of the fourth century, was brought in 1587 from the Circus Maximus (the celebrated imperial racecourse lying between the Tiber and the foot of the Palatine Hill), and re-erected on the northern side of the Basilica.[22] More than 65,000 scudi were spent on this cluster of related projects, the raising of the new obelisk costing almost two-thirds of the corresponding venture at St Peter's.[23]

St Peter's and St John Lateran were two of seven Roman churches which had a special niche in the liturgical pattern of the Catholic church. They were allocated particular responsibilities in the programme for the celebration of the most important Church festivals, Holy Week and Christmas.[24] Above all, they formed a chain of illustrious churches to which pilgrims from all quarters would proceed in a carefully-organised pilgrimage sponsored, recognised and encouraged by the authorities of the Church. These pilgrimages had been popularised by Philip Neri, the saint of Santa Maria in Vallicella, who was accompanied by ever-increasing crowds until, in the Jubilee Year of 1575, they could be accommodated only with the greatest possible difficulty. Pope Pius V had completed the pilgrimage in the company of many of his Cardinals and Church dignitaries; Gregory XIII had done likewise in spite of his great age, neglecting the strain on his physical resources and probably shortening his life in the process.[25] The pilgrimage was established as one of the ambitions of the devout. Corps of pilgrims several hundreds strong assembled at St Paul's Outside the Walls, where they prayed and performed their devotions. They passed along the Via delle Sette Chiese to the basilica of San Sebastiano, then to the Lateran and on to Santa Croce in Gerusalemme and San Lorenzo fuori le mura. From there they turned back towards the city, stopping at Saint Mary Major before completing their circular journey to St Peter's. They were generally accompanied by guides and spiritual leaders, often by distinguished clergy in their robes, or papal officials who lent them official encouragement and recognition. At each of the churches the pilgrims, joined by fresh followers at each of the stations, offered prayers or joined in a service, listened to a preacher and lit a candle or offered alms. The journey led them around the outskirts of the city, three of the churches being actually outside the ancient walls, until they passed near to the foot of the Quirinale. The ascent to the Lateran was the most difficult stage of the task, but stretches of the roads were in such bad condition that long before they reached Ponte Sant'Angelo, many were footsore and physically exhausted. Their circuit completed, they arrived at St Peter's where they performed their final devotions and received a blessing. Those who had completed the entire circuit in a single day were rewarded with a special papal indulgence. As the sun went down behind the dome of St Peter's, polyglot groups stood in square, pondering with amazement on one of the most moving and memorable religious experiences of the sixteenth-century world.

All these basilicas, except Saint Mary Major, had been founded by the Emperor Constantine during his reign or had replaced one which he had established. Santa Croce had once been a part of an imperial palace; San Lorenzo combined one of the fourth century basilicas with one built two centuries later, the older forming the chancel, the latter the nave of the new basilica; Saint Mary Major, the youngest of the seven, dated from the fifth century.

All were buildings of architectural note and impressive dignity. They all reminded their visitors of the time when Christianity triumphed over all other gods and became the official religion of the Empire; each told its own story. Each had special features of compelling and relevant interest to the pilgrim. St Paul's was erected over the tomb of the Apostle to the Gentiles and stood near the place where he had been beheaded.[26] San Sebastiano was connected by a staircase to the tomb of St Sebastian, an imperial official, who was executed for his faith early in the fourth century: it stood above the vast network of the catacombs of St Sebastian and St Callixtus. Santa Croce preserved the relic of the Holy Cross which Helena, the mother of Emperor Constantine, had miraculously discovered; from San Lorenzo access was given to the tomb of St Lawrence, "one of the most famous saints of the Roman church",[27] martyred in AD 258 reputedly by being slowly roasted on a gridiron, but in fact by being beheaded.

Saint Mary Major was devoted to the honour of the Blessed Virgin Mary. Above the high altar it displayed a magnificent set of mosaics dating from the fifth century designed to accentuate the beauty and glory of the Virgin, and it also houses the *Salus Populi Romani*, an image of the Virgin believed to have been that processed around the city by Pope Gregory the Great at a time of plague, and which successfully invoked God's aid. The basilica also preserves a relic of the holy crib of Bethlehem. Adjacent to the church stood an oratory or small chapel built to resemble the grotto of the Nativity at Bethlehem.[28] This basilica was of particular topical and contemporary interest. Situated near to the Villa Montalto, it had become Sixtus' personal church. His favourite architect, Fontana, built the Sistine chapel to form a transept on the right of the nave and fashioned in it an elaborate tomb for the Pope himself, and another for Pius V, whose remains were transported to the Church in 1587. The following year the Pope had the body of his nephew, Francesco, transported from Santa Maria degli Angeli to this chapel, and that of his niece was moved almost at the same time to the adjoining Oratory so that Saint Mary Major was virtually designated as the family church.[29] Again in 1587, outside the Basilica, beyond the apse, at the cost of a mere 3,000 scudi,[30] Sixtus erected an obelisk which he had transported from the Mausoleum of Augustus near the heart of the city, symbolising—as at St Peter's and St John Lateran—the triumph of Christianity over paganism.

The pilgrimage of the Seven Churches offered a feast of religious experience to the pilgrims. They enjoyed the satisfaction of forming part of a cosmopolitan procession of hundreds of the devout. They were forcibly reminded of the sacrifices made by the ancient martyrs and of the triumph of truth over paganism. The pilgrims would return home, their faith renewed, their religious conviction strengthened, their spirits alive with fresh resolution to withstand the continuing onslaught of heresy and to restore apostates to Mother Church. The impact of the pilgrimage cannot be exaggerated: it was without doubt one of the outstanding experiences of the time.

In addition to his notable works at the Vatican, the Lateran, and Saint Mary Major, Sixtus V made two highly important contributions to the development of this pilgrimage of the Seven Churches. Firstly, he introduced the Piazza del Popolo and the comparatively recent and beautiful church of Santa Maria del Popolo into the pilgrimage circuit, in substitution for San Sebastiano. The latter, though valued for its association with the Christian catacombs, was remote and not easy of access, in spite of efforts made by Gregory XIII to improve the road between Porta San Sebastiano, Porta Metronia and the Lateran; moreover, years of neglect had reduced it to such a state of disastrous disrepair that a complete restoration was required in the following century. Santa Maria del Popolo, by contrast, had been built by Sixtus IV between 1472 and 1477 to replace a mediaeval church erected by Gregory IX in 1227 on the site of an earlier chapel, commonly reputed to mark the site of Nero's tomb. The latest church had been richly patronised by the della Rovere family to which Sixtus IV belonged and has been described as one of the artistic treasure houses among the Churches of Rome[31] with a magnificent chapel designed by Raphael for the famous Sienese banker, Agostino Chigi, whose family had been so much a part of the Renaissance city. The Piazza del Popolo stood at the end of the Via Flaminia, the main highway into

Rome from the north and north-east, by which very large numbers of travellers and pilgrims entered the city. This entrance was guarded by the Porta del Popolo, only re-built twenty odd years previously under Pius IV, and here travellers stopped to present their certificates of good health and character and to be examined for any heretical literature they might have carried. An array of roads led from there to the city—the Corso, racing-track in times of the Carnival, led to the Palazzo San Marco, Pius IV's favourite palace; Via Babuino, developed by Clement VII for the Jubilee of 1525, linking the Piazza del Popolo with Piazza di Spagna and the Via di Ripetta, followed the line of the Tiber to the port at the Ripetta, which in turn was linked by road and river transport to Ponte Sant'Angelo and the Vatican. Piazza del Popolo was one of the chief focal points in Rome's system of communications and formed a central gateway to the countryside beyond. Sixtus V, having selected it as one of the stations of the pilgrimage of the Seven Churches, placed in it in 1589 the second oldest obelisk in the city which had been brought from Heliopolis by the Emperor Augustus, whose massive mausoleum and column stood between the Corso and Via di Ripetta a short distance away. This irregular, wedge-shaped piazza, one of the most superb of its kind,[32] acquired a fresh focal point and gave the travellers a fascinating vista at the Porta from the obelisk, along the Corso to the Palazzo San Marco at its head. Similarly, the pilgrim who arrived at Santa Maria del Popolo from Saint Mary Major saw, across the river, Castel Sant'Angelo and the dome of St Peter's. The last stage of his pilgrimage was triumphal. The introduction of Santa Maria del Popolo between Saint Mary Major and St Peter's making the concluding stations better related, and the final entry to the Vatican more dramatic.

Secondly, Sixtus planned a network of roads to support and underline the route of the pilgrimage of the Seven Churches. His roads would be broad and straight so that uninterrupted views should be opened from one stage to the next. His more important road was the Strada Sistina from SantaTrinità dei Monti to Saint Mary Major with extensions from the former to Santa Maria del Popolo, and from the latter to Santa Croce, and a branch road from Saint Mary Major to San Lorenzo. This remarkable hill road intersected the Via Pia described as "one of the most splendid highways in the whole city",[33] and which had been improved and reinstated by Pius IV. At the point of intersection Sixtus had the Via Pia lowered four feet so that the view from this point of vantage should not be impaired, and ordered his architect, Fontana, to erect Four Fountains to concentrate attention on this exceptional crossing. Looking from north-west to south-east, a spectator saw Santa Trinità, a fine, impressive structure in a superbly elevated position which Sixtus himself consecrated in 1585, recently built with funds supplied in part by the King of France, and in the other direction the splendid Esquiline piazza with its lofty obelisk and at its head, the Pope's favourite church, Saint Mary Major. Looking from south-west to north-east, the spectator saw the Pope's new palace, the Quirinale, as one end and Michelangelo's Porta Pia at the other. Surrounded by open countryside and untilled fields, he was able to survey the inhabited city below and in the distance the incomparable St Peter's. If he moved only as far as the farther side of Saint Mary Major he would obtain a similarly remarkable but much shorter view along the Via Merulana, another broad, straight dignified street laid by Pope Gregory XIII, to St John Lateran, and its famous obelisk. Unfortunately, the extension of this road to Santa Maria del Popolo never proceeded beyond the outline planning stage, and pilgrims continued to follow a detour route into the Via Babuino (neither the Spanish steps nor any alternative road being available). The engraving of Giovanni Mercati, *De rebus gestis a Sisto V Pontifex Maximus* of 1588, shows the scale of Sixtus' civic design.

Sixtus developed the schemes of Pius IV and Gregory XIII to urbanize local spaces, but adapted them to a larger scale. Instead of the rather haphazard arrangement of road junctions, he introduced a street system radiating from the seven early Christian basilicas, which stood some considerable distance from each other. Essentially Sixtus' scheme emphasized religious symbolism: the basilicas were to be connected by processional routes. Six roads were constructed and countless others planned.

The plans of Sixtus and his architect, Domenico Fontana, provided Rome with a structure that was genuinely progressive—a comprehensive solution that accommodated the large-scale monuments dating back to the construction of the ancient imperial city to the densely crowded medieval quarter. New roads made the expansion of the city possible while leaving the centre intact. But this form of urban renewal "clearly involved community disruption".[34]

Sixtus planned, but was unable to implement, drastic and far-reaching changes at each end of the pilgrimage of the Seven Churches which, if completed, would have dramatically enhanced the splendour of pilgrimage and made them easier. He shaped in outline a plan for a new road from San Salvatore in the Trastevere to St Paul's without the Walls and at the final station of the pilgrimage he projected a fresh road from a point on the river facing San Girolamo degli Schiavoni to St Peter's. The former would have necessitated a new bridge across the river where Ponte Sublicio now stands, a road, and a new gateway through the ancient walls; the latter would have called for a new bridge at the Ripetta on the line of the present Ponte Cavour, and a new road on the western side of the river. Both were for those days formidable undertakings and would have required extensive demolition of inhabited properties and extremely heavy expenditure. Sixtus rarely failed his ambitions for want of courage or inability to surmount obstacles but the length of his pontificate did not allow such gigantic tasks. Sixtus also considered the construction of a series of steps to link his Via Sistina from the platform in front of S. Trinità dei Monti to the Piazza di Spagna below, from which the Via Babuino would have led pilgrims easily and quickly along their penultimate station to Santa Maria del Popolo. If all these projects had been completed the pilgrimage could have followed, within a single day, one of the most magnificent circuits in the world, studded with some of the historically richest and most moving monuments of all time and the participants would have circulated one of the most inspiring and splendid cities of all time.

Sixtus also laid a road from Porta Salaria crossing the line of the Via Pia to San Lorenzo and planned another from Ponte Settimiana, near the far bank of the Tiber, to St Paul's, though he was unable to put this in hand. These were considered as subsidiary routes to the circuit of the Seven Churches and were intended to augment the flow of visitors by multiplying the points from which ready access could be given. By extending the Via Panisperna, he opened a road from Saint Mary Major to Trajan's column and forum, still on the edge of the city. Here he found a dramatic method of reminding the city and all its visitors that Christianity had subjugated the Roman Empire, vast and powerful as it had become. Trajan's statue was removed from the top of the column and that of the great apostle, St Peter, put in its place. The column of the Emperor Marcus Aurelius, adjacent to the Corso, was treated similarly, the statue of the Emperor being hauled down and that of the Apostle Paul hoisted in its stead. As at St Peter's, the religious significance of these changes was emphasised. The new columns were exorcised and prayers said "that they might be cleansed to bear the image of the Apostles and remain free from every taint of paganism". The erection of the new statue of St Peter was preceded by the celebration of High Mass at S. Lorenzo in Lucina (some distance down the Corso), by the Patriarch of Jerusalem, the raising of the new statue to replace that of Marcus Aurelius followed Mass celebrated by the Patriarch of Alexandria. Such exploits, though technically interesting, may seem trivial or irrelevant now but their symbolic significance was not lost on Sixtus' generation. Trajan's column, even to this day, when massive structures have impinged on the skyline and buildings have crowded into the area round it, is unmistakably striking, and even that of Marcus Aurelius is sufficiently lofty to demand attention. In Sistine Rome they genuinely commemorated the triumph of Christianity over paganism and the power of

Christian faith. These twin statues linked with the obelisks planted in notable places associated with the Seven Churches form a co-ordinated expression of the unfailing dominance of Christianity in its capital city.

But Sixtus V had little patience with ornamentation for its own sake. This ring of churches rivetted together by the intricate network of roads was to become the basis of an immense and comprehensive town planning exercise. Rome presented many complex problems. At the inauguration of the Roman Empire, the capital covered fifteen square miles and had a population of 400,000—a massive city with an extremely high density of population for those days.[35] But the ravages of one horde of barbarians after another, epidemics and other disasters reduced its population. At the beginning of the fifteenth century following the catastrophic visitation of the plague and the departure of the Papal Court to Avignon it was no more than 17,000—a tiny city in comparison even with others in Italy—and only a quarter of the old city area was occupied.[36] From that period onwards the tide turned; by 1513 it had 40,000 inhabitants, and by the time of Sixtus' accession, in spite of the devastating effects of the Sack of 1527 and renewed epidemics, the number was approximately 90,000. The return of the Popes and their court from Avignon brought a substantial influx to the city and created an immense demand for clerks, legal staff, administrators, teachers and above all, perhaps, for servants and suppliers of personal services, tailors, shoemakers, fabric makers.[37] Bankers, financiers, money lenders and money changers, property-dealers, tax farmers and customs collectors migrated to Rome from other Italian cities. The development of new palazzi, churches, streets, monuments, vastly extended the construction, furnishing and artistic industries and the blossoming of the new city attracted legions of visitors and caused a massive and continuing extension to the tourist industry. Rome lived on service industries which were highly labour-intensive. Yet its needs could be met, for skilled labour in central Italy was mobile and the depopulation of the countryside provided a ready-made fund of semi-skilled and unskilled labour. Prosperity may have raised the birth-rate somewhat, improved sanitation and a subsequent decline in epidemics almost certainly reduced the death rate. Nevertheless, though the population grew rapidly, the extension to the city area was marginal; indeed, luxury and grandiose construction of great public buildings and elaborate and spacious private palazzi diminished the area available for normal residential purposes. During the century there had been some fresh development in the Borgo, in Campo Marzo and in Trastevere, and towards the Palazzo San Marco, but there was no large scale extension, Trajan's column was still on the periphery of the habitable city.[38] Some villas had been planted on the Quirinale, a few on the Esquiline, the Palatine and on the Vatican and Janiculum hills, but the mass of the Roman people remained herded inside an area bounded by the bow of the Tiber and the feet of the Seven Hills. In the four *rioni* within the bow of the Tiber—Ponte, Parione, Regola, Sant'Eustachio—lived forty-two percent of the total population of the city—occupying less than 7% of the total area; two city parishes—San Lorenzo in Lucina and San Lorenzo in Damaso had more than 9,000 inhabitants.[39] In the city area as a whole living conditions had become intolerable; it was low-lying and swampy, liable to recurrent epidemics, especially of malaria. When heavy rains on the mountains caused the flow of the Tiber to swell, the river frequently overflowed its banks, flooded the lower reaches of the city, demolishing numbers of houses, driving the citizens from their homes and leaving a trail of havoc in its wake. In 1589, for example, there was severe flooding in the city, the waters even reaching Santa Maria sopra Minerva.[40] Streets were narrow, dark and intertwined; they formed a confused and pattern-less maze; for the most part they were not metalled and the growth of wheeled traffic caused clouds of dust to invade the houses and placed an added premium on air. The supply of water was completely inadequate.[41] The limit of relieving population pressure by further in-filling had almost been reached. There were two fundamental alternatives—to control the size of the population itself or to inaugurate a substantial extension of the city's habitable area. It would have been possible to decentralise papal government and establish a series of provincial capitals allowing them to surround themselves with their own dependent establishments. Such a possibility ran directly contrary to papal policy and if ever considered was clearly rejected. Rome was essentially the single centre of a unitary church transcending geographical boundaries; its function was to welcome the faithful from far and wide and the intention of the Pope and the church was to be accessible to them all. The alternative was therefore inescapable. The River Tiber though to some extent a highway from the sea to the countryside beyond the city, was a genuine barrier to expansion to the south, where in any event the terrain was unreceptive to habitation. Geography therefore determined that expansion should be towards the Roman hills and before Sixtus' election this had already begun, particularly in the Quirinale where Piazza Santi Apostoli and Palazzo and Villa Colonna formed a ready bridgehead. Here the population of the city could be allowed to double without creating fresh problems, except those of roads and water.

The re-shaping of the route of the pilgrimage gave Saint Mary Major, situated on the most elevated spot in the city, a central and dominant position. Extensive demolitions of property were undertaken, especially in the direction of Santa Prassede and Santa Pudenziana, to enhance its location. In the plans for the extended city, it shared its key situation with St John Lateran. From both were to radiate new, broad, straight, commanding roads to points on the periphery of the inhabited city. From Saint Mary Major a road was projected passing near to the Arch of Constantine to the Coliseum; an extension was to lead across the Forum to the Capitol, the centre of the city administration which Michelangelo had already done so much to re-shape.[42] This would have linked with a new road planned to run from Trajan's column across the Piazza San Marco and the head of the Corso to St Peter's.[43] From St John Lateran, Sixtus sketched a road to the Quirinale and put another going past the chapel of Santa Balbina to the Baths of Caracalla. Unfortunately, these projects were little more than ambitions which would have anticipated later undertakings by three centuries or so. Nevertheless, they show that what Sixtus had in mind was a soundly-conceived and carefully co-ordinated extension of the city into the hills so designed that controlled and orderly developments would be possible within predetermined contours. The final product was to be a city of great grandeur, dignity and composition.

Sixtus was never content with fantasy. Notwithstanding the brevity of his reign and the multiplicity of his commitments, a beginning was made on the residential development of the hills. The Via Sistina and the Via Pia formed the foundation and each became main limbs from which secondary systems could emerge. To encourage development in these areas Sixtus granted substantial privileges to new residents: security of tenure with guarantees against eviction, full rights of citizenship, exemption from papal and other dues.[44] Full use was made of the City Building code published by Gregory XIII in 1574. This facilitated the development of new building by curtailing obstruction by unwilling vendors, encouraged the amalgamation of small neighbouring properties, assisted their by the occupiers, arranging for compensation to be fixed by officers of the city authorities.[45] His two Bulls, *Decet Romanum Pontificem* (1587) and *Suprema cura regiminis* (1590) dealt with the subject of Roman town planning. He offered tax relief to those who built their houses along the avenues, prohibiting any wooden extensions to the buildings as they would impede the movement of goods. He ordered that house fronts should be aligned and for aesthetic reasons that washing should not be hung across the streets. He also prohibited by papal decree the emptying of waste and excrement on to the thoroughfare. The total length of new road laid by Sixtus amounted to almost eight miles and many miles of existing roads were paved for the first time, so greatly facilitating their use by wagons for the transport of materials and by carriages and horses for the movement of people.

On the Esquiline substantial development took place after a large number of small and ailing properties had been demolished in the vicinity of the newly constructed Villa and Palazzo Montalto where the Pope's sister and her relatives lived and where the Pope himself was a frequent visitor. Authority was given for an annual fair to be held in the nearby Baths of Diocletian; a weekly market was transferred to it from the Campo dei Fiori; stalls were erected for those who wished them, shops were built for traders in silks and large wash-houses were constructed so that the whole Piazza delle Terme area rapidly became a thriving commercial centre,[46] a model point of prosperity in this hill region.

The exploitation of the hill areas was impossible unless an adequate water supply could be ensured. At the time of Sixtus V's accession, Rome was dependent on three sources of water—private tanks, the Tiber and an ancient aqueduct—the Aqua Vergine—built by Marcus Agrippa in 19 BC and reinstated in the middle of the fifteenth century but still weakened by leakages and extraction for private use outside the city. Surprisingly, water from the Tiber, though often typhoid-infected, was in great demand (there were more than sixty water-carriers in the city of whom somewhat less than a half operated in the rione Regola on the banks of the river) and was popular with some of the nobility and even with some Popes, including Sixtus' predecessor, Gregory XIII. The Aqua Vergine brought softer water from Salone, about nine miles to the east of the city and supplied a number of fountains including Trevi and the Pantheon, all in the lower reaches of the city. A few fountains, like the one near S. Giorgio in Velabro at the foot of the Palatine, operated from individual springs. As fountains dependent on the Aqua Vergine multiplied (Gregory XIII built at least thirteen),[47] the need for an alternative supply increased. Gregory XIII had already proposed the idea but had been unable to do anything to forward it except initiate a fund for its development.

Almost immediately after his election, however, Sixtus purchased from Cardinal Medici's brother land between Zagarola and Palestrina, nineteen miles to the east of the city. On the recommendation of Cardinal Medici, Sixtus engaged one of the Grand Duke's architects to undertake the project but quickly replaced him by his trusted Domenico Fontana and his brother, Giovanni, who, suspecting the quality and extent of the intended springs, sought out alternatives at a higher level. A special congregation under Cardinal Medici was established to supervise the work. Sufficient money was guaranteed to the engineers; the Pope made personal inspections of the work and repeatedly incited the work-force to greater efforts, and when sickness struck a workman he was immediately replaced. The water flowed in conduits underground for some twelve miles until it came to the surface about seven miles from the city: materials from the ancient waterway were used in the building of the aqueduct which was carried on massive arches until it again went underground at the Villa Montalto, emerging finally in the Piazza San Bernardo on the Esquiline. There, a waterhead was constructed with a monument designed by Fontana depicting Moses facing the square. An average of 2,000 men were employed on this work but the number rose as high as 4,000 when progress slackened or difficulties increased; the Pope maintained his visits to the works and even forbade the burning of stubble in the vicinity lest smoke should slacken the efforts of the workmen. Nothing—neither the wrangling of Cardinal Medici, nor nature itself—was allowed to impede progress. Within twelve months the waters had reached the Pope's Villa at the head of the Esquiline though not with adequate force to be effective. But by the end of 1586 it was supplying properties on the Via Pia and by the following spring it had reached the Pincio so that in June 1587 Sixtus was able to undertake a five-day triumphal tour of the new aqueduct, and on the feast of the Nativity of Our Lady in 1589 completion was celebrated with impressive ceremony as water flowed from all its fountains.[48] The cost of this gigantic enterprise exceeded a quarter of a million scudi—approximately equal to all Sixtus' expenditure on St Peter's, St John Lateran, the Quirinale and his hospital for the poor, and in brief, about 45% of his total outlay on public works. Before his death seven large fountains, some of considerable merit as works of art, had been sculpted and connected to the new supply. Fresh and uncontaminated water was available on the Quirinal, the Capitoline, the Esquiline and the Coelian hills. Maintenance of the aqueduct was made the responsibility of the Congregation charged with the supervision of water supplies, streets and bridges. Aqueduct and fountains had to be inspected by two Roman citizens appointed annually once every three months and they were obliged to report to the Pope. Severe penalties were imposed for any damage done to either aqueduct or fountains.[49] Almost thirty years were to pass before a further supply was developed by Pope Paul V and then this was bought from the west to the Janiculum from where it fed the Trastevere. With these supplies Rome had to be content until modern times.

Completion of Aqua Felice was a momentous triumph for the engineers as well as for the Pope. The planning of the project owed little to Sixtus, but its implementation owed him everything—his was the determination to have it undertaken, his was the drive which never flagged until the moment of completion, his was the responsibility for choosing its master engineers and above all for ensuring that its development was never interrupted for lack of money. The Aqua Felice rendered feasible the development of the whole hill area from the Lateran to Pincio and as far as the Capital; pure water, fresh air, new broad, straight roads, opportunity for the development of planned residential areas were made available. These new areas were closely linked with the eastern arc of the pilgrimage of the Seven Churches, underlining in a visual sense the religious character of the capital and creating the possibility of a city development with its own highlights and focal points, most of them of religious significance. Property development in the new areas would be of a very high standard and essentially suburban in character, for land prices were quite extraordinarily high. Had progress continued smoothly after Sixtus' death, not only could congestion and squalor have been reduced in the city but Rome might have evolved as a capital beyond comparison. When the new Italy was born almost three centuries later a vast and ugly railway station replaced the Pope's villa, the dominant monument to Vittorio Emanuele described as "the least beautiful in the city"[50] was erected, and a dull, undistinguished new Corso Vittorio Emanuele was constructed to lead to the new Ponte Vittorio Emanuele—a bridge which offered no centre of interest, leaving St Peter's to one side and Sant'Angelo to the other. Sixtus' vision was never fulfilled.

Sixtus V's energetic transformation of Rome was, however, extensively and savagely criticised by his contemporaries. It had necessitated widespread and drastic demolitions and frequent invasion of private property rights: the urgency with which he undertook his building works seemed to indicate an insensitivity to past traditions and historic associations as well as an imperviousness to established interests and a stubborn indifference to reasonable resistance. The agent of the Grand Duke of Tuscany grieved at the wholesale destruction of property between the Lateran and Saint Mary Major and particularly at the removal of several venerable sanctuaries. On behalf of the city, the Conservatori instructed Cardinal Santorio to protest at the demolition of the Arch of Janus at the foot of the Palantine, a historic monument of Constantine's reign. Opposition to the proposed destruction of the outstandingly splendid tomb of Cecilia Metella, one of the wealthiest women of the late Republic, near the Basilica of San Sebastiano, was so intense that even Sixtus abandoned his intention and the tomb was saved and stands today on the Via Appia Antica. The severest and most sustained criticism was reserved for what appeared as the wanton and unnecessary destruction of the *Septizodium*, an imperial palace by the Emperor Septimus Severus (AD 146–211) at the foot of the Palatine, a fine impressive building once lavishly decorated with fountains and the last imperial palace to be used for a Conclave (in 1241). This palace was used quite unscrupulously as a quarry to provide stone for the Vatican, for the base of the obelisk erected in the Piazza del Popolo, the Lateran palace and the Sistine chapel at Saint Mary Major.[51] Energetic town planners who need to overcome the inertia of tradition have learned to expect accusations of iconoclasm and regard as normal the stiff resistance of established interests and the indiscriminate demands of the conservationists. Progress and indifference to clamour must often go hand in hand. Sixtus' determination to portray the triumph of Christendom over paganism probably rendered him unappreciative of classical beauty and certainly his own upbringing and his absorption into Franciscan traditions made him positively hostile to luxury and ostentation. Veneration was reserved for God. His missionary zeal for the urgent establishment of a new Rome as the capital of Christendom made him ruthless and undeviating in the pursuit of his plans. His sense of purpose was obsessive and gave him many of the characteristics of a bigot: his intense determination to achieve his objectives made him autocratic, unreasoning, even callous. Men who are intent on accomplishing ambitious designs regardless of the time allowed them must often lay themselves open to such condemnation and be found guilty at the bar of posterity.

History has likewise stigmatised Sixtus V's building works as second-rate. He had no distinguished architect. Fontana's style has been described as severe, stiff and lacking in imagination; little of his work for Sixtus had grace or inspiration.[52] He was best when confronted with some task of massive dimensions; faced with a project which demanded lightness of touch and deftness of execution, like the Sistine Chapel at Saint Mary Major, he found difficulty in re-orientating himself within smaller, less expansive limits. Some of the works undertaken for the Pope betray unmistakable signs of undue haste and were of indifferent quality. Sixtus V's skill lay in his ability to scan Rome as a whole, to envisage the co-ordination of its several areas and to plan a long-term expansion of its area. Detail was apt to be neglected. Consequently it was Fontana's skill as an engineer rather than architect which was appropriate to Sixtus V's demands. Architecturally, Sixtus V's reign fell into one of those recurring periods of ebb tide; the first outburst of Renaissance inspiration was spent, the torrent of baroque splendour was not yet prepared. The Pope's nature and his concern with instant output made him accept much that was mediocre and commonplace.

It has also to be conceded that he worked without originality or inventiveness. Scarcely any of his projects were creations of his own initiative, almost all had already been conceived by his predecessors. Even his plans for the settlement of the hill region of the city had been foreshadowed during the previous reign: the transfer of the obelisk at St Peter's and the bringing of the Aqua Felice to the city had been considered by others for several years. The building of St Peter's dome was part of the overall plan for the rebuilding of the basilica. What Sixtus contributed was neither inventiveness of mind nor creative fertility of design, but resoluteness of spirit and a determination to overcome obstacles. Above all he possessed a willingness to meet whatever expenditure was required to permit the implementation of his schemes and an unshakeable faith in his assistants such as gave them confidence and initiative and a capacity to work enthusiastically under their own momentum. He was a genuine realist impressed by accomplishments, outrageous in his demands but never carping in criticism or petty in recrimination. Fontana, to whom he owed so much, he treated with great generosity.

Yet when account has been taken of these justifiable criticisms, it has to be conceded that few Popes have made so distinctive a mark upon the development of the capital. Sixtus V was a giant in its history. Considered individually the more outstanding of his projects—the completion of the dome of St Peter's, the transportation and re-erection of the obelisk at St Peter's, the re-development of the Lateran complex, the bringing of the Aqua Felice to the city—were stupendous feats, outstandingly expensive in monetary cost and in human labour. That they were successfully completed in an age when scientific knowledge and skill in calculations, though increasing, were still restricted and when engineering apparatus and equipment were still quite elementary is almost beyond belief. Certainly they made an indelible impression on the age. Taken together, Sixtus V's achievements in the city are beyond comparison: no Pope of the century could match his accomplishments in amount or claim so extensive a catalogue of permanent additions to the city's treasures. From the Vatican to St John Lateran, from San Girolamo degli Schiavoni to Saint Mary Major, it was impossible to escape his handiwork: in almost every quarter of the city can be found solid, compelling evidence of his genius. No one who plots the works of Sixtus V on a map of the city will fail to recognise the immensity of his contribution to sixteenth-century Rome. Perhaps his most characteristic achievement was the creation of piazze with obelisks: the piazza being an impressive, ordered space, the obelisk serving as a vertical foil to the solid mass of the main structure. Consequently, each of the Sistine piazze employs an ordered geometrical pattern and a symmetry of design to give dignity and controlled splendour to the church which forms its centrepiece. Rome had fourteen obelisks (Egypt—from which most came—has eight) and Sixtus erected four in their present locations. These, along with the fountains are the glories which render Rome unique amongst the capitals of the world.

All this enrichment of the capital was motivated by religion. During Sixtus V's reign the city was conscious of the tireless inspiration and unconquerable energy of the papacy. The Pope worked with an infectious assurance, a profound sense of the supremacy of the Church and a conviction that all human gifts were held in trust for the service of God. At a time when the division of Europe amongst separate churches was becoming permanent and accepted, his generation recognised that the Pope personally was inspired with a consuming faith in the destiny and divine purpose of the Catholic Church. His personal vitality, his sense of urgency, his indomitableness and his singleness of objective permeated his Court and spread through all ranks of the city. The completion of the Gesù the year before his election, the erection of Philip Neri's new church now in full swing, his own completion of San Girolamo degli Schiavoni, and the extension and enrichment of Saint Mary Major were portents of the new age. The energy which had been concentrated on the construction of palaces for noble families and cardinals was now transferred to the erection, adornment and enrichment of churches as remarkable in their magnificence and splendour as the palaces had been. The faith, the earnest devotion, the practical piety and social conscience of Cardinal Charles Borromeo which had transformed men as eminent as Cardinal Altemps and Cristoforo Boncompagni, Archbishop of Ravenna, and profoundly influenced men like Cardinals Pallotta and Serbelloni, now captivated the city. Borromeo had died only a year earlier at the age of forty-six, but he was to be canonised at an early date and the city was to raise a most handsome and imposing church in the Corso to his memory. Already the spirit of Borromeo had descended on his friend and disciple, now Sixtus V. None of Sixtus V's works in the city was so much in accord with it as his recognition and re-organisation of the Pilgrimage of the Seven Churches (which Charles Borromeo himself had made in 1575). The substitution of Santa Maria del Popolo for San Sebastiano made the pilgrimage a much more closely integrated institution with a more even balance of stations. Four of the seven now had a piazza with an obelisk to remind the pilgrims of the replacement of Egyptian sun worship and imperial paganism by Christianity and to testify to the vitality and assurance of the contemporary Catholic church. Inevitably the religious fervour awakened by the pilgrimage linked with the statues of the great apostles, St Peter and St Paul, now surmounting the columns of Trajan and Marcus Aurelius and showing prominently over the old city from almost all points of the pilgrimage round the capital's periphery. Saint Mary Major became the central point of the pilgrimage at about the half-way mark, and the superb and allegorical view at the intersection of the Via Pia and the Strada Felice at the Quattro Fontane created an incomparable prelude to the descent to Santa Maria del Popolo and the triumphal return to St Peter's.

Sixtus V's works and particularly his development of the Seven Churches had a spiritual and religious significance which though now perhaps unconvincing was then clear and unmistakable. It was a facet of the Counter-Reformation movement and though its effect may have been somewhat transitory it had a vital impact on Roman society and because Rome was so cosmopolitan in character and such a unique pilgrimage centre, this impact was transmitted to every quarter of Europe.

Moreover, Sixtus V's achievements were cut short by his death, and his vision of what ought to be done is as significant as his accomplishments. For example, how greatly changed would Rome have been had he lived to build bridges over the Tiber at the Ripetta and Santo Spirito as he had planned? The city was to wait more than three hundred years for these. Similarly, he intended to raise obelisks at Piazza Navona and in the Piazza delle Terme di Diocleziano,[53] and it must be evident that he would have undertaken much more work at St Peter's and would have constructed many more roads had his reign not been so brief, though it may well be that the delay at St Peter's was to the church's advantage.

Perhaps his plans for the new Rome are equally significant. Rome has always presented formidable problems, many of them still unsolved: they were scarcely less so, comparatively at least, in Sixtus V's day. First, the Tiber, formed a constraining limit to development, preventing all large-scale growth on one side of the river. In Rome this had the further disadvantage that the Borgo and the Vatican remained a detached island difficult to integrate in the city. Second, the residue of classical Rome in the old city and medieval Rome itself formed a heritage too valuable to destroy or diminish. Between the river and Piazza del Popolo in one direction and the Forum in another, there was scarcely a square yard which was not historically sacrosanct.

More than three centuries later Mussolini planned "to make the mass of the Pantheon visible through a vast opening from Piazza Colonna", but the necessary and widespread demolition in the old city rendered the scheme impossible.[54] Even the cutting of the Corso Vittorio Emmanuele and the development of Piazza Venezia as the centre of Fascist Rome destroyed much of the character of old Rome without producing a satisfactory focal point of a new city. One authority has said, "The objective of emphasising both classical Rome and the centrality of Piazza Venezia was actually self-contradictory."[55] Third, the fact is that Rome had and still has no natural centre. The centre of the ancient capital, the Capitol, was then on the fringe of the old city, bordered by the ancient Forum; then still an open waste where cattle grazed, it was quite detached from the Court or commercial activity of the city. In spite of the work of Michelangelo it had no substantial significance, and in any event Sixtus V's policy was to subordinate the city administration to the Papal curia and this would have modified any attempts to develop the Capitol. The Campo de' Fiori was in many senses the administrative centre of the old city (papal orders being displayed there), the Chancellery was adjacent to it and the Via Giulia with several government buildings, was not far away. To develop this as an adequate city centre would, however, have been as difficult as developing from the Pantheon. Palazzo San Marco, so dear to Pius IV, though it stood commandingly at the head of the Corso, had never seriously claimed any dominance in the city. Similarly, the Vatican, in spite of its outstanding importance and historic associations, was remote, isolated and particularly in summer, unsanitary and oppressive. One modern alternative was "to shift the centre of the city and the railway station at the Termini to the east so as to drain traffic from the historic centre and permit its conservation"[56] while developing residential quarters outside the walls of ancient Rome and around the perimeter of the twentieth-century city. Faced with the saturation of the site of the old city and a phenomenally rapid increase of population, but not with the enormous increase initiated by Unification, Sixtus was able to achieve a compromise solution which enabled the old city to be maintained intact, indeed restored to its pristine splendour, and provided for expansion and re-development on the hills lying to the east and north-east of the old city. This solution, logical and natural, perhaps even inescapable, satisfied the conservationists and yet met the needs of the progressives and the realists. Sixtus V's perceptive vision of the future enabled him to plan with prudence and foresight and provided area sufficient to encompass developments until Unification: it was an ordered framework which would enable all reasonable contingencies to be coordinated within its outline.[57] The establishment of the Aqua Felice and the construction of new roads translated this theoretical design into a realistic practicality, and at the same time established close links with the old city, so obviating rivalry between the old and the new. In particular, the focal position created for Saint Mary Major, the linking of the Quirinale with one of the main arteries of the new city and the connection of the new Via Felice with the old Via Babuino and so with the Piazza del Popolo, made practicable a development of the new area as a logical expansion of the old. As a city planner, therefore, Sixtus combined imagination with realism, foresight with acceptance of the practical, and so made possible the creation of a new Rome, combining the vast treasures of the classical with the immense wealth of the Renaissance and at the same time opening unobstructed highways into the future—a typical act of faith. History cannot blame him that his vision was unfulfilled.

Nor must it be thought that Sixtus sacrificed the welfare of the people of Rome to his ambitions to endow the city with great physical amenities. He worked indefatigably to restore law and order, to suppress banditry and lawlessness and to remove the danger of violent assault, wrongful duress and victimisation. In his domestic policy he gave unqualified priority to the restoration of peace and good order and spared neither expense nor personal effort to achieve his plans. His compassion for the poor of the city was evidenced by his concern for the well-being of tourists and visitors, and by his erection of the extremely costly hospital for the poor and by his diligent supervision of the Corn Laws. During his reign the supply of corn and vegetables was maintained unhindered and prices were strictly controlled so that the most essential needs of the lowest classes were consistently met until the final year of his pontificate. Whilst the gulf separating rich from poor was vast, Sixtus did his utmost to ensure that the latter did not fall below the subsistence level and his concern for their welfare appears genuine and practical.

The price of Sixtus V's achievements was the maintenance of an absolute autocracy and the increased centralisation of the machinery of state. From the officials of his court he expected unquestioning subordination, a zealous and energetic performance of their duties in conformity with his personal wishes and an unflagging tenacity in the face of opposition. His government was ruthless and unrelenting in the strict enforcement of rigid and arbitrary laws. Rome had many of the aspects of a police state where punishment was intended to be exemplary, where people were regularly intimidated and cowed, where the informer was encouraged and incriminating gossip was valued. The Pope's own belief in severity, repression and exact compliance permeated the state and bred an atmosphere of suspicion and insecurity. In such a situation it was important that the city administration should be wholly subordinated to the Pope and the Papal court and that the Capitol should be completely dominated by the Vatican. The powers of the Senator and Conservatori had long been reduced to shadows; they were now still further restricted so that the Caporioni and the Maestri di Strada who were responsible for the day-to-day administration of the city operated virtually as papal officials who, if they sought independence, met hostility and circumvention. By these means the citizen body was squeezed into subservience.

In spite of all his developments and plans, Sixtus left Rome much as he had found it—a highly vulnerable city with no industry, almost wholly dependent for employment on the Papal Court and for sustenance on an extensive countryside devoted (often compulsorily) to supplying the needs of the city. His efforts to introduce industry failed dismally. Notably unlike London or Paris in the sixteenth century, Rome remained without manufacture. It was not a port of any significance; the city had no important export trade, its imports were restricted and generally introduced by road. Much of the city's commerce was handled by foreigners. The bulk of trade with the Papal States was handled in Ancona, and the Papal States were not one of the foremost commercial centres even in Italy. Only in the money market were its resources significant. Florentine, Spanish, French and German money-dealers had settled in Rome in considerable numbers and the floating of loans and changing of coinage on an international scale were valuable occupations to the city. In consequence, it remained dependent on employment at the Papal Court or in the city administration, in the service and luxury industries which the Court sustained, on work generated by the pilgrim trade of the City, or in meeting the demands of a vast and growing construction industry and the building trades. Such a city could only be stable and prosperous so long as its food supply was guaranteed by the surrounding countryside and the import of papal revenues from foreign countries saved it from balance of payments problems. A city as vulnerable as Rome was obliged to be concerned about the social and economic equilibrium of the Papal States and the status of the Church in Europe. Papal policy like education was a seamless robe and almost wholly dependent on the international situation.

## Notes

[1] J. Lees-Milne, *Saint Peter's: the story of Saint Peter's Basilica in Rome* (London: Hamish Hamilton, 1967), p. 125.
[2] Orbaan, *Sixtine Rome*, p. 118.
[3] *Bullarium* 8, p. 807.

4   Lees-Milne, *Saint Peter's*, p. 92.
5   *Ibid.*, p. 82
6   *Ibid.*, p. 91
7   It is important to remember that St Peter's faced west, not east, therefore the North direction lies to the right of its axis
8   Lees-Milne, *Saint Peter's*, p. 90.
9   Pastor 23, p. 415; and Lees-Milne, *Saint Peter's*, p. 127.
10  Lees-Milne, *Saint Peter's*, p. 83.
11  *Ibid.*, pp. 233, 142.
12  Delumeau 1, p. 253.
13  *Ibid.*, p. 764 n. 3.
14  Pastor 22, p. 309.
15  Lees-Milne, *Saint Peter's*, p. 124.
16  *Ibid.*, illustration, p. 119.
17  See Delumeau 1, plates 12 and 13 after p. 272.
18  See *ibid.*, plate 10 after p. 256.
19  See drawings by Martin van Heemskirk (1498–1574) on p. 127 of Lees-Milne, *Saint Peter's* and in Pecchiai, *Roma nel Cinquecento*, Plate 7.
20  The story is told in full by Fontana himself, a copy of whose *Della transportatione dell'obelisco Vaticano e delle fabriche di Sisto V* (Rome: 1590) is to be found in the Vatican Library. There is a more readily available account in Orbaan, *Sixtine Rome*.
21  Delumeau 1, p. 263.
22  Massimo, p. 309.
23  Orbaan, *Sixtine Rome*, p. 171.
24  Pecchiai, *Roma nel Cinquecento*, p. 368.
25  *Ibid.*.
26  Massimo, p. 425.
27  ODCC.
28  Regrettably, in spite of Fontana's elaborate precautions, this oratory collapsed in the course of being removed to a position below the altar.
29  Pastor 23, p. 289 n. 1.
30  Orbaan, *Sixtine Rome*, p. 171.
31  Massimo, p. 215.

32. Both phrases are from Masson, *Italian Gardens*, pp. 211, 213.
33. Pastor 23, p. 224.
34. J. R. Short, *The Urban Arena* (London: MacMillan, 1984), p. 141.
35. Fried, "Planning the Eternal City", p. 15.
36. *Ibid..*
37. Delumeau 1, p. 372, Table II.
38. *Ibid.*, p. 272, Plates 13 and 19.
39. *Ibid.*, p. 284.
40. Pope Sixtus' final illness was linked to persistent malarial symptoms.
41. I. de Feo, *Sisto V. Un grande papa tra Rinascimento e Barocco* (Milano: Mursia, 1987), p. 167.
42. Delumeau 1, p. 316.
43. See E. Bacon, *Design of Cities* (London: Thames and Hudson, 1967).
44. *Bullarium* 8, pp. 914–916.
45. Pastor 23, p. 603.
46. Delumeau 1, p. 322.
47. *Ibid.*, p. 331.
48. Pastor 23, p. 212.
49. *Ibid.*, p. 217.
50. Massimo, p. 81.
51. Pastor 23, pp. 236–237; Orbaan, *Sixtine Rome*, p. 237; Massimo pp. 71, 357.
52. Orbaan, *Sixtine Rome*, p. 142.
53. *Ibid.*, p. 266.
54. Fried, "Planning the Eternal City", p. 32.
55. *Ibid..*
56. *Ibid.*, p. 33.
57. In the event, the increase in population slackened in the seventeenth-century and growth virtually ceased between 1750 and 1850. (See Fried, "Planning the Eternal City", p. 18.)

# CHAPTER 7

### The Worth of his Ambitions

*Like Napoleon in a later day, Sixtus V possessed in a singular degree the gift of impressing his immediate surroundings with his personality and of passing this impression to others at a great distance.*

Count Ugo Balzani (1905)

SIXTUS V'S RESTORATION of the Eternal City as the capital of Christendom by harnessing the inspiration of the Renaissance to religious objectives was the triumphant expression of spiritual revival. It provided a visual canvas on which the spiritual forces of Catholicism could operate, and created an unequivocal focus from which a Church with restored confidence and command could radiate vitality into new worlds and alien cultures and perhaps even recapture some of the states which had been led astray by heresy. Yet the Pope's building work in Rome remained only a symbol: and even in a century in which the allegorical was profoundly appreciated, only the reality would truly satisfy. The reform of the Church had dominated papal policy throughout the whole of the second half of the century. But even as the end of the century approached the daunting task remained incomplete, the success already achieved had been intermittent and remained uncertain and its further progress was dubious. A reverse would have been disastrous and Sixtus was conscious of how much depended on a fresh momentum.

Three events, the most recent of them twenty years old, dictated the main lines his policy had to follow and outlined the area in which he could operate. First the collapse of Paul IV's struggle in Italy with Philip II and his ignominious defeat clearly demonstrated that any papal political ambitions and hopes of territorial aggrandisement which survived were vain, especially since the Treaty of Cateau-Cambrésis in 1589 had ended the period when Imperial and French rivalries could be involved in the affairs of Italy. Future Popes might manoeuvre to diminish Spanish influence in Northern and Southern Italy; they might seek to manipulate the policies of other Italian states, especially of Tuscany and Venice; their moral support, financial resources and religious prestige would remain valuable to European rulers but henceforth a belligerent or chauvinistic policy was impracticable. Prudence dictated that Papal policy should concentrate on enhancing its spiritual influence and leadership and on deepening the loyalty and moral allegiance of its supporters.

Second, the Peace of Augsburg (1555) had recognised for Germany the principle *cuius regio eius religio*; the union of church and state was unbreakable and the religious persuasion of each state was to be determined by its ruler. The partition of Germany between Lutheranism and Catholicism was formally recognised and became permanent, but no recognition was given to other Protestant creeds. It was open, therefore, to the Catholic authorities to re-establish their control in Lutheran states by bringing about the re-conversion of their rulers; it was particularly important to maintain an effective surveillance of the ecclesiastical states where temporal and religious authority were completed united. The apostasy of Catholic princes and the spread of Protestantism other than Lutheranism had to be prevented by every possible means. Moral, intellectual and scholastic standards of the clergy had to be raised; genuine religious conviction, practical charity and piety had to be encouraged in Catholics. The Jesuits had already shown skill, energy and determination in efforts for the expansion of Catholicism in Germany, and though the complete restoration was impracticable, a fluid situation was being consistently exploited.

Third, the Tridentine decrees had still not been fully promulgated. Their insistence on the authority of the Papacy and their emphasis on the unity of the Church in belief and jurisdiction provoked widespread suspicion, and in many quarters were viewed with cautious non-cooperation. The decrees were accepted without delay in Venice and the other non-Spanish states in Italy, by Portugal and the Emperor and by many of the South German princes and the Catholic cantons of Switzerland. But in the Spanish possessions, though they were received promptly their acceptance was subject to the reservation of the rights of the king and country.[1] The Imperial and Polish Diets bluntly refused to accept them, and in France there was sustained and bitter opposition to their publication, led by the Parliament of Paris.[2] The Council had elucidated many of the controversial doctrines of the Church with great care and accuracy but was unable entirely to avoid compromises. It gave to the Church a positive and authoritative definition of many of the most debatable beliefs so that disputes within the Church might be stilled. But clarity of belief achieved by cold intellectual decisions does little galvanize the human spirit: this is more likely to be achieved by personal contact with those who combine firmness of belief with spiritual conviction, and human compassion by personal example. The restoration to the Church of pristine fervour and integrity was inevitably a slow and difficult process. Progress had been made in the elimination of simony, and corruption had been reduced. Nevertheless, the regular Orders continued to cause successive Popes great anxiety. Many monastic houses were ill-disciplined or even anarchic; the standard of morality was often low, monks and even more nuns were allowed to live in idleness or luxury; scholarship and charity were frequently neglected. But the greatest clerical abuse was the non-residence of the secular clergy. Very many sees were occupied by bishops who transferred their responsibilities to vicars, often ill-paid, sometimes incompetent and neglectful of their pastoral duties. It was inevitable that the hollowness of the diocesan administration should grievously affect the parish clergy on whom the restoration of morality, purpose and sense of social responsibility ultimately depended. Churches and their furnishings were allowed to deteriorate, the sacraments were administered rarely, or casually and irreverently, sermons were preached irregularly, congregations were neglected. The intellectual capacity of many of the clergy was poor and they remained untrained and ill-fitted to exercise substantial influence over their flocks.

Reform of the church was therefore Sixtus' pre-eminent task and in this he would be following faithfully in the tracks of his predecessors, Gregory XIII and Pius V. Sixtus' reform of the Church combined two elements of quite outstanding importance; first, his own personal undeviating devotion to the Church for which he lived and died, together with a solid determination that its direction should spring from his own judgement and initiative. Second, to guarantee any permanency to his reforms the Church should possess a logical and efficient form of government. He made the utmost use of his right of nomination to the highest ecclesiastical offices and used this power to stamp his personal policy and opinions throughout the ranks of the Church from himself to the Sacred College, from the College to the bishops and their clergy. The basis of papal control over a world-wide Church was the establishment in the Roman Curia of a system of Congregations, comprising of Cardinals, appointed by the Pope himself and meeting weekly to discharge their responsibilities and to report directly to the Pope. Sixtus established a system of government by Committee in which the initiative was his. Opposition was largely illusory and organised resistance excluded. Success ensured the direct transmission of the Pope's personal ideals to the remotest parish and its congregation. The Holy Father loved his flock but he kept them under an eternally vigilant eye. Largely independent of this system, he established direct contact with the regular Orders. They had sworn personal allegiance to him; though they were intended to accept the surveillance of the bishops, the Pope maintained supervision of the Orders, rewarding and recognising their work, but also imposing upon them duties and tasks with penalties for non-compliance for which they were held responsible directly to himself. Such a Church faced the grave dangers of stagnation, but Sixtus foresaw that expansion into the New Worlds—East and West—could mitigate against that danger. In this expansion he therefore took an unswerving interest. His vision was as expansive as his energy was boundless.

His personal example gave him great influence in the governance of Western Christendom, for he was devoted to the responsibilities of his pontificate. He was conscientious and industrious, working regularly and earnestly, often far into the night with the aid of the palace candle-light: to his major tasks—the raising of St Peter's obelisk, the construction of the Aqua Felice aqueduct, the translation of the Vulgate—he gave his personal attention without sparing himself or considering his years. His enthusiasm became infectious and his boundless expectation notorious. Yet he remained personally modest and unostentatious; simple in dress, frugal in habit, an enemy to luxury, pomp, flattery and bribery. His justice was impartial; he spared neither powerful nobles nor Church dignitaries. The devoutness of his character was beyond dispute; he attended the regular religious offices with meticulous care, received the sacraments with unfailing regularity and reverence, officiated frequently at major services in the principal basilicas and at the recognised festivals of the Church calendar. He himself preached rarely on these occasions, but he listened with close critical attention to the preachers wherever he went, and made evident his regard for correct liturgy and effective preaching. A rigorous austerity descended on the papal court; the more ostentatious and those who had lived on favour left for more palatable conditions. His recognition of scholarship continued and the Papal Court was replete with officials possessing the highest academic and juridical distinctions and with theological writers of acknowledged eminence. If there was criticism of the Pope's elevation of his great-nephew, Alessandro Peretti, not yet fifteen, the new Cardinal responded by accepting the guidance of the Pope and devoted himself to his responsibilities with considerable natural ability. Similarly, if the Peretti palazzo on the Esquiline titillated the gossips, the Pope insisted on his sister, Camilla, living with great frugality and modesty. Though the Pope was prone to promote members of the religious Orders, particularly his own, and inhabitants of his native Marches, their elevation was never unmerited and their appointments rarely regretted. In short, the standards of personal conduct in the inner circles of the Papal entourage were unexceptionable and the canons of papal administration were unusually exacting and severe. No serous accusation against the integrity of Sixtus' pontificate could be justified.

He gathered around himself officials who could reflect his own standards and would bring honour to his reign. Among his principal officials were the Camerlengo, the Cardinal Datario,[3] and the Cardinal Vice-Chancellor and the Treasurer.[4] During the sixteenth century the Cardinal-nephew had tended to establish his primacy amongst these papal officials, but Sixtus' (great) nephew was so young that he necessarily worked under the Pope's direction or in close association with one of these principal officials. Only towards the end of Sixtus V's pontificate was he sufficiently experienced to exercise the influence normal to a Cardinal-nephew. These principal officials were selected by Sixtus with the greatest possible care.

The Sacred College of Cardinals were picturesquely described as stars in orbit round the sun; he himself being the life-giving sun. The dignity of their office needed to be matched by their outstanding personality, and it seemed prudent to Sixtus that the qualities required of them and the deficiencies which would debar them from office should be precisely defined. One of the Pope's early bulls, *De S.R.E. Cardinalium creandorum praestantia* (December 3rd, 1586) stipulated that a Cardinal should be at least thirty years of age, unless he were a Cardinal Deacon in which case he had to be at least twenty-two, and had to be ordained within a year on pain of disqualification from voting in the Sacred College. He must have received at least the four minor orders, and be free of all blemishes (which would exclude him from orders), he was to be of exemplary conduct, sincere piety, ardent zeal, blameless purity of faith and great learning. Those who were illegitimate were totally excluded; fathers with children living, even though legitimate, were debarred from elevation. Anyone having a brother, cousin, uncle, nephew or relative of the first or second degree in the Sacred College was ineligible. Within the Cardinalate there were to be, in addition to doctors of jurisprudence and masters in theology, at least four Cardinals drawn from the Mendicant Orders. The Sacred College was to include men of different nationalities. Any Cardinal not resident in the Curia was required to go to Rome within a year to take the oath of loyalty to the Holy Father and to have his title conferred on him, on pain of forfeiture.

The standard of these requirements was above reproach. Membership of the Sacred College was to be restricted to men of impeccable character and personal distinction; learning in a variety of faculties, and adequate representation of the regular Orders, was to be characteristic of the College, and cliques founded on family influence were to be prevented. A number of Cardinals promoted in the earlier decades of the century would have been ineligible on grounds of age alone,[5] and Sixtus' own promotion of his great-nephew only the previous year would have been rendered impossible. Some cardinals in the past had not been in Holy Orders and so would have been ineligible under the new law.[6] The Bull's insistence on representation of different nationalities had not been observed before, for the Sacred College was numerically dominated consistently by Italians, yet this requirement in the Bull was so imprecise as to allow the situation to continue unchanged. In any event, though the Church was vociferous in its claim to be the universal Church, Italian Popes and Italian Cardinals were quite unwilling to forego their hold on power.

A Bull *Postquam Verus* determined that "the number of Cardinals should not exceed seventy and that any promotion beyond that number should be void." 6 cardinal bishops, 50 cardinal priests and

14 cardinal deacons—the number was retained until the reign of Pope John XXIII. Because Cardinals who died were not regularly or systematically replaced, the size of the Sacred College varied greatly; ranging from 33 during the second decade of the sixteenth century to 69 on two occasions during Pius V's reign. It had never exceeded seventy. The number was consistently higher from the reign of Paul III (1534-50) onwards. The danger was that after a period in which the number was allowed to fall the College could become impracticably small, so that sudden promotions would change the character of the College. For example, In 1517 Leo X created thirty-three Cardinals and doubled the size of the College; in 1565 by his elevation of twenty-three Cardinals, Pius V increased the College by almost fifty per cent; and the promotion of sixteen Cardinals by Pius IV in 1561 increased the size of the College by more than a third. There were ten other years in which the number of promotions exceeded ten. Small colleges deprived the Pope of adequate assistance and prevented the effective representation of diverse views within the church; large ones could render the College an inadequate instrument of control over papal policy and favour manipulation within its ranks. Large numbers of promotions by a single Pope tended to establish a clique and could perpetuate his influence into his successor's pontificate. Some statutory control over the Pope's power of making Cardinals was therefore advisable and the establishment of a maximum number of its membership was a reasonably flexible method of achieving this. Judged by the experience of the sixteenth century, the figure of seventy did not impose an undue limitation on the Pope's prerogative.

In fact, during his pontificate Sixtus created thirty-three Cardinals, his great-nephew less than three weeks after his election, eight in December 1585, a further eight in 1586, one in August 1587, and eight in the following December, one in July 1588 and two in December of the same year, and finally four in December 1589. The appointment of his great-nephew gave widespread offence to the Sacred College because of Alessandro's youth. Subsequent promotions were condemned in the Consistory, and those of 1588 were particularly resented and bitter opposition was voiced in the College, especially by Cardinals Paleotti and Santorio. More recently critics have compared Gregory XIII's elevation of thirty-four cardinals in a pontificate of thirteen years with the thirty-three promoted by Sixtus in his five years on the throne. In fact, Sixtus' own election to the papal throne, twenty-three deaths of Cardinals and Medici's resignation should be offset against the new appointments in his reign to show a net increase of eight in the membership of the College. At his election there were sixty Cardinals, at his death there were sixty-eight; the proportion of Gregorians in the Conclave of 1585 was considerably larger than that of the Sistine elevations in the Conclave of 1590. In neither Conclave could the late Pope's followers alone achieve the two-thirds majority required for a pope's election: in both Conclaves they could, if united, prevent such an election. The criticism of Sixtus' use of his prerogative in elevating Cardinals seems therefore to have little justification, and the imposition of a limit to the total number of Cardinals probably reduced for the future the domination of the Conclave by the followers of any single Pope.

Sixtus V, in fact, chose his Cardinals with the greatest care, exercising to the full his own judgement and discretion. Even a critical Consistory found little occasion to be hostile to his selection. Sixtus returned to the practice prescribed by the old books of ceremonial,[7] indicating several days in advance his intention to announce the creation of new Cardinals and so gave members of the College an opportunity to make recommendations to him. This opening to public discussion produced great pressure by individual Cardinals for the advancement of their protégés[8] and some vitriolic criticism of the Pope by, for example, Toledo, the Jesuit. As Sixtus did not accept nominations but entirely followed his own judgement, the procedure apparently so even-handed, produced only frustration. Sixtus obstinately turned a consistently deaf ear to the insistent recommendations of foreign princes, including Philip II of Spain, Henry III of France, the Emperor Rudolph II, and a number of rulers of Italian States.[9] These pressures were severe and persistent;[10] to have surrendered to them would have given access to nationalistic ambitions and would have subjected the Sacred College more than ever to non-religious domination. Sixtus refused to allow the Cardinalate to be regarded as a political office or reward, and when he agreed to promote William Allen in 1587 out of respect for the Spanish King and in preparation for the invasion of England he shrewdly used the occasion to urge a more conciliatory attitude to papal claims in Spain.[11]

Sixtus V's Cardinals were remarkable in virtue and in talent. Not surprisingly, more than half these new men were middle-aged: eleven in their fifties, seven in their forties. Only Bonucci (aged 66) and Drascovics (aged 63) were elderly, and died in 1589 and 1587 respectively. But at the other end of the age scale, eight were in their thirties and five more were distinguished by their youth; Pepoli was twenty-eight when promoted Cardinal, Colonna twenty-seven, Federico Borromeo twenty-three, Charles Duke of Lorraine twenty-two, and the Pope's great-nephew, Alessandro Peretti was only fourteen. All these five were created Cardinal-Deacons and therefore none was disqualified by age, though Alessandro Peretti would have been ineligible had the Bull of December 3rd 1585, been in operation when he was promoted. The suitability of the men in their twenties for the Cardinalate is open to debate: the promotion of a boy of fourteen, though not without ample precedent in the sixteenth century, was contrary at least to the spirit of the Council of Trent, seems quite unwarrantable and was widely criticised at that time. Whereas the average age of the Conclave of 1585 was fifty-five, the average age of Sixtus' elevations was forty-four. Youth marched into the Cardinalate and as a result half of Sixtus' creations lived into the next century, six surviving into the third decade, and one (Federico Borromeo) into the fourth decade. It would appear that Sixtus was attracted by youth: its vigour and determination, its promise and its optimism, its spontaneous capacity for dedication, its sense of purpose and its loyalty.

He may well have found stimulation and inspiration in their company. He evidently chose those who sympathised with his ideals and ambitions, whom he would be able to galvanise quickly into action and whom he hoped to shape in his own mould. They were not spineless sycophants; Sixtus despised flatterers, preferred independence of judgment and counted on reasoned allegiance not passive subservience.

Sixtus' cardinals formed an attractive collection of men. Lénoncourt was notably good-looking with manners so elegant and cultivated as to be noticed even in that courteous century. De' Rossi was extremely handsome and of such attractive character that it was said that "a certain divinity shone in him so that everyone was obliged to honour and revere him". His charm was matched by Gonzaga, a great wit, an effervescent character, always elegantly dressed and groomed with unusual suavity of manner; del Monte's affability and genial good humour was proverbial; Drascovics and Federico Borromeo were easy in conversation and outstandingly persuasive and eloquent in the pulpit. De' Rossi, Bernerio and Mendoza had established reputations for compassion, understanding of those in distress, and a willing charity. Mendoza, Dean of Talavera, was also known for his unstinted care of the sick, visiting them personally and providing a suitable funeral if they died in poverty. Bernerio too was a diligent visitor and protector of the poor, and the imprisoned Colonna kept open house so long that his generosity became famous in Italian society. All the new Cardinals were of unblemished character. Pierbenedetti had sown a lavish crop of wild oats in his youth in and around Camerino (birthplace of Sixtus' mother), but he had gone to Rome at his uncle's instigation and had been overwhelmed by one of the preachers at Santa Maria dell'Anima. This was the church of the Germans living in Rome and housed the tomb of the last non-Italian Pope, Adrian VI (1522–3). It was not far from the site where St Philip Neri's Chiesa Nuova was to be planned, near the Piazza Navona. Pierbenedetti's conversion was complete; he took orders, studied diligently to obtain his doctorate in philosophy and theology at the Jesuit Collegio Romano, and became a Bishop. All Sixtus' elevations to the Cardinalate justified his confidence in their capacities and qualities, with the possible exception of Sauli, who lived to the great age of eighty-two, and in his later years lost his religious devotion and became somewhat worldly.[12] On the other hand the integrity and piety of the others was unquestionable, and their attention to religious duties exemplary. Morosini was a model of zeal, keeping all regular church festivals with evident devotion, confessing with great humility and fasting three times a week. Del Monte was widely known for his devotion to the Blessed Virgin Mary in whose honour he fasted on bread and water every Saturday, and distributed alms in her name.

There is no evidence to suggest that Sixtus' Cardinals were noted for artistic taste or interest; none except del Monte was a patron of the painters still working in Rome. Several, notably de' Rossi, Bernerio and Pallotta, were concerned in the restoration and embellishment of churches in Rome or in their bishoprics. Pallotta, for example, was a collector of religious sculpture, and Sauli had a most striking altar surmounted by a remarkable Madonna erected in S. Maria del Popolo. Della Rovere and Colonna were both collectors of books and eventually amassed libraries of outstanding quality, the formers being remarkable for its codices and Greek and Latin books, the latter for rare books, especially in Greek and Latin.

Two-thirds of Sixtus V's Cardinals were of noble birth; all but one of the remainder were descended from well-connected families. Only Bonucci, and perhaps Petrocchini, could match the Pope's humble origin. Born at Arezzo, forty miles south-east of Florence, Bonucci was the son of a textile worker or a mason who had moved from the neighbouring country to Arezzo to live with a relative belonging to the Order of the Servites. Bonucci entered the Order and followed a career singularly similar to Sixtus V's. Of Petrocchini's parentage almost nothing is known. It would appear that origin in poverty was, in Sixtus V's judgement, no inevitable advantage for Cardinals, though when accompanied by merit, it was no disqualification. His Cardinals included Charles, Duke of Lorraine (of the French royal house of Valois), and della Rovere (of the lineage of Sixtus IV and Julius II and seven other Cardinals). Colonna was a member of one of the most famous noble Roman families, Cornaro and Morosini were Venetian patricians of the first order and Guistiniani came of a correspondingly elevated family in Genoa. Aldobrandini was a brother of a Cardinal who had died and Gonzaga also had a near-relative in the Cardinal's College. Though the Marches produced few nobles of higher rank, Cardinal Pallotta came of one of their best families. As a group, therefore, the social origins of Sixtus V's Cardinals were comparable with the College of other eras. Nobles and well-connected men predominated, there was only one Cardinal of humble birth, and Sixtus was assisted by men for the most part deeply imbued with the traditions and connections of the upper class. A Pope of humble origin proved himself highly conservative in his choice of Cardinals.

Deeply versed in Franciscan traditions, Sixtus regarded proven scholarship as one of the essential characteristics of a Cardinal. Eleven of his promotions—a third of the total—were distinguished jurists, almost all of whom had attended Universities in Italy, France and Spain. Nine more were famous for their erudition in the Humanities or theology; della Rovere, a student at Padua and Paris, had an international reputation for his skill in Greek and Latin; Colonna studied Greek and Latin at Salamanca and Alcalá and graduated also in philosophy, theology and canon and civil law. Gonzaga had a profound knowledge of Greek and Latin, studied mathematics and philosophy at Bologna and Padua Universities, graduating as a doctor in these subjects. Borromeo also took his doctorate in philosophy and mathematics at Bologna University and Pierbenedetti took his degree in philosophy and theology at the Collegio Romano. Six of the Sistine Cardinals were professors, Pinelli at Padua, Bernerio at Cremona, Boccafuoco at Perugia, Padua and Rome, Allen at Douai, Bonucci at Padua and Bologna and Cusani at Pavia. In few other establishments could a comparable muster of scholastic talent and learning be assembled.

Four of Sixtus' Cardinals were members of established Regular Orders. Bernerio was a Dominican who had been an Inquisitor in Genoa and had been appointed Prior of the Convent of S. Sabina, a large Dominican Monastery in Rome. Petrocchini belonged to the Order of the Hermits of Saint Augustine and after graduating in theology rose to the highest rank in the Order and became a preacher with a considerable reputation. He had been appointed General of the Order by Sixtus two years before being promoted Cardinal. Bonucci was a Servite, one of the strictest of the religious orders, founded in 1240 in Tuscany and following the rule of St Augustine with additions from the Dominican constitutions.[13] He had been both Procurator-General and in 1572 General of the Order; he was also an examinee of the Index and after Sixtus' election Consulter of the Holy Office. Boccafuoco joined the Conventuals at the age of twelve, an eminent scholar, a graduate in and professor of theology, and a writer on biblical, theological and philosophical subjects. The promotion of four such men to the highest honour open to them except the Papacy itself reflected the reformation which had been sweeping through the regular Orders since the middle of the century and the disappearance of the widespread hostility to them which had been characteristic of earlier decades. Sixtus had selected with perspicacity some of the most eminent leaders of the Orders and they brought to him and to the College of Cardinals singleness of purpose and dedication in addition to scholastic eminence and vast experience of theological debate and the popular search for personal conviction.

At least five more of Sixtus' Cardinals had given clear proof of their faith and confidence in the resources and the devotion of the regular Orders. Cornaro had established the Theatines, one of the youngest and strictest Orders, in Padua where he was Bishop; Pinelli had introduced both Priests of the Oratory and the Jesuits in his diocese of Fermo and was himself the Protector of the Carmelities and

Carthusians. Della Rovere had brought the Jesuits to Turin; Morosini introduced into Brescia the Capuchins and the Minims, both Orders following strictly the rule of St Francis to which the latter added "a fourth vow of perpetual abstinence not only from flesh meat and fish, but also from eggs, cheese, butter and milk".[14] Bonucci had founded a convent for the Capuchins at Arezzo. Cusani, Aldobrandini and Federico Borromeo were close friends of St Philip Neri and fervent supporters of his Oratory: and Federico had subscribed heavily to the building of Neri's Chiesa Nuova and administered the last rites to St Philip on his death in 1595. In the College of Cardinals, therefore, the Pope could readily find guidance and help in his relations with the Orders and count on solid support for their activities both in Europe and the New World. Moreover, Drascovics, Cornaro, de' Rossi and Bonucci had attended the Council of Trent and had taken an influential part in its debates. They were energetic adherents of the cause of reforming the church to which they pledged all their intellectual and personal resources, having helped in the fashioning of the Tridentine decrees they were eager to see them implemented.

Sixtus was a man of action and the Cardinals he chose were selected for their skill in devising effective methods of re-invigorating the church, of restoring discipline and inspiring genuine religious devotion and zeal. No fewer than seven of his thirty-three Cardinals had held high office in the Papal administration, Castrucci in the Dataria, Aldobrandini as Auditor of the Rota (the most important papal tribunal for civil affairs), Mattei and Cusani as Auditors of the Camera, Pepoli as Clerk of the Camera; Pinelli had served as Lieutenant of the Auditor of the Camera and Gaetani as Referendary of the tribunals of the Apostolic Signature of Justice and of Grace, Morosini had been Venice's ambassador in Savoy, France, Spain and Poland, had also twice been an inter-nuncio and then papal ambassador to the Ottoman court, Sauli had served as nuncio to Naples and Portugal and Gondi as ambassador to Spain. In addition, Cornaro had been in the service of the Venetian Republic and Castrucci in that of Lucca.

Gondi had presided over the French Estates General in Paris in 1577. These men together amassed an impressive fund of political experience and brought to the Cardinal's College great skill in statecraft. Others were equally distinguished in ecclesiastical service for they included the Patriarchs of Jerusalem and Alexandria, and Archbishops of Cologne, Chieti, Genoa and Paris, ten bishops and the coadjutor of Pavia. In short, half Sixtus' promotions had already had experience of administering a diocese and were therefore fully conversant with the problems of the Church and with the need to ensure that the standards set by the Council of Trent were implemented with firmness and conviction. Some of these had been outstanding in the performance of their Episcopal duties. Cornaro had carried out a most rigorous visitation of the churches in his diocese of Verona, had convened a diocese synod on three occasions and had attended four provincial councils called by Charles Borromeo, Archbishop of Milan, della Rovere had convened and presided as Archbiship of Turin at a provincial council, Gondi had convened diocesan synods in Paris and had been most energetic in the repression of heresy and in the enforcement on his clergy of the proper performance of their ecclesiastical duties. Drascovics, Cornaro and Allen had founded seminaries for the training of clergy.

In fact, it is evident that Sixtus surrounded himself with a group of high-principled, splendidly qualified and experienced Cardinals who reinforced those who in Conclave of 1585 had chosen a Pope of humble origin, great learning, Franciscan discipline and love of simplicity and an intense and consummate devotion to religion. The Conclave and the Consistory, the various Congregations and all the ranks of papal administration were pervaded by a sense of purpose, a judicious capacity for rigorous and impartial examination of problems and a stern determination to accelerate the progress of reform which the Tridentine decrees had initiated. The character of the new Cardinals guaranteed that Sixtus' intentions would not be frustrated by opposition but would be effectively implemented with zest and enthusiasm

Nevertheless, although his choice of Cardinals was impeccable, it produced, whilst Sixtus lived, a clique based on a personal relationship to the Pope which to the outside world and posterity could appear to be little short of favouritism. Azzolini, Pallotta and Pierbenedetti all hailed from the Marches and were in a special sense the Pope's countrymen—perhaps the nucleus of an anti-Roman faction. They and Galli had served in Sixtus' household during Gregory XIII's pontificate and had shared Sixtus' eclipse; by the Pope's influence whilst Cardinal, Castrucci, Azzolini and Pallotta had obtained canonries. Bonucci had served with Sixtus when in 1565 Cardinal Boncompagni was sent as Legate to Spain to investigate the Carranza case;[15] Pinelli succeeded Sixtus as Bishop of Fermo; Pierbenedetti was consecrated by Cardinal Montalto as Sixtus then was, and Gonzaga's brother was Minister General of the Frati Minori Osservanti; Caetani was a relative of Cardinal Carpi, Sixtus V's former protector and master. Whilst none of these was unworthy of the Cardinalate, yet it does appear that Sixtus' selection was greatly influenced by his own acquaintanceship and his personal knowledge of men. It was therefore narrowly based and created the danger of forming an inner coterie of personal followers. Had the Cardinal's nephew been older or had Sixtus reigned longer, a genuine faction might have appeared in the College.[16] Yet these new Cardinals with their senior colleagues, some of whom had half-willingly elected their master, would be the kingpins of the papal administration and bear its many burdens to earn the Pope's gratitude and praise.

Perhaps the most serious criticism of Sixtus V's use of his prerogative in appointing Cardinals to the Sacred College was that he failed to make the college representative of the geographical extent of the Church. Of Sixtus' thirty-three Cardinals all but six were Italians, two of the six hailing from Lorraine, the remaining four being Spanish, Hungarian, English and Maltese respectively. Of the new Italian

Cardinals, three came from Venice, Genoa and Tuscany respectively, five Northern cities—Milan, Turin, Parma, Modena and Mantua - provided one each; four were Roman, one Bolognese and eight were citizens of the Marches. Thus more than a third of all Sixtus' elevations came from the Papal States, and these comprised almost a half of the new Italian Cardinals. Not a single new Cardinal came from Southern Italy. At his accession the Sacred College was overwhelmingly Italian; he made no attempt to change or modify its character and the representation of foreign states in the supreme governing body of a Church which claimed to span the world remained totally and undisguisedly unrepresentative. The dominance of Northern and Central Italians was riveted even more firmly on the Sacred College. The government of the Church which was stirring so determinedly to restore its claims to universality was narrowly based. As nationalism grew amongst European states, rulers were less and less inclined to acquiesce in the mediaeval unity of a Church in whose direction they had so little influence, however well it might be managed. Sixtus who wished to re-create a united Christendom under Papal control discovered no means of establishing the supremacy of Rome over the rivalries of individual states or of overcoming their resistance to the supra-national claims of the Church

    The Cardinalate was designed to be the fulcrum of the papal administration, the prime mover by which energy and momentum were transmitted to the church at large. The Cardinals met in Consistory at least once a week: they were provided with clear agenda, and there were often lengthy and sometimes acrimonious discussions. Though the Pope was almost invariably able to have his wishes accepted, he was frequently made to note the strength of the opposition and to re-examine the wisdom of his proposals. Often groups of Cardinals consulted together so as to take concerted action in the consistory and made formidable representations which even Sixtus could not neglect even though finally he over-rode them. Consistory also transacted much important business; for example, the appointment of bishops and abbots. But because of its size, the Consistory was unsuitable for the transaction of detailed business. Certain Congregations or Commissions had therefore been formed already and had an official and permanent recognition; such were the Congregations which respectively supervised the operation of the Index, directed the Roman Inquisition, spurred on the implementation of the decrees of the Council of Trent and regulated the Pope's dealings with the Bishops. Other Congregations were established from time to time to undertake particular temporary responsibilities.

Sixtus wished to extend these arrangements, to co-ordinate them into a consistent and systematic pattern so that each Congregation became a permanent organ of government with a precise constitution and with well defined duties and specific powers. By a Bull *Immensa Aeterni Dei* published in January 1588, which he himself prepared personally, fifteen congregations were recognised, five being concerned with predominantly secular responsibilities—food supplies, defence, the lightening of burdens in the Papal States, roads and water supplies, and public business—the remainder being charged with duties directly affecting the church. The four permanent Congregations with outstandingly important functions were retained, and six new ones were established to deal respectively with the affairs of the regular clergy, the supervision of rites and ceremonies the control of papal graces and favours other than those reserved to the Consistory, the affairs of the Consistory itself, the Vatican Press and the Roman University.[17] Each congregation comprised small groups of Cardinals—normally four or five—and was required to have the agreement of at least three of them before publishing any decree: they normally net weekly and had the assistance of such theologians, notaries, scholars and canonists as they required. The congregation for the Index was urged to seek the co-operation of Universities as far flung as Bologna, Louvain, Paris and Salamanca. Inevitably they removed a substantial volume of business from the deliberations of the Consistory and malevolent critics of Sixtus V accused him of elaborating this machinery of government by Congregation with that purpose in mind. This is unjust. Pastor's judgement is more acceptable, namely, that "it bore witness to his far-seeing vision and to his brilliant gifts as an administrator".[18]

Certainly this form of administration facilitated rather than impeded the Pope's personal direction of papal policies and his control of their interpretation and implementation. For example, he personally presided at the Congregation for the Inquisition and though the Congregation for the enforcement and interpretation of the Tridentine decrees was authorised to interpret doubts or difficulties in the Council's enactments on morals, discipline, judicial charges and ecclesiastical tribunals. It operated under strict instructions from the Pope and all its decrees were subject to the Pope's approval. The Congregations were vehicles for the effective implementation of papal policy under the Pope's guidance. Because of his intense desire to achieve rapid change in the spiritual direction of the church and because lengthy debates wearied him unless they produced clear decisions, and because of the clarity of his own views and his unwillingness to change them, he fashioned the instruments of government so as to give effective and speedy effect to his own policies. Many of the Cardinals resented the re-orientation and re-moulding of papal government. Some were opposed by nature and personal inclination to change: others were unwilling to sacrifice their own influence merely to allow the advance to power of the Pope's personal friends and supporters; others perceived that the increasing autocracy of papal government represented a fundamental change in its character. Cardinal Paleotti one of the Pope's contemporaries, twenty years a Cardinal, a man of principle and unadulterated integrity, a learned man an deeply respected, a traditionalist of deep-rooted conviction, considered that the dignity of the Sacred College as the Senate of the Papal States was being undermined and that the free speech and political influence of the Consistory were threatened. His views won widespread support.[19]

To do justice to Sixtus, he did not exclude opponents of his own views and he did not treat the Consistory as a nonentity. He was stubborn and unmoving in defending his policies and only those whose resistance was based on genuine conviction and matched by persistent spirit could expect attention. He would not brook obstruction though he was prepared to listen to constructive propositions even though he finally adopted few of them.

But every system of administration, however well conceived, is dependent for success on the quality of its leaders and of those who operate it. Administrators may bring to their labours personal initiative and independence of judgement and action but those who work under tight control and within strictly defined rules may shelter behind the final responsibility of their masters, avoiding genuine decisions and taking refuge in the monotonous recital of their instructions. Sixtus was able to man the Congregations with Cardinals of drive, of integrity, of vision and purpose, and during his pontificate a system which would readily have ossified, operated with energy and determination. For example, Cardinal Facchinetti, a noted Gregorian who had bitterly resisted Sixtus' election in the Conclave, but an eminent scholar of great learning, was a member of the Congregations of the Inquisition for the affairs of the Regular clergy. Cardinal Paleotti,[20] a well-connected Bolognese, a doctor of law, a Cardinal of considerable seniority—a man calculated by temperament, training and experience to irritate Sixtus—was a consistent critic of the Pope in Consistory, and yet became a member of the Congregation responsible for Consistorial business. He had served at the Council of Trent and having succeeded to the Bishopric of Bologna was most assiduous in pastoral visitations, preaching, holding diocesan councils and teaching the catechism. A close friend of Charles Borromeo and Cardinal Sirleto, he had worked diligently on the revision of the Index and had convened a Provincial Council at Bologna as recently as 1586. His immense talents and his undisputed adherence to the interests of the Church far outweighed any personal reluctance of the Pope to admit him to the inner circles of the Sacred College.[21] Even his opposition to the transfer of the abbey of Farfa to the Pope's nephew on the death of Cardinal Farnese did not remove him from Sixtus V's counsels.[22] The energetic Castagna, the noble Genoan, who was to succeed Sixtus on the papal throne, the Spaniard Deza, the noble Roman Colonna, all found themselves immersed in the work of the Congregations. They systems was no refuge for sycophants: it demanded and used merit, natural talent and loyalty to the church.

The Congregation for the enforcement of the Tridentine decrees, by way of example, was directed by Cardinal Carafa. A member of the most influential aristocratic family in Naples who had entered the Papal service under the Carafa Pope, Paul IV(1555-59), he had shared the disgrace of the family when the Pope's nephews were accused of the most desperate and heinous crimes for which they were finally sentenced to death. The Cardinal had turned religiously to the study of Greek; tutored by Cardinal Sirleto, he quickly acquired a great reputation for his scholarship: he was made a Cardinal in 1568 at the age of thirty and subsequently began the task of revising the Vulgate. A man of immense religious fervour and unflagging devotion and now in the prime of life, he was profoundly respected in the Sacred College for his learning, his patience, sound judgement and imperturbability. He was often chosen as leader to make representations to the Pope on controversial subjects. In spite of his refusal to attend the Consistory, called for the promotion to the Cardinalate of the Pope's nephew, Carafa[23] was appointed Cardinal Prefect of the Congregation of the Council in 1586 after serving on the Congregation of the Index and on several ad hoc Congregations, and he brought inspiration as well as organised and sustained method to its work. For him regulations were intended not to furnish the papal archives but to be systematically implemented. The Council of Trent had directed that Diocesan Synods should be held annually and Provincial Councils triennially: Cardinal Carafa as Prefect of the Congregation wrote to the Papal Nuncios instructing them to ensure that these were regularly summoned in accordance with the Council's decree, and evolved a system of reminders by which Bishops promptly had their memories jolted if the appropriate interval passed without the Council or Synod being convened. These Provincial Councils were obliged to submit reports to the Congregation and the Prefect studied, corrected and annotated them before returning them to the Province for action. When the Bishops of Tours and Bordeaux published the reports without the Congregation's amendments, they were sharply and unequivocally reproved. Patriarchs, primates, archbishops and bishops before being consecrated or taking up their diocesan duties were obliged to make a personal visit to Rome and present themselves officially to the Pope. Only for very special reasons and with precise papal sanction were they allowed to and send a deputy of appropriate rank, and this mode of control had a very salutary effect, especially in the Empire, though it provoked some friction with Philip II of Spain, always jealous of his royal prerogatives. Bishops were also obliged to visit Rome at prescribed intervals after their appointment, these varying according to the distances from the Vatican at which they resided. For example, Italian bishops were required to make this *ad limina* visit once every three years, Irish bishops once every four years. The interval for an African bishop was five years.[24][25] They then reported on their duties, the discipline of their clergy and the state of the people in their care. Failure to fulfil these obligations was traced by the Prefect, and the Bishops of Bagnoreggio, Senigallia and Camerino were ordered to complete penitential pilgrimages for not having paid their *ad limina* visits within the prescribed time. In turn, the Bishops were ordered to enforce residence on parish priests and to investigate resignations from holy orders to ensure that the reasons given were genuine and sufficient. The Congregations also directed them to enforce discipline on the Regular Orders, especially to ensure that the clausura was thoroughly observed on nunneries, that the regular clergy took communion in their own churches and that instances of those living outside their monasteries were closely investigated. The Congregation also obliged the Bishops to insist on church festivals being properly observed within their dioceses and to ensure that communion was made available to the laity as well as to the clergy every day, without exception. Through the work of the Congregation, therefore, clergy, both secular and regular, were made to realise the reality of the church's concern for the proper observance of discipline and good order.

The Congregation of the Inquisition similarly continued its dedicated pursuit of heresy, witchcraft, divination and prohibited books. When, in 1588, the system of fifteen congregations had been established, it was the largest and the most carefully chosen of all, and evidently worked most closely under the Pope's personal direction. He himself frequently attended its weekly sessions. It included Cardinal Madruzzo, a middle-aged man at the height of his considerable powers, a Cardinal for more than a quarter of a century, Bishop of Trent for more than twenty years, and papal legate to the Emperor. He knew well the continuing problem of heresy in Northern Italy and having taken a considerable part in the proceedings of the Council of Trent, he was a most enthusiastic protagonist of its decrees. Facchinetti, the fierce and outspoken Gregorian, now completely committed to the work of reform in Rome and standing on the threshold of the Papacy itself, was also a number and brought his scholarship and experience to its operations with the assistance of Cesare Speciani, Bishop of Novara.

These were notable reformers who perpetuated the pervading spirit of Borromeo. They had already reformed their respective dioceses and were fully experienced in the deficiencies to be discovered and the reforms to be introduced. They drew up a detailed plan for the examination of the ecclesiastical administration of the City, including the establishments of the Regular Orders, universities, colleges and seminaries and the main departments of papal government, and named a Commission for each of the nine headings under which the investigation was to be undertaken.[26] They failed to reckon with the Pope's sense of urgency. The remaining two were Cardinals promoted by Sixtus—both members of Regular Orders. Bernerio was a stern Dominican who had been Inquisitor in Genoa and Protector of the Servite Order, and Boccafuoco, a member of Sixtus' own Order and a Professor of theology in the Universities of Perugia, Padua and Rome, was acknowledged to be a scholar and preacher of outstanding merit. He gave the sternest possible admonition to every bishop to fulfil the obligation of residence as defined in the Tridentine decrees and made it evident that no exceptions were to be permitted. Even Cardinals were to comply with these Decrees. He also issued a Bull to state that the Church would not look with favour on anyone who took the sacrament of the Eucharist between Palm Sunday and the end of Easter week outside his own parish unless he had the licence of his own parish priest.[27]

Yet, perhaps surprisingly, no outbursts of persecution marked Sixtus' reign. Only five sentences of death were passed in Rome, there was only one auto-da-fé outside the Dominican church of Santa Maria sopra Minerva and on that occasion only four were condemned to death, twelve abjuring their apostasy. Of the four who were condemned to death, two were guilty of heresy, one was a Franciscan friar who, with the support of forged bulls, posed as the Patriarch of Jerusalem and the other was a priest who had violated the seal of confession. But while the Inquisition in Rome sought no spectacular activity, Sixtus missed no opportunity of establishing its authority in foreign states. He succeeded in having two men against whom the Inquisition had laid charges extradited from the Low Countries. He had two suspects arrested in the Spanish possessions of Naples and the Duchy of Milan respectively and brought to Rome for investigation. He had an escaped prisoner arrested in the Tyrol and brought him to Rome even though he was a Venetian citizen. Perhaps, most remarkable of all, he induced the Viceroy of Naples to allow a representative of the Holy Office in Rome to attend the trials of heretics held in the Kingdom. In Rome he extended the office of the

Inquisition by adding a prison to its buildings. He established new tribunals at Ascoli, Fermo, Camerino and Aosta. He confirmed the bull of Paul IV which made it a capital offence for anyone to celebrate Mass who had not been ordained and he reserved to himself appeals in matters of faith. The suppression of astrologers and soothsayers was pursued with particular intensity.[28] The work of the Inquisition cannot be justly assessed by the number of cases brought to its tribunals. Moreover, the Holy Office preferred conversion and recantation and was often content to intensify its hunt for heretics and to be satisfied with an undertaking of future conformity. The tribunals were generally concerned with the obdurate and cases of repeated apostasy. There is no reason to doubt that under Sixtus' personal direction and initiative the work of the Inquisition continued without interruption. Effective and persistent repression often forestalled more overt heretical activity.

The congregation of the Inquisition operated in a firm partnership with that for the Index. The latter consisted of five members, comprising Marcantonio Colonna, a close friend of Sixtus for many years, and four of Sixtus' own promotions, Rovere, Lénoncourt, Allen, and Ascanio Colonna, a member of one of the younger branches of that famous family and a relative therefore of Cardinal Marcantonio. The elder Colonna belonged to one of the most famous families in Rome, he was Librarian to the Vatican and was a member of the Commission engaged in the correction of the Vulgate.[29] Rovere came of a family which included two Popes and seven Cardinals in its ranks. He was a notable Greek and Latin scholar and a boy genius in poetry and rhetoric was developed into an outstanding orator who preached at the funerals of Henry II and Charles IX. He was the Protector of the Franciscan Conventuals, and amassed a library of quite exceptional value. Lénoncourt was an influential Frenchman, bishop in two French dioceses, eminently experienced to advise on dealing with French Protestants, having already been on a mission to persuade Henry of Navarre to enhance his future claim to the French crown.

Allen, an English nobleman who had been declared guilty of treason by Queen Elizabeth and obliged to flee from one European country to another, had founded two seminaries, and presided over one for fourteen years; the English College in Rome. Finally Ascanio Colonna, son of the hero of Lepanto, was a brilliant scholar in Greek and Latin and took his master's degree in Philosophy, theology and Canon and Civil Law in the Spanish Universities of Salamanca and Alcalà. He was created with a phenomenal memory, acquired a large library (possibly that of the deceased Cardinal Sirleto) and was widely respected for his generosity and liked for his open house.[30] Even more than the Congregation for the Inquisition, this was a Congregation in which the influence of Sixtus dominated, all but on of its members being his creation. He could count without reservation on their loyalty. Nevertheless, it was a Congregation whose learning, reforming zeal and varied experience gave it an indisputable capacity for its task of surveying the products of all the printing presses in Europe and made it well qualified to decide on the inclusion in the Index of books, authors or publishers with calm, stoical judgement free from fanaticism. Including a Frenchman, an Englishman and a former student of two Spanish universities, it was comparatively free of Italian bias.

During the sixteenth century the Press had greatly increased its importance and influence. The Reformation itself had relied very substantially on its capacity for producing books and circulating them over a very wide area. Writers and printers were men of considerable social standing and the printing trade, as to-day, exercised political influence out of proportion to its numbers of its revenues. Succeeding religious disputes produced a demand for the printing of argument and counter-argument. The Renaissance created an intellectual readership eager to be engaged in controversy. Preaching from the pulpit enabled simplified versions of these arguments to be circulated in wider circles, and though peasants, and artisans generally were often illiterate and sometimes apathetic, amongst them were substantial numbers who were better-informed and had a taste for sifting information and arriving at independent conclusions.

Religion was common ground on which all classes met. The cities and small towns, Rome and Milan, Bologna or Siena, Macerata or Caserta, richly endowed with churches and monasteries, effectively organised around civic centres, were well planned to preserve a regular exchange of information. Control of the press therefore was an essential prerogative shared by church and state.

The Index of Prohibited Books had been found by the Church to be an essential weapon of control; by the majority of clergy and laity alike, excepting the free-thinkers and the curious. It also a conveniently marked with firmness and clarity the limits which thirst for knowledge should observe. Nevertheless, acceptance in principle and agreement in detail were as widely separated then as now. The Index published by Paul IV 1557 had been subjected to sustained and often bitter criticism; the Council of Trent was agreed on extensive modifications. Sixtus in 1587 ordered a new edition to be prepared and immediately sought the assistance of the Universities of Paris, Salamanca, Alcalá and Coimbra. A Bull was prepared ready for the publication of the new List, but this had not been completed when Sixtus died. Sixtus ordered those members of the Congregation of the Index who knew Hebrew to undertake a revision of the Talmud. The whole Congregation also contained the examination of Jewish books which Gregory XIII had inaugurated.[31]

It would, however, be a great mistake to think that Sixtus contented himself with the repression of heresy or with preventing the circulation of false doctrine. He shared deeply and with conviction the Franciscan veneration for scholarship; as the editor of St Ambrose he favoured research into Biblical exegesis, the traditions of the Church and the works of the Fathers. He believed with profound sincerity that every generation had an obligation to enlarge the theological and philosophical heritage which had been bequeathed to it by the past. Sixtus' most ambitious project to which he devoted much of his personal attention throughout his reign and on which he regularly worked far into the night, was the production of a new edition of the Latin bible brought completely up to date and textually accurate so as to warrant recognition by the Church as the only authentic version of the Scriptures. This was an academic exercise of unprecedented difficulty. The Council of Trent had recommended the publication of just such a text. The Council was well aware that a large number of Latin texts of the bible existed and that printed versions had multiplied greatly during the previous century so that confusion had become widespread, and divergent readings of the text gave rise to serious differences of interpretation and application. Under the influence of Cardinal Cervini (elected Pope Marcellus II in 1555) Sirleto set to work on a revision of the Greek text of the Old Testament and subsequently Maggiorano joined him on a comparable revision of the New Testament. As the Council of Trent prepared for its final sessions, Manutius and a Commission of four Cardinals were engaged in the production of an amended Latin Bible and this they completed in 1565. Pius V, loyally anxious to fulfil the Council's intention as quickly as possible, established another Commission charged with the production of an amended Vulgate, but though it was able to make some progress it encountered difficulty in finding a suitable press for printing its work, and the new edition never appeared.

During his examination of the works of St Ambrose, Sixtus V, then Cardinal Montalto, noticed that many of Ambrose's quotations from the scriptures did not completely correspond with those in the current editions. Knowing that the Vulgate (in Latin), the work of St Jerome, a contemporary of St Ambrose, was based largely on the Septuagint Greek text of the Hebrew Bible dating from the second century before Christ, Montalto examined the Septuagint more closely. His own knowledge of Greek was negligible. When in May, 1585, only a month after Sixtus' election, Cardinal Sirleto died and his work on the Old Testament came to a premature end, fresh measures were needed if the Council's plan for a definitive text of the Vulgate were to be completed. In November, 1586, Sixtus established a Commission under the Presidency of Cardinal Carafa, including Cardinal Allen and Robert Bellarmine, a noted Jesuit, to produce a new edition of the Vulgate which would, when completed, become the sole authentic edition recognised by the Church. This would enable Carafa use his own work on the Septuagint (which was now in its final stages), to complete Sirleto's work on the Old Testament and to bring it up to date. To facilitate the work Sixtus had the manuscript Codex Amiatinus brought from Monte Amiato in Tuscany; this was the oldest text of the Vulgate extant and was reckoned the best text available. Carafa was to concentrate on the production of an equally commanding version of the New Testament, and both Testaments together would be published as the new Vulgate. Colonna was probably the best exegetical scholar alive at that time; he was painstaking and conscientious. There could be no doubt of his orthodoxy.

Two years later, in November 1588, the work was complete, but when Carafa presented it to the Pope, Sixtus was overwhelmed by the number of alterations made. In a violent interview, the Pope launched totally unwarranted attacks on the Commission's work and ordered the Cardinal from the room. Sixtus estimated, probably correctly, the dangerous impact Carafa's work would have on the Protestant world, which would hail the new Vulgate as a damaging admission of the shallow foundations on which the teaching of the Church rested. In an era in which Renaissance scholarship and criticism dominated philosophical thought, every revelation of error was liable to become a perilous dagger in the body of a Church which claimed infallibility. From that point expediency superseded scholarship.

On the following day the Pope ordered all the work done to be submitted to him. From then on, with the assistance of an Augustinian monk and a Jesuit, he read everything and decided personally the text to be printed. By June 1589 he had completed the work as far as the Apocalypse, and five months later the whole of the Old Testament was in print—at the newly established Vatican Press. Taking wholly irrational and incredible risks, the work was sent to print before revisions could be completed and the whole text was presented to the Cardinals and Ambassadors and placed on sale in May 1590. The unfortunate Carafa warned the Pope of the inevitable consequences of this frenetic pace and expressed his apprehension that the Papacy and its Curia would be disgraced. Sixtus retorted by threatening to summon him before the Inquisition. Undaunted, Carafa was instructed by the Cardinals of the Index to make the most spirited remonstrances to the Pope. Three months later Sixtus was dead. The Curia was left to survey the results of the Pope's obstinacy and to repair the damage.

In fact, this edition of 1590 included a very large number of simple printer's errors—mistakes which to-day a proof-reader would eliminate. But there were also errors of much greater significance: much of the earlier scholarly work of the Commission was cast on one side: where the Commission had used amendments to the Antwerp Bible of 1583, these were removed by the Pope: it is said he lent too much authority to the Louvain Bible of 1546 merely because he knew it best; he accepted many additions made during the previous centuries which properly formed no part of the original text, and correspondingly he omitted phrases whose inclusion was warranted. This was Sixtus at his worst—impatient, unreasonably dogmatic, irascible and ungrateful. Having chosen an excellent and erudite Cardinal to head a team of distinguished scholars, he was incapable of accepting their conclusions or of spending time in resolving disagreement. Relying on his own judgement and ignoring his own limitations, he rejected their considered judgements as if with contempt. Having set himself an impossible objective, he refused to admit defeat, but proceeded inexorably to an outcome which was inevitably disastrous.[32]

Sixtus had the Bull prepared which was to have declared his new edition of the Vulgate the only authoritative version. Publication of unauthorised versions was to be forbidden. The 1590 version was not to be re-printed during the following ten years except at the Vatican

Press and then only in absolute conformity with the Sistine Edition under pain of excommunication. But this Bull was never published. A few days after the Pope's death, the Cardinals suspended the sale of the Vulgate and the Bull. Copies already sold were recalled as far as possible and work was begun on a fresh edition. In 1592 when Clement VIII (previously Cardinal Aldobrandini, promoted by Sixtus V) had succeeded to the Pontificate, the new edition embodying more than 3,000 corrections, was published as a revision to the Sistine version. This "Sixto-Clementine" edition became the standard version of the Latin Bible in the ancient Vulgate edition until the recent New Vulgate.[33]

Not all Sixtus' academic enterprises ended so badly. A noteworthy literary achievement of his reign was the amendment and republication of the Martyrology and the publication of the first two volumes of the *Annals*, both dedicated to Sixtus; all the work of Cesare Baronio, one of the leading members of Philip Neri's community, and from 1584 the Librarian of the Vallicelliana. Baronio was a profoundly pious and ascetic man, a devoted follower of Neri, firmly attached to the philanthropic work of the Oratorians among the poor and the sick, who rejected repeated offers of favour, including ecclesiastical benefices and preferment. In 1582, Cardinal Montalto had commissioned him to write a life of St Ambrose as part of Montalto's revised edition of St Ambrose's work and this Baronio completed in 1584, though publication was delayed until after Sixtus V's accession. The Pope indeed offered him a pension which he at first refused, though subsequently he accepted it on the understanding that it should finance a Commentary on the Acts of the Apostles. Baronio's work on the *Annals* was of much greater and more extensive significance. Between 1559 and 1574 under the direction of Flacius Illyricus, described as "the most learned, militant and quarrelsome churchman of the sixteenth century",[34] with the help of the Centuriators of Magdeburg, the Lutherans produced the *Historia Ecclesiae Christi*, "the first serious and scholarly survey of the history of the Church, tracing with zeal and care the slow corruption of the Church from the New Testament times into the Middle Ages".[35] Baronio, in the *Annals*, produced the answer of the Catholic Church—these were published with its authority and support. Using the resources of the Vatican Library, Baronio was able to take advantage of the liberties Flacius had taken with original texts and redress the balance and justify the Church. Subsequent generations learned that Baronio's work also was biased and inaccurate, but for many years the brilliant persuasiveness of the *Annals* was acknowledged and their authority respected.[36] Sixtus arranged that they should be published at the newly established Vatican Press. Also published from 1588 onwards were the Works of St Bonaventure in seven volumes compiled by Cardinal Boccafuoco on Sixtus' instructions and printed with his authority. Bonaventure was the most famous theologian, preacher and Minister General of the Franciscan Order of the thirteenth century and the author of an official biography of its founder. Other writers of lesser note also enjoyed the Pope's encouragement and assistance, but they were required to be unequivocally orthodox in their views and incontestably conforming to the conclusions of the Council of Trent. Criticism had to be muted, originality was circumscribed, and authors were always conscious of the eagle eye of authority scanning and sifting all their works. Sixtus was particularly apprehensive and suspicious of books published in foreign languages, especially Oriental tongues of which obviously he understood little if anything. A bull was passed, therefore, specifically to ensure that books in Arabic, Turkish, Persian and Chaldean were not published unless they had first been examined by the Cardinals of The Congregation for the Index.[37]

One triumphant weapon of this tight censorship was the Vatican Press. The work of publishing and that of printing went hand in hand, but the former was parent of the latter and of greater value.[38] At this period the collection, transcription and translation of manuscripts, the examination of their dating and authorship and the study of their content and philosophy was incessant. Access to a press made the publication of this work more efficient. Rome was badly equipped with presses and much of the work done in its richly endowed libraries had to be printed elsewhere. As early as the beginning of the sixteenth century Venice had more than 150 presses, many of them internationally famous for the remarkable quality of production, their experimentation with various types of print and their advanced techniques. Rome, it would appear, though it had more than twenty book shops, a lively and extensive coterie of authors and an exceptionally numerous book market, had no more than five presses.[39] Even the publication of a corrected edition of the Vulgate had been prevented by the absence of adequate printing facilities.[40]

Sixtus, by personal experience, was a scholar who knew the thrill of gazing at the text of works composed in antiquity and revered through the centuries: he was an author who had had the satisfaction of going into print, and he understood the value of preachers' words being preserved for posterity. Now he recalled student nights spent under the dim light near the altar of the monastery at Fermo, and was driven to present a worthy offering to generations of students who would follow his example.

On 1586, therefore, Sixtus took the decisive step of establishing the Vatican Press. The following year he appointed the Venetian Domenico Basa to direct it,[41] and when in 1588 he brought into existence the fifteen Congregations he named one specifically to be responsible for the supervision of the publication of religious books and the proper use of manuscript material.[42] Its members comprised the formidable Carafa, the French Cardinal Joyeuse, and three of Sixtus V's own creations—the Franciscan Boccafuoco, the Greek and Latin scholar, Cardinal Gonzaga, Patriarch of Jerusalem, and Giustiniani, the Papal Treasurer.[43] Under such direction and with its unique relationship to the Vatican Library and the papal court, the Press quickly accelerated the production of religious books and achieved an enviable reputation throughout Catholic Circles.

Meanwhile, Sixtus V, following in the footsteps of his predecessors since Pius IV, maintained an enthusiastic and sustained interest in the development of the Vatican Library. The collection had already reached quite exceptional dimensions and included many original manuscripts, medieval and Renaissance publications, and was unique in the world's literary resources. It was used intensively almost every day by large numbers of serious students and was quite invaluable to the Church and the world. Sixtus built new accommodation for the Library[44] at the centre of the Vatican Palace across the Cortile Belvedere. He enlarged its collection and encouraged some of the best scholars in the city to assist it, including the celebrated Baronio, who in 1597, after Sixtus' death became its Chief Librarian and directed its development with great distinction. Sixtus was also keenly interested that church documents and manuscripts should be carefully preserved and so he ordered that in all the states and districts of the Papal States, the cities of Rome and Bologna excepted, Archives should be established and that a director of archives should be appointed with privileges and prerogatives sufficient for the discharge of his duties.[45] Similarly, he issued a bull forbidding the withdrawal or moving of books from the library of the Franciscan Observants and specifying orders for their preservation.[46]

One other facet of the re-invigoration of the Church which received Sixtus V's assistance and encouragement was the development and strengthening of the cult of its historic traditions. These traditions strengthened the Church's authority and preserved its teaching. They and the ritual in which they were enshrined made people amenable to successive generations of leadership, and critical of innovation. They created a spontaneous atmosphere of docility and acceptance, of contentment and satisfaction. For priesthood and laity alike, church festivals and celebrations provided opportunities for participation and active involvement so that together they shared the satisfaction of common achievement. They were therefore a fundamental element in the life of the historic church.

One of the traditions of the Church in East and West was the conferment of the title of Doctor of the Church on those who were outstandingly eminent for their sanctity, their orthodoxy, and above all for their learning, particularly as evidenced by their writings. Until the sixteenth century they were limited to writers of later antiquity. They numbered only eight: Ambrose, Jerome, Augustine, Gregory the Great, Basil the Great, Gregory Nazianzen, John Chrysostom and Athanasius. Pius V had added Thomas Aquinas, Sixtus added the Franciscan St Bonaventure, Aquinas's contemporary.[47] Bonaventure's most famous writings were the *Itinerarium Mentis in Deum* and his *Commentary on the Sentences of Peter Lombard*—one of the essential texts of the schools.[48] His festival was to be observed on 14th July every year.[49] Sixtus' intention evidently was to extend Pius V's recognition of mediaeval scholars by adding to a list which was quite selective. Choosing from the previous millennium a candidate for elevation to such an honour must always be a thankless and unenviable task, but posterity has judged St Bonaventure worthy of that honour. He encouraged Bernadine's devotion to the Name of Jesus by authorising in 1597 the invocation "Praise be Jesus Christ". Sixtus canonised St Didacus, an Observant Franciscan professor with an annual festival celebrated on 12th November. He instituted festivals to commemorate the Presentation of the Blessed Virgin Mary in the Temple (21st November); for St Francis de Paola, the founder of the Minims, who had been canonised in 1519; for St Nicholas of Tolentino (10th September), a pious Augustinian preacher and hermit of the thirteenth century, who was canonised in 1446; for St Antony of Padua (13th June); for St Januarius (19th September), the patron saint of Naples, a martyr of the third to fourth century; for St Peter the Martyr (29th April), a Dominican inquisitor of the thirteenth century who was assassinated whilst journeying from Como to Milan; and finally for St Placid (5th October), a notable disciple of St Benedict. All these feasts except those of St Januarius and St Placid were to be celebrated by the clergy with the reciting of both the major hours of the day,

Lauds and Vespers, and the minor hours, Prime, Terce, Sext, None and Compline.[50] The feasts of St Januarius and St Placid entailed the celebration of the minor hours only.[51] Sixtus also decreed the papal chapels in the basilicas and other churches of the city should be used for celebration on the Sundays of Lent and Advent and on other holy days.[52] Individual Orders of Regular Clergy were put under pressure to honour their saints on the appropriate festival days. For example, the brothers and sisters of the Reformed Congregation of the Discalced Carmelites were instructed to recite the canonical hours in accordance with the reformed Roman Breviary and to celebrate the saints of their own order.

The addition of festivals to the calendar and the desire to instil greater dignity into the liturgy threw into prominence the part which music should play in church worship. Some at the Council of Trent would have totally excluded music as a distracting triviality belonging to the secular world, just as they forbade applause in church, but the Council as a whole was less dogmatic. After prolonged discussion the Council declared that profane and flippant music should be avoided and that music in church should be sung in such a way as to be both audible and intelligible to the congregation. History has not informed us of Sixtus' skill or taste in music. Nevertheless, as a Pope who subscribed very readily to the views of the Council, he was obliged to give attention and thought to the development of church music. Moreover, although the celebrated Palestrina was not appointed as Master of the Apostolic Chapel in 1586 when Giovanni Antonio Merlo was preferred, he was appointed *Compositore della Cappella*.[53] Palestrina was already Italy's foremost and most prolific composer and was involved in Vatican musical affairs in a variety of capacities for almost forty years. His appealing music and his fluency of phrasing enabled him to advance the wishes of the Council of Trent to a notable degree. His melodies were dignified and sonorous, his contrapuntal sequences were arranged so as not to obscure but to enhance the phrases they were intended to accentuate. He was able, in fact, to demonstrate that musical creativity was in no sense incompatible with audibility, and that music and words could be happy and effective partners without rivalry. Sixtus himself would have been involved at this time in securing and enlarging the powers of the Cardinal Protector, the College, the singers and the Papal chapels.[54] Then, as now, choirs were not always distinguished for their tranquillity, and some twenty years earlier Palestrina himself had been engaged in the reform of the Papal choirs. Now Sixtus evidently wished to enlarge the authority of the Cardinal Protector and to arm him with the appropriate powers. Whatever Sixtus' personal contribution to the development and reform of church music, that of certain of his Cardinals is indisputable. Galli, Bernerio and Boccafuoco were all musically inclined; the first two provided funds for their Cathedral choirs from their own pockets and the last presented a new organ to the church of Sant'Eusebio. The Vatican's reception of the latest of the Renaissance arts was greatly to its credit and advantage. Italian church music which had owed much to Flemish sources during the middle of the century, established its own distinctive style and quality. Italy, and particularly the Vatican and the other papal churches in Rome became pre-eminent. If Sixtus did no more, he shared willingly in this exuberant explosion of musical achievement.

In the church's ecclesiastical administration bishops were the lynch-pins, the indispensable links between the Pope at one end of the chain and the parish priest at the other. This had been recognised by the Council of Trent and by many writers, such as Contarini, the author of *De Officio Episcopi* (1516), who tried to paint the picture of the ideal bishop, the manifold qualities necessary for success.[55] The Bishop was responsible for the doctrinal guidance and stimulation of the clergy, for impressing on them the doctrine of the Catholic faith, for maintaining reverential respect for unchanging truth, for inspiring in them a profound and unshakeable regard for the value of the individual, for stimulating love, consideration and the amelioration of suffering. They were also armed with extensive powers of judgement: they had to adjudicate between rival disputants in the church, to determine claims made by lay interests on Church rights or property, they had to licence teachers and books, and to investigate the affairs of a whole range of charities. They needed to be men of character and stature, capable of exercising decisive influence in social and political affairs without becoming ensnared in partisan intrigue. They were not only bulwarks of the state, they were to be also effective and persuasive upholders of social order. The deterioration in the episcopate, and the growth of corruption and worldliness within it had contributed to a considerable extent to the decline of the Catholic Church in the sixteenth century. There was, however, much religious feeling of genuine depth, much goodwill and concern for human welfare. Restoration of integrity and intellectual and spiritual quality to the episcopate would be the basis of the recovery by the church of its pristine power and influence. Consequently, the selection of bishops and their advancement with due preparation for diocesan responsibility were two of Sixtus V's most exacting and important tasks. Bishops were appointed in a plenary session of Consistory and a special Congregation existed to determine dispute involving their jurisdiction, claims for immunity put forward by them or by appellants against them. During his five-year pontificate Sixtus appointed twenty bishops in the Papal States and the papal enclave of Benevento where his right of appointment was unfettered. Each was an exemplary choice. One was the transfer from the diocese of Cagli to that of Fano, an important see adjacent to the Duchy of Urbino, of Giulio Ottinelli mentioned above as a reformer of his own diocese, who was employed by Sixtus to undertake the visitation of all the churches and colleges in Rome and subsequently as Nuncio to the Imperial Court. Another of the choices was Antonio Maria Galli, the Pope's private prelate, treasurer and secretary, who was raised to the Cardinalate a month later. Six of the bishops appointed were from the regular orders, one a Dominican and five from Sixtus' own order of the Conventuals.[56] This recognition of the Religious Orders was, however, balanced by the appointment of six secular priests, including an Auditor of the Rota, the supreme Vatican law court. Other appointments included a clerk from Pesaro who was a doctor of theology, a canon of the Vatican and a vicar of the church of Pesaro; in one instance note is made that Marcus Antonius Bizonus was only in minor orders but he was a clerk of the Roman court, and a notary of the consistory.

The number of promotions assigned to members of his own Order and to men who hailed from the Marches has often been used to accuse Sixtus of unjustifiably favouring his Order and his own native country, a form of patronage if not of corruption. There is, of course, no doubt that Sixtus wished to encourage the Regular Orders and to make the best use possible of their resources in reforming and invigorating the church. It would be understandable that in selecting men for promotion to bishoprics he should rely on ecclesiastics he knew or about whom he could obtain reliable and critical information. Neither should it be thought that an Order such as his—one of the largest established Orders—was deficient in men of devotion, energy, scholarship and a profound experience of the needs of Italian cities and communities: friars when genuinely motivated by sincere convictions and deep-rooted loyalty to their Order, had an exceptional skill and an intimate acquaintance with the influence of religion on normal secular life. There is no evidence that the friars who were promoted bishops by Sixtus failed to fulfil his expectations. Moreover, the numbers of bishops in the Papal States and Benevento chosen from the Orders of regular clergy by Sixtus was no more than the average for the period 1565 to the end of the century. On this criterion both Friars Minor and Dominicans had escaped from the disrepute under which they had suffered in earlier decades. The number of Franciscan bishops was not without precedent for although it was the highest for any five-year period in the sixteenth century, yet it was equalled by Dominican appointments in the quinquennium 1565–70. More important than any of these facts, advancement to the episcopate from the Regular Orders was a prudent and realistic method of increasing understanding between the regular and the secular clergy and of diminishing rivalry between the two. Disputes between their respective jurisdictions had been almost continuous through the century: measures which could terminate them were of very great importance.[57] In fact, Sixtus promoted to bishoprics men of quality, scholarship and energy, men whose views and religious attitudes corresponded closely to his own. He had enemies enough without; at least, he could save himself from feuds and disagreements with his own followers. He was carefully promoting unity by drawing the ecclesiastical community together, by selecting for promotion men who in fundamentals were in agreement with his own ambitions for the renewal of the church.

Nevertheless, it does appear that Sixtus insufficiently appreciated the difficulties under which bishops operated, even though he himself had had responsibility for two moderately-sized dioceses, Sant'Agata and Fermo, for eleven years. In his determination to increase the central resources of the Papacy, especially the treasury in the Castel Sant'Angelo, he neglected to see that his bishops and their clergy received sufficient funds to enable the reform of the church to be pursued with the thoroughness and the speed he thought necessary. In this he was less liberal to his bishops than to his architects. He did not adequately recognise the extent to which inflation and rising prices added to their difficulties and curbed their resources. Moreover, his concern with the maintenance of the Pope's temporal powers within his dominion deterred him from resolving inevitable friction between the bishops and his own officials responsible for the central departments of his government.

The position of many of the reforming bishops was exceedingly difficult. They were instructed to be resident both by the Tridentine decrees and by the Papal Court. If they wished to keep contact with Rome their expenses were heavy; for example, Cardinal Paleotti's visit to Rome for the Conclave of 1585 cost him 6,000 lire.[58] Although their revenues were often considerable, their dioceses were encumbered with equally burdensome charges, such as pensions paid to former holders of their office or other impoverished bishops.[59] Many of their clergy had been granted directly by the Papal Court privileges and favours which reduced the income of the diocesan treasury.[60] The reforms which these bishops attempted to effect generally formed part of the implementation of the Tridentine decrees, and were entirely in conformity with papal policy and often were initiated under papal directions, yet the cost of carrying them into effect was usually not matched by any allocation of funds from the Treasury and frequently entailed additional expenditure charged against a fixed or even diminishing income.[61] The founding of seminaries and the establishment of diocesan libraries and archives were projects which were strongly supported by the Papal authorities, but the cost of implementing them fell on the bishops, generally without assistance from papal funds.[62] Parish clergy were often in a similar position and many churches were closed simply because none of the clergy was prepared to take them on account of their inadequate revenues.[63] So, far from rescuing such bishops from these financial pitfalls, the Papal Court often added to them by raising additional taxes to pay for projects such as the re-building St Peter's[64] and by using its own officials to collect its levies even though the clergy were unable to pay their dues to the diocese.[65] Indeed, some of the clergy in the diocese of Bologna were placed under interdict for failing to pay taxes to the Papal Court.[66] As today, central government in pursuit of progressive social policies, frequently enlarges the responsibilities falling on local authority but fails to increase the grants by which these responsibilities are financed. In the sixteenth century, Italian dioceses were charged with implementing the Decrees of the Council and the policies of the Popes and yet were denied funds adequate for the purpose. Both bishops than and local authorities today face the dilemma of failing to reach the standards set by central government except by increasing local levies and provoking local discontent. Both are driven to expedients designed to minimise the local burden by spreading it over as wide a field as possible.

The administration of the temporalities of a diocese was in any event a burdensome chore, which could only be efficiently carried out if additional and specially qualified staff were added to the diocese and this greatly distracted the bishop from his spiritual duties. Cardinal Paleotti, with the support of many of his colleagues, notably St Charles Borromeo, advocated the separation of responsibility for the temporal affairs of the dioceses and the appointment of separate officers to deal with them[67]—a proposition naturally unacceptable to the Papal Court. This divergence of the temporal interests of the Papacy from its spiritual responsibilities produced frequent and violent conflicts between these bishops and the independent administration of the Papal Court. For example, Papal Legates were often instructed to intervene in purely domestic affairs where Papal interests were involved and in one instance in Bologna the Legate imprisoned one of the bishop's notaries.[68]

Because ecclesiastical boundaries frequently did not coincide with the network of state frontiers, these bishops were regularly involved in disputes with the secular authorities. For example, the diocese of Bologna extended to parishes within the Grand-Duchy of Tuscany and the Duchy of Ferrara.[69] Even within Bologna itself the bishop had repeated disputes with the City authorities and the Pope's Governor there.

Even his purely ecclesiastical responsibilities had pitfalls for the bishop. The bishop of Bologna was prevented from appointing to any of his benefices clergy who were not Bolognese.[70] His attempts to establish his authority over the hospitals and rest houses for the sick, beggars and orphans (of which there were thirty in the city and a total of ninety in the diocese[71]) in order to enable him to discharge his responsibilities for welfare an relief met with considerable resistance. He had many difficulties in his own Chapter,[72] he found himself entangled in conflicts with the Inquisition.[73] Above all, in bishoprics generally, the effective independence of the Regular Orders from his control and jurisdiction constituted a perpetual threat to his authority, frequently invalidated his efforts at reform and on occasions produced scandalous disputes. In Bologna there were fifty churches where regular clergy had responsibility for the parishes.[74] Many of the Regular Orders had similar responsibilities in other places; they were authorised to preach, to administer the sacraments, to hear confessions and grant pardons; their preaching was generally of a high standard and drew large congregations to their churches. Between such parishes and those for which the bishop and his clergy were responsible there was often considerable rivalry or animosity. The Jesuits were particularly jealous of their wide-ranging privileges and their independence of Episcopal controls. This system by which spiritual duties were shared by the Episcopal organisation and the regular orders was wasteful of effort and resources, produced much confusion, competition and serious friction, and probably was one of the most serious obstacles to reform.

Sixtus was not unsympathetic to the difficulties under which the bishops operated. He dealt with individual problems as they arose and when they came to his notice.[75] Yet when the authority of his own Court was involved or the interests of his Treasury were concerned, the wishes of the Papal administration almost invariably prevailed. For instance, special powers which his predecessor had granted to Cardinal Cesi as Legate to Bologna were widened in favour of three succeeding legates[76] and the bishop's authorities continued to be severely circumscribed. What was needed was a radical and far-reaching examination of the bishoprics, their resources and their duties, and a survey of the best means of enabling them to play a full part in ecclesiastical reform. Such an examination would have been obliged to look critically at the relationships of the diocese with the administration of Papal government. Sixtus was concerned to uphold and strengthen the latter; he was not therefore sufficiently impartial to be disposed to produce solutions to the basic problems of the bishops.

So far as the Regular Orders were concerned, Sixtus wished to see their work extended and their organisation strengthened. Nevertheless, he resolutely made his assistance dependent on their willingness to reform abuses, promote men of high morals, learning and unquestioned orthodoxy, and to observe with strict conviction the Rules of their Founders. Even before the establishment of Congregations on a permanent basis in January, 1588, the Pope found the machinery for controlling the Orders and imposing his designs upon them ready to hand since a Congregation for dealing with the Orders was already in existence. It met regularly, acted with conspicuous diligence, and comprised five distinguished Cardinals of outstanding qualities of intellect, personality and spirit. They were Alessandrino, the Dominican Cardinal—nephew of Pius V's reign, and Vicar-General of Rome, Santorio, a Neapolitan and Cardinal of great experience and ability, Facchinetti, the future Urban IX, Spinola, a notable and enterprising Genoan, and Sarnano, one of Sixtus' own creations and a member of the Congregations concerned respectively with the Inquisition and the Press.

These were the men charged with responsibility for the control and guidance of the Orders, with the effective communication of the Pope's wishes to them, and the resolution of problems which might arise between one Order and another or between an Order and some civil or religious authority. The separation of the affairs of the Orders may not have been entirely well-conceived, especially as a comparable Congregation had responsibility for business concerning the bishops; indeed, this may have added to the existing and inevitable conflict of interests; nevertheless, it did provide for the Pope effective control and manipulation.

Sixtus' assistance to the Regular Orders was wide-ranging in character. He confirmed the privileges of a historic and coenobitic Order like the Cistercians,[77] encouraged the development of its stricter branch, leaving it under the jurisdiction of the Superiors of the Order but forbidding the latter to recall any of its members from their separate establishments. Indeed, he ordered disputes between the Order and its stricter dependencies to be submitted directly to himself and authorised the latter to establish monasteries "even without the licence of the Ordinaries," an undertaking directly forbidden by the Council of Trent.[78] He granted to the ancient Camaldolese Order the right to admit brethren from other Orders and yet prohibited all its own brethren from leaving it to join another even though these might observe a stricter rule. He confirmed and extended the privileges of both the Observant and the Conventual branches of the Franciscan Order. He confirmed the former in the possession of the properties they held with the proviso that the consent of the Ordinary should be obtained for their ownership of property acquired in the previous decade. Both the Observants and Conventuals were empowered to establish Confraternities,[79] and Sixtus charged the Conventuals with the training and maintainence of twenty-one papal singers under masters of the Papal chapel.[80] He enthusiastically encouraged the Franciscan Conventuals to return to the strict rule of their Founder, and in 1586 approved their establishment of reformed houses as a Congregation with a habit and privileges of their own, and some years later they were authorised to take over the Houses of the Discalced of the Franciscan family in Italy. Proliferation of quasi-independent sectors of the Order was a disease among the Franciscans of the fourteenth and fifteenth centuries as it was in the eighteenth and nineteenth centuries. More drastic measures could therefore have been justified and might have forestalled the extensive suppressions of the following century.[81] Sixtus also extended the powers of the Third Order of the Observant branch,[82] and confirmed an amended constitution for the Mazalotti, an offshoot of the Third Order of the Franciscans, founded in the fourteenth century and devoted to a strict ascetic life[83] and ordered it to be observed in the Romagna. He confirmed, renewed and extended the privileges and indulgences already granted to the sodality of the rosary of the Blessed Virgin Mary which was associated with the Dominicans through the use of a Psalter complied by St Dominic, and he gave to their Master and Vicar General the authority to found other Confraternities of the Rosary.[84] He similarly confirmed the constitutions of the Hospital of St John of Jerusalem.[85]

He was also aware of the theological debate between the Jesuits and the Dominicans on the interplay in divine grace between freedom and God's efficacious action. The Commission *De Auxiliis* which had been set up in 1582 would continue until 1607. Sixtus was acquainted with the issues and imposed mutual silence between the two sides, binding them to avoid further recrimination. He thus avoided taking a stand on an extremely complicated matter, and that position would be maintained by subsequent pontiffs.

Yet in no sense was the Pope's help reserved for the better established or historic Orders. He approved the constitution of the Barnabites, a small Order founded at Milan in 1530 and especially devoted to the study of the Pauline Epistles, gave them autonomy, the right to celebrate the divine offices and to build regular houses.[86] He established the Somaschi in a position of quite singular independence. This was a small Order founded in Northern Italy in 1532 which specialised in work among the poor of the Western Venetian Republic and which worked closely with the Theatines. The latter was one of the strictest of the Religious Orders, founded by St Cajetan and Bishop Carafa, subsequently Paul IV; it had been joined to the Somaschi from 1547–1555. Pius V had already raised the Somaschi to the rank of an Order in 1568 and gave it particular responsibility for the care of orphans in Northern Italy. Sixtus gave them exemption from the jurisdiction and authority of the Ordinaries, authorising them to administer the sacraments even to members of other parishes at any time except Easter and guaranteed their integrity by forbidding transfer to any Order other than the Capuchins and the Carthusians.[87]

Sixtus himself took a notably personal and intimate interest in religious organisations which undertook philanthropic and social work. To deal with disputes which might arise from lack of definition in their functions or through serious rivalries, he enlarged the powers and independence of the judge charged with hearing cases which might arise about the admission to one of these charitable institutions of wandering beggars in the city.[88] He also made provision for the establishment of a separate prison for lay and regular clergy, Jews and Christian wrongdoers. The reasons for imprisonment were legion, and conditions in prison were generally dire for all those without financial resources.[89] He also gave to the Archconfraternity of *Pietas dei Carcerati* (which his predecessor had founded) the duty of placing condemned men on the papal galleys and of visiting the prisons in the City and gave them authority to release a prisoner on the second festival after the first Sunday of Lent, even though he had been condemned for a capital crime.[90]

St Philip Neri's oratory was an outstanding testimony to the effectiveness of joining profound religious motives to the relief of human suffering and in uniting the efforts of devoted men pledged to the religious life with laymen who had been brought under their influence and were willing to remain under it. Thirty years earlier, during his first period of residence in Rome, he had established a Confraternity with the title of *Compagnia de Santissimo Sacramento* with the object of carrying the Blessed Sacrament to the sick with proper dignity and decorum, and with the agreement of Ignatius Loyola and the consent of Pope Julius III this had been joined to the Confraternity of the Twelve Apostles. This joint organisation was given papal authority to collect alms for the poor and to support twelve knights for this work. After his election as Pope, he conferred the honoured title of Archconfraternity on this organisation and charged it with the direction of all similar establishments throughout the world.[91] He confirmed the recent establishment of a Society of Regular Clerks to minister to the sick, granting them licences to collect alms in the City and authorising them to tend the spiritual and temporal needs of the sick and even to hear their confessions and to give them absolution.[92] He similarly empowered a number of hospitals established in Pius V's pontificate (and maintained by a number of separate Confraternities) to unite in a single Congregation with a common rule and a single Superior, and granted the Congregation exemption from interference by other authorities. He gave his approval to the establishment of a college for virgins and widows at the monastery of the monks of St Bernard in the City, enlarged its financial powers and gave it exemption from all extraneous jurisdictions, including that of the Vicar of the City. He also provided for the admission to the College of poor girls who were unable to raise the dowries normally required.[93] Another social problem in those days of violence was the capture of citizens by raiding pirates or Turkish privateers. These were then carried off into distant lands or sold into servitude, often leaving behind them destitute families and helpless dependents. Sixtus confirmed the rules and privileges of the Mercedarian Order, devoted to the ransoming of Christian captives,[94] and granted it the use of the Church of Sant'Adriano in the City.[95] He also gave official recognition to the Archconfraternity of the Blessed Virgin Mary at the Gonfalone, established by Gregory XIII, with the duty of financing the ransom of captives. This Archconfraternity was authorised to receive for this purpose money, goods and rights over property not only in the capital but throughout the Papal States and bishops were charged to give it every encouragement and assistance.[96] The Archconfraternity was given authority to nominate Protectors who should elect a judge with autonomous jurisdiction over disputes arising within it or arising from its work.

Throughout a large part of the sixteenth century the social conscience which the Reformation had awakened increased its influence on public policy. Sixtus readily recognised the responsibilities of public authorities and accepted fully and without reservation the social emphasis of the Franciscan Order. On the one hand, he did not scruple to govern with exceptionable severity and rigour imposing a strict and unyielding uniformity of belief and doctrine. The streets of the City were meticulously patrolled by police and watched by paid agents; the informer's services were extensively used. Sumptuary Laws restricted the tastes of the rich; books were rigorously censored and the presses kept under the strictest control; prostitutes were swept from the streets. An atmosphere of repression hung heavily over Rome and the rest of the Papal States. But on the other hand, there existed a lively awareness of the injury inflicted on the poor, the sick, the handicapped, by the forces of nature and of the injustice sometimes imposed on them by the rich and the powerful. Sixtus' generation was content to stir human ideals, to preach the virtue of charity and to press upon people the eternal benefits which would reward acts of benevolence.

Many Protestant states, including England, found themselves driven by economic circumstances and the dispersal of the immense resources of the medieval church to undertake, usually reluctantly, works of relief as a predominantly secular function. In the Republic of Venice, in contrast, the government was able for many decades to avoid this responsibility because it was possible to extend and energise independent semi-religious institutions. In the Papal States, on the other hand, the church continued to accept responsibility for social relief and promoted organisations independent of government resources. State and Church were completely integrated and by their remedial social work united in preserving the fabric of society. Both were concerned that the sources by which this work was financed should be coordinated and that the distribution of funds should be selective and consistent. Genuine need was to be carefully distinguished from plausible subterfuge and relief was to match but not exceed requirement. The organisation of relief for the poor, the sick, the needy was an orderly operation, and indiscriminate charity was clearly seen as inimical to the social order. Clearly the Church was not content with merely restoring uniformity of belief, repressing overt vice and compelling regular church attendance, and formal observance of religious rites. "Sunday Piety" did not suffice.[97] The reform of the church called for compassion for human suffering. In this context the Religious Orders formed one of the foremost allies of the secular authority and one of the most essential forces of the reforming church. The salvation of men's souls and the strengthening of their bodies were barely distinguishable parts of a single objective.

Support for the Regular Orders by the Pope and his Court was, however, subject to strict conditions, and re-organisation was the price they were required to pay for papal assistance. Extensive reforms of various orders had already been carried out, particularly by Paul IV and Pius V, but the basic deficiencies of the Regular Orders had been ameliorated rather than eliminated. These arose in large part from the admission of candidates lacking in intellectual and moral qualities, and often in genuine motivation. Frequently families committed sons and, more particularly, daughters to a Religious Order who were likely to become liabilities to them; admitted at an early age and sometimes under a measure of coercion some might find the Order's Rule irksome. This then created the perpetual threat of monastic vagrancy and the ensuing scandal of monks on the run with no permanent means of support. To resolve these problems in 1587 Sixtus V issued a Bull forbidding the admission to any Order those had been born illegitimate even though they might subsequently have been legitimised, and debarring any already enrolled from being promoted or receiving any dignity of the Order. Criminals and those suspected of crime were similarly ineligible for admission and severe penalties were imposed on any monk who received such into his Order.[98] By the same Bull it was ordained that any member of an Order who transferred from one province in his Order to another should carry a licence from the Provincial authority, and if he were found trying to obtain entrance to a hospice when he could not produce a licence he was to be imprisoned by the ordinary.[99] Sixtus believed that though the relations between the three branches of the Franciscan family was generally satisfactory and the work of the Observants—especially overseas—was exemplary, their rigid separation and the multiplication of tiny houses at very small distances from each other was illogical and debilitating. The Observants and the Conventuals were probably approximately equal in numerical strength and the Capuchins had about half the number of either of the two senior branches of the Order.[100] The union of the stricter sectors of the Observants would be a rational reorganisation of the Order, and this Sixtus tried to bring about but was not successful.[101] Similarly, Sixtus V ordered the Decollati of St Paul (later called the Barnabites) to refuse admission to the illegitimate, criminals and those with money problems. Because admissions could only lawfully be authorised at the General Chapter which met only every three years, authority was given to the President of the Order and his assistants to approve admissions individually in the intervening periods provided they were in accordance with the Constitutions of the Order.[102] In such a society the obligation to be celibate proved a great strain on many monks and nunneries therefore needed the strictest possible supervision. In the Duchy of Ferrara, for example, a Papal bull forbade all contact between the Regular Orders even the Medicants, with nunneries, even though the nuns were their responsibility and subject to their jurisdiction.[103]

Sixtus not only believed in the power of statutes and ordinances, he attached great importance to the organisation and structure of religious bodies. He followed the founder of his own Order and his own experience in the Order in believing in the advantage of precise regulation of the governance of an Order and in the involvement of its wholly body in the regular and periodic selection of its rulers.[104] So rigid were his notions of the elements of good government that something of the doctrinaire appears in his regulations. While he reduced the term of office for which, in accordance with a decree of Pius V, the Minister-General of the Observants was appointed, from eight years to six,[105] he ordained that chapters of the *Eremiti* where the officials of the Order were chosen, should no longer be convened annually, but should be summoned every third year,[106] yet he chose six years as the period for the summoning of the General Chapter of the Order of Friars Minor of St Francis de Paola.[107] When the constitution of the Order of the Mercedarians gave rise to internal dispute, Sixtus ordered that a Minister-General should be elected every six years, and provided that if he died in office, the prior of the monastery should automatically succeed to the office and complete his term.[108] Whereas Pius V had obliged the Augustinian Order to hold a chapter general and to appoint a General Prior and visitors every third year, Sixtus ordained in addition that other abbots and the prior's vicars should similarly be elected for a period of three years and that when a General had completed his three years in office he should not be re-elected until an interval of six years had elapsed.[109] All abbesses of the Observant branch of the Franciscan family were ordered to submit an account of their work at the end of their triennium so that the state of their monasteries and their finances could be kept under regular review.[110]

The structures of other Orders were carefully regulated. The Cistercians were empowered to elect abbots from those who had held minor office for two years. The considerable number of hospitals and confraternities of St John of God which had been founded in the Spanish possessions and in Italy were brought under a unified control when Sixtus ordered two confraternities from each hospital and confraternity to attend a constituent chapter in Rome so that a single Congregation should be established to associate them all under a common rule.[111] Sixtus similarly intervened to impose on the Magalotti, a group of hermits established as a fourteenth-century offshoot of the Franciscan Order, the reforms which a commission under Cardinal Santacroce had recommended.[112] When an attempt to amalgamate the Augustinian houses in the Congregation of St Ambrose in Milan with those in the provinces of the March and Genoa was resisted, the Pope issued a Bull compelling the Union to be observed throughout the Order.[113] The management of monastic finances also left much to be desired and there was widespread mismanagement of their properties. So Sixtus issued a Bull ordering the congregation of the Lateran, the Carthusians and the Camaldolese and other Orders to maintain inventories of their goods, their revenues and their documents, papers and books.[114]

He employed Jesuits to carry out a rigorous visitation of the German, English, and Roman Colleges and the College of the Maronites, and following a favourable report on the last he made a grant to it. Sixtus also gave the Society support in its difficulties in Spain. Two former Provincial Ministers, a Rector and a teacher who had been seized by the Spanish Inquisition, were protected by the Papal Nuncio against the Grand Inquisitor who finally was instructed not to proceed with their trail and to restore the copies of papal bulls and the books which he had seized in an effort to compile evidence against the Society.[115] In due course the four Jesuits were released. Similarly when the Grand Inquisitor, Cardinal Quiroga, on instructions from the King, forbade Spanish Jesuits to leave the country, Sixtus procured the withdrawal of the prohibition and instructed the Papal Nuncio to order the Grand Inquisitor to restore all the papal bulls to the Society on pain of excommunication and loss of his Cardinalate.[116] In a dispute with the King about the appointment of visitors to carry out a visitation of the Order in Spain, Sixtus gave the Society his full support and succeeded in persuading the King to accept the Society's proposals.[117]

In brief, during Sixtus' pontificate the Regular Orders enjoyed papal favour and encouragement; the threat of extinction which had been so menacing in the earlier decades of the century was dispelled. But in return they were obliged to accept not merely the overall direction and guidance of the Pope but his extensive intervention in their affairs and an expectation of their compliance. Not surprisingly, therefore, Sixtus V's relations with the Jesuit Order were particularly difficult. He had shared a close friendship and much common interest with its founder, Ignatius Loyola. Robert Bellarmine, the Professor of Christian Controversy at the Jesuit Collegio Romano was a friend and had assisted him in his work on St Ambrose.[118] His sponsor, Charles Borromeo, had made great use of Jesuit skill in educating children and had established colleges under Jesuit direction and built a professed house for them at Milan.[119] Sixtus greatly admired their devotion and zeal and recognised without reserve their success in establishing missions, more particularly in the East, and in combating Protestantism in the Low Countries and in Germany. He increased his grant to the Church of Japan and its seminaries from 4,000 to 6,000 scudi per annum on representations made by the Jesuit General Acquaviva, and granted the Society a special indulgence.[120] When Sixtus issued a bull obliging all Regular Orders to admit novices only at Provincial and General Chapters, the Society was expressly exempt from this requirement.[121] He authorised the Rector of the Jesuit College at Bitonto to have possession of an adjoining priory,[122] and he prolonged the papal grant to a University of General Studies newly established by Archduke Charles of Austria at Graz and extended its privileges.[123] Neither personal animosity nor disregard of the value and genuine success of the Society was therefore responsible for conflicts during Sixtus' pontificate.

Differences between the Pope and the Society were, in fact, substantial. The very name of the Society gave wide spread offence. It seemed to imply a primacy over all other Orders which was greatly resented and the attempt to appropriate the name of the Redeemer of the World to a particular Order (as it appeared to many) smacked of arrogance and a superiority completely at variance with the Christian faith. Sixtus did his utmost to induce the Society to change its name and was still engaged in this exercise when he died.

The Society had no General Chapter though it had a General Congregation with no elective foundation which met on the death of a General to select his successor. They had no convents governed by abbots or priors; instead they had colleges and houses, rectors and superiors. Each house or college enjoyed a large measure of autonomy, houses being established for particular purposes to meet specific needs or to take advantage of individual endowments. The links of their superiors were with the General and his Assistants rather than with each other. At the election of Lainez as General in 1558 there were four Assistants responsible respectively for Italy, Spain, Portugal and the northern countries.[124] This freedom of the individual member and the flexibility of the Society's organisation contributed greatly to its success. Ignatius had formulated no Rule for the Order but his *Spiritual Exercises* were the unfailing guide of every individual Jesuit. Self-imposed discipline achieved during long years of rigorous training produced a spontaneous devotion to duty and drove the individual Jesuit to the limit of his personal resources.

The organisation of the Society was highly autocratic. The candidate for admission, after a rigorous examination for selection, served a novitiate of two years, followed by a scholasticate of indefinite length; after that, if acceptable, he was ordained and proceeded to a tertianship, lasting one year. He then was incorporated in the Society either as a formed spiritual coadjutor with limited responsibility, or as a fully professed member, or as one who professed the fourth vow. The members of this final category were pledged to accept any instruction of the Pope and to hold themselves directly responsible to him if he ordered them to work in a foreign mission.[125] It was those "professed of the fourth vow" who elected the General when a vacancy occurred and constituted a group responsible for the direction of the Order. The multiplicity of grades was a unique feature of the Society's organisation and enhanced the influence of the General and his immediate associates. By prolongation of one of the phases of probation or of service in a particular grade, membership of the higher grades was restricted. At the time of Lainez's election to the Generalship the Society had about 1,000 members, but only 43 were professed of the fourth vow.[126] As the Society expanded it became flooded with large numbers of students but the higher grades remained restricted.[127] Only the professed, namely those who had completed their novitiate, their scholasticate and their tertianship, and excluding the formed spiritual coadjutors, were bound by solemn vows, the remainder having taken only simple vows. This led to disputes and some contended that only those who had taken solemn vows were true members of the Order. At the time when Sixtus became Pope there was a strong movement to subject the formed spiritual coadjutors to solemn instead of simple vows, and the reformers also wished to see all superiors elected by a majority of their subjects.[128] Pius V had obliged the Jesuits to make their profession as a prerequisite of ordination but Gregory XIII had revoked this order.[129] Jesuits did not normally attend the celebration of the divine office but recited it privately, and even those who had not advanced to the priesthood were allowed to celebrate certain minor offices. Perhaps the most unusual feature of the Society was that the General held office for life and when a new General was elected there was scandalous intrigue or open dispute. The Jesuits in less than a half century had created many enemies and there was a growing demand both within the Order and outside for radical reform.[130] To Sixtus the structure of the Society was unfamiliar and strange: as a Franciscan he looked for a more traditional organisation and he wished to systematise, consolidate and unify many of its procedures. These problems Sixtus approached in a determined but doctrinaire spirit. He called for the Society's Constitutions and had them examined in detail by members of the Curia, many of whom fully shared the Pope's desire to amend them. He particularly insisted on future Generals being elected for a three-year period and repeated his demand with increasing emphasis. But he was resisted courteously but firmly by Acquaviva, the first Italian General, described as "the greatest of Jesuit Generals".[131] Acquaviva was a superbly energetic and resourceful man in his forties who had been a member of the Society for eighteen years, a professed of the fourth vow for eight years and General for four. He was steeped in canon and civil law and had had charge of the Society in Naples and Rome. He was a fair but formidable adversary in any conflict, and though he had never known the Founder closely, he was steeped in the traditions of the Order and was prepared for any trespass on its prerogatives.[132] Sixtus never succeeded in effecting the revision of the Society's constitutions, and at his death the problems raised were totally unresolved.[133]

Possibly because the constitutions and organisation of the Order left so much scope for local and individual initiatives, and the Jesuits were determined to maintain what they regarded as right regardless of consequences, possibly because they relished controversy and dialectics, they became inextricably entangled in European politics. In Spain, in particular, the Jesuits were seen as emissaries of Rome and the Spanish Jesuits went to great lengths to gain extensive powers of self-government for themselves. They agitated for the appointment of a special representative of the General to be resident in Spain and who would have overall responsibility for the Spanish establishments and they demanded that Spanish Jesuits should appoint their own superiors. Antonio Araoz, the first Spanish Provincial Minister, wanted the General Chapter to be held in Spain;[134] and his colleagues in Castile tried to bring into existence a Spanish congregation elected on a broad basis, to formulate reform, but his Spanish colleagues were not yet ready for so radical step. The Jesuit seminaries in Spain with the exception of the English and Irish Colleges at Salamanca, Valladolid and Seville, were kept exclusively under Spanish control. When Suarez, an eminent Jesuit lecturer at the Roman College and the foremost authority of the day on St Thomas Aquinas, was sent to Spain to lecture, the Jesuits at Salamanca and the Examiners of the Province of Castile refused to admit him, even though he was a Spaniard and was well received by the Provincial Minister.[135] There was widespread resistance by the Spanish authorities to the collection of alms by the Jesuits because they would be forwarded to Rome to support the Jesuit College there.[136] This quasi-nationalist movement within the Order was used by King Philip to undermine the authority of Rome even though he had little regard for Jesuits. When, therefore,

Araoz was called to Rome to become an Assistant to the General, Philip forbade him to leave Spain and Araoz preferred to obey the King rather than be exiled in Rome.[137] In the middle of the century, the Dominicans in Spain who dominated the Spanish Inquisition, led by Melchior Cano, the Professor of Theology at the University of Salamanca who also vigorously supported the King's anti-papal policy, launched a bitter and tortuous attack on the Jesuits. The calm which followed Cano's death in 1560 was shattered again when Diego de Chaves, the King's Dominican Confessor, reported on the Society to the King and encouraged opposition to it. When, in 1582, a young Jesuit left the Order to marry, his action revived the old dispute about the validity of simple and solemn vows for the Professor of theology in the Dominican convent and the University of Salamanca contended that the young men's action was lawful since having attained only one of the lower grades in the Order he was bound by simple vows. The General of the Order appealed to the Pope and Gregory XIII issued two bulls to make it clear that canonically student Jesuits were bound by solemn vows. In spite of papal support of the Order, both Professors continued the fight and the Professor at Avila went to Rome to contest the views of the Roman Inquisition, and finally after years of acrimonious controversy, he appealed to the Pope. In the year of his death Sixtus again proclaimed in favour of the Jesuit Order, but even this failed to silence the strife in Spain.[138] Meanwhile, however, the Jesuits continued to evolve one of the most efficient systems of education in the world of that day under the influence of the *Ratio Studiorum* which Diego Ledesma, a student at Alcalá, had initially developed until in many parts of Europe, the Jesuits had a virtual monopoly over the instruction many of the well-to-do.

There were similar internal dissensions within the Order in France. The privilege granted to the Jesuits to hear confessions and to teach and preach even in churches for which they had no parochial responsibility was bitterly resented by other Orders. The bishop was hampered in the control of his diocese and in some instances this contravened the decrees of the Council of Trent. In Parish there was a continuing feud between the Order, the diocese and the University—both ancient institutions steeped in their own traditions and resistant to most reform. The Bishop of Paris refused to ordain Jesuits and forbade those who had already been ordained to hear confessions, to preach or administer the sacraments in his diocese. The Parliament of Paris had earlier refused to register a royal edict allowing the Jesuits to own property, and when the dispute had been referred by the Parliament to the bishop and the University, Bishop du Bellay pronounced quite dogmatically that, "The Pope had no power to approve an Order in this country but only in his own State. Neither has the King such power, the matter being spiritual."[139] As conflict developed between the Church and the Huguenots and between the Crown and those who resisted the growth of autocracy, the French Jesuits found great difficulty in remaining neutral and became more and more involved in the political disputes of the time, some of them even welcoming it. While the country was shattered by political and religious battles and reduced to chaos, the Jesuits added to the philosophical and juridical confusion.[140]

In the Spanish Low Countries also the Jesuit Order was foremost in attacks on Baianism. About the middle of the century, Michael Baius, a Professor in the University of Louvain, published views which revived the strife which previously had locked St Augustine and Pelagius in fierce conflict about the part played by human works in men's salvation. Baius' views were repeatedly declared heretical and he was condemned by Pius V and Gregory XIII, but he was powerfully supported by the Faculty of theology in the University, by the Archbishops of Cambrai and Malines and the Bishop of Roermond, and most vehemently by the University of Douai which violently denounced the Jesuit teaching. Moreover, Baius enjoyed the protection of King Philip and represented his University at the Council of Trent. The Jesuit, Bellarmine, was despatched by the Jesuit authorities in Rome to lecture in their College at Louvain, a task he discharged with great zest, energy and success. On Bellarmine's return to Rome, another Jesuit theologian, Leonard Lessius, a native of the Low Countries, took his pace and continued the attacks on Baius and the Belgian Universities and clergy with equal vehemence. In 1587 the struggle reached its height when Baius induced the Faculty of theology in the University to condemn thirty-four propositions in Lessius' teaching, having won the support of Domenico Bañez, Professor of theology in the University of Salamanca,[141] a former pupil of Melchior Cano and an opponent of Jesuit Order in Spain. On the other side Lessius' views were supported by the Jesuit Professor of theology in the University of Evora in Portugal, Luis de Molina, whose writings in turn won the favour of the Grand Inquisitor of Portugal. Molina was subsequently summoned before the Portuguese Inquisition and cleared of all suspicions of heresy. He also sent a copy of the accusations against him to Acquaviva, the Jesuit General in Rome, who in turn referred them to Bellarmine for examination. These religious disputes created a tremendous stir in the areas where they arose and produced a flood of polemics on either side, they shook theological and philosophical circles to their roots, and indeed, posed serious threats to the stability of the Church. Sixtus found these sharp theological controversies wholly unwelcome and recognised their debilitating effect on the Church. Moreover, he was clearly how rulers quickly took advantage of these feuds within the Church to challenge the claims of the Papacy and to reduce its authority.

The situation was exacerbated by conflict which developed between Sixtus and Bellarmine. Since returning from Louvain, Bellarmine continued to follow the strict Jesuit line in the interminable arguments about the relationship of grace and works in the salvation of man. As Professor in the Jesuit College at Rome he enhanced his reputation as a theologian, a preacher and a dialectician of immense skill and resourcefulness. He began his great work—*Disputationes de Controversiis Christianae Fidei*[142]—described as the most systematic and cogent defence of the Counter-Reformation against the Reformation,[143] dedicated it to Pope Sixtus, and was pressed by him to accept from him the gift of 400 gold pieces.[144] When the Pope launched his excommunication of Henry III of France following the murder of the Cardinal of Guise and a fiery controversy ensured, Bellarmine sprang eagerly to the Pope's defence.[145] In a larger portion of his book, Bellarmine, however, denied that the Pope was lord of the world in temporal matters and particularly that he had the right to depose princes. Only as the supreme spiritual authority could he make civil laws, invalidate the decrees of a secular prince or deprive him of his prerogatives, and then only if it was necessary for the salvation of the people's souls.[146] In view of the political situation in Scotland, England and France and of the mounting opposition of Philip II to Rome and its claims, Sixtus found Bellarmine's teaching dangerous and subversive. These views on the limits of national sovereignty consorted well with Bellarmine's suspected Gallican sympathies, and Sixtus was incensed that a theologian with whom he had been so closely and agreeably associated should add to the complications of the religious and political situation in France. An examination of his works was begun in spite of Bellarmine's absence in France whilst assisting the Cardinal Legate, Caetani. On his side, Bellarmine made a most spirited and scholarly defence of his position, circulated a statement to the Cardinals and won substantial support.[147] In August 1590, on the very eve of the Pope's death, in spite of Jesuit General Acquaviva's defence of Bellarmine's contentions and in spite of the fact that there was widespread resentment at the Pope's high handed and bigoted action, Bellarmine's works were placed on the Index. Only a few days after Sixtus' death, his successor Urban VII, who was only to reign twelve days, had Bellarmine's name removed from the Index.

Sixtus' reign had produced an explosive situation in which fundamental controversy went to the very basis of political philosophy. Developing states—whether Protestant or Catholic—inevitably emphasised the unity of the church and government on which law and peace depended. Sixtus, on the other hand, looked back to the triumphs of Gregory VII, and above all, to the great days of Innocent III who had done so much to encourage St Francis and the establishment of his Order.[148] Those Popes had created the powerful medieval tradition which the Babylonian Captivity and the Great Schism had undermined; it was natural that a Franciscan Pope should return to philosophical doctrines on which the new supremacy of the Church could be re-founded. The resulting controversy reached its greatest intensity in the Spanish dominions where the Pope's conflict with the Jesuits formed part of a deeper and more combustible division of interests.

The kingdom of Spain to which Portugal had been recently annexed (1580) caused Sixtus profound and continuous concern. Its area was almost twice that of the British Isles or Italy; its coastline extended approximately 1,700 miles. Yet its population was little more than half that of Italy.[149] Substantial stretches of the Iberian Peninsula comprised nothing but mountain ranges. Much of the Peninsula was inhabited by Moriscos, some nominally Christian, the majority recently Moslem in faith and culture. These Christians lived in constant fear.[150] For the numerous Regular Orders, the country was studded with intellectual and moral temptations, while their superiors were preoccupied with pressing political and social problems. The moral standards and spiritual integrity of their founders were difficult to maintain, discipline buckled at every succeeding wind of change. Rome, suspected in all official circles, commanded little respect in religious quarters and was obliged to fight on every occasion for its own authority and control. Within the kingdom the re-organisation of the Church, initiated by Cardinal Ximénes at the beginning of the century, had never been fully completed, and there remained recurring rivalries between the constituted kingdoms. The incorporation of Portugal within Philip II's kingdom added to the confusion and the animosity. Gregory XIII's Hispanophilism added to the problems set for his successor since he issued privileges and exemptions to various ecclesiastical bodies which proved to be seriously divisive in their effects. Philip was profoundly religious, well read in the doctrines of the Catholic Church, well versed in its ritual and genuinely receptive to the guidance of his religious advisers. On the other hand, he was conscientiously aware of the responsibilities of the crown and diligent in the preservation of the royal prerogatives. He was jealously suspicious of Papal claims which he recognised as threats to his own authority and security. At almost every point a distinction would be drawn between spiritual powers, and political responsibilities: and their interpretation opened the gateway to ambiguity and controversy and created divided loyalties. Philip had the right (which he preserved with meticulous care) of appointing bishops and other ecclesiastical dignitaries within his dominions: he had accepted the Tridentine decrees only subject to his own rights. He expected royal interests to be set above ecclesiastical claims. In no Catholic state in Europe, therefore, was a closer watch kept on Papal interference or a more determined resistance offered to papal claims. Though the king readily accepted the need to reform the church, he expected this to be achieved by his own initiative and without any independent papal policies which might appear to weaken the authority of the crown. The extensive and radical reform of the Carmelite Order begun by St Teresa under Gregory XIII was still incomplete and there was a danger that the growth of the stricter branch of the Order (the Discalced) would be thwarted. To prevent this, Sixtus gave the Discalced a carefully constructed constitution so that although they remained under the ultimate authority of the General Prior of the Order they were permitted to elect their own Vicar-General and subordinate to him provincial Priors. The former was elected for six years and was not to be re-elected until an interval of six years had elapsed; the latter were elected for three years and were debarred from re-election for a further three years. Thus a schism in the Order was prevented but encouragement and a large measure of independence was given to the Discalced establishment with the Order.[151] Sixtus also gave papal confirmation to the constitutions drafted by the Discalced in 1581, and prohibited interference with their affairs even by bishops.[152]

Similarly a reformation of the government of Benedictine houses in Portugal had been begun by Pius V, whilst Portugal was still an independent kingdom. Pius V had ordered that all the houses in the kingdom should elect priors to hold office for three years and that these houses be united in a single Congregation under an Abbot-General who also was to hold office for three years. This orderly system had only been established in part and as a result many houses were governed by superiors who held office for life and did not accept the instructions of the Abbot-General; in these houses abuses and deficiencies often went uncorrected. At Philip II's request, Sixtus placed all these independent houses under the Abbot-General whom he authorised to take possession of them, transferring their members to other houses as he thought best and of applying their revenues to more isolated monasteries.[153] In the kingdom of Aragon Sixtus had to revoke measures introduced by his predecessor.

In Valencia it was necessary to forbid the advance of the illegitimate to canonries, prebendaries and other dignities,[154] and to prevent foreigners from other parts of the Kingdom of Spain being appointed to Valencian benefices. Disputes between the Cardinal Archbishop and his Chapter at Seville had had to be brought before the Congregation of the Council whose decisions the Pope confirmed.[155] Sixtus confirmed the detachment of Teruel from the diocese of Saragossa and its establishment as an independent diocese effected by Gregory XIII in 1577.[156] In the kingdom of Portugal, to safeguard the position of the heads of monasteries, Sixtus enacted that parish churches in the car of Regular Canons of the congregation of St John the Baptist were to be provided by the Superiors of the Congregation and not by the diocesan authorities.[157] Parish priests appointed by the Benedictines in Portugal were not longer to hold their appointment for life but were in future to be removable by the General of the Order or by the abbots.[158]

The annexation of Portugal to Spain caused confusion in the Augustinian Eremite Order in Portugal. To remedy the situation, Sixtus V united the two Congregations, Spanish and Portuguese respectively, each electing its own General to hold office for three years, and the General taking overall command in alternate triennial periods.[159] Each monastery was placed under the direction of a superior. A year later, in 1589, he ordered the holding of annual chapters to be discontinued and substituted triennial chapters. He also had to revoke licences which permitted Ministers General or other superiors to keep revenues or property for their own use, and he forbade the issue of such licences in future.[160] Sixtus also settled disputes which had arisen between the bishop and chapter of Avila by assigning the right of visitation in the diocese to the bishop.[161]

In the Spanish kingdom of Naples, he approved the establishment of a home for nuns who were exempt from the jurisdiction of the bishop and set out detailed regulations for its management.[162] Sixtus also resolved doubts which had arisen about ecclesiastical incomes in the kingdom by declaring that they belonged wholly to the Apostolic Camera[163]—a declaration easy to make but no doubt much more difficult to enforce.

Throughout Europe perhaps the most difficult problem was to enforce *clausura* in monastic houses for nuns. In 1585 Sixtus instructed the bishops of Portugal to forbid nuns to converse with anyone not belonging to the nunnery otherwise than in the *locutorio* where a grille separated the nun from her visitor. Even there she could only converse with the outsider with the permission in writing of her superior. Each of the bishops was to satisfy himself that these restrictions were meticulously observed.[164] Moreover, nuns in any of the Spanish dominions, even if belonging to noble families, were forbidden to leave their monasteries, and penalties were provided against any of their superiors who consented to their leaving.[165] Similarly, women were absolutely prohibited from entering any monastery in the Spanish possessions[166] and a bull was issued specifically to enforce the *clausura* in nunneries in the Spanish Duchy of Milan.[167]

Reorganising the Central Government of the Church in Rome, improving the spiritual and intellectual quality of those holding senior offices in its hierarchy, purging and re-invigorating the Regular Orders, all those would prove ineffective in the longer term unless the Church could be assured of a sufficient flow of new entrants into its priesthood of good intellectual quality and spiritual dedication who could be thoroughly and systematically trained for their vocation. Continuing spiritual health was dependent on effective recruitment and efficient training. Sixtus made great efforts to increase and improve facilities for training. He paid the debts of the Sapienza, the Roman University established by Leo X, where he himself had lectured in earlier years, and added two wings to it.[168] He approved the establishment of a University at Pont a Mousson (Lorraine),[169] and converted the Jesuit College at Graz into a University;[170] he confirmed the privileges of doctors in the University of Bologna;[171] he revived the *Studium Generale* at Fermo[172] and recognised another at Valencia. At Santi Apostoli in Rome he founded and endowed the Collegio San Bonaventura, and placed it in perpetuity under the protection of the Cardinal-nephew, or some other member of the Peretti family or some distinguished citizen of the Marche. Provision was made for the education of twenty who already held the degree of Bachelor (which gave no entitlement to teach) and who after three years' study would take the master's degree.[173] In Bologna he founded the Collegio Montalto where fifty young scholars were to be provided with places for seven years with free lodging and clothing, a communal chapel and refectory and library. The College was to enjoy all the privileges of the University of Bologna and was exempt from the jurisdiction of the Papal Legate of Bologna, the Archbishop and of the Judges of the ordinary courts. Like the College of San Bonaventura, it was to be under the protection of the Cardinal-nephew, a member of the Peretti family, a Cardinal from the Marche or, in the last resort, a Protector was to be chosen by the pupils of the College.[174] Sixtus authorised those qualified by study in theology or philosophy in the Order of St Jerome at the Escorial to be admitted to the degree of doctor or master in any university in the kingdom of Spain.[175] He gave recognition to deacons and sub-deacons trained at the Greek College in Rome[176] and made students of the German College in Rome who had been taught in the Jesuit Gregorian College eligible to take Holy Orders.[177] He helped to solve the serious problem of student overcrowding in Rome by enlarging the Congregation of the Annunciation of the Blessed Virgin Mary, and establishing others for students of the Jesuit College.[178] He approved the establishment of a seminary for secular clerks in the town of Saint Trond in the diocese of Limburg,[179] and he commended the College founded at Rheims for the training of English priests to the support of the Emperor and other Christian kings and princes.[180] This long list of measures to assist teaching institutions, not only in Italy but in imperial and Spanish dominions and beyond the shores of Europe, bear testimony to the Pope's deep concern with the enlargement of educational facilities and his personal involvement in these projects which he regarded as of prime importance.

Unfortunately, the history of the English College, near the Palazzo Farnese, greatly discouraged Sixtus V. Situated in Via Monserrato, almost adjacent to Philip Neri's church, San Girolamo della Carità and within a brief walk of the Chancellery, the Palazzo Farnese and the Campo de' Fiori, the English College had originally been a medieval hospice for English pilgrims. It was a conspicuous setting for an exiled community whose activities were hard to hide from the busy quarter around it. After England's breach with Papacy, it became a refuge for English exiles under the care of a Cardinal Guardian appointed by the Pope and under the immediate direction of a Rector. Pope Gregory XIII not only lent it his personal favour but endowed it generously with money and property. In 1576 Dr Allen (later

Cardinal) the founder of the English seminaries at Douai and Rheims, together with Dr Owen Lewis, a Welsh exile, Professor of Law at Cambrai, and a personal friend of the Rector of the hospice, recommended to the Pope that a seminary for young English men should be attached to the hospice where they would be trained to become secular priests who would be expected to return to England to stimulate the faith of Catholics there and to win back the heretical Protestants. With the Pope's ready approval, students were sent by Dr Allen from Douai, Rheims and elsewhere, and Jesuit priests were attached to the seminary to be responsible for the teaching and training of the students. The work of the Jesuits was outstandingly efficient and some of the initial students had already taken orders as priests or deacons: consequently the College "quickly took a position as one of the first in Rome for the excellency of its studies". Nevertheless, almost from the outset there were serious student troubles. The College suffered from the inept administration with which it was inaugurated. The Rector was incompetent, failing to keep records or to establish any rapport with the students, and as numbers were allowed to increase, physical conditions deteriorated and students looked for contacts outside the College. Dr Allen had no confidence in the Rector who had been appointed against his better judgement. Within the College national factions were bitter, and the Rector, with the support of Dr Lewis, was thought to be excessively partial to his countrymen, the Welsh minority in the College. The students generally were boisterous and sensitive to every appearance of ill-treatment; the Welsh were said to be quarrelsome and uncouth. The division of authority between the Rector, charged with control of the hospice as well as the administration of the College, and the Jesuits responsible for teaching in the College only, was difficult, even though the latter took no part in the unrest and, indeed, were ordered by their General to avoid every possible involvement in it. The students found Jesuit discipline irksome, petty and arbitrary: training to be secular priests they failed to appreciate the value of the Jesuits' self-control and personal direction. They were restless and impatient, obsessively concerned with their return to their native land. Even after an open riot in 1579 had led to the removal of members from the College, even after the Rector had been pensioned-off by the Pope and a Jesuit appointed to succeed him, wounds were unhealed and ugly scars remained.

Scarcely had Sixtus been elected than a fresh revolt of the students broke out against their superiors, but this time they were much more activated by antagonism to the Jesuit regime. Indeed, one of the most serious accusations was that the Rector was unduly partial to those students who showed an inclination to join the Jesuit Order, even though in fact only six students had done so. The students also complained that the Jesuit government, though suited to the Jesuit Order, was not appropriate to the training of secular priests. English agents were even suspected of being embroiled in the student discontent and in stimulating their hostility to the Jesuits. There was now also a Scottish minority, and a deep rift of feeling developed concerning the succession to the English throne. The Jesuits accepted the Infanta of Spain as the rightful contender by reason of her descent from John of Gaunt, and no doubt looked forward to the day when England would be restored to the Catholic fold as part of Philip II's Spanish Empire. The Scottish students, on the other hand, were not unnaturally in favour of Mary, Queen of Scots. Sixtus appointed a commission comprising the Bishop of Piacenza (later promoted Cardinal Sega) and the Bishop of Castro, assisted by an accountant to examine the College finances. Unfortunately, the investigation was allowed to become extremely protracted and its report was not completed until after Sixtus V's death. Meanwhile, Sixtus ensured that a compromise was accepted pending the outcome of the Commission's report. Eight of the dissidents were expelled but the Jesuit rector was also removed and an Englishman and former student of the College, also a Jesuit, installed in his stead. Sixtus subsequently withdrew the annual papal subsidy of 3,000 scudi from the College and the number of both students and Jesuit teachers was reduced. After six months Father Holt surrendered the post of Rector and was then succeeded by another English Jesuit, Father Parsons, who remained in that position until 1589. Then a further English Jesuit, Father Creswell, succeeded to the post. As a mark of his regard for the work of the College, Sixtus appointed Dr Lewis in 1588 to the bishopric of Cassano in the kingdom of Naples, but continued to employ him in Rome. The Jesuit Order had never had enthusiasm for its involvement in the College and General Acquaviva was prepared to surrender the Order's responsibilities to Sixtus, but because of the acknowledged efficiency of Jesuit education the Jesuits were retained as teachers. Experience had shown beyond doubt that administration and teaching needed to be under the same control and so to the end of Sixtus' reign the English College remained under Jesuit management and direction. The problems of the College had not, however, been resolved, and a number of years were to elapse before a further re-organisation of the College could be effected. Sixtus had been plagued by the College disorders which he could not wholly dissociate from his disputes with the Jesuit Order.[181]

Revitalised by Sixtus' prodigious reforms, assured of its doctrinal positions and spurred by a vast chain of groups pledged to spirituality, the Church was ready to resume its attempt to reconquer Protestant Europe and its crusade in the New World—the third World of that day. The Union of Portugal with Spain in 1580 brought together under one monarch two immense empires of substantially different characteristics whose independence was guaranteed when Philip undertook to leave the administration of the Portuguese Empire in Portuguese hands—a promise which in general he faithfully kept. The Spanish Empire included lands which rendered the Caribbean virtually a Spanish Lake, and an area of incalculable wealth, Peru the richest source of silver in the world, Chile as yet less important, and in the Eastern Pacific, the Philippines, a land with coveted resources and a splendid springboard from which to forge links with China and Japan.

From the beginning this was an Empire of orderly settlement under closely coordinated Crown control with land settlements allocated to the settlers, by official royal licence, and the administration in the charge of Viceroys or governors, assisted by regularly constituted royal courts. By the time of Sixtus V's accession, Spanish trade with America was organised into twice-yearly convoys and trading expeditions outside the convoy system was forbidden. The whole system of Spanish administration concentrated on the production of silver and was designed to ensure that the Crown revenues reached the Spanish Treasury without interruption. Thus the health of the Empire overseas could be judged by the state of the revenue in Seville.

The Portugal was a maritime Empire, based on a chain of fortresses on the edge of the Atlantic, the Indian and the Pacific Oceans and the Chinese Seas, guarding a series of interlocking trading stations. Control by the crown was less obsessive, settlements were more restricted, and no single product could match the preponderance of silver in the Spanish Empire, though pepper and other spices were clearly dominated in the Portuguese economy. This oriental empire depended on the entrepot trade between one sector and another, and on its protection by squadrons of the royal navy, and it remained more dynamic and less predictable and circumscribed than its Spanish counterpart.

The size and wealth of these two empires must have astonished the Sistine cartographers. The Spanish and Portuguese strongholds united on each side of the Equator—an immense new Iberian monopoly. If Philip was jubilant at his accession to the Portuguese throne, other nations were apprehensive, even terror-stricken. By that time the Indies provided about a quarter of the total Iberian revenue, and in the Potosi silver mines about one-seventh of the total adult male Indian population was conscripted to labour.

The Spanish and Portuguese Empires were Catholic from the outset, the missionaries accompanying the invading soldiers, merchants and settlers, and establishing large, even elaborate, churches, schools and hospitals alongside imperial buildings, settlers' houses and factories, and customs houses. For these pioneers it was an obvious duty to convert the pagan natives, and in the East they felt a particular commission to oppose Islam (which had so recently been removed from Spain itself). In Mexico the Christian settlers razed Aztec temples to the ground and built Christian churches on the sites. The strict Franciscan Observants began the evangelisation of Mexico only five years after its conquest, and were joined by the Dominicans the following year and by the Augustinians eight year later; by 1553 eighteen Dominican houses formed the Province of Lima, and there were over a hundred Dominicans in the state of Peru. The Franciscans were organised identically. These groups of Regular clergy settled in towns, built themselves monasteries, and encouraged the indigenous population in the neighbouring countryside, affording them protection against Spanish oppression. One of the three initiators of the Spanish conquest of Peru, with Pizarro, was a priest, Luque, who though he took no part in the campaign, nevertheless found most of the capital needed for the expedition. The Franciscans established themselves in Goa where they founded a friary as a base for their mission work. In 1534 they also settled in Southern India, where the pearl-fishers, the Parevas, accepted Christianity in return for protection. They founded monasteries and managed schools, hospitals and orphanages. These older Orders maintained effective activity into the second half of the century. The Dominicans established a mission in the Lesser Saudi Islands in 1562. The Augustinians set out to evangelise the Philippines in 1565 (only four years after the Spanish occupation), founded a settlement in India in 1573 and another in China twelve years later. Throughout the period these ancient Orders followed hard on the heels of the conquerors, remaining with the settlers to teach the gospel, to organise religious communities and to educate the young. But the most notable of these religious colonists were the Jesuits. In 1542, only two years after the recognition of the Order by the Pope, they began a conversion campaign in India; seven years later they were established in Brazil. In Peru they founded churches and schools in almost every city, and by 1580 there were more than fifty preaching in one of the native languages; the area was organised as a Province, and by 1582 it numbered more than 1,300 Jesuits. By 1580 the Jesuits were active in Japan and took over control of the developing port of Nagasaki. Wherever they settled the Jesuits developed a close contact with the local people, learned their languages, often preached in the native languages and wrote and printed books and pamphlets in the vernacular. Everywhere they were disposed to accept the indigenous culture they found, recognising it and embodying it within the Christian faith and tradition, so facilitating the acceptance of Christianity amongst native populations. At Goa, Francis Xavier established a College to train youths of various nations to return as missionaries to their own countries, and began to translate catechisms, creeds and prayers into a number of local tongues.

The Inquisition was introduced in 1560. The activities of the clergy were fully supported by the Crown and its local administrators. Church and State were united in a common cause and the Crown developed a clerical administration to match its civil organisation: metropolitans, bishops and parochial clergy matching viceroys, governors and district officers. The first bishop of Mexico was appointed in 1527, but by 1545 Mexico was an Archbishopric with six dependent bishoprics. In Peru, Lima was an archbishopric, and there were bishoprics at Arequipa, Casco and Trujillo. In India, Goa was established as a bishopric in 1558 with jurisdiction from the Cape to China, and nine years later was elevated to an Archbishopric with suffragans at Cochin and Macau. In 1576 the latter was given the status of a bishopric with responsibility for China and Japan. Royal control over the Church was strictly and rigidly enforced. All bishops, heads of religious houses and parish priests were crown appointments; the royal sanction was needed for the erection of a church, a convent or a school. Communications with colonial establishments had to be approved by the crown and the proceedings of a colonial synod had to be sanctioned by the Viceroy or Governor and could be vetoed or referred to the Council of the Indies in Spain. Under these conditions, life for the regular clergy could be difficult and uncertain, for the policy of the Crown was to uphold the Authority of the diocese against them when disputes arose. Relations between the Crown and the Papacy were therefore crucial to the welfare of Christian establishments overseas.

Everywhere the Catholic clergy played Moses to the native peoples, defending them against the oppression of European Pharaohs and delivering them from their bondage. The Spanish and to a less marked extent, the Portuguese, pursued a largely enforced and surprisingly enlightened policy to the native. As early as 1512, the Laws of Burgos, described as the first European colonial code, ordered that indigenous people should be treated as freemen, not as slaves, that they should be converted by peaceable means and not by force and that the Christian clergy's duty was to persuade the idle to work in return for wages fixed by the courts. In 1542 the New Laws published in Peru and Chile substantially enforced the standards and practices of the Christian missionaries in the treatment of the native inhabitants. Thirty years later, in 1573, the *Ordenanzas sobre Descubrimiento* forbade warfare, ordered the settlers not to engage in inter-tribal strife and prohibited the seizure of native property. Enlightened laws needed enforcement and the missionaries and clergy were regarded as the natural defenders of indigenous rights.

Sixtus V came to deal with the religious problems of this Iberian Empire when its fortunes had reached a crucial stage and when problems inherent in its relatively short history were demanding resolution. Firstly, the Spanish appetite for expansion was sated. Empires were immensely expensive in men, in money and in natural resources: moreover, these real costs would rise as prices rose in the last quarter of the century. New lands, if conquered, were unlikely to prove as easy to acquire or to exploit as those already developed, and the spirit of pioneering expansion had been exhausted by the continuing disillusion with the profits of the existing empire. Secondly, the Spanish concentration on the production of silver became increasingly costly as more advanced techniques, usually more profligate of manpower, developed, and the increasing demand for both native and slave labour raised its value. Moreover, in Europe the importation of silver was to a substantial extent self-defeating. As the volume of silver imported increased, prices of other international products rose; indeed, the economy began to experience difficulty in paying for the imported silver and shortages of foodstuffs developed. Thirdly, in the Empire exploitation of its natural resources increased the demand for labour and so reduced the standard of agricultural maintenance and development. The excessive breeding of sheep, which reduced much valuable soil to a wilderness and soil erosion, the plague of South America, set in. A rich native culture disintegrated and a stabilising tradition disappeared. Similarly in the East, Portuguese administrators found their costs rising rapidly, control by the parent government was restricted and weakened, and the value of empire became more and more questionable. Commercial developments became increasingly dependent on private enterprise, and government interest declined. Venice, which had never suffered disastrously from the opening of the Cape route by the Portuguese, began to handle a growing trade between Central Europe and the Far East. Portuguese trade via Antwerp had closed before the middle of the century and increasing European entanglements prevented her from returning to her Low Countries trade. The effects of these changes on the Church overseas were serious. Firstly, shortage of native labour brought the building of churches, convents and schools to a virtual halt and the maintenance of existing buildings was neglected. Religious establishments in towns began to lose their splendour, an appearance of decay settled on their walls and their furnishings. Epidemics, though spasmodic, became frequent, further reducing the native population, and at the same time presenting the clergy with immense charitable demands they could no longer afford: faced with unavoidable failure, they lost spirit. The older Orders of regular clergy which had been so successful in evangelising the Empire now faced two alternatives—either to retire and return to Europe though that would require the royal consent, or to transfer to areas on the colonial frontiers where they could resume their old tasks amongst less highly civilised communities; this many did.[182]

Sixtus could do little to help the Western Empires, though he did his utmost to encourage the Regular clergy. All the overseas clergy were dependent on the Spanish crown, and Sixtus had little influence in the Escorial to shape the views of Philip II or induce him to initiate new efforts for religion's sake in America. Nevertheless, his contribution to the church in America was not inconsiderable. He authorised the General Commissioner of the Franciscan Observant to take part in the General Chapter of the Order and to exercise his rights in full,[183] and he confirmed and extended the privileges granted by previous Popes to the General and priests of the Missions.[184] In Mexico he safeguarded the entry of deacons, archdeacons and canons into new appointments,[185] and he confirmed the proceedings of the synod held in Mexico so that its recommendations might be implemented.[186] In Spanish South America he authorised the Dominicans to elect a Provincial General and other officers,[187] and he authorised the establishment of a University at Quito.[188]

By contrast he took a remarkably keen interest in developments in the Far East. He raised the establishments in the Philippines from the rank of custody to that of a Province and authorised the Provincial to found convents in both India and China; he established a Province of the Most Holy Rosary in Luzon.[189] By that date it was estimated that half the 600,000 Filippinos subject to Spanish rule had been converted to Christianity.[190] But his special concern was reserved for Japan. A Japanese deputation to the Pope was despatched in 1577 and was still in Rome when Sixtus V succeeded to the papal throne. The new Pope took noteworthy steps to do them every honour; he made the envoys Knights of the Golden Spur,[191] allocated to them places of special distinction at both his coronation and *possessio* ceremonies,[192] and on their departure gave them a farewell audience, a brief to the Japanese king and 3,000 ducats towards their expenses.[193] In the early part of 1588, at the very time when Sixtus was deeply embroiled with Philip II in frustrating negotiations about the Armada, Sixtus established an independent bishopric for Japan based on Funai and persuaded Philip to patronise and endow it.[194] The Jesuit Provincial in Portugal was named as the first bishop but unfortunately died before he could take up his appointment. By this time there were more than 15,000 converts in the central provinces of Japan, even though no financial or commercial favours were offered them, schools, seminaries and resplendent churches and been established in all the provincial cities. The Jesuits were exuberant with their success, established two new seminaries and a college for novices where native entrants to the Order could be trained, and a College at Funai. They were generally received with enthusiasm for, with great diligence and foresight, they had learned the native language and absorbed much of the native culture and regarded the natives as equals to be treated with every human respect and solicitude. Even though after they had been suspected of involvement in Japanese politics and had been ordered to leave the country within twenty days, they were able to outstay their expulsion, and eventually came to terms with the native rulers.[195] Sixtus supported them by increasing their papal grant by fifty per cent.

To his great delight Sixtus learned in 1586 that largely due to Jesuit initiatives entry had at last been effected into China. This success had been achieved substantially by a Neapolitan, Ruggierio, who had studied the Chinese language closely and developed a talent for winning the confidence and the hearts of the Chinese. The Jesuit mission was given every papal encouragement and Sixtus planned to send a mission to the Emperor. Ruggierio was called to Rome to prepare himself for this task, but unfortunately French affairs occupied so much of Sixtus V's attention and energy that the mission was not dispatched. China had proved the most resistant country to Christian penetration, but by the time of Sixtus V's death the way was open and the will and the means of evangelisation were ready.

The magnetic attraction of the Far East did not cause Sixtus V to ignore the Middle East. From his predecessor he inherited a mission intended to examine closely and purposively the possibility of reunion with the Eastern Churches. Following a prolonged and serious dispute about the one Personhood and two natures of Christ during the fifth century, a series of Churches was recognised in the Middle East which were excluded from the Roman Catholic Church and which never fell under the sway of the Eastern Orthodox Church when that finally established its independence of Rome in AD 1054. Groups developed in Asia Minor and Persia, with dependencies in South-West Asia and Cochin. There were others, especially Syrians who acknowledged the jurisdiction of the Patriarch of Antioch and Armenians under the authority of the Patriarch of Cilicia, who retained their connection with Rome but were enabled to use their own languages, rites and canon law. Lastly, there was the Egyptian Church which became more and more isolated from both Rome and Constantinople and the Coptic Churches of Upper Egypt which were organised under the jurisdiction of the Patriarch of Alexandria and twelve bishops who elected him. After the Arabs succeeded in conquering most of the region and after Islam had taken over control in matters of religion, these fragmented Christian churches were subject to sporadic persecution, but generally succeeded in maintaining their independent existence. From time to time there were attempts to effect reunion with Rome but this had not been achieved. The mission which Gregory XIII had despatched under the leadership of the Bishop of Sidon reported to Sixtus in 1587. It found little enthusiasm for reunion with Rome except in certain districts of Lebanon, Armenia and Chaldea. A Mission from certain Middle East churches was received the following year and the Patriarch of Chaldea submitted a profession of that area's faith. This, however, did not enable a formal act of reunion, but the relations of Rome with these Eastern churches was improved by this fresh examination of their respective doctrinal positions and by the better understanding which was promoted. In the last year of his pontificate Sixtus also wrote to both the newly appointed Patriarch of Alexandria and his Vicar-General urging them to take steps to bring about a reunion of the Copts with Rome since the differences between them seemed too narrow to justify a separate organisation. He also despatched a mission of Jesuits to Constantinople to improve the relations of Rome with the East, but unfortunately plague killed both the Jesuit missionaries and the Capuchins who followed them. Sixtus, obsessed with the continuing advance of the Turks into Eastern Europe, recognised the importance of maintaining Christianity in the midst of Islam and of uniting all the Christian churches in the face of a common threat.

From the middle of the century Papal policy had been set firm in the direction of reform and rejuvenation. The last two phases of the Council of Trent had provided the Church with a unity which gave strength and purpose to its objectives, and both in doctrine and practice set standards capable of attainment and yet stimulating of effort and devotion. Above all, Trent had strengthened the authority and restored the leadership of the Pope. Sixtus, well aware that the time was ripe, brought to his pontificate an iron determination to accelerate the pace of reform. These were five remarkable years and highlight Sixtus as perhaps the most devoted reformer of the century. He reorganised the papal central government, defining the qualities of members of the Sacred College, from which evolved all the major instruments of papal administration. He established on a permanent footing the Congregations into which were recruited the resources and energies of every Cardinal, and these became the effective means by which Papal policy was imposed through the bishoprics into every religious establishment under Rome's control. This highly centralised government worked efficiently, motivated by a clear and unwavering policy, and activated by a closely knit inner caucus of men attached personally to the Holy Father and ideologically to the philosophy he represented. The permanence of this new system gave it strength and assurance so that its operation was consistent and fundamentally dominant. There was one basic limitation on the effectiveness of papal government. Outside the Papal States, and certainly amongst the leading Catholic powers, the authority of the church was wholly dependent on the support of the states. In all these quarters the Pope's supreme task was to gain the active involvement of the rulers in the implementation of ecclesiastical policy. The pace of reform in Europe and overseas was dictated by the co-operation of the princes. Papal foreign policy was therefore largely directed to maintaining an understanding and agreement about religious affairs with the major states and their satellites.

Sixtus recognised that obedience to church law and acceptance of centralised administration required the active support of subordinate rulers in the church. To strengthen their loyalty to Rome and to stimulate their willingness to be involved in the implementation of its wishes, Sixtus increased the extent and improved the quality of religious literature available, re-invigorated and extended the regular celebration of historic traditions and multiplied the Universities and seminaries from which church workers were drawn. While bishops were encouraged, cajoled or compelled to use to the utmost their talents in the service of the church, the Pope strove with utmost diligence to develop the work of the Regular Orders and to multiply associations of layman and clergy pledged to the observance of religious sites and the fulfilment of charitable missions in the name of the church. He capitalised on the growth of settlements and commercial foundations, especially in the East, to ensure that in the New World the authority of the Catholic Church was established and that its influence was guaranteed by its philanthropic work amongst the indigenous people, especially through their education.

## Notes

1. *CMH* 3, p.54.
2. *Ibid.*, p. 53; and J. H. Elliott, *Europe Divided 1559–1598* (London: Collins, 1969), p. 150.
3. The Dataria was a Commission, originally forming part of the Chancellery which was primarily concerned with grants and favours and with the conferment of those benefices which were not reserved to the Consistory.
4. There is a summary of the organs of Papal and Roman government in Delumeau 1, pp. 17–22.
5. Cardinal Medici was created Cardinal at the age of fourteen and Cardinal Farnese at the age of fifteen, Alessandro Peretti at the age of fourteen.
6. Since the beginning of the century there had been only three years in which no Cardinal's death occurred; there were thirty-eight years in which no Cardinal was appointed.
7. Prodi 1, p.505
8. Pastor 21, pp. 8, 232, 235, 239.
9. *Ibid.*, 21, pp. 231, 235, 242
10. In the Vatican Library is preserved a list comprising 27 names of those to be considered for the Cardinalate in December 1587 (*Codice Barberiniano Latino*, 1055, f. 493).
11. Letter dated 7th August 1585 in the Vatican Library; see *Codice Vaticano Latino*,10445, f. 1.
12. Pastor 21, p. 237.
13. *ODCC*, p. 1244.
14. *Ibid.*, p. 903.
15. Bartolomé Carranza (1503–1576), Archbishop of Toledo, accused of heresy.
16. Information about Sixtus V's Cardinals has been taken from L. Cardella, *Memorie storiche de' cardinali della santa romana Chiesa scritte da Lorenzo Cardella parroco de' SS. Vincenzo, ed Anastasio alla Regola in Roma* (Roma: Stamperia Paglierini, 1793) and from *Dizionario della Romana Chiesa* (Roma: 1893), Vol 5.
17. *Bullarium* 8, pp. 985–999; Pastor 21, pp. 245–261.
18. Pastor 21, p. 261.

19  See P. Prodi, *Il Cardinale Gabriele Paleotti*, vol. 2 (Roma: Storia e Letteratura, 1967), pp. 484–485, 512, 523 and 525.
20  Pastor 21, p. 246.
21  Article in *EC* by Professor Pachini.
22  G. Cugnoni, "Autobiografia di Monsignor G. Antonio Santori cardinale di S. Severina" in *Archivio della Società Romana di Storia Patria* 13 (1890), p. 185.
23  *Ibid.*, p. 165.
24  Pastor 21, pp. 132–135.
25  *Bullarium* 8, p. 641.
26  *Codice Ottoboniano latino* 2473 in the Vatican Library.
27  *Bullarium* 9, p. 249.
28  Pastor 21, p. 193.
29  *Ibid.*, pp. 206–207 and p. 207, n. 1.
30  Cardella 5, p. 265.
31  Pastor 21, p. 197.
32  *Ibid.* 21, pp. 198–222.
33  See *ODCC*, articles on "Vulgate" and "Septuagint", and corresponding articles in *EC*. See also J. Brodrick, *The life and work of Blessed Robert Francis Cardinal Bellarmine, S.J. 1542–1621* (London: Longmans Green, 1950), pp. 276–287.
34  O. Chadwick, *The Penguin History of the Church 3, The Reformation* (London: Penguin, 1976), p. 143.
35  *Ibid.*, p. 303.
36  See *ODCC*, articles on "Flacius", "Centuriators of Magdeburg" and "Baronius", and articles on "Baronio" by A. Pincherle in *DBI*.
37  *Bullarium* 8, p. 894.
38  The famous printer Aldus Manutius the Younger was primarily a Professor of Eloquence.
39  Delumeau 1, pp. 371–381 with first table.
40  Pastor 21, p. 205.
41  *Ibid.* 21, p. 209.
42  *Bullarium* 8, p.841.
43  See *EC*, articles on family of "Manutius", "Tipografia".
44  Ambrosini & Willis, *Secret Archives of the Vatican*, pp. 168–169.
45  *Bullarium* 8, p. 23.
46  *Ibid.* 8, p. 928.

47  See G. Carandente, "Dottori della Chiesa" in *EC*.
48  See *ODCC*, article on St Bonaventure.
49  *Bullarium* 8, p. 1005.
50  See *EC*, article on "Ufficio Divino".
51  For festivals see *Bullarium* 8, pp. 591–592, 592–593, 645–646, 654–655, 662–663.
52  *Ibid.* 8, pp. 663–666.
53  EC article on "Palestrina" by Luigi Ronga.
54  *Bullarium* 8, p. 736.
55  O. M. T. Logan, *Studies in the religious life of Venice in the sixteenth and early seventeenth centuries. The Venetian clergy and religious Orders 1520–1630* (Cambridge: PhD thesis, 1964), pp. 114f. The theme was continued throughout the century and was developed by Cardinal Paleotti in his *Archiepiscopale bononiense, sive De bononiensis ecclesiae administratione* in1594; see P. Prodi, *Il Cardinale Gabriele Paleotti*, vol. 2 (Roma: Storia e Letteratura, 1967).
56  Appointed Bishop of S. Agata. He thus followed in Sixtus V's own footsteps, having been appointed to that See while Vicar-General of the Order in 1566.
57  Sixtus attempted to heal divisions in the Franciscan Order, see Pastor 23, p. 142.
58  Prodi 2, p. 108.
59  *Ibid.*, pp. 270–291.
60  *Ibid.*, pp. 324–327.
61  *Ibid.*, p. 291.
62  *Ibid.*, pp. 26, 472.
63  *Ibid.*, p. 295
64  *Ibid.*, p. 353
65  It should be added that Gregory XIII had made generous grants towards the restoration of Bologna Cathedra (Prodi 2, p. 58).
66  Prodi 2, p. 297.
67  *Ibid.*, p. 311
68  *Ibid.*, pp. 328, 333 and 358 n. 88.
69  *Ibid.*, p. 327
70  *Ibid.*, p. 73
71  *Ibid.*, p. 191
72  *Ibid.*, p. 51

73  *Ibid.*, p. 328 n.
74  *Ibid.*, p. 173.
75  For example, he established a commission to examine the finances of the diocese of Bologna. (Prodi, p. 300)
76  *Ibid.*, p. 383.
77  *Bullarium* 8, pp. 706–709.
78  Schroeder, *Disciplinary decrees of the General Councils*, p. 219: Council of Trent 25$^{th}$ Session, Chapter III.
79  A Confraternity was an ecclesiastical corporation, normally associating together clerics and lay people. It was normally associated with a church or chapel or a particular altar and was pledged to the regular observations of religious festivals and rites related to the altar, church. A confraternity was usually under the jurisdiction of a bishop or one of the Regular Orders, and it frequently took some particular charitable function as its purpose. (See article on "Confraternity" by P. Paschini in *EC*). There were large numbers of confraternities in the Italian States and many of them had very strong memberships. Montaigne records an occasion when 12,000 confraternities each with a lighted torch in hand passed him on their way to celebrate Holy Thursday. See Pastor 20, p. 558.
80  *Bullarium* 8, pp. 630–632, 736–740.
81  *Bullarium* 8, p. 934; 9, p. 138. See also A. Coccia, *La Provincia romana dei frati minori conventuali dall'origine ai nostri giorni* (Roma: Amati, 1967), Document 2.
82  *Bullarium* 8, pp. 931–933.
83  *Ibid.* 8, pp. 916–928.
84  *Ibid.* 8, pp. 659–662.
85  *Ibid.* 8, pp. 671–672.
86  Pastor 21, p. 139, n. 3.
87  *Bullarium* 8, pp. 663–666.
88  *Ibid.* 9, p. 33.
89  *Ibid.* 8, p. 9.
90  *Ibid.* 9, p. 104.
91  Tempesti, *Storia della vita e geste di Sisto Quinto*, p. 49.
92  Pastor 23, pp. 141–142.
93  *Bullarium* 8, pp. 877–888.
94  *Ibid.* 9, pp. 97–98.

95   *Ibid.*, pp. 94–96.
96   *Ibid.* 8, pp. 673–681.
97   A phrase from L. Elliott, *I will be called John* (London: Fontana, 1973), p. 167.
98   Admission of a novice was to be authorised by a General or Provincial Chapter.
99   *Bullarium* 9, pp. 656–657.
100  L. Di Fonzo, G. Odoardi, A. Pompei, *I Frati Minori Conventuali. Storia e vita 1209–1976* (Roma: Curia Generalizia Conventuali Roma, 1978), pp. 40, 57.
101  Pastor 21, p. 142.
102  *Bullarium* 8, p. 957.
103  *Ibid.* 9, p. 248.
104  See Bettenson, p. 128.
105  *Bullarium* 9, pp. 270–271.
106  *Ibid.* 9, pp. 71–72.
107  *Ibid.* 8, p. 856.
108  *Ibid.* 9, p. 256.
109  *Ibid.* 9, p. 270.
110  *Ibid.* 9, pp. 72–73.
111  *Ibid.* 8, pp. 761–765.
112  *Ibid.* 8, pp. 916–928.
113  *Ibid.* 8, pp. 81–94.
114  *Ibid.* 9, p. 20.
115  Pastor 21, pp. 158–159.
116  *Ibid.* 21, pp. 160–161.
117  *Ibid.* 21, pp. 164–169; Hübner 2, p. 46.
118  Brodrick, *The life and work of Blessed Robert Francis Cardinal Bellarmine*, p. 126.
119  Pastor 19, p. 91.
120  Pastor 21, p. 179.
121  *Bullarium* 8, pp. 458–459.
122  *Ibid.* 8, pp. 352–355.
123  *Ibid.* 9, pp. 158–164.
124  Brodrick, *The life and work of Blessed Robert Francis Cardinal Bellarmine*, p. 26.
125  *CMH* 1, p. 294.
126  *ODCC*, p. 734.
127  In about 1575 the Jesuits numbered 3,905, but 210 Colleges and missions

contained about one-third of the total and these were in training; see Brodrick, *The life and work of Blessed Robert Francis Cardinal Bellarmine*, p. 269.

[128] Pastor 21, p. 152. In 1570, there were still only 47 professed of the fourth vow, of whom 26 were Spaniards; see Brodrick, *The life and work of Blessed Robert Francis Cardinal Bellarmine*, p. 268, n. 4.

[129] Brooke, *Early Franciscan Government*, p. 204, n. 2.

[130] Pastor 21, pp. 152–153.

[131] Brooke, *Early Franciscan Government*, p. 180.

[132] *ODCC*, p. 78.

[133] Brooke, *Early Franciscan Government*, pp. 274–276.

[134] Pastor 21, pp. 152–153.

[135] Brooke, *Early Franciscan Government*, p. 268, n. 4 and p. 285.

[136] *Ibid.*, p. 139

[137] *Ibid.*, p. 176.

[138] Pastor 21, pp. 147–149.

[139] Brooke, *Early Franciscan Government*, pp. 32, 33, 40, 42, 43.

[140] J. Brodrick, *The progress of the Jesuits (1556–79)* (Chicago: Loyola, 1986), pp. 62–63.

[141] See Brooke, *Early Franciscan Government*.

[142] *ODCC*, article on "Bellarmine".

[143] Chadwick, *The Reformation*, p. 304.

[144] Brodrick, *The life and work of Blessed Robert Francis Cardinal Bellarmine*, p. 270.

[145] *Ibid.*, p. 198.

[146] *Ibid.*, p. 264.

[147] *Ibid.*, p. 273.

[148] Ambrosini & Willis, *Secret Archives of the Vatican*, pp. 113–115.

[149] F. Braudel, *The Mediterranean and the Mediterranean world in the age of Philip II*, trans. S. Reynolds (New York: Harper and Row, 1972), p. 395.

[150] *Ibid.*, pp. 780–795.

[151] *Bullarium* 8, pp. 871–877.

[152] *Ibid.* 8, pp. 203–208.

[153] *Ibid.* 9, p. 303.

[154] *Ibid.* 9, p. 30.

[155] *Ibid.* 9, p. 380.

156 Ibid. 9, p. 286.
157 Ibid. 9, p. 60.
158 Ibid. 9, p. 317.
159 Ibid. 9, pp. 30–32.
160 Ibid. 9, pp. 94–95.
161 Ibid. 9, pp. 275–281.
162 Ibid. 9, p. 359.
163 Ibid. 9, p. 431.
164 Pastor 21, pp. 131–131.
165 *Bullarium* 8, p. 204.
166 Ibid. 9, pp. 286–300.
167 Ibid. 9, p. 337.
168 Hübner 2, p. 11.
169 Pastor 22, p. 198, n. 5.
170 Chadwick, *The Reformation*, p. 310.
171 *Bullarium* 8, pp. 721–724.
172 Ibid. 9, pp. 99–103.
173 Ibid. 8, pp. 978–985; Coccia, *La Provincia romana dei frati minori conventuali dall'origine ai nostri giorni*, p. 20.
174 *Bullarium* 8, pp. 593–598; Pistolesi, *Sisto V e Montalto da documenti inediti*, p. 97.
175 *Bullarium* 8, p. 198.
176 Ibid. 9, pp. 250–252.
177 Ibid. 9, p. 319.
178 Ibid. 8, p. 826.
179 Ibid. 9, pp. 125–127.
180 Ibid. 9, pp. 352–355.
181 This section is based on Cardinal F. A. Gasquet, *The History of the Venerable English College, Rome* (London: 1920).
182 See *NCMH* 1 Chapter 15; 2, Chapters 19 and 20; 3, Chapters 2 and 17. See also Brodrick, *The progress of the Jesuits*, p. 127.
183 *Bullarium* 8, p. 855.
184 Ibid. 9, p. 265.
185 Ibid. 9, p. 124.

[186] *Ibid.* 9, p. 350.
[187] *Ibid.* 9, p. 96.
[188] *Ibid.* 8, p. 733.
[189] Pastor 20, p. 183.
[190] *NCMH* 3, p. 555.
[191] Pastor 20, p. 179.
[192] *Ibid.* 21, p. 155.
[193] *Ibid.* 20, p. 179.
[194] *Ibid.* 20, p. 181.
[195] *NCMH* 3, pp. 551–552.

# CHAPTER 8

### The Papal States and the Italian Peninsula

*Much of his leadership was thus a form of pragmatic extremism, extreme action and threat of more extreme action to come, but used in the cause of more limited objectives.*

John Ramsden, *Age of Balfour and Baldwin*

THE POPE EXERCISED temporal suzerainty over the Papal States, Avignon and Benevento, the latter a small enclave of papal power enclosed within the Kingdom of Naples. The Papal States were somewhat larger than the Tudor principality of Wales, somewhat smaller than Mary Stuart's kingdom of Scotland, though its population was considerably greater:[1] they formed the link between the states of the valley of the Po, Tuscany and the kingdom of Naples, of which at that time the Abruzzi was a spire. Its axis, running from North West to South East, spanned the area between the Mediterranean on the West and the Adriatic on the East; its Mediterranean coastline extended somewhat more than 160 miles, the Adriatic exceeding 120 miles. At the widest point, only 160 miles of land lay between the two seas, a distance approximately equal to that which lies between the Irish Sea at Dublin and Connemara on the Atlantic Ocean.[2] The Apennine Range crossing any strict East-West axis formed a natural and formidable obstacle between the very narrow Adriatic coastal plain and the very much wider plain on the Mediterranean.[3] Both the coastal plains included very substantial areas of marsh which had been neglected for centuries and maintained only intermittently, so that both on the Adriatic and on the Mediterranean sides the area suitable for intensive cultivation was severely restricted in size and quality. Clearly nature had never designed the medieval Papal States to blossom either as a maritime power or as a skilled exploiter of physical resources. The absence of any large-scale port and failure to develop advanced forms of industry allowed only limited growth and serious handicaps in agriculture never permitted it to accumulate surpluses sufficient to play any significant part in the international market. Nevertheless, amongst the Italian states it remained the greatest of the independent states after Venice. The time for political warfare and for the involvement of European powers in Italian affairs had passed; now the Papal States only had a role in European diplomatic engagement. Papal policy was therefore to preserve the self-sufficiency of the Papal States, to reduce its demands on the products of other states, to raise their own level of productivity and to enlarge its own banking and marketing affairs, so attracting to its own Treasury a surplus of international monetary and commercial revenues.

Few people had a more illuminating introduction to the geographical structure, economic resources and natural weaknesses of the Papal States than the traveller from the shrine of Loreto to St Peter's, Vatican. Loreto was the site of the Holy House where the Blessed Virgin Mary resided when the Archangel Gabriel made the announcement of her conception to her. Pious tradition asserted that angels had miraculously transported the household from Nazareth to Dalmatia in 1291 and thence to Loreto on 9th December 1294. As the devotion grew, and its authenticity was accepted, a scheme was formed of erecting a venerable and spectacular basilica alongside the site of the Holy House, and this was begun with great pomp and celebration by Paul II and work continued through the remainder of that and the following century. By Sixtus V's time there was an unending procession of pilgrims to it, to whom ecclesiastical favours were regularly granted. The Basilica, constructed lavishly in marble and filled with artistic treasures of the period, was supremely impressive and evoked such wonder that sceptical or scientific enquiries were set aside. In the phasing of the new Bull the Pope wished to "increase the devotion of faithful Christians to the honour of the Blessed Virgin Mary".[4] People were in a mood to believe; they were searching for assurance: consequently religion and devotion stood not far apart. From the plateau on which the Basilica had been planted the traveller could look out over the Adriatic Sea towards the misty outline of the Dalmatian mountains stretching to the East. From Loreto the traveller followed the valley of the River Potenza, and beyond its rolling folds of mountains, three to four thousand feet high. The soft green of the spring fields in the valley contrasted sharply with the bleakness of the foothills and the stark towering rocks of the mountains beyond.

Continuing his journey, the traveller headed between the foothills of the Potenza valley, where he was soon surrounded by the mountains of the Marches. He passed through the Cathedral city of Recanati and on to Macerata, the capital of the Province. Two miles further on the Chienti valley provided westward route through Tolentino, and on to Camerino and Foligno. This was a region of small rival towns, often perched precipitously on the edge of an escarpment and generally walled against the incursions of local brigands. Small communities provided defence, protection and administrative direction. Near Camerino, Monte Igno rose to 1,500 metres and Monte Ferino to 1,700 metres. A river valley led through dangerous, forbidding, mountain territory stretching north and southwards. These were the Pennines of Central Italy, where a lost traveller could find himself trapped in a vast chain of mountain peaks. This was ancient Etruscan territory, bordering Perugia and Assisi. From Foligno the road led along a deep river valley to Spoleto, and then to Terni. Now only a third of the journey was left — just sixty miles of easy travel. Terni is approximately 300 metres above sea-level, the air fresh and clear. A small town, Terni has a Roman amphitheatre, a medieval Cathedral and a church dedicated to San Salvatore built in the twelfth century as an extension of an ancient Temple of the Sun. Now the route lay along the valley of the river Tiber, the road to Narni led to the main stream of the river. From Borghetto the Tiber was navigable and the journey into Rome offered no further obstacles.[5] As the river valley steadily opened, the Tiber flowed through rich and well cultivated agricultural land.

No sixteenth-century traveller who completed such a journey could fail to register firstly, the absolute dependence of the Papal States on its rivers—both as communications and as places of human residence and development—and secondly, the total domination of the entire States by Rome. Climate determined the States' prosperity and fixed the level of major crops: floods or drought reduced or destroyed them; variation in the melting of the snows was sufficient to turn spring promise of bumper harvests into autumn catastrophe for those who were normally self-sufficient. The river valleys were the essential link between one rural town and the next; floods made the roads impassable for protracted periods during which the local inhabitants were left entirely dependent on their own resources. Frequently flood-waters surrounding Santa Maria sopra Minerva reminded the rulers of the capital that control of the upper Tiber was the only permanent solution.

Rome then was an irresistible magnet. The government of the Church made its own steadily increasing demand for services in the capital, and officers were steadily recruited from a variety of countries in Europe and even from further afield: peasants and other working people were inevitably attracted from outlying areas. The pressure on the City presented a constant problem which remains with it today.[6]

Rome, therefore, required the products of the Mediterranean coastal plain and the foothills behind, but the growth of its population, the continued enlargement of a non-productive court and the emergence of a money-driven transfer from agriculture to cattle breeding and sheep rearing made this source of supply inadequate and, in times of exceptional difficultly, hopelessly insufficient. The area from which supplies had to be drawn were pushed more and more into the hills, and government restrictions were used to place the foothills and even the more distant river valleys under contract to the City. These tendencies reached their height in the difficult climatic conditions of the last two years of Sixtus' reign.

The Papal States' unique geographical situation made them the natural land highway between the Adriatic and the Mediterranean.[7] They had developed with great foresight and skill a whole labyrinth of roadways closely linked with the river valleys. "Rome" says Delumeau, "is situated on one of the great axes of Philip II's Empire;" and the *Avvisi* recorded in 1588 "an intense coming and going of couriers between Spain, Rome and Naples." A particularly brisk and flourishing trade in textiles developed between Rome and Naples, the luxuries of Florence and the cloths of Tuscan and Umbrian towns being carried via Rome to Naples, and in return the fine silks, velours and damasks were brought back for distribution to northern Italy.[8] Rome became "the best informed city in the world". There was always fierce competition between water carriage and land transport; the former was cheaper but slower and less reliable; so long as corsairs and pirates roamed the eastern and western Mediterranean seas and so long as Christian shipping was poorly organised, regular shipping routes remained precarious. Normally, in spite of their technical advantages, the sea routes did not enjoy the dominance which might have been expected. Efficient systems of transportation then developed and expanded throughout the second half of the sixteenth century till they were established as the major bases of European transport and communication. This was particularly so because the limitation of financial resources in commerce kept trading ventures comparatively small. The main enemies of road transport were brigandage and highwaymen; on many occasions carriages were set upon, overturned and ransacked, not only under cover of the wild country of the Romagna or the Marches but almost at the gates of Rome. Travellers went in perpetual fear of these onslaughts and coaches preferred the shelter of night to the nakedness of daylight travel. In 1589 Huguenot bands so decimated Philip II's convoy from Barcelona that he ordered further expeditions to embark at Genoa and travel by sea to Barcelona.[9] But, in general, land travel was more easily subjected to a convoy system escorted by a heavily guarded escort which could hold its own with all but the best organised brigands. Road and river transport was essential to the maintenance of Rome's dominance over the European international communications system.

There were five international postal lines centred on Rome, with a predetermined service of which the departure dates and the routes to be followed were invariable. The Spanish line ran every month from Barcelona to Lyons, thence to Genoa, from where a spur connected with Milan. From Genoa the main line ran onwards to Florence and Rome and so to Naples—a total distance of 1,220 miles which in circumstances of urgency were covered in sixteen days.[10]

Secondly, a French post ran every ten or fifteen days from Lyons following the same route as the Spanish line to Rome and Naples, covering the journey at best in ten to twelve days. Much of the traffic on this route arose from the need of the Papal Court to be fully informed of the state of the French beneficiaries. Since the Concordat of 1516 the succession to many of the benefices not reserved to Consistory or in the gift of the French king were, to varying degrees, under the Pope's power of nomination. The political power of the French clergy being extremely pervasive and decisive, it was of great importance that the Roman court should have up to date and detailed information of impending vacancies and the electoral prospects and difficulties, and likewise that Roman views and tactics should be very speedily transmitted to the diocese.

The third postal line belonged to the Republic of Genoa and a weekly courier reached Naples via Florence and Rome in about eight days. A fourth line departing weekly from Rome connected Venice with Naples by way of Ravenna, Rimini, Fano, Foligno and Rome, the journey occupying three days. A spur from this line connected Venice with Bologna and Ferrara. By way of the alternate passes through the Alps, the Venetian route linked with the whole of the highway system of Central Europe—to Antwerp in the West, to Vienna and Poland in the East. Lastly, the Pope organised a service over all the other national routes. In addition, there was a weekly service to Bologna and a similar one to Ancona, both within the Papal States. He similarly provided services to Alatri and Benevento—the latter an important link with what could have been an isolated enclave surrounded by a foreign and often a hostile country. Rome itself was therefore an outstanding centre of international communications from which radiated permanently, and normally with regularity and punctuality, connections which threaded their way across the whole map of Europe. There information acquired over several decades was stored under the control of a staff who knew its value, edited its pages with discretion and guarded its publication. Primarily a diplomatic and state service under the direction of the respective heads of state, members of the public were allowed to use it, the receivers paying fees according to the weight of the letter or packet and the distance it was carried.[11] These fees were farmed, the purchase price forming part of the Papal revenues. Isolated travellers and pilgrims thronged all these routes, some perhaps joining the coaches for the most difficult stages of the journey, many on horse and more on foot. Each line was under the control of the General of the Posts, but the Papal General had established a sort of hegemony, not extending to any form of censorship but constituting a form of priority and directional control over the rest. All letters passing in and out of Rome had to be registered with the Papal Master of Posts. Every courier arriving in Rome or being despatched from the city had first to report to the Papal Master of Posts. Only the official foreign posts could be exempt from this requirement as special circumstances demanded. Such a system offered a measure of security and a comprehensive service to its clients, whose demands for regularity of despatch and punctuality of delivery over these considerable distances could be very largely met. Merchants of a large number of nationalities soon used these services to maintain an efficient correspondence and to deliver many of the smaller items of merchandise. Among the foremost mercantile clients were the foreign bankers, Florentine, Genoese,[12] and Neapolitan, who maintained a regular correspondence with their clients in other cities, and who transferred moneys from Rome to their customers. In particular, they were responsible for collecting information on bank failures, which were frequent,[13] and transmitting it with all speed to other cities. "The roads to Rome were therefore more busy than all the other routes of Europe, and the axis Madrid—Lyons—Rome was the most heavily used of the postal itineraries of the sixteenth century."[14]

Rome was the unequalled international capital of communications and this, to a considerable extent, offset the lack of commodity commerce and the absence of manufacture from which she suffered. Sixtus V's immense floating of *Monti* through the Genoans, Pinelli and Guastavillani, helped to create a buoyant market in the city whilst its ecclesiastical transactions provided it with funds for substantial monetary activities.[15] This was a resourceful state whose magnetic power attracted important financial business and probably made Rome during Sixtus' reign an international financial market.

One other city, Bologna, was exceptional and had a population of 60,000. It had been conquered by Pope Julius II when the local despot, Giovanni Bentivoglia, was driven from the city, his magnificent palace destroyed, and Bologna incorporated in the Papal States. Factions, however, died reluctantly and Bologna long remained a turbulent and often disorderly city where in the latter half of the sixteenth century bandits could find temporary refuge from their pursuers. Standing at the foot of the Apennines, it overlooked the central portion of the rich valley of the Po, shared its wealth and engaged in its East/West trade; it was a city of obvious wealth with a textile industry of some note, of great grandeur, and it nourished with unstinting munificence a powerful University that enjoyed an international reputation, particularly in law. An intellectual as well as a commercial city, it was noted for its civic pride, its independence and its arrogance; few communities were more jealous of admission into its society. Its tradition was closely wedded to its historic artistic standards and it retained much of the character of a Renaissance city. Furthermore, it was the seat of a distinguished archbishopric which maintained a desultory but recurring campaign against the municipality.[16]

The Papal States had two main ports, Ancona on the Adriatic, and Civitavecchia on the western coast. Neither could claim to be in the first rank of European ports, yet both were of considerable magnificence. Ancona was the main papal port on the Adriatic and constituted the meeting place of treasures, the agricultural products imported from the East, and exports intended for the Ottoman Empire. It had special importance in Sixtus V's policy of developing the resources of the Marches.

Civitavecchia on the Mediterranean coast was unique. It was the main bastion of the Papal States' maritime defence, was provided with an independent supply of drinking water and was heavily fortified so as to be able to defend itself against even the heaviest attacks. It kept watch over international trade between Naples and Tuscany and Genoa, and with a considerable number of small ships provided an efficient if limited Mediterranean port for the city of Rome. In the centre of the town was the great custom house, impeccably maintained, whose records have proved a priceless hoard for historians. But the main trade from Civitavecchia was in alum. This was a mineral used as a tinting material in art, and an essential dyeing and finishing material in the textile industry. Its chemical properties made it invaluable for fixing colours in the final stages of fabric processing. The alum mines of Tolfa, some ten miles inland from Civitavecchia, had been discovered in the middle of the fifteenth century, and because of their superior quality and ready supply had quickly begun to supplement other sources of supply such as Syria, Egypt, Greece, North Africa and, especially, Anatolia. With varying success the church tried to impose a complete monopoly in the alum trade, ensuring for itself a steady, reliable income of a very sizeable level. In later decades English, Low Country and Spanish shipping developed a bitter rivalry with the Italian suppliers, but for the moment the trade from Civitavecchia was at its zenith. The working of the mines was let to a series of mine exploiters and was based on a system of the most carefully constructed papal contracts which gave generous opportunities to the farmers of the assignments. The industry sustained a work force of some seven or eight hundred, brought 36,000 containers to the surface and provided an income of 335,520 écus annually for the papal treasury. Almost all this was exported, and was shipped by sea, making Civitavecchia a splendidly thriving port so that the alum industry has been described as "probably the greatest mining undertakings in Europe".[17]

The Papal States were studded on the east and the west of the Apennines with numerous small towns, whose populations ranged from 2,000 to 10,000. These had some limited measure of local autonomy and were economically largely self-supporting; their life was unpretentious and provincial. The local churches and the municipal authorities together preserved, for the most part, a quiescent acceptance of the established way of life, until some arbitrary interference with the natural outlets of their small scale trade, or some disaster made their situation desperate, and drove them to sudden and destructive change.

Outside Rome, the society of the Papal States remained largely medieval in character. There were the Roman nobility (some related to the princes of the lesser Italian states) maintaining their provincial castles to which they escaped from the city's summer heat and the rule of the Papal and City authorities. They seemed powerful and opulent and yet were heavily and incurably in debt because of their predecessors' extravagant patronage of the Renaissance arts and their imprudent investment in sumptuous buildings which their descendents were obliged to maintain. On the fringe of the nobility were the leaders of the bandits, some of them descended from the *condottieri* of the previous century, others virtually professional mercenaries hired for their military training, prowess and ruthlessness, who lived through periods of unemployment on the proceeds of their marauding raids. Moving not merely from place to place, but from one Italian state to another, and even enlisting in the recognised forces of Central Europe, they were homeless, roving bands who preferred the adventures of unofficial wars to the prospects of a regular, organised and legitimate livelihood.

The population of the Papal States comprised a considerable number of clergy. It included the six dioceses in the vicinity of the City assigned to the six Cardinal bishops; thirteen in the Province of Rome, fourteen in that of Umbria and twenty-one in the Marches, and eight in the Province of Ravenna—a total of sixty-two.[18] Subject to the bishops were a very large number of parish priests on whose training and supervision the Council or Trent had laid so much emphasis. The papal war on pluralism and non-residence no doubt ensured that vacancies were few and short. In addition, there were numerous establishments of male and female religious. For example, in the Province of Rome, divided into six custodies and comprising seventy-eight individual houses, the Friars of the Conventual branch numbered over five hundred. The number of houses exceeded those in the whole of England at the time of the Dissolution, though they appear to have been at least on average somewhat smaller.[19] The Observants may have had an equal number; the Capuchins would have been less numerous. The Dominicans may have equalled the Franciscans in number, and there were houses of Cistercians, Benedictines and other Orders in the Papal States. To these must be added clergy who were attached to schools and Universities, novices and the like, who were in training, and numerous unofficial residents of the various monastic establishments. In total, clerics must have made up a substantial proportion of the population outside the capital City, and they certainly exercised considerable influence over local society. Sixtus added to the problem by replacing many laymen with clerics.

In almost all the towns of the Papal States there were hordes of minor officials, some representing the Central Administration, others appointed by the local communes, some attached to the ecclesiastical authorities and their courts. Lawyers, notaries, advocates, scribes and petty clerks abounded whilst in the ports there were large numbers of customs officials. Alongside these professional administrators, there were the minor moneyed men—moneylenders, bankers, brokers, auditors and cashiers. The scarcity of industry and the concentration of financial establishments in Rome and the consequent need for contact men enlarged the demand for professional services in the provinces and exaggerated the reputation, influence and importance of the men of training and administrative experiences. Among these everyone had his price, and corruption was rife.

Nevertheless agriculture was the basis of the economy of the Papal States and the smallholder its mainstay. True, changes in rural society were beginning to develop; holdings were amalgamated to make larger arable units. Merchants and financiers, particularly in the vicinity of the larger centres of population, above all in the Roman Campagna, began to invest in land on which to rear cattle and sheep to satisfy the growing demand especially in urban areas for fresh and salted meat and the by-products—cooked meats and offal—of the butchers' abattoirs. Meanwhile the peasant, the smallholder, the tied worker and the simple landless wage-earner continued their precarious and uncertain livelihoods. Feudal serfdom had been much reduced, but other forms of semi-servitude continued. Mezzadria and similar forms of land holding by which the smallholder cultivated his land substantially at his own volition in return for rendering annually to the proprietor a share of his product were popular, especially in the east of the State.[20] At fairs and markets surplus stocks were accumulated and acquired by merchants from the cities within the Papal

States, and to a lesser extent by foreign buyers or their agents. Agricultural products were, however, of prime importance to the central government and foreign trade was severely curtailed in the interests of Rome. Profits, it would seem, were probably modest and did not compare with those of the speculative financiers in the cities. There was therefore a continuous temptation for the ambitious to drift into the towns and for the local producers to control their hours of working and their output once the need to sustain their families and to pay their money dues had been satisfied. The era of intensive cultivation and scientific development had not yet arrived.

Briefly, the society of the Papal States had substantial elements of stability built into it. Its great scourge and curse were the ravages of the bandits. A ruler who could bring them under control was certain of support from all quarters and would bring cohesion and solidarity to the State.

The population of the Papal States in Sixtus V's reign amounted to approximately 1,500,000,[21] not quite one-third of that of England and Wales.[22] For administrative purposes, the Papal States were divided into six provinces—Campagna to the West and South of the capital, the Patrimony of St Peter with its centre at Viterbo[23] to the North and East; Perugia was the centre of the Province of Umbria, and to the East lay Bologna, Ravenna and the March of Ancona. Among the six provinces there was some rivalry for supremacy: the Romagna was said to be the richest, having surpassed Bologna during the past century; however one authority says the March of Ancona also was "the richest of all",[24] but Campagna and the Patrimony of St Peter were "so impoverished" as to be exempt from certain forms of papal taxation.[25] The Papal States as a whole were, by comparison with others, of only modest resources, with an export surplus of goods only in good years. Ordinarily its people were content to raise enough for their family's subsistence and the payment of their taxes and dues, leaving nature or the government to accumulate capital for future developments. It was not unusual, for example, for wine and oil produce in the States to be markedly inferior in both quantity and quality to that of Tuscany.

To each of the Provinces a Nuncio—a Cardinal—was appointed, and though ecclesiastical causes were always intended to take precedence over his other duties, church and secular affairs lay so tightly together that he inevitably wielded both secular authority and influence as well as ecclesiastical prerogatives. The real rulers, however, were the Vice-Legates or Presidents. Throughout the century, central government had consistently squeezed the power of the Provinces, withdrawing local privileges, limiting local jurisdictions and overriding local interests by the use of Papal powers. Nuncios and Vice-Legates, therefore, were the Pope's representatives and the links between Rome and the Provinces by which the dominance of central government was firmly and irresistibly fastened on the Provincial authorities. Provincial finances were also organised so as to leave them dependent on income under the control of central government.[26] The Nuncios and Vice-Legates were indispensable keys in the administration of the Papal States and were accordingly chosen by the Pope with the utmost care. The appointment of Nuncios in the Romagna and Bologna were particularly critical for these were (comparatively) recent annexations to the Papal States standing on its perimeter and inhabited by people of proud and belligerent traditions with strong and often divergent interests.

Most of the Communes retained the semblance, for the reality, of a former autonomy. The largest cities, such as Bologna and a port as important as Ancona, warranted the appointment of a Governor, one of the latter being one of the Pope's great-nephews, and were allowed to keep most of the trappings of independence. In lesser cities a *podestà*, or chief magistrate, whose functions were largely judicial, was elected by the citizens subject to confirmation by the Pope; in this way he retained the appearance of deriving his power from the people but was the representative of the Pope and bore such authority as the Pope delegated to him. He was responsible to Rome and the Pope was his master. In the smaller towns, similarly, vicars were appointed by the Vice-Legates; Rieti, Todi, Viterbo and Spoleto were under the Pope's direct rule. The obligation to military service remained, though in many instances it had been commuted into a monetary fee rendered either to the papal authority direct or to a noble to whom the town had been enfieffed. In his crusade against the bandit, Sixtus made a general call on the local militia and imposed heavy penalties on those who tired to evade their duty, in addition to employing the trained professional armies of the day.[27] The towns generally had their own courts presided over by the judge, usually a local man chosen by the citizens, and these dealt with civil disputes between citizens and registered contracts and transfers of land. The communal council was now largely a ceremonial rather than an executive body, but preserved the appearance of former times of independence. In fact, the government of the Papal States as a whole had an orderly and logical pattern with political rights precisely defined mainly by papal grants, and though individual rivalries and factions of long standing continued unabated, serious threats to papal power were few. Most provincial and local offices could be purchased and almost all changed hands at the death of the Pope. Justice was therefore uncertain and administration arbitrary and conflicts with papal policy or interests were predominantly unsuccessful. Though the appearance of popular control might remain, the Papal States were in fact highly centralised and power was exercised by the Papal Court in the Vatican.

Sixtus V's domestic policy had four main threads: first, the overthrow of the bandits and the restoration of internal peace and security; second, the provision of an adequate and secure supply of food for the capital; third, the improvement of local administration, particularly in the Adriatic region; and fourth, the enhancement of the prestige and the prosperity of the Marches and its port, Ancona. The main defect in the administration of justice in the Marches was the scarcity of professionally trained staff in the face of competition from both Rome and Bologna and the inadequacy of the training they received. Sixtus therefore confirmed and extended the privileges of the College of Advocates and Procurators of the Province,[28] established a Rota in Macerata, its administrative centre, to hear criminal cases and gave it authority to appoint notaries and scribes.[29] He established the offices of procurator and fiscal advocate in the Province, and of commissioners-general to deal with cases of fraud.[30] In Ancona he confirmed the right granted by Pope Paul III of choosing and removing notaries for civil cases,[31] and he founded the office of secretary and chancellor to the Governor.[32]

Following complaints of inadequate service from Ancona, Sixtus established a public convoy of horses for passengers, vehicles for the conveyance of goods, baggage, letters and packets, with special provision for gold, silver and other valuables. This *procaccio* ran from Rome direct to Ancona on Monday each week.[33] He intended to rebuild the bridge across the Tiber at Borghetto in accordance with an earlier demand from the port, but due to floods destroying the foundations in 1589 he was unable to complete the work which was, in fact, not finished until 1600.[34] He developed schemes for the improvement of the river Tiber from Borghetto southwards and for its canalisation from Rome to the sea. Unfortunately, he was unable to put this far-sighted scheme into effect for fear of Turkish attacks, and navigation on the river remained limited and unsatisfactory.[35] Ancona, like Civitavecchia, was already heavily fortified against the attacks of the Turks and other corsairs, and Sixtus gave his close personal attention to the maintenance and strengthening of these fortifications. When Venice tried to compel all ships trading with Ancona to call at the port of Venice the Pope vigorously supported the city in resisting this, and he also reprimanded the Order of Malta for interfering with shipping intended for the Jews of Ancona.[36] Indeed, Sixtus reversed the intolerant attitude of some of his predecessors, especially Paul IV and Gregory XIII, towards the Jews, allowing them to settle in towns of the Papal States as they wished. Not only did the Jewish population of the capital increase to 3,500 but that of Ancona increased by more than 2,500, so that the building of a third synagogue was undertaken.[37] Under papal encouragement Ancona rapidly became a prosperous international port with a growing cosmopolitan population reaching 23,600 in 1581,[38] including Florentines, Luccans, Sienese, Venetians, Turks, Armenians, Dalmatians, Sicilians, Germans, French and Flemings.[39] It imported hides from Hungary, spices, handicraft, tapestries and leathers from the Orient, and exported fine cloths and leather goods from Florence to the East. When the imposition of new taxes on leather and skins in 1589 produced fierce resistance and a flood of protests, Sixtus exempted the city.[40] Ancona was the essential link between the Papal States and the wealth of the East and the main resource of the Papal economy. With its natural harbour capable of dealing with the very large ships of the Adriatic, with an array of civic and ecclesiastical buildings in the upper reaches of the town, with a large and skilful population, prosperous and richly endowed surrounding countryside to supply its needs, and a system of fortifications capable of guaranteeing it a large measure of security from outside attack, Ancona, though not comparable with the largest ports in Italy like Naples or Venice or Genoa, was already the dominant mercantile unit in the Papal States, and the key centre of the Adriatic coastal plain. It had its own Governor, a member of Sixtus' own family and an Archbishop.

The towns of the March, like Camerino and Macerata, also received papal favours. Montalto, Sixtus V's native town, was given exemption from Papal taxation for eight years.[41] There were five mints in the Papal States, at Rome, Bologna, Ancona, Macerata and the ducato di Castro (near Viterbo), and in addition casual supplementary issues of coins were made during Sixtus V's reign at Perugia, Camerino, Fano and Montalto. Permanent mints at Ancona and Macerata, the chief port and the provincial capital respectively, of the Province, indicated their importance in the economy of the State and enabled a regular and adequate flow of coinage to be available to meet the mercantile needs of the region.

By his personal initiative Sixtus greatly strengthened the educational resources of the Marches. He revived the University of Fermo, originally established by Boniface VIII (1294–1303) and granted it the privileges of other Universities.[42] He confirmed the privileges of the University of Bologna[43] and established in it a Collegio Montalto with places for fifty students so that they might proceed directly to the study of philosophy, medicine and law without having first to enrol in the more preparatory studies of the Faculty of the Humanities.[44] Poor students were to be accommodated in the College for seven years without charge and provided with free lodging and clothing. The College had all the privileges of the University of Bologna and was exempt from the jurisdiction of the Papal Legate of Bologna, the Archbishop and of the state judges. The Pope's own great-nephew was its Protector.[45]

Sixtus V also re-shaped a section of the diocesan organisation of the March to make Fermo the centre of a group of bishoprics in the Adriatic coast plain lying between Ancona to the north and the Kingdom of Naples (the Abruzzi, south of Ascoli). This has often been represented as favouritism to the area in which he was born and in which he spent much of his life, and to provide opportunities for the advancement of his fellow countrymen.[46] It is true that the Bull which elevated Montalto to the status of a bishopric described it as the place "whence the Pope himself derived his birth",[47] and the one similarly elevating Tolentino refers to the Pope's involvement in its promotion and to his being its protector and supporter whilst he was Cardinal.[48] It is, however, questionable that the Pope's personal attachment to his native country was the sole motive for considerable changes. Moreover, the introductions to the respective Bulls indicate that the elevations were part of a plan to raise the religious standards of the area—to increase the devotion of the people, to ensure that the divine liturgy should flourish and that places formerly of little note should be rendered famous by more worthy titles and splendid favours. These were no doubt typical phrases used habitually, by the papal court, but nevertheless they are clearly intended to associate an increase of bishoprics with attempts to impress on the humble cultivators of the Marches' fertile soil the value of faithful follower of the Catholic faith and to encourage them in spiritual devotion and a continuing acceptance of the guidance of the Church and its priesthood. Moreover, these changes were of sufficient importance as to require scrutiny by the Congregation for Bishops and subsequently by the Consistory itself. The establishment of a bishopric was not dealt with trivially or casually. The proposal to transfer the bishop's see from Recanati to Loreto was referred to Cardinals Farnese, San Giorgio, Lancellotti, Medici and Guastavillani—a formidable group with exacting standards—and the later proposal to establish a bishopric at Montalto was referred to the same group.[49]

Although the bishopric of Osimo was no more than ten miles from Loreto and about fifteen from the bishopric of Recanati, Sixtus V decided that the improvement of facilities for the veneration of the Blessed Virgin Mary, the recognition of her supreme role in the function of the church and the special importance of the pilgrimages to the Holy House fully justified the establishment of a new bishopric at Loreto. Osimo is an ancient see dating from the early days of Roman Christianity, with records continuous from the tenth century: it was a centre of revival in the Catholic Church of the sixteenth century. Its bishop, Bernardino de Cupis (1547–74), had taken an active part in the Council of Trent and was succeeded by an equally zealous successor, Cornelio Fermani (1574–88), who called a synod and founded a convent of the Capuchin Order.[50] If some reduction had to be made in the number of dioceses in this area to permit the elevation of Loreto, it was only Recanati which could be demoted. Within a year of becoming Pope, Sixtus replaced the bishopric of Recanati by a new bishopric located at Loreto, only five miles away. This brought the Sanctuary of the Holy House and its pilgrims—many en route for Rome—under direct episcopal supervision. The bishop now had the opportunity to direct and encourage the development of the Holy House, to improve the provision for pilgrims and to enhance the international reputation of this splendid monument. Territory, including Castelfidardo, Santa Maria del Ficardo and Montefiascone, was transferred from the bishoprics of Ancona, Osimo and Fermo respectively to the new diocese. This was provided with a monetary dowry transferred from Cacerata, and Cardinal Guastavillani was appointed its Protector. Recanati ceased to be an Episcopal see and Macerata with which it has been united from 1573 was relieved of the responsibility for its affairs.[51]

Seven months after the elevation of Loreto to be an Episcopal see, Sixtus established a new bishopric at Montalto, his hometown. The Bull itself sets out in some detail the reasons for the creation of the new See. Not only was it the Pope's native land, but the town was sited very famously and with great distinction and was surrounded by walls. In addition, its collegiate church was artistically built and was well endowed with appropriate clerical posts. The city had about 300 houses (perhaps 1,200–1,500 residents) and a fair. In short, it was represented as having all the essentials of a cathedral town. Certain additional areas taken from the dioceses of Ripana, Fermo and Ascoli were added to Montalto to give it an adequate area to make the bishopric viable.

Only four days later, Sixtus named San Severino as a separate bishopric, cancelling its connection with the bishopric of Camerino, a very distinguished and flourishing see. San Severino was effectively twenty-five miles from Camerino and a new bishopric was not therefore an embarrassment to Camerino in terms of the accepted pattern of episcopal structure in the Marche at that time, especially as henceforth the bishopric of San Severino was exempt from contribution to the revenues of Camerino.

Then, a fortnight later, Sixtus created a new bishopric of Tolentino, by separating it from the bishopric of Camerino. The justification for this new bishopric was similar to the rest—"to strengthen the devotion of the people, to make the divine cult flourish and the well being of souls to be kept in progress"[52]—and the town is credited with great fame, town walls and a substantial population. Nevertheless, the establishment of a bishopric of Tolentino must have created some difficult situations, for it was united to the bishopric of Macerata whose bishop became bishop of the united sees and in affairs affecting Tolentino he was to use that signature appropriately.[53] Tolentino was to have a single Vicar "who will not recognise a superior, nor have recourse to the vicariate of the said city of Macerata but rather to its own bishop".[54] Tolentino was also provided with an annual income of 400 scudi in currency of the Marches. Apart from the particular complications in the relationship of Tolentino with Macerata, the new structure created a debatable situation in which three bishops, in a triangular formation, were respectively 30 (Camerino–Tolentino), 15 (Tolentino–San Severino) and 25 (San Severino–Camerino) miles from each other. Was such a concentration of bishoprics in this area justified? It is easy to accept that this was personal favouritism on the Pope's part. On the other hand, none of the elevations is totally unjustified, that of San Severino being perhaps the most vulnerable and the Marche reorganisation entailed in total only a net increase of two bishoprics, Montalto and San Severino, Loreto being a transfer and Tolentino a titular alteration of status. In a more general sense, if the modern adage that "larger is better" is rejected, it is possible that Sixtus wished to bring the elevated clerical appointment of the Marche into closer association with the small towns of the village and to encourage them to participate in the effective organisation of the bishoprics. If this was a philosophical part of Sixtus' policy, how much success did he enjoy? The whole of the Marches reorganisation could well be investigated more closely.

It is of great interest to note that at the time of their respective elevations all those bishoprics were exempt from the local Episcopal organisation and were made responsible directly to the Apostolic Chamber and presumably under its direct guidance, surveillance and inspection. Sixtus encouraged the local development of autonomy and initiative but made the new bishoprics dependent on the Camera's approval and control. In May, 1589, a great change was made when Fermo was raised to the metropolitan rank, given authority over the bishoprics of Montalto, San Severino, Macerata with Tolentino and Repana. Bishop Sigismondo Zanettini, a most venerable Bolognese, appointed to the bishopric of Fermo in January 1585, four months before Sixtus' election, was elevated to the new metropolitan chair and received the pallium in July 1589.

Sixtus V's establishment of a properly coordinated ecclesiastical organisation of this area of the Marches complemented his political and economical policy for the Adriatic sector of the Papal States. He aimed to reduce the dependence of Ancona and the Marches on the capital, whilst ensuring that the supplies of Rome were not endangered. He hoped to strengthen the prosperity of the Marches, so diminishing the social powers of the nobility and increasing the social and economic stability of the Adriatic coastal area. Had Sixtus V lived longer, posterity would have known both how far these designs formed a central part of his domestic policy and how far it could be developed to consolidate the strength of the Papal States.

Had all his plans for the development of the province within the Papal States been capable of fulfilment and could the abandonment of the implementation of some of the most far-sighted of them, such as the improvement and canalisation of the Tiber, been avoided, the Papal States must have emerged as vastly strengthened un economic power and status, with the means to eliminate banditry and with the capacity for taking advantage of the decline of Spanish power in the next century. It is possible, therefore, to understand the sense of urgency under which Sixtus lived and to realise how he never felt that time was his ally.

A State so strategically situated, whose government was so well endowed with riches collected and stored by ruler so determined as Sixtus, and which was supported by the vast prestige and spiritual authority as the Papal States could not fail to exercise a powerful influence throughout the Italian peninsula. Its blessing and assistance were regularly sought by its neighbours: its guidance and views were accepted with respect and consideration. Though Italian states were notoriously individualistic often tortuous and unreliable and always reluctant to unite in concerted action, they nevertheless recognised that the Italian peninsula had interests in common which they tended to expect the Pope to defend. Yet his influence was strictly restricted; firstly, Paul IV's struggle with the King of Naples had demonstrated the impossibility of Papal resistance to Spain being pursued to the point of open war; secondly, Italian states had learned by more than a half century of bitter and devastating experience the peril of becoming involved in the conflicting interests of France and Spain and of their own territories becoming the battlefield over which these rivals might fight. A policy of non-intervention and non-belligerency was forced on the Papal States and its Italian associates.

Italy was dominated to an incredible extent by the power of Spain which held it in a relentless grip. The Pope's persistent resistance to Spanish influence was limited by the sheer inability of the other Italian states to confront Spanish power, and the Pope was driven to invoke ecclesiastical and spiritual weapons in his aid. Politics and religion was irrevocably and inextricably involved with each other. Spain ruled the kingdoms of Naples, Sicily and Lombardy (approximately one-half of what could be described as geographical Italy). But, in addition, the Republic of Genoa was so completely involved in Spanish finances as to have become virtually a satellite of the Spanish possessions and Tuscany was traditionally dependent on Spain and responsible for the leadership of the Spanish party in the Roman consistory. Piedmont-Savoy, though pretending independence, was basically controlled by Spanish power and the Duchy of Milan. Only the Republic of Venice was genuinely independent and in a position to give substantial support to whatever policy the Pope cared to follow. Confronted by this array of Spanish-controlled and pro-Spanish states, Sixtus V's task in the Italian peninsula was formidable. His difficulties were substantially increased by the highly centralised and despotic governments which ruled all the Spanish possessions. Throughout the latter half of the sixteenth century, the Spanish crown was under very severe financial difficulties and found it impossible to avoid squeezing its dependencies. This in turn obliged the Viceroy to try to curtail the royal levies demanded of them, and so to keep the danger of popular outbursts and rising against them. Neither the King nor the Viceroy were able to live peacefully for long periods and the Pope was able to take advantage of the Viceroy's dangerous financial situation and to resist the Spanish kingdom more strongly.

Both the city and kingdom of Naples which the Pope had known, first as Director of Studies at the Franciscan friary of San Lorenzo in 1552–55, and later as Bishop of Sant'Agata (1566–71), were changing. In both, the population was rising in a spectacular way; the kingdom excluding the city increased between 1573 and 1595 from 487,000 to 540,000, an average of 10% per year, though, because of the size of the mountain terrain and the organisation of cattle breeding and rearing industries in Apulia, population density remained low. Population was concentrated in the ports such as Bari and Taranto, the latter having also flourishing textile industries.[55] Meanwhile, however, the city increased even faster by sustaining a wave of immigration from the neighbouring countryside. Its population—about 220,000 when Felice first saw it—had grown perhaps to 243, 000, including soldiers, clergy and inmates of hospitals, etc., and rose to perhaps almost 300,000 by the time of Sixtus' death. Moreover, many of the provincial nobility and many more of those who had amassed wealth during the first half of the century, were induced by a variety of exemptions and concessions from the viceroy to move into the city where they built luxurious residences on the hills behind the centre of the city. They had fresh air, pure water and a superbly charming view over the Bay below. Monastic building and church restoration were adding to the beauty of the skyline and there were 70 monasteries for men with 1995 religious resident in them and 22 monasteries for females with 1774 nuns resident.[56] The Viceroy's court became more and more magnificent and the feudal nobility of the Kingdom and the Spanish courtiers and officials surrounded him with extravagance as they exchanged the management of their domains for the frivolity or serious culture, the immorality and corruption of the city.

At Sixtus V's accession the Viceroy had surrendered his office and a year's prorogation ensured so that the new Viceroy only took up his duties in November, 1586. He was Juan de Zúñiga y Avellaneda, Count of Miranda del Castañar, a man in the middle span of life, of great eminence in the Spanish nobility and immense wealth. He became known for his conspicuous caution and skill in avoiding political traps and indiscretions: like many contemporary politicians he was temporising and ready for compromise and believed consistently that time was necessarily on his side. Deeply attached to his family, he tended to saddle subordinates with heavy responsibilities and cared little for their success, provided his personal peace was not disturbed. His main policy was to safeguard the interests of the King and his Spanish countrymen in Naples; to crush the ubiquitous bandits on land and the pirates and Turks on the sea and the coasts: he had also to preserve the prosperity of the kingdom and ensure the safety of its supplies. Unfortunately, the negative and wholly defensive policy of the viceroy, combined with the excessive taxes and rising prices, tended to outrage the people of the realm and to create anti-Spanish feeling in many parts of the kingdom, including the capital and the provincial capitals. Though the Count of Miranda was able to complete his period of office in 1595, these were ill omens for his successors which anticipated the widespread discontent of the seventeenth century. Much of Miranda's success in preserving order in the Kingdom was due to his successful understanding with the people's representative in the Council of State, Giovanni Battista Crispo, whose luxurious residence near Camaldoli aroused deep suspicion.

Sixtus was happy to encounter so accommodating a neighbour: the repulse of the bandits and the Turks were objects they shared in common. Sixtus did his utmost to prevent the Neapolitan bandits from entering the Papal States, was glad to have the Viceroy's assistance in the arrest of bandits who escaped from the Papal States to the Kingdom and readily concluded treaties of extradition with the Viceroy.[57] He was greatly pleased when the Viceroy succeeded in having Benedetto Mangone, one of the most famous of the southern bandits captured near Eboli and executed after being subjected to some of the most brutal tortures known at that date. He admired the Viceroy's attempts to capture Sciarra, one of the most famous bandits left alive who operated in the mountains of Abruzzi, even though success was not achieved. He launched no special measures against the Turks but he used their attacks as an excuse for the levy of the *donativo*, which was appropriated for defence.

Nevertheless, this considerable area of common interest and policy did not prevent the continuance of the traditional animosity between church and the state in Naples. The Pope was extremely energetic in maintaining vigilance over ecclesiastical affairs in the Kingdom. After Cardinal Savelli left his office as Nuncio in Naples in June, 1585, Sixtus appointed Giulio Rossino his successor, and in turn in May 1589 he was succeeded by Alessandro Glorieri.

When Glorieri's instructions were drafted by the Cardinal Nephew (clearly under direction, as he was still in his teens), they began, "There are two principal duties of nuncios and especially of the Nuncio to the Kingdom of Naples; one is the maintenance of the papal jurisdiction in that Kingdom, the other is diligence in collecting all the profits and revenues of vacant sees belonging to the Apostolic See." Guidance in these duties was elaborated on at length, the successful example of earlier Nuncios was cited and he was advised of the need to resist, from his initial reception by the Viceroy, all attempts to encroach on papal prerogatives. At the audience with the Viceroy at which he was to present his credentials, he was to be accompanied by Mgr Scudi, doubtless one of the family of Genoan bankers, who was heavily involved in financial dealings with both the Pope and the King of Spain. In short, every effort was made to present the Viceroy with the strength of the Pope's resources in the Kingdom. He was specifically instructed to resist without the slightest hint of compromise an attempt by the Viceroy in 1573 to limit the prerogatives of the Pope and to establish the right of the Pope to all his traditional powers. The Nuncio clearly went to Naples prepared for instant diplomatic battle.[58] Revenues from vacant sees were obviously of great importance to the Papal Treasury for in Charles V's time there were twenty archbishoprics and a hundred and ten bishoprics in the Kingdom, of which eight and sixteen respectively were in royal patronage.[59] So, although the Pope and the Viceroy had common interests which encouraged them to keep peace and although there were certain areas in which their interests tended to coincide, nevertheless their relationship was conducted against a background of rivalry, intrigue and legal dispute. The Popes of the sixteenth century, indeed, returned to the conditions of the eleventh, twelfth and thirteenth centuries when conflict to determine the boundaries of supremacy in matters of church and state was the major issue of European politics. Sixtus was well versed in the historical and philosophical bases of those disputes, especially since Innocent III, the protagonist of the Emperor Frederick II had been largely responsible for the recognition of the Franciscan Order. Moreover, in the sixteenth century the importance of this issue was enhanced since the Reformation had made it possible for Protestant princes to escape from all the financial and jurisdictional claims of Rome, and Sixtus found himself facing the problems of states which were Catholic in belief and ritual but independent in politics. This was a problem not of abstract religious philosophy but of everyday administration. From time to time every archbishop or bishop might find himself challenged by some suppliant in his court who claimed his case lay within the jurisdiction of the secular authorities, or he might feel obliged to defend some clerical subordinate against whom the secular authorities had preferred a charge which in his submission concerned the ecclesiastical authorities. In such cases there were no independent arbiters and the arena was set for a direct conflict between the contestants and in which neither side was prepared for compromise. Sixtus' reign was therefore a period of continual conflict with the power of Philip II's Spanish Empire, where apparent trivial claims and counter claims were amplified into disputes of the first dimension and the financial and theological resources of the respective Powers were massed but not committed to battle lest the more dominant quarrels over the map of Europe should explode into a holocaust. This situation, however, did not prevent the Pope and his Curia from pressing on with a much needed reform of the Dominican Order —one of the fiercest adherents of Philip's authority in the Kingdom.[60]

In the separate Kingdom of Sicily, described as "the chief granary of the Western Mediterranean," exporting mainly to Spain and her ally Genoa, "but also in varying quantities to all the hungry cities of Mediterranean Europe and North Africa".[61] Indeed the situation was similar in Sicily, the King possessed the right of *Monarchia*, the right and powers of a permanent apostolic legate.[62]

At the opposite end of the peninsula, the Duchy of Milan constituted the upper jaw of the vice in which Spain relentlessly held the Italian states. Milan itself was a very large, densely populated city: in 1500 its population was reckoned at 100,000, a century later it had doubled.[63] Twice as large as Rome, its rate of growth similar; it was one of the ten largest cities in Europe and was the centre of a flourishing textile trade.[64] In farming and in industrial products Milan was an opulent city of immense resources. Strategically it was the centre of movement northwards into Germany and Flanders, southwards into Italy. Its dominance as a centre of arterial highways was reflected in the number of its hotels.[65] It was rich, for it was a control point for the movement of Spanish silver and gold from America to the Empire, from Naples and Sicily to the Duchy. It was the Headquarters of Spanish direction of the movements of troops garrisoned in other cities of Lombardy. In spite of the grandeur of its Cathedral square which dominated the city, it was a dirty city with many offensive slums.[66] Yet the influence of cultural progress in Europe generally made itself felt in Milan; improvements in its structure began to appear, Cardinal Charles Borromeo initiated many new ecclesiastical buildings and set an example to the laity which they followed until the city had points of magnificence but fell heavily in debt. A social conscience was awakened and a Monte di Pietà was established to rescue the poor and the unfortunate from the ravages of the moneylender.

The city was ruled by the Governor, Count Alfonso Gonzaga, the current representative of one of the great Italian noble families. Supported by the nobility he ruled wholly in the Spanish interest and wielded despotic powers, seriously obstructed neither by ancient privileges nor by the people. So weary were the Milanese of the battles of the past half-century that only a religious issue—the proposed introduction of the Spanish Inquisition—roused them to action. Indeed, in the Duchy no issue was more inflammatory then state–Church relations. For eighteen years Charles Borromeo had been resident as Archbishop and had proved so energetic and determined in enforcing the Tridentine decrees that he had been involved in ceaseless conflict with the Ducal authorities and in bitter campaigns with the clergy themselves. An order as reformist as the Theatines conspired to kill him. But Charles had died one year before Sixtus V's accession and was succeeded as Archbishop by Gaspare di Gonzaga, a member of one of the foremost families in the Duchy. Gaspare was typically Milanese in detesting strife and in being prepared to make sacrifices to create peace. Indeed, it is said his occupancy of the archbishop's office was "a period if not of demobilisation, at least of relaxation, specially for the clergy".[67] This had Sixtus V's agreement for by this time he saw that direct conflict with Philip II's temporal power achieved no permanent advantage for Papacy. Indeed Sixtus took positive steps to diminish the bitterness with the Duke of Milan. A marriage was arranged between the Pope's great-nephew (son of Camilla's daughter) and the Duke's only daughter. Michele, eleven years old, was the Pope's favourite, whom he had already made Governor of the Church and he was, in fact, to live almost a further half-century (he died in 1631). Philip II facilitated the marriage by allowing Michele to enjoy the revenues of his dowry without being obliged to live in the Duchy as the law required.[68] Sixtus ensured that Michele was well endowed for his marriage, buying for him a marquisate and a county in the Duchy of Mantua, and subsequently Philip made him Prince of Venafro.[69] The Pope who had grown up in poverty and who had advanced in his career by his own efforts in the Church was anxious to establish his own House in its own right and with its own distinctions. Michele was the only Perelli who could fulfil this ambition but Sixtus' introduction of Michele to the intimacies of the Duke's court was a skilful means of gaining influence in the affairs of Spain. Sixtus V's reign was unfortunately too short, but at least the Pope's foresight in the affairs of Northern Italy must be applauded and encourages the belief that with greater opportunities and a longer reign an extension of his influence might have developed.

Parma was little more than an extension to the more extensive Duchy of Milan. Alessandro Farnese, Duke of Parma, was already very closely connected with Spain, for he had married the Spanish King's niece, the Infanta Maria of Portugal. During his early years he was educated at the court of Madrid and subsequently much of his time was spent in Spain. Moreover, since 1586 he had been Governor-General of the Low Countries and performed outstandingly in overcoming Philip's rebel subjects and restoring Spanish power in several Low Country towns. When the Armada was prepared he was given command of the 30,000 troops which were to be transported across the Channel once the Spanish fleet had liquidated English maritime resistance. His conduct and outlook were Spanish and until his death in 1592 he was deeply involved in Spanish affairs in the Low

Countries and conversant with the policies and plans of the Spanish royal family. During Sixtus V's reign, though the Duke himself was normally absent in the Netherlands, the Duchy was completely involved in the Spanish sphere of influence, and the transfer of troops from the Duchy to the Low Countries kept the Duke continuously aware of the essential part which he and the Duchy played in policies of the Spanish Empire.

To the east of the Duchy of Parma lay lands dominated by the d'Este family to which the protection of French interests in Italy were entrusted: these were Rezzio, Modena and Ferrara. Ferrara had established a tradition for a progressive and innovatory culture which earlier in the century had bred suspicions of heresy, and reflected the literary genius of Torquato Tasso, perhaps the supreme poet of late sixteenth century Italy. Its town planning probably imitated Sixtus' planning of Rome,[70] and its ducal palace, its churches and its majestic avenues were as dignified and impressive as those of other northern Italian cities—features which had not failed to attract the French traveller, Montaigne, three or four years before Sixtus' accession. It has been described as "a cosmopolitan place for meetings of erudite men of letters, artists, philosophers and scientists".[71] The d'Este family's domains covered the central area of the lush valley of the River Po, the largest plain in Southern Europe, well watered in winter and spring and fed by a number of major tributaries from the Alps to the north and the Apennines to the south. The area offered no obstructive physical features and communications were profuse and well maintained. The soil was rich and fertile and in spite of backward methods of cultivation, produced lavish crops of cereals of all kinds and sustained vineyards and orchards of high quality. Profits from the land were sufficient to attract capital investment and support a high level of maintenance, judged by the standards of those days. Montaigne was struck by the orderliness of the area and the energies devoted to making it attractive. Roads, easily laid across the plain, were tidily enclosed by ditches, their surface was solid and carefully drained, and their dimensions generous and well designed. Montaigne had much praise for the valley's road system which he contrasted acidly with those around Florence and even Rome.[72] Ferrara, larger and far more attractive than Florence,[73] lay a short distance from the Lower Po, shortly before it broadened into the delta area. Modena was within sight of the Adige, one of the River Po's most important tributaries, and Reggio, at a distance of some twenty miles, on the banks of the Crostolo, one of the Po's lesser tributaries. Cardinal d'Este, owner and developer of Tivoli at Sixtus V's accession, was one of the Cardinals whose support for Sixtus at his election was decisive. But rich though they were and prolific as its crops undoubtedly were, they were a most meagre counterbalance to the might of Spain to the north and west. The area itself in total was small compared, for example, with the Duchies of Milan and Modena; they were vulnerable to attack and because of the open character of the country, difficult to defend. But more important still, throughout the whole of Sixtus V's reign, France was hopelessly divided by rival claims to the throne and distracted by issues of religion and political philosophy. Weakened though he was by civil war in the Low Countries and his ambition to bring England and Scotland within his Empire, Philip II could rest confident in the security of his possessions in Northern and Southern Italy. For the whole of his five year reign, Sixtus was held tightly in Philip's grip. Cardinal d'Este was in no doubt about the matter, "What Philip was aiming at is dominion over the whole of Christendom".[74]

## Notes

[1] The size of Scotland's population is regarded with considerable uncertainty, but with great reservation it has been estimated at 750,000. See A. G. R. Smith, *The Reign of James VI and I* (London: 1973).

[2] In Italy of the late sixteenth century it ranked in size next to Venice, was slightly larger than Lombardy, substantially larger than Tuscany.

3   A great deal of the mountain area, especially in Umbria, was of little agricultural value, much of it arid and sterile, even though on the lower slopes olives and some hardy species of vines were grown.
4   *Bullarium* 8, p. 667.
5   Delumeau 1, pp. 1–2.
6   See *Financial Times* (16 February 2008) on the need to improve urban infrastructure.
7   Delumeau 1, pp. 57, 58 and 59.
8   Ibid., pp. 84f..
9   Ibid., p. 72.
10  Ibid., p. 55.
11  Ibid., p. 67.
12  "In Sixtus' reign we know of only two *Monti* which were not bought by the Genoese" see Delumeau 1, p. 885.
13  Hale, *The Civilization of Europe in the Renaissance*, pp. 385ff.
14  Delumeau 1, pp. 39ff.
15  Pecchiai, *Roma nel Cinquecento*, pp. 282ff.
16  G. Hanlon, *Early Modern Italy 1550–1800* (London: Macmillan, 2000), pp. 83ff.
17  Delumeau 1, p. 77.
18  Pastor 20, p. 519.
19  Sixty houses with 1200 friars; see F. N. A. Gasquet, *English monastic life* (London: Methuen, 1910).
20  Hanlon, *Early Modern Italy 1550–1800*, pp. 94–96.
21  Delumeau 2, p. 32.
22  *CEHE* 4, p. 32.
23  J. J. Martin, *The Renaissance: Italy and Abroad* (London: Routledge, 2002), p. 96.
24  Compare P. Partner, *The Lands of St. Peter. The Papal State in the Middle Ages and the Early Renaissance* (Los Angeles: University of California Press 1972), p. 89, with Pastor 16, p. 375 and Delumeau 1, p. 94.
25  Partner, *The Lands of St. Peter*, p. 114.
26  Pastor 21, p. 121.
27  *Bullarium* 8, p. 586.
28  Ibid. 8, pp. 602–604.

[29] *Ibid.* 9, pp. 81–84.
[30] *Ibid.* 9, pp. 281–283.
[31] *Ibid.* 8, pp. 292–294.
[32] *Ibid.* 9, pp. 300–302.
[33] Delumeau 1, pp. 47, 81.
[34] *Ibid.*, pp. 101, 104.
[35] *Ibid.*, pp. 110, 114.
[36] *Ibid.*, p. 100.
[37] *Ibid.*, pp. 96, 99.
[38] P. Earle, "The Commercial Development of Ancona, 1479–1551" in *The Economic History Review* 22/1 (April 1969), pp. 28–44.
[39] Delumeau 1, p. 96.
[40] *Ibid.*, p. 837.
[41] Pistolesi, *Sisto V e Montalto da documenti inediti*, p. 93.
[42] *Bullarium* 8, pp. 593–598.
[43] *Ibid.* 8, pp. 721–724.
[44] *Ibid.* 8, pp. 771–776; 9, pp. 45–57.
[45] Pistolesi, *Sisto V e Montalto da documenti inediti*, p. 83.
[46] He received relatives kindly, but gave them no preferment; see Pastor 21, p. 67.
[47] *Bullarium* 8, p. 800.
[48] *Ibid.* 8, pp. 817–819.
[49] In 1586, and the first bishop was Paolo Emilio Giovannini.
[50] *EC* article by Serafino Prete Braudel, p. 765.
[51] It was merged with the diocese of Loreto in 1591, see *NCE*, article on "Diocese of Recanati and Loreto (*Recinetensis*)".
[52] *Bullarium* 8, p. 817.
[53] *Ibid.* 8, p. 818b.
[54] *Ibid.*.
[55] *CEHE* 4, p. 21.
[56] C. De Seta, *Città territorio e mezzogiorno in Italia* (Torino: Einaudi, 1977), pp. 237, 258, Tav. 56–57.
[57] Pastor 21, p. 80.
[58] *Codice Vaticano Latino*, 7080.

59 147 sees according to Bl J. H. Newman, *Tracts for the Times*, 33 "Primitive Episcopacy", p. 11.
60 See M. Miele, O.P., *La riforma domenicana a Napoli nel periodo post-tridentino (1583–1725)* (Roma: 1963).
61 *CEHE* 4, p. 157.
62 *CMH* 3, p. 258.
63 *CMH* 3, p. 33, and Delumeau 1, p. 360.
64 Delumeau 1, p. 503.
65 *Ibid.*, p. 142.
66 *Ibid.*, p. 360.
67 See *EC*.
68 Delumeau 1, p. 460.
69 *Ibid.*
70 *Ibid.*, p. 292.
71 I. Montanelli & R. Gervaso, *Storia d'Italia 4. L'Italia della Controriforma* (Milano: Rizzoli, 1997), p. 342.
72 M. de Montaigne, *Essays* (1774 edition: 3 volumes), Vol. 2, pp. 34–35, 50, 162.
73 *Ibid.*, Vol. 2, pp. 50 and cvi.
74 Letter of October 1585 as in Pastor 21, p. 121.

# CHAPTER 9

### Foreign Diplomacy and Final Days

*As he is the head and leader of the Church, a society of human beings, the Pope must naturally come into contact with the earthly governors of those human beings.*

Giuseppe Sarto, Pope St Pius X, 1903

TO THE NORTH and west of the Papal States lay the Grand Duchy of Tuscany ruled by the Medici. This was one of the larger and stronger states of Central Italy: much of its territory was mountainous, rugged and of low productivity, but the long Mediterranean coastal plain was rich and fertile. Its capital, Florence, was one of the most resplendent Renaissance cities whose architecture, painting and sculpture were world famous and drew great numbers of scholarly, well cultivated students and patrons to the city. It had profitable commercial links with Bologna, Ravenna and Venice, and stood on the main routes between Southern France, Liguria, Rome and the south. During the sixteenth century it acquired both Lucca and Siena, and at Sixtus' time was beginning to develop Leghorn as a free entrepot port next in importance to Genoa in Mediterranean Italy. By skilled management, "almost alone among contemporary princes they were always solvent".[1] Since about 1550 the royal house had occupied the Pitti palace in great splendour, and at Sixtus V's accession Francesco I was in the twelfth year of his reign. He had little interest in statecraft and was content that heavy taxation should sustain his riches and that despotic methods of government should keep is throne secure whilst he attended to scientific investigations and the cult of classical learning. The Medici owed their throne to Spain and never succeeded in freeing themselves from Spanish influence. The Spaniards held the *presidios*, five maritime barrier fortresses on the Tuscan coast, anticipating the French and Low Countries barrier of the next century. Nevertheless, the relationship with the Duchy and Spain was that of an ally rather than a satellite,[2] especially as Catherine de' Medici, a descendant of Lorenzo the Magnificent, married Henry II of France, reigned with him for twelve years and produced for him three princes who succeeded him in turn on the throne. During the reign of Charles IX (1560–74) she directed the government of the kingdom and continued to exercise great influence until her death in 1589. Rome was only a hundred and seventy miles from Florence to which it was connected by a well constructed highway running almost wholly over pleasant, easy and undulating country, along which ran frequent courier services. A *courier extraordinaire* could complete the journey in twenty-four hours, and the weekly convoy service needed no more than four to eight days.[3] It was natural, therefore, that Sixtus V, who had been financially dependent on the Duke, particularly after he lost his pension as a poor Cardinal, and owed his election in no small measure to Cardinal Medici, should cultivate the closest possible relationship with the Grand Duke and with the Cardinal now installed with great dignity and magnificence in the Villa Medici on the Pincio. The Grand Duke in turn maintained close contact with his Cardinal brother and with the Florentine contingent who formed a considerable proportion of the population of Rome and lived closely knit and in substantial opulence in the neighbourhood flanking the Tiber and adjoining the Via Giulia.[4] These close and effective links notwithstanding, Pope Sixtus V was infuriated by the Grand Duke's harbouring of some of the most notorious bandits from the Adriatic region of the Papal State, notably Piccolomini and Malatesta.[5] But in 1587 Francesco died and was succeeded by his brother, Cardinal Ferdinando, and a great change came over the relationship of the two states.

At first the Pope frowned angrily at the new Duke's decision to surrender the purple and to marry. But on the day of his coronation, Ferdinando published his decision to marry Christina of Lorraine. Christina was the daughter of the Duke of Lorraine and his wife, Claude, daughter of Catherine de' Medici, the French Queen Mother, so that from that time the Grand Duchy moved even more forcefully in the French ambit. Moreover, the Grand Duchy was already internationally famous for its manufacture of gunpowder, cannonball and matches, and this gave her increased influence on the European stage.[6] As part of Christina's dowry, Catherine surrendered all her rights over the Grand Duchy. Ferdinando passed from the Spanish field of influence to the French.[7] The Pope and the Grand Duke had many mutual interests; they were both earnest reformers, though the Grand Duke did not entirely share the Pope's single-mindedness; both were interested in the development of their Mediterranean coastlines, particularly the draining of the marshlands,[8] and in combating the great harvest failure and consequent famine of 1589. During the last years of Pope Sixtus V's reign there developed between the two states and their rulers a close, friendly and politic relationship which became the basis of a growing counter-balance to the predominance of Spain. In the last year of the Pope's reign the Grand Duke joined others in urging recognition of Henry IV's conversion to Catholicism and his accession to the French throne.[9] Events in the Grand Duchy strengthened the Pope's persistent resistance to Spanish influence in Italy. Spain dominated sixteenth century Europe but at the end of the century France was preparing to overhaul her, and in this change in the balance of power Sixtus played his cards in the interests of the future. Indeed Philip II recognised the challenge to his position so clearly that when Sixtus died, he revived Spanish influence in the Conclave to such effect that a pro-Spanish Pope, Urban VII was elected. When a few months later Urban died of malaria, he was succeeded by Gregory XIV, whose election was due to Spanish influence, and yet again in October 1591, following

Gregory's early death, the pro-Spanish Innocent VIII was elected by the determined and unscrupulous activities of the pro-Spanish Cardinals. The reign of three Spanish Popes in succession demonstrated to the nations the wisdom of independent Popes, liberated from national pressures.

North of the Ligurian Alps there reigned a young, fledgling prince, aged twenty-three, Charles Albert of the Duchy of Piedmont. His impetuosity and vigour made him popular with the people, but five years on the throne had not matured him in public affairs nor sobered his judgements. In politics he entertained numerous outrageous ambitions, but was determined enough to carry a proportion into effect: he married the Infanta Catherine of Spain, Philip II's youngest daughter and enjoyed the intimate encouragement of the Spanish royal house. Charles Emmanuel's father, Emmanuel Philibert, had commanded the Spanish forces with skill at the Battle of St Quentin and had forced the French to sign the decisive Treaty of Cateau-Cambrésis. He thereupon married Margaret of France, sister of Henry II and made a secret Treaty with Philip to allay his suspicions of Savoy's policy if Emmanuel Philibert should die without heirs. Yet the House of Savoy was so closely associated with the French royal family that it was regarded almost as part of France. Charles Emmanuel's father, Emmanuel Philibert, had restored the Duchy after its exhausting entanglements with Geneva, had re-taken the towns which the French had occupied in Savoy. He rigorously upheld the authority of the central government and made himself one of the most absolute rulers in Europe.[10] He broke the powers of the nobility by bestowing on them titles and possessions at court and had his own power secured by amassing immense revenues so that he could dispense with Parliament. The Duchy was richly endowed with natural resources, the intensively cultivated hills of Monferrato and Langhe, south of the Po, supporting a prosperous dairy industry, and in the valleys the cultivation of wheat, rice, vegetables, fruit and milk prospered. Asti and Barbera produced some of the best wines in Italy.

Emmanuel Philibert had practised the cultivation of the mulberry, planted 17,000 trees at Tronzano and obtained a papal loan for the silk merchants.

This headstrong prince created many problems for Pope Sixtus V who, though personally very friendly with the Duke, recognised clearly the European perils of Savoy's ambitions. The prince revived his father's designs on Switzerland, won the approval of Philip II for a renewed attack on Geneva which was easily approved, particularly as Henry III of France had joined in an alliance of Berne and Solothurn to defend Geneva's independence. Charles Emmanuel then appealed to Sixtus who, in spite of warnings by Cardinal d'Este of the dangers of Henry II of France taking up Savoy's challenge, rashly recognised the war as a miniature war of religion, established an account for the assistance of the Catholic armies and authorised recruitment in the Papal State and the raising of contingents under Antonio Orsini and Count Sarno. Nevertheless, with characteristic ambivalence he insisted that should Geneva be overrun neither Philip II nor the Duke of Savoy should take possession of it. The money amounting to 100,000 golden scudi was available only till the end of 1589, and when the Duke slackened his efforts against the Genevans the Pope insisted on the return of the money to the Papal Treasury in Rome, and shortly afterwards he dissociated himself from the venture.[11] Fortunately for the peace of Europe, Geneva succeeded in resisting the attacks and Charles Emmanuel was glad to call off the campaign and look elsewhere for the outlet of his ambitions.

When in July 1589 Henry III was assassinated, the Catholics saw with alarm the almost immediate prospect of the succession of a Huguenot, Henry of Navarre. Charles Emmanuel immediately took advantage of the situation to advance his claims to the French throne, but his claim had little substance and found little support. When the Cardinal of Bourbon died in July 1590, the contest for the throne of France was intensified and opposition to Henry of Navarre became so hot that candidates who in other circumstances might have realised their prospects of the succession were remote could now see their hopes more brightly: Charles Emmanuel was one such. He shelved his claim and was rapidly persuaded to substitute one for the establishment of a kingdom in Provence. In support of this he despatched Savoyan troops and the campaign against Geneva was abandoned in spite of the prospects for success being good. This was the situation when Sixtus V died.

Saluzzo lay some thirty-five miles from Turin, the capital of Piedmont. It stood partly on a spur of the Cottian Alps and partly at the head of fertile Piedmont, combining the character of a small hill town with a rich commercial centre connecting the riches of the valley of the Po with some of the main commercial routes linking South-west France with Northern Italy and Austria.

The Duke of Savoy became entwined in the affairs of the Marquisate of Saluzzo. It was part of the French kingdom on whose frontier it lay, but Emmanuel Philibert had taken it from the French and for some years it belonged to the Duchy of Savoy. By the time of Charles Emmanuel's accession in 1580 it had reverted to the Kingdom of France. In October 1588, seeing the French king's hands tied by the civil war in his kingdom, Charles Emmanuel attacked and overran the Marquisate. Ostensibly he occupied it to prevent it falling to the heretic Huguenots and to protect Henry III's suzerainty—a deceit which the French king treated with scorn. To assuage Henry's wrath, Charles Emmanuel undertook to restore his conquests to their French owners when the conflict had finished, but the King demanded not only the fulfilment of this undertaking but also payment in full of the expenses involved. Sixtus now saw the danger of reprisals by the French king and the possibility of a general conflagration developing out of this quite minor dispute. He began to press the duke to meet Henry's demands and the Cardinal Secretary reiterated the Pope's view by letter. Montalto's correspondence with the Papal envoy to Savoy even made it clear that repression of heretics in the Saluzzo area was less urgent than the pacification of France. Sixtus told his

Legate to inform Henry III that the Duke of Savoy had given his assurance that he would retain Saluzzo as part of the French kingdom and "in the obedience of his Majesty". At the same time when his Legate informed the Pope of pressures on Henry III to revenge himself on the Duke, he was urged to persuade the King to attend to the repression of the Huguenots and the unification of his own kingdom, since the restoration of the Duchy was bound to follow. Such was the limited and vacillating support from the Pope on which a Northern Italian prince could count.

On the Papal side these minor expeditions were a recurring embarrassment. It was difficult for Sixtus to refuse help to princes whose avowed object was the repression of heretics. On the other hand, the religious motives of these excursions quickly became submerged beneath political and personal ambition and the church's name and honour were invoked in aid of projects which quickly became almost wholly political in motive and character. Overwhelmed by the constant supremacy of Spain in the Italian peninsula, the Pope had to give priority to the preservation of a Catholic kingdom of France. This was the only possible counterbalance to the menacing pressures of the vast Spanish Empire on a relatively small area divided into a large number of autonomous states, each with its own divergent interests and independent policies. To Sixtus therefore these minor outbreaks were dangerous: he could not avoid their support because of their religious entanglements, and yet they presented to the French king a tempting distinction from his main task of preserving his kingdom. The Duke of Guise, for example, saw the Saluzzo affair as "the ruin of the whole realm and religion in France, for in order to be able to make war with the Duke of Savoy, his Majesty would have agreed to make peace with Navarre and the heretics, not being able at the same time to maintain two expeditions.[12] The Pope himself described the affair as "the intrigue of a wicked world which sought to ruin his Majesty so that he should be always occupied and never make himself obeyed in his kingdom".[13]

In addition, there was the perpetual danger that one of these local disputes would be extended until they became part of a general upheaval. The Pope and other Italian rulers knew how dangerous was the fragmentation of the peninsula. He was aware of the deliverance from foreign intervention the treaty of Cateau-Cambrésis had brought to Italy, he perceived the knife's edge on which Italian politicians tried to preserve their balance and he understood the absolute necessity of maintaining peace.

Sixtus V's brief five year reign, crowded with activities in the ecclesiastical affairs of the Catholic church, made no impression on the foreign policies of the numerous Italian states or on their relationships with each other. The rigid domination of Italian politics by the unshakeable power of Spain, supported when necessary by the might of the whole of its Empire, kept Papal political power completely fettered and constrained. The danger that resistance to Spain would produce conflict with France, especially when the kingdom of the Most Christian King was torn by deeply divisive internal religious and political strife; Sixtus V had to avoid conflict at all costs. A policy of neutrality and non-belligerence was inexorably imposed upon him and papal inactivity was made inevitable by the continuing rivalries of the individual states, their individual domination by Spain and their insistence on the preservation of peace. For Italy there was, as yet, no unifying rallying call, no over-riding cause to give them common loyalty and purpose. To them indeed, papal intervention in their internal affairs loomed as largely as the enemy of Italian autonomy—Spain. The Duke of Savoy, for example, claimed the right to nominate the bishops of his Duchy, and when Sixtus himself appointed the Bishop of Vercelli there was a sharp clash in which the Pope vigorously defended his right to select the bishops of all lands except France where, by virtue of a privilege granted by Clement VII, the right of making such appointments was reserved to the King. The Pope pressed his contentions so tenaciously that Charles Emmanuel was obliged to withdraw his claim.[14] Remoteness did not permit this

Italian state to preserve its independence when papal prerogatives were involved. The great medieval issue which had shaken Europe throughout the centuries was totally unresolved, and whereas Protestant states had been able to exclude papal claims altogether by embracing some reformed creed, Catholic states—however orthodox in faith and doctrine—met the promulgation of clerical pretensions by a deepened resistance to the contentions of an international church. In all these states Sixtus V was involved in the dispute whether the Pope, in defence of a man's soul and to preserve the unity of the Christian Church, could dictate to him a course of conduct contrary to the wishes of his political ruler. Until this issue was resolved the task of the Council of Trent could be only partially fulfilled. Sixtus' dilemma was to make his religious powers effective without being involved in the political entanglements which the states would design for him. His policy was therefore essentially and inevitably negative.

Although Sixtus' earlier experiences as Inquisitor in the Venetian Republic had not been without their problems, he remained on good terms with the authorities there. Venice combined efforts to avoid conflict with a robust defence strategy in case these efforts failed. In the matter of the French succession they allied themselves with Henry of Navarrre, in accord with their attitudes of religious tolerance. They also instructed their ambassador to Rome, Alberto Badoer, to urge the Pope to consider the merits of the case. Venice feared the expansionist tendencies of Spain and pointed out that Philip II was not in the Italian peninsular for the good of the papacy. It seems that Sixtus was by that time thinking on these lines, because he muttered to Badoer, "They want to conquer the world."[15]

Sixtus V's initial admiration for Elizabeth I of England went hand in hand with his abhorrence of her heretical beliefs. He is recorded as saying, "She is a valiant woman... She is certainly a great Queen. Were she only a Catholic she would be our dearly beloved. Look how well she governs. She is only a woman, only master of half an island, and yet makes herself feared by Spain, by France, by the Empire, by all."[16]

Ugo Balzini considered that Sixtus hoped "to transform Elizabeth into a Countess Matilda."[17]

However, with the execution of Mary Queen of Scots in 1587, Sixtus realized that his hopes for Elizabeth's conversion[18]—which she had laughed at, when she heard a report of Sixtus' remark—were illusory. He renewed the excommunication delivered by Pius V, and issued a proclamation to justify it, *An Admonition to the Nobility and Laity of England*. She became the "new Jezebel".[19] Sixtus supported Philip II's plan for an armada with the secret convention of July 29, 1587. By this he promised one million crowns for the enterprise. But this was not unconditional. Five hundred crowns were to be paid when the armada had successfully landed. The remainder was payable in instalments of 100,000 crowns every four months. The papal treasury in the event was not burdened. The subsequent course of events in England was marked by treason laws against Jesuits and priests, the activities of the pursuivants and the subsequent arrest and savage execution of those apprehended.

Sixtus's accession had coincided with the arrival of a Japanese embassy in Rome (one of the princes of this mission took part in his inaugural Mass). Since the time of Francis Xavier, the Catholic population of Japan had risen to two hundred thousand and Sixtus created the first diocese of Japan, Funai (Oita) on February 19th, 1588. He also favoured missions to the Philippines and South America, using the Franciscan and Dominican Orders. At the same time he urged a crusade against the menace of the Turks, suggesting a campaign launched from Poland or an assault on Algiers. At the beginning of his pontificate he mused, "If I had the necessary money I would set on foot a great expedition against the infidel".[20] He sent an envoy to the Shah of Persia, who was then at war with Ottoman Turkey. The Shah took four years to reply. Rather than leave the Holy Sepulchre in infidel hands, Sixtus conceived a project to bring it stone by stone to Italy. All these projects remained pipe dreams.

*Foreign Diplomacy and Final Days* 391

The succession to the throne of Poland in contrast proved to be one of Sixtus' diplomatic triumphs. Two chief claimants presented themselves: the twenty-nine year old Sigismund, Prince of Sweden, and the Hapsburg, Archduke Maximilian. When Maximilian was defeated Sixtus' envoy, Cardinal Aldobrandini, managed to negotiate an honourable compromise whereby Maximilian surrendered his claim and was granted his freedom, and Sigismund ascended the throne with papal blessing. This result would be recorded for history on Sixtus' tomb.

At what would be his final Consistory, he was able to announce that the papal galleons had captured three corsair ships — the medal struck to commemorate the occasion stated grandiloquently "Terra marique securitas".[21]

In the summer of 1590, the sixty-eight year old pontiff, suffering from the heat and the effects of 'marsh fever', began to decline visibly. According to the contemporary accounts, he did not put much faith in doctors or their prescriptions. However, the prevailing wisdom for a hot fever was something cold. Sixtus had wine mixed with snow —Hübner adds "more wine than was his wont"[22]—and some of his favourite melon. The fever subsided, Sixtus got out of bed and worked for four hours. He celebrated the conversion of the Margrave of Baden. He found time to take half a million ducats from his Treasury in Castel Sant'Angelo—two strong boxes had been constructed by Fontana—to buy grain from Sicily to help the poor during the bad harvest following torrential floods. But this was only a respite and the fever returned with greater intensity, preventing him even from receiving Communion because he was not able to swallow.

Legend has it that Sixtus expired without the consolation of the Sacraments,[23] but more substantiated accounts say that he made his confession at six in the evening and received the sacrament of Extreme Unction from Cardinal Aldobrandini.[24] He died at ten o'clock in the evening of August 27, 1590. The exact cause is unknown, but his body was opened "and found to be in a perfect state (*nettissimo*)".[25] In accordance with his instructions, part of his heart (the *praecordia*) was placed in the apse of the ornate baroque church of Santi Vincenzo e Anastasio. This custom was continued under subsequent Popes until Pius X ended it in the twentieth century. Sixtus was immediately buried in the Vatican, but on August 26, 1591 in a procession led by his great-nephew, he was re-interred in the chapel of the Presepio in St Mary Major on which he had lavished so much care, near the tomb of his friend Pope Pius V. The marble soldiers portrayed on Pius' tomb displayed the severed head of a bandit chief. For both Popes the suppression of banditry was a matter of unfinished business.

Sixtus' careful husbandry of his office is witnessed by the fact that, in contrast to his predecessors, on his death he left five and a half million scudi in the Treasury. The Roman mob—presumably composed of many of those who had been victims of Sixtus' urban planning and of his tax regime—were frustrated in their attempt to topple Taddeo Landini's statue of the Pope. The Senate had erected it in the Palace of the Conservatori in recognition of his work for Rome, but aware of the possible reaction after his death instructed the Constable to cover it up. The Jewish moneylenders on the Piazza Navona, who had benefited from Sixtus' tolerance, hearing of his death, fled the city.

## Notes

[1] *CMH* 3, p. 261.
[2] *Ibid.*
[3] Delumeau 1, p. 54.
[4] *Ibid.*, p. 207.
[5] *Ibid.*, pp. 544, 552. See Chapter 5 above.
[6] Braudel, *The Mediterranean* 2, p. 839.
[7] I. Montanelli & R. Gervaso, *Storia d'Italia 5. L'Italia del Seicento* (Milano: Rizzoli, 2010), pp. 157–159.
[8] Delumeau 1, p. 349.

*Foreign Diplomacy and Final Days* 393

9   Sixtus initially favoured his own nephew for the succession.
10  *CMH* 3, p. 260.
11  Tempesti, *Storia della vita e geste di Sisto Quinto*, 2, pp. 353–366. See also Hübner 2, pp. 396–406.
12  Tempesti, *Storia della vita e geste di Sisto Quinto*, 2, p. 168.
13  *Ibid.*, p. 192.
14  Tempesti, *Storia della vita e geste di Sisto Quinto*, 1, p. 684.
15  Pastor 21, p. 368.
16  J. E. Neale, *Queen Elizabeth I* (London: Penguin, 1960), p. 284.
17  "Rome under Sixtus V" in *CMH* 3, p. 435.
18  Hübner 1, pp. 343–344.
19  Pastor 22, p. 33.
20  *Ibid.* 22, p. 145.
21  *Ibid.* 21, p. 120.
22  Hübner 2, p. 364.
23  G. Leti, *Vita di Sisto V* (Lausanne: 1609). Brumani wrote to Tullio Petrozani on 27 August 1590 that the Pope did go to confession (Pastor 22, p. 180, n. 2). See also Sangaletto to Grand Duke Ferdinando I (27 August 1590), as mentioned in Hübner 2, p. 351.
24  Hübner 2, p. 351. Donna Camilla, Cardinals Giustiniani, Pinelli, Aldobrandini and his great nephew were at his bedside.
25  *Avviso di Roma* (29 August 1590). Hübner 2, p. 351 n.

# EPILOGUE

### A Pope in a Hurry

*This is a friar with energy in him, and he does not intend to be in the world to no purpose.*

Antonio Tiepolo, Ambassador of the Venetian Republic, 1578

IN HIS DAYS, Sixtus V was known as one of the great reforming Popes. Since that time, he has been largely forgotten. Sixtus IV is remembered for the Sistine Chapel, the Sistine Choir and the Ponte Sisto, Sixtus V is remembered largely in unsupported legend.

The truth behind the legend is relatively prosaic. Sixtus was a serious religious, driven by a sense of destiny. Such people are frequently intransigent and over-zealous. The Venetians would accuse him precisely of those faults as Inquisitor. But against that we must weigh his erudition in theological debate, his skill as preacher and his conscientiousness as Vicar-General of the Franciscans. He was responsible for more than one thousand three hundred friaries, many of which he visited on foot, and he appointed a series of Visitors to ensure observance of the Rule.

The same characteristics surfaced when he became Pope. He did not suffer fools gladly, but he had a clear sense of what needed to be done without fear of offending people. Gregory the Great says that "negligent religious leaders are often afraid to speak freely and say what needs to be said for fear of losing favour with people."[1] Sixtus V attempted what others considered impossible, such as raising the obelisk of St Peter's, and he completed the dome in record time. He was responsible for thirteen new streets and associated piazzas, the reconstruction of St John Lateran, St Mary Major and the papal apartments in the Vatican. Hübner says that "he understood the art and had a technical knowledge about construction which few Popes possessed".[2] He built the first twenty-four kilometre aqueduct since Roman times, restored two others along with numerous fountains, and generally improved hygiene in the city and civic amenities. Some hold it against him that the Septizodium of Septimus Severus was destroyed to provide building materials, but the plundering of antique and mediaeval buildings for new construction was considered normal practice among his contemporaries and continued up to modern times.[3] In his book *Roma dal cielo* Cesare d'Onofrio makes the accusation that Sixtus' improvements to the landscape of Rome were largely motivated by a desire to enlarge his villa—but this is only partly true. In the second stage, the Palazzetto Montalto dwarfed surrounding structures (it was itself finally demolished for the building of Termini Station in 1869). Sixtus' master plan included his villa, but that was only part of the ten kilometre square area that was mapped out. "Sixtus V provided the structural and legal basis for the growth of the Baroque city. None of the later popes, not even Alexander VII was to undertake such extensive urban projects."[4] His reliance on his close friend Domenico Fontana (and also Fontana's son) as architects and brilliant engineers (erecting the obelisk in the Piazza of St Peter's) meant that many of his projects were solid and also possessed artistic merit.

Was he ruthless? Undoubtedly, but he could not be described as "the most inexorable of despots".[5] His edicts were draconian in regards to brigands, but he exercised strange restraint over the murder of his nephew. For a former Inquisitor, he was not over-vigorous in the pursuit of heterodoxy. Unlike previous or subsequent Popes, he adopted a most enlightened policy towards the Jews, exempting them from many petty restrictions (the 1559 Index of Paul IV had prohibited the Talmud and all works based on it; Venice burnt the books).

Augias calls Sixtus "one of the most open-minded of the sixteenth-century Popes."[6]

As ruler of the Papal States, he did have responsibilities to the people of his kingdom as well as to the faith he represented. Both were interrelated since he was also a temporal ruler. The Doge of Venice referred to "the public utility which springs from the protection of the Catholic religion".[7] Treatment of heretics was severe throughout sixteenth-century Europe—they were seen as a danger to the commonweal. In fact, only five were executed under Sixtus' jurisdiction during his pontificate.

Some of his nominations to the Cardinalate aroused resentment—in particular his grand-nephew because of his extreme youth—yet such an appointment was common at the time (cardinals Carafa, Boncompagni, Bonelli and Borromeo were all nephews of a Pope). Sixtus did not particularly favour the Franciscans (although he did canonize Diego of Alcalá and made St Bonaventure a Doctor of the Church), he created only one of them Cardinal but he did exercise his preference for those well qualified academically and he appointed his fellow religious to other posts. He gave advance warning of his Consistory, allowing objections to be made—which probably invited them. By limiting the number of Cardinal to seventy (a restriction to last until the pontificate of Pope John XXIII in modern times) he also made it less likely that any Pope's nominations would come to dominate the election of the next Pope and the future pontificate (Gregory XIII had favoured Bolognese, and these were in a majority on the conclave that had elected Sixtus).

Critics would say that his foreign policy was marked by a certain irresoluteness and changeability.[8] It could be argued that his dealings with Philip II showed some measure of shrewdness that did not deplete the treasury. His delaying tactics in France ensured the succession of Henry IV, the frustration of Spanish interests and ended the possibility of civil war between the factions. Hübner would assert that "Sixtus saved France from innumerable miseries and has deserved well of the Church and of history".⁹ He indirectly stemmed Philip II's expansionist ambitions.

One of the most interesting facets of Sixtus' character is shown in his attitude to the English Queen, Elizabeth I. Unlike his predecessors, he admired her spirit and her leadership qualities while abhorring her religious beliefs. He rather naively thought he could convert her, in which speaks the religious preacher and mission-giver. He rightly assessed that the attempt to overthrow her would as likely as not fail.

How can we explain the apparent contradictions in his personality —his admiration for Elizabeth, his tolerance for the Jews, his frugality as against his relentless pursuit of banditry, his policies of taxation and centralization, his insistence on clerical dress? He was first and foremost a religious (albeit not an *Observant* Franciscan) and considered obedience to the rule as paramount. This fitted strangely with Papal court life, designed to cater to aristocratic tastes and ways of operating. We must also bear in mind that he had experienced years of opposition—in Venice, in his own order, and finally from Gregory XIII both before he was Pope and during his pontificate.

History has recognised Pope Sixtus V as a significant figure in the Counter Reformation. He was open to large ideas and threw himself into his undertakings with great energy and determination, and this often led to success. His pontificate saw great enterprises and great achievements. He slept little and worked hard. He had inherited a bankrupt treasury, administered his funds with competence and care, and left five million crowns in the coffers of the Holy See at his death.[10] He built the Lateran Palace; completed the Quirinale; restored the Church of Santa Sabina on the Aventine; rebuilt the Church and Hospice of San Girolamo dei Schiavoni; enlarged and improved the Sapienza; founded the hospice for the poor near the Ponte Sisto; built and richly ornamented the chapel of the Presepio in the Basilica of St Mary Major; completed the cupola of St Peter's; raised the obelisks of the Vatican, of St Mary Major, of the Lateran, and of Santa Maria del Popolo; restored the columns of Trajan and of Antoninus Pius, placing the statue of St Peter on the former and that of St Paul on the latter; erected the Vatican Library with its adjoining printing-office and that wing of the Vatican Palace which is inhabited by the pope; built many magnificent streets; erected various monasteries; and supplied Rome with water, the *Acqua Felice*, which he brought to the city over a distance of twenty-four kilometres, partly underground, partly on elevated aqueducts. Sixtus left the Church, the city of Rome and the world a better place.[11]

## Notes

[1] Pope Gregory the Great, *Pastoral Rule*, 2, 4.

[2] Hübner 2, p. 118. J. H. Plumb, for instance, does not mention Sixtus V in his book on the Renaissance.

[3] K. Nille, *St Peters* (Harvard: Harvard University Press, 2007), p. 77. He did however strip the marble facing from the tomb of Cecilia Metella in the Via Appia.

[4] W. Jung, "Architecture and city in Italy from the early Baroque to the early neo-classical period" in R. Toman, A. Bednorz, C. Bindman (eds.), *Baroque : architecture, sculpture, painting* (Cologne: Ullmann & Konemann, 2007), p. 16.

[5] V. Pirie, *The Triple Crown. An account of the Papal Conclaves from the fifteenth century to the present day* (London: 1935), p. 114. Under Sixtus there were only 5 executions for heresy.

[6] C. Augias, *The Secrets of Rome: Love & Death in the Eternal City* (New York: Rizzoli, 2007), p. 359.

[7] N. S. Davidson, "Il Sant'Uffizio e la tutela del culto a Venezia nel '500" in *Studi Veneziani* 6 (1982), p. 85.

[8] Pirie, *The Triple Crown*.

[9] Hübner 2, p. 372.

[10] *CE* 3, p. 241.

[11] The changes wrought by Sixtus on the street plan of Rome were documented in the film, *Rome: Impact of an Idea*, featuring Edmund N. Bacon and based on sections of his book *Design of Cities* (London: Thames & Hudson, 1967).

# *Bibliography*

Amann, F. *Die Vulgata Sixtina von 1590: Eine quellenmassige darstellung ihrer geschichte mit neuem quellenmaterial aus dem Venezianischen staatsarchiv. Freiburger theologische Studien: Vol. 10* (Freiburg im Breisgau; St. Louis, MO: Herder, 1912).

Ambrosini, M. L. &. W. M. *Secret Archives of the Vatican* (New York: Little Brown, 1996).

Augias, C. *The secrets of Rome: Love & death in the eternal city* (New York: Rizzoli, 2007).

Balzani, U. *Sisto Quinto: [Sixtus V]* (Roma: A. F. Formíggini, 1924).

Baumgarten P. M. *Die Vulgata sixtina von 1590 und ihre Einfurungsbulle. Aktenstucke und Untersuchungen* (Munster:1911).

Black, C. F. *Italian confraternities in the sixteenth century* (Cambridge: Cambridge University Press, 1989).

Bordini G. F. *De rebus praeclare gestis a Sixto V Pont. Max.* (Romae:1588).

Borsi, S. *Roma di Sisto V. La pianta di Antonio Tempesta, 1593* (Roma:1986).

Braudel, F. *The Mediterranean and the Mediterranean world in the age of Philip II* (New York: Harper & Row, 1972).

Brooke, R. B. *Early Franciscan Government: Elias to Bonaventure. Cambridge studies in medieval life and thought. New series: Vol. 007* (Cambridge: Cambridge University Press, 1959).

Brown, H. F. *The Venetian printing press: An historical study based upon documents for the most part hitherto unpublished, with twenty-two facsimiles of early printing* (London: John C. Nimmo, 1891).

Burkart, B. *Der Lateran Sixtus V. und sein Architekt Domenico Fontana* (Bonn:1989).

Canestrari, R. *Sisto V* (Torino: Società Editrice Internazionale, 1954).

Cartechini, P. *La Marca e le sue istituzioni al tempo di Sisto V. Pubblicazioni degli archivi di Stato: Vol. 20* (Roma: Ministero per i beni culturali e ambientali Ufficio centrale per i beni archivistici, 1991).

Chambers, D. *Popes, cardinals, and war: The military church in Renaissance and early modern Europe* (London; New York: I. B. Tauris, 2006).

Coccia, A. *La Provincia romana dei frati minori conventuali dall'origine ai nostri giorni* (Roma: Amati, 1967).

Corkery, J., & Worcester, T. *The papacy since 1500: From Italian prince to universal pastor* (Cambridge; New York: Cambridge University Press, 2010).

Dalla Santa, G. *Un documento inedito per la storia di Sisto V* (Venezia: Tip. ex Cordella, 1896).

Duffy, E. *Saints and Sinners. A History of the Popes* (New Haven & London: Yale University Press, 2006).

Dumesnil, M. A. J. *Histoire de Sixte-Quint. Sa vie et son pontificat* (Paris:1869).

Fagiolo, M., & Madonna, M. L. *Sisto V* (Roma: Istituto poligrafico e zecca dello Stato; Libreria dello Stato, 1992).

Feo, I. de. *Sisto V: Un grande papa tra Rinascimento e Barocco* (Milano: Mursia, ²1987).

Fontana, D. *Della trasportatione dell'obelisco vaticano et delle fabriche di Nostro Signore papa Sisto V* (Roma; Napoli: D. Basa; C. Vitale, 1604).

Forlani Tempesti, A. *Capolavori del Rinascimento: Il primo Cinquecento toscano. I Disegni dei maestri, vol. 1* (Milano: Fabbri, 1970).

Galesini, P. *Ordo dedicationis obelisci quem S.D.N. Sixtus V. Pont. Max. in foro vaticano ad limina apostolorum erexit et benedictionis item Crucis quam in eius fastigio collocauit ... ;: Adiuncta est initio breuis quasi historia ordine contexta qua praeclarum obelisci Crucisq[ue] erectae opus sempiterna memoria dignum* (Romae: ex typographia Bartholomaei Grassij, 1586).

Gasquet, F. N. A. *English monastic life* (London: Methuen, ⁵1910).

Gasquet, F. N. A. *A history of the Venerable English College, Rome: An account of its origins and work from the earliest times to the present day* (London: Longmans Green and Co, 1920).

Gatti, I. *Sisto V papa "piceno": Le testimonianze e i documenti autentici. Bibliotheca Sixtina* (Ripatransone (AP): Maroni, 1990).

Gatti, I., & Tassoni, R. *Ancora su Sisto V papa piceno: Commento ad un recente opuscolo* (Acquaviva Picena (AP): Tip. Fast Edit, 1999).

Graziani, A. M. *Vita di Sisto V* (Romae:1587).

Grendler, P. F. *The Roman Inquisition and the Venetian press, 1540-1605* (Princeton NJ: Princeton University Press, 1977).

Grendler, P. F. *The Universities of the Italian Renaissance* (Baltimore, MD: The Johns Hopkins University Press, 2004).

Grünbacher, T. *Sixtus V. und seine städtebauliche Tätigkeit: [Hauptseminararbeit ; Seminar: Von der Stadt der Päpste zur Kulturhauptstadt: Rom im 16.–19. Jahrhundert]* (München: Grin-Verlag, 2004).

Hale, J. R. *The civilization of Europe in the Renaissance* (London: HarperCollins, 1993).

Hübner, A. von. *Der eiserne Papst: Sixtus V. und seine Zeit* (Berlin: Paul Aretz, 1932).

Jode, P. de. *Sixtus V. pont. max: Creatus anno 1572, obijt 1585* (Antverp: P. de Iode axcudit, 1635–1674).

Kalman, J. T. *Sixtus V, and late XVI century Roman civic design* (Davis, CA:1973).

Kneller, K. A. *Zur Geschichte der Jesuiten unter Sixtus V* (Innsbruck: F. Rauch, 1928).

Lees-Milne, J. *Saint Peter's: The story of Saint Peter's Basilica in Rome* (London: Hamish Hamilton, 1967).

Leti, G. *Vita di Sisto V, Pontefice Romano* (Amsteldamo:1731).

Logan, F. D. *Excommunication and the secular arm in medieval England: A study in legal procedure from the thirteenth to the sixteenth century. Pontifical Institute of Mediaeval Studies. Studies and texts: Vol. 15* (Toronto: Pontifical Institute of Mediaeval Studies, 1968).

Madonna, M. L. *Roma di Sisto V: Le arti e la cultura* (Roma: De Luca, 1993).

Magnuson, T. *From the election of Sixtus V to the death of Urban VIII* (Stockholm: Almquist and Wiksell, 1982).

Mandel, C. *Sixtus V and the Lateran Palace* (Roma: Istituto poligrafico e Zecca dello Stato, Libreria dello Stato, 1994).

Masson, G. *Italian Gardens* (London: Thames & Hudson, 1961).

Montanelli, I., & Gervaso, R. *L'Italia della controriforma (1492-1600)* (Milano: Rizzoli, 1968).

Montanelli, I., & Gervaso, R. *L'Italia del Seicento (1600-1700)* (Milano: Rizzoli, 1970).

Orbaan, J. A. F. *Sixtine Rome* (London: Constable & Company Ltd, 1910).

Orbaan, J. A. F. *How Pope Sixtus V lost a road* (Liverpool: Liverpool University Press, 1928).

Ostrow, S. F. *The Sistine Chapel at S. Maria Maggiore: Sixtus V and the Art of the Counter Reformation* (Ann Arbor, MI:1987).

Paoli, M. *Sisto V e i banditi (1585-1590)* (Sassari: Tipografia e Libreria G. Gallizzi & C., 1902).

Papa, G. *Sisto V e la diocesi di Montalto: Erezione e consolidamento. Biblioteca storica (Maroni): Vol. 2* (Ripatransone (Ap.): Maroni, 1985).

Parisciani, G. *Sisto V e la sua Montalto. Ricerche francescane* (Padova: Ediz. Messaggero, 1986).

Partner, P. *The lands of St. Peter: The Papal State in the Middle Ages and the early Renaissance* (Los Angeles: University of California Press, 1972).

Paschini, P. *Venezia e l'Inquisizione Romana da Giulio III a Pio IV. Italia sacra: Vol. 001* (Padova: Editrice Antenore, 1959).

Pastor, L. *Sisto V il creatore della nuova Roma* (Roma: 1922).

Pecchiai, P. *Roma nel Cinquecento. Storia di Roma: Vol. 013* (Bologna: Cappelli, 1948).

Peretti, G., & Peretti, A. *Sixti Quinti Pont. Max. Creatio: Ad Alexandrum Perettum Cardinalem Montaltum S.R.E. vicecancellarium* (Romae: Apud Iacobum Ruffinellum, 1591?).

Personè, L. M. *Sisto Quinto, il genio della potenza* (Firenze: Le Monnier, 1935).

Pistolesi, F. *Sisto V e Montalto da documenti inediti* (Montalto:1920).

Pistolesi, F. *La Prima Biografia Auteutrea di Papa Sisto Quinto* (Montalto:1925).

Polichetti, M. L. *Il progetto di Sisto V: Territorio, città, monumenti nelle Marche* (Roma: Istituto poligrafico e zecca dello Stato, 1991).

Polverini Fosi, I. *La società violenta: Il banditismo nello Stato Pontificio nella seconda metà del Cinquecento* (Roma: Ed. dell'Ateneo, 1985).

Pronti, D. *La cappella eretta da Sisto V nel Vaticano: Magnifico portico della Basilica Vaticana* (In Roma: presso l'Incisore Domenico Pronti, 1795).

Pullan, B. S. *Rich and poor in renaissance Venice: The social institutions of a Catholic state to 1620* (Oxford: Blackwell, 1971).

Quast, M. *Die Villa Montalto in Rom: Entstehung und Gestaltung im Cinquecento. Tuduv-Studien: Vol. 45* (München: Tuduv, 1991).

Rebaschi Carotti, L. *Il conclave di Sisto V* (Mantova:1919).

Regnard, V., Collignon, F., & Pecci Blunt, A. L. *Sixtus V. pont. max. Bibliothecae Vaticanae aedificationem praescribit.* (Roma: Francesco Collignon formis, 1650).

Renwick, A. M., & Harman, A. M. *The story of the Church* (Leicester: Inter-Varsity, 1998).

Ricci, C. *Statue e busti di Sisto V* (Roma: Tip. Dell'Unione Ed., 1916).

Romani, M. *Pellegrini e viaggiatori nell'economia di Roma dal XIV al XVII secolo* (Milano: Università del Sacro Cuore, 1948).

Roscius, I., & Gioacchini, D. *Epigrammi in lode di Sisto V. Quaderni dell'Accademia dei Signori della città di Orte: Vol. 3* (Orte: Accademia dei Signori Disuniti, 1989).

Rossi, G. G. de. *Sixtus V Pont. Opt. Max. aquas Felices senatui P.Q.R. adduxit.* (Roma: Giovanni Iacomo Rossi le stampa alla Pace, 1648–1691).

Russo Caro, E. de. *Sisto V e Carlo Emanuele di Savoia, 1585-1590* (Roma:1987).

Sanità, G. *Sisto V e la lotta al brigantaggio nello Stato Pontificio* (Roma: Pubblicità progresso, 1967).

Sansolini, C. *La spiritualità di Sisto V nei suoi sermoni prima del pontificato* (Roma: Tipografia Poliglotta Vaticana, 1989).

Santori, G. A., & Tacchi Venturi, P. *Diario concistoriale di Giulio Antonio Santori, cardinale di S. Severina* (Roma:1903).

Schiffmann, R. *Roma felix: Aspekte der stadtebaulichen Gestaltung Roms unter Papst Sixtus V* (Bern: P. Lang, 1985).

Servanzi Collio, S. *Un bastone ad uso del pontefice Sisto V.* (Urbino: co' tipi della Cappella per E. Righi, 1879).

Sette, M. P., & Benedetti, S. *Architetture per la città: L'arte a Roma al tempo di Sisto V : Roma, Palazzo Venezia, novembre 1991. Storia, architettura: Vol. 1* (Roma: Multigrafica, 1992).

Sette, M. P., & Benedetti, S. *L'arte a Roma al tempo di Sisto V: Architetture per la città Roma, Palazzo Venezia, novembre 1992. Storia, architettura: Vol. 1* (Roma: Multigrafica, 1992).

Sixtus V. *Sixti Papae V. Diplomata, una cum officiis ipsis S.S. Francisci de Paula, Petri martyris, Antoniii de Padua, Nicolai Tolentinatis & Januarii sociorum ejus: Ab omnibus ecclesiasticis ipsius pontificis jussu recitandis : accesserunt quoque officia B. Annæ & præsentationis Deip. Virg. Mariæ* (Leodii: apud Christianum Ouwercx, 1588).

Sixtus V. *Roma di Sisto V: Arte, architettura e città fra Rinascimento e Barocco* (Roma: De Luca, 1993).

Spagnesi, G. *La pianta di Roma al tempo di Sisto V (1585-1590)* (Roma: Multigrafica, 1992).

Spezzaferro, L., & Tittoni Monti, M. E. *Il Campidoglio e Sisto V* (Roma: Carte Segrete, 1991).

Tagliaventi, F. *Sisto V Papa e principe* (Fermo: La rapida, 1969).

Tempesti, C. L. *Storia della vita e geste di Sisto Quinto* (2 vols.) (Roma: a spese di Remondini di Venezia, 1754).

Torre, D. *L'igiene a Roma durante il pontificato di Sisto V* (Roma: Tip. F. Centenari, 1982).

Trollope, T. A. *The papal conclaves* (London: Chapman & Hall, 1876).

van Aelst, N. *Sixtus V Pont. Opt. Max. aquas Felices senatui P.Q.R. adduxit.* (Roma: Nicolaus van Aelst Bruxellen. feliciter easdem formis aeneis expressas dicavit, 1589).

Williams, M. E. *The Venerable English College* (Leominster: Gracewing, ²2008).

Witcombe, C. L. C. E. *Sixtus V and the Scala Santa* (Philadelphia: Society of Architectural Historians, 1985).

Zuccari, A. *I pittori di Sisto V* (Roma: Palombi, 1992).

Zugaj, M. *Sisto V tra Oriente ed Occidente. Collectanea croatico-hieronymiana de Urbe: Vol. 001* (Roma: Edizioni Miscellanea Francescana, 1987).

# *Glossary*

*Ad limina (Apostolorum) visits*: A diocesan requirement to visit the thresholds or *limina* (of the Apostles), to meet the Pope and the curia on a regular basis.

*Apostolic Camera*: An office more directly dependent on the Pope, in charge of temporal affairs—especially during a vacancy.

*Basilica*: In Rome there are four major basilicas : St Peter's, St John Lateran, St Mary Major, St Paul's outside the Walls.

*Barnabites*: A religious order founded in Milan in 1530 by St Anthony Maria Zaccaria, known as the clerks regular of St Paul.

*Bull* (from the Latin *bulla* or lead seal): The term for a papal document stamped with a lead seal bearing the images of Saints Peter and Paul on one side and the name of the Pope on the other.

*Camaldolese*: Monastic order of hermits founded around 1012 by St Romuald at Camaldoli.

*Camerlengo* (or *Camerarius*): The Cardinal Chamberlain of the Holy Roman Church who was the highest fiscal official. In the event of a vacancy he assumed control of the administration of the Church, certified the death of the pontiff and organised the conclave.

*Canonical Hours*: Portions of the Divine Office to be recited at various hours of the day.

*Canon Law*: A compilation of laws and decrees governing the discipline of the Roman Catholic Church, reviewed and re-issued between 1560 and 1582.

*Capuchins*: A reform of the Franciscan Order instituted by Matteo di Bessi of Urbano from 1525.

*Cardinal-nephew*: Title given to a nephew or close relative given the rank of Cardinal and acting as first minister in the papal curia. Innocent XII (1691-1700) put an end to the practice.

*Concordat*: A legal agreement between a civil authority and the Pope.

*Condottiere*: Mercenary soldier in Europe from 13th to 16th centuries.

*Confraternity*: A Catholic association of laymen having some special religious work or devotion. The Confraternity of the Standard (del Gonfalone) was erected in Rome in 1260.

*Conclave*: The place for the election of a pope (the Apostolic Palace) or the assembly itself of Cardinals.

*Conventuals*: A branch of the Franciscan Order, first approved in 1332, which held that property could be accumulated. It separated from the Observants in 1517.

*Curia*: The Papal administration made up of several departments, called Congregations.

*Doge*: Supreme elected magistrate of the republic of Venice and of Genoa.

*Dominicans*: Also known as Friars Preachers founded by St Dominic in 1215.

*Exequatur*: A legal instrument issued by secular authorities in Roman Catholic nations to ensure that Papal teachings have legal force within their jurisdiction. The tradition began during the time of the Western Schism, when the legitimately elected Pope gave secular leaders permission to verify the authenticity of papal degrees before enforcing them.

*Gabelles*: Various types of taxes placed on consumer items like salt.

*Holy Office of the Inquisition*: An institution entrusted with upholding the faith of the Catholic Church and of prosecuting heresy, magic, obscenity and blasphemy, established by Pope Paul III in 1542.

*Index*: One of the Congregations of the Papal Curia, linked with the Inquisition which investigated books for their doctrinal content, established by Pope Pius V and reorganized by Sixtus V.

*Inquisition*: An institution established in the Middle Ages for the eradication of heresy. The Roman Inquisition was distinct from the Spanish version (q.v.). The Congregation of the Inquisition was renamed the Congregation for the Doctrine of the Faith in 1965.

*Jesuits*: The Society of Jesus, a Religious Order approved by Paul III in 1540. Their church of the Gesù was begun in 1567.

*Locutorio or Locutory*: A room or parlour in a religious house set aside for conversation.

*Lateran Basilica*: The Cathedral Church of Rome and a major basilica, the Church of the Saviour.

*Minims*: Members of an order of hermits founded by St Francis of Paola (1416-1507).

*Mezzadria*: A form of sharecropping by which the crops and the profits are split fifty-fifty with the landlord. The equivalent to the French *metayage*.

*Monte de Pietà* (*Mons pietatis*): An institution lending money or various goods to the poor at little or no interest, against the security of items left on deposit.

*Monti*: Public loans at interest. These could be *vacabili* if they were redeemable in a stated time, or *non vacabili* if they were assumed as part of the permanent debt. Sixtus issued 11 *monti* of which 8 were vacabili.

*Nuncio*: Official representative of the Pope to a civil administration. The term is derived from the ancient Latin word, *Nuntius*, meaning envoy.

*Observant Franciscans*: Originally a protest movement in 1368 which urged return to the primitive rule of 1223. They split into the Observants, Reformed, Discalced and Recollects. Leo XIII reunited them in 1897 under a Minister General, as Friars Minor.

*Papal States*: Also known as the Patrimony of St Peter. At the time of Sixtus V they included parts of Central Italy, Ravenna and the cities of Rimini, Pesaro, Fano, Senigalia, Ancona and Emilia as well as the French portion purchased by Clement VI from Joanna, Queen of Naples in 1348.

*Pontifex Maximus* (Pont. Max.): Supreme Pontiff. A title given to the Pope since the late fourth century, but originally accorded to the Emperor as Head of the College of Roman pagan priests.

*Regular Clergy*: Clergy living in community governed by a rule.

*Rota*: The supreme Roman Catholic tribunal for judging cases brought to the Pope and a final court of appeal. The judges are called Auditors and the President is called the Dean. The court is named *Rota* (wheel) because the Auditors originally met in a round room to hear cases.

*Pallium*: The circular band of white woollen material worn on the shoulders by the Pope and granted by him to metropolitan archbishops.

*Ratio Studiorum*: The study plan and set of rules governing the teaching activity of the Jesuits from 1599–1773.

*Saint Mary Major/Santa Maria Maggiore*: One of the four major basilicas, founded by Pope Liberius in the fourth century and rebuilt by Sixtus III in the fifth century.

*Sbirro*: Policeman employed by the local magistrate to serve summonses and to make seizures of people and goods.

*Spanish Inquisition*: Church tribunal established by the Spanish Crown in 1479, as distinct from its Roman counterpart. Its jurisdiction included Sardinia and Sicily.

*Theatines*: A Congregation of Regular Clerks founded in 1524 by Bishop Carafa (later Pope Paul IV) and St Cajetan.

*Third Orders*: Religious organizations affiliated to the mendicant orders. Its members either live outside (tertiaries) or inside the community.

*Trent, Council of*: The nineteenth general Council of the Church, held in three stages from 1545 to 1547; 1551 to 1552 and 1562 to 1563.

*Trinitarians*: Religious Order founded in Rome by St John of Matha in 1198 to redeem Christian captives from slavery (it ransomed 30,720). In 1218, the Military Order of Ransom was established by King James I of Aragon and St Peter Nolasco with the same ends.

*Uskoks*: A Serbian word applied to the Christian refugees inhabiting the eastern coast of the Adriatic, much given to piracy.

*Vatican Library*: Established by Pope Nicholas V in 1448 and containing some 75,000 manuscripts and over one million printed books, it was opened to scholars by Leo XIII in 1881.

*Viceroy*: A nobleman chosen by the king of Spain to represent him and to transmit his instructions.

*Vulgate*: The Latin version of the Bible authorized by the Roman Catholic Church, first translated by St Jerome at the end of the fourth century.

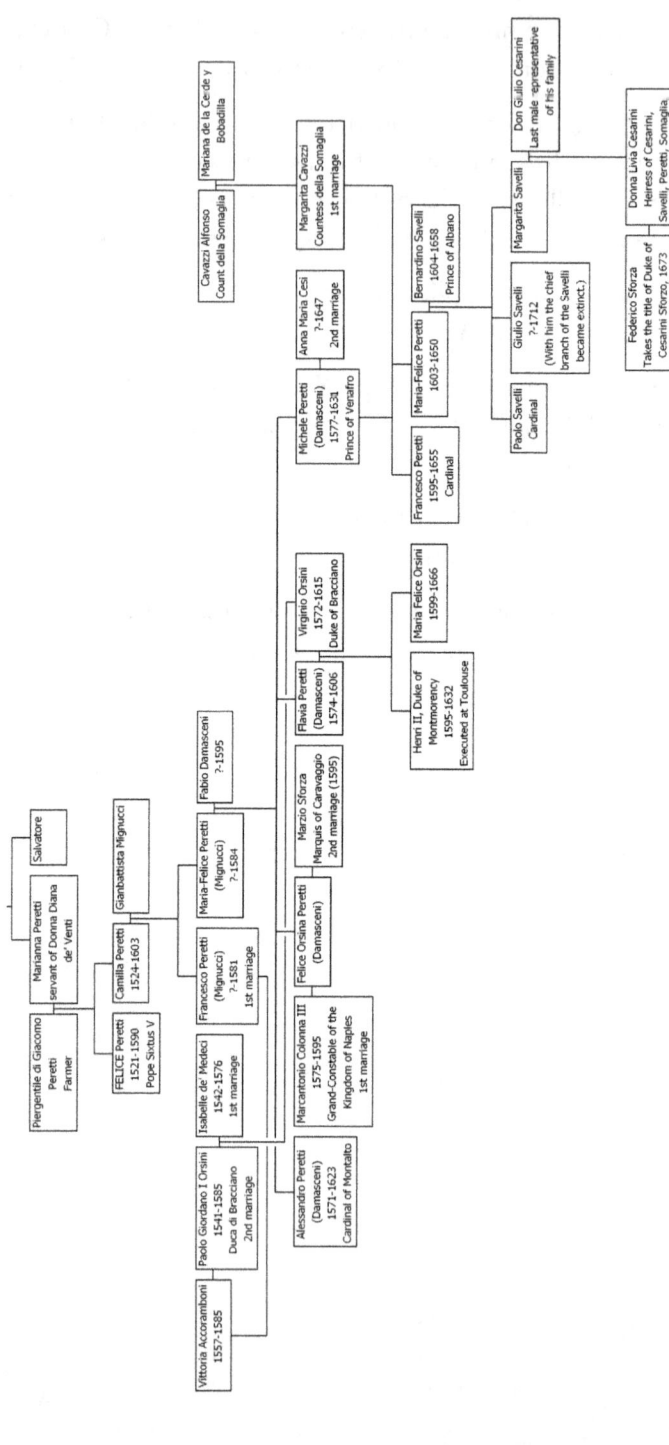

*Appendix 1: Family Tree of Felice Peretti*

# Appendix 2

## The Conclave of 1585

**Cardinals who attended:**

Alessandro Farnese, Bishop of Ostia e Velletri, Dean of the Sacred College

Giacomo Savelli, Bishop of Porto e Santa Rufina, Vicar of Rome

Giovanni Antoni Serbelloni, Bishop of Frascati

Afonso Gesualdo, Bishop of Albano

Gianfrancesco Gàmbara, Bishop of Palestrina

Girolamo Simoncelli (or Simonelli)

Mark Sittich von Hohenems (or Altemps), Bishop of Konstanz

Ludovico d'Este, Archbishop of Auch

Ludovico Madruzzo (or Madruccio), Archbishop of Trent

Innico d'Avalos d'Aragona, Knight of the Order of Santiago

Ferdinando de' Medici, son of the duke of Florence

Marco Antonio Colonna (senior), archbishop of Taranto

Antonio Maria Galli, bishop of Perugia

Prospero Santacroce, bishop of Kisamos, Crete, nuncio in France

Guglielmo Sirleto, protonotary apostolic

Gabriele Paleotti, Archbishop of Bologna

Michele Bonelli O.P., Great-nephew of Pope St Pius V

Antonio Carafa, protonotary apostolic, canon of the patriarchal Vatican basilica

Giulio Antonio Santorio (or Santori), archbishop of Santa Severina

Pier Donato Cesi, senior, cleric of the Apostolic Chamber

Charles d'Angennes de Rambouillet, Bishop of Le Mans

**Felice Peretti, O.F.M. Conv.**

Girolamo Rusticucci, personal secretary of His Holiness, protonotary apostolic

Nicolas de Pellevé, Archbishop of Sens

Gian Girolamo Albani, protonotary apostolic, governor of the Marches

Filippo Boncompagni, Grand Penitentiary

Filippo Guastavillani, Camerlengo of the Holy Roman Church

Andreas von Austria, son of Archduke Ferdinand of Austria, Bishop of Brixen

Alessandro Riario, titular Patriarch of Alexandria

Pedro de Deza, President of the Council of Valladolid

Giovanni Antonio Facchinetti de Nuce, senior, titular patriarch of Jerusalem

Giovanni Vincenzo Gonzaga, knight of Saint John of Jerusalem, prior of Barletta

Gianbattista Castagna, former archbishop of Rossano

Alessandro Ottaviano de' Medici, Archbishop of Florence

Giulio Canani, Bishop of Adria

Niccolò Sfondrati, bishop of Cremona

Antonmaria Salviati, bishop of Saint-Papoul, France, nuncio in France

Filippo Spinola, Bishop of Nola

Matthieu Cointerel, datary of His Holiness

Scipione Lancelotti, auditor of the Sacred Roman Rota

Francesco Sforza di Santa Fiora, Canon of S. Nicola in Carcere

Guido Luca Ferrero, Governor of Faenza

## Cardinals who did not attend:

Georges d'Armagnac, ambassador of King Francis I of France in Rome
Niccolò Caetani, protonotary apostolic
Charles II de Bourbon-Vendôme, bishop-elect of Saintes
Antoine Perrenot de Granvelle, bishop of Arras
Albrecht von Austria, archduke of Austria, son Emperor Maximilian II
Charles de Lorraine de Vaudemont, bishop of Toul and Verdun
Charles I de Guise de Lorraine, archbishop of Reims
Gaspar de Quiroga y Vela, Archbishop of Toledo
François de Joyeuse, Archbishop of Narbonne
Michele della Torre, Bishop of Ceneda
Agostino Valeri (or Valier), Bishop of Verona
Vincenzo Lauro, bishop of Mondovì
Alberto Bolognetti, Bishop of Massa marittima
Jerzy Radziwill, Bishop of Vilnius, Lithuania
Simeone Tagliavia d'Aragonia, abbot
Charles III de Bourbon de Vendôme, Coadjutor Archbishop of Rouen
András Bathóry, Bishop of Ermland, ambassador of Poland to the Holy See
Rodrigo de Castro Osorio, Archbishop of Seville

# Appendix 3

## *Monetary values and Papal coinage*

There were two kinds of florins, the papal florin, which maintained the old weight, and the florin di Camera, the two being in the ratio of 69 papal florins = 100 florins di Camera = 1 gold pound = 10 carlini. The ducat was coined in the papal mint from the year 1432; it was a coin of Venetian origin that circulated with the florin, which in 1531 was succeeded by the scudo, a piece of French origin (écu) that remained the monetary unit of the Pontifical States. At the same time, there appeared the zecchino. The ancient papal florin was equal to 2 scudi and 11 baiocchi (1 baiocco = 0.01 scudi); one ducat was equal to one scudo and 9 baiocchi. The scudo also underwent fluctuations, in the market and in its weight: the so called scudo delle stampe (1595) was worth 184·2 baiocchi, that is, a little less than 2 scudi. Benedict XIII re-established the good quality of the alloy, but under Pius VI it again deteriorated. In 1835, Gregory XVI regulated the monetary system of the Pontifical States, establishing the scudo as the unit, and dividing it into 100 baiocchi, while the baiocco was divided into 5 quattrini (the quattrino, until 1591, had been equal to ¼ of a baiocco). The scudo was coined both in gold and in silver; there were pieces of 10 scudi, called Gregorine; and pieces of 5 scudi, and of 2½ scudi were also coined. The scudo of the eighteenth century was equal to 1·65 scudi of Pius VII, which last was adopted by Gregory XVI; the zecchino was worth 2·2 scudi. The scudo is equal to 5·3 lire in the monetary system of the Latin Union. The fractional silver coins were the half scudo, and the giulio, called also paolo, which was equal to 0·1 seudi. Julius II created the latter coin to put the carlini of Charles of Anjou out of circulation, those coins being of bad alloy.

There were pieces of 2 giulii that were called papetti, at Rome, and lire at Bologna, a name that was later given to them officially. A grosso, introduced in 1736, was equal to half a giulio (25 baiocchi); there were also the mezzogrosso, and the testone = 30 giulii. The copper coins were the baiocco or soldo (which was called bolognino, at Bologna) and the 2 baiocchi piece. The name baiocco is derived from that of the city of Bayeux.

Ducat (Ducato stretto, Gold gulden, Grand Ecu) = 24 carats : 3.386 grams of gold = 6 livres

Scudo (of gold) = 22 carats 3.043 grams

Scudo (of silver) = 30 grams = 10 giulii

Écu/Petit écu (of gold) = 1.693 grams = 3 livres

Écu (of silver) = 30 grams of silver

Giulio = 2.940 grams of silver

Pope's Crown= 2.822 grams = 5 livres

# Index of names

## A

Accoramboni, Marcello, 130, 186
Accoramboni, Vittoria, 127, 130, 138, 166, 186
Acquaviva, Fr Claudio, 309, 311, 315, 316, 325
Adrian VI, Pope, 265
Alaleone, P., 175, 178
Albani, Cardinal Gian Girolamo, 147, 148, 157, 158, 162, 163, 191
Alciati, Cardinal Francesco, 100
Aldobrandini, Cardinal Ippolito (See also Clement VIII, Pope), 103, 120, 267, 269, 286, 391, 393
Alessandrino Cardinal (See also Bonelli, Cardinal Michele), 146, 299
Alessandro da Montefalco, 14
Alessandro, relative of Giovanni Beroaldi, 117
Alexander III, Pope, 150
Alexander VI, Pope, xii
Alexander VII, Pope, 396
Allen, Cardinal William, 264, 267, 270, 280, 281, 284, 322, 323
Altemps, Cardinal Mark Sittich von, 146, 147, 148, 149, 151, 157, 160, 172, 188, 215, 247
Altemps, Roberto, 157, 188
Ambrose, St, 107, 121, 127, 282, 283, 286, 290, 307, 309
Ambrosini, M. L., 23, 337, 341
Andrew of Austria, Cardinal, 147, 158
Antoninus Pius, 399
Antonio di Montalcino, 74
Antony of Padua, St, 290

Aquinas, St Thomas, 290, 312
Araoz, Fr Antonio, 312, 313
Aretino, Pietro, 61
Armagnac, Cardinal Georges d', 146
Athanasius, St, 290
Augias, C., 397, 399
Augustine, St, 107, 122, 156, 290, 314
Avalos, Cardinal Innico d'Aragona d', 147, 148, 149
Avalos, Francesco Fernando d', 41
Azzolini, Cardinal Decio, 215, 271

## B

Bacon, Edmund N., 254, 399
Badoer, Alberto, 389
Baius, Michael, 314, 315
Balzani, Count Ugo, 255, 390
Baronio, Cardinal Cesare, 286, 287, 289
Bartolomeo de Luga, 74
Basa, Domenico, 288
Basil the Great, St, 290
Bathóry, Cardinal András, 147
Battistella, A., 89
Bañez, Fr Domenico, 315
Bednorz, A., 399
Bellarmine, St Robert, 284, 308, 314, 315, 316
Bellay, Bishop Jean du, 314
Bellini, Giovanni, 51
Benedict XI, Pope, xi
Benedict XII, Pope, xi
Beneducci, G., 136, 137
Benoffi, F. F., 88
Bentivoglia, Giovanni, 352
Bergamo, Andrea di Micheli da, 62, 90

Bernardine of Siena, St, 20, 290
Bernard, St, 303
Bernardino of Ochino, 15, 19
Bernardus de Fremeda, 105
Bernardy, A. A., 216
Bernerio, Cardinal Girolamo, 265, 266, 267, 268, 279, 292
Berni, Francesco, 61
Bernini, Gian Lorenzo, 222, 225
Beroaldi, Bishop Giovanni, 116
Bettenson, H., 340
Bigio, Nanni, 83
Bindman, C., 399
Bizonus, Marcus Antonius, 294
Boccaccio, Giovanni, 40
Bolognetti, Cardinal Alberto, 147
Bonaventure, St, 58, 287, 290, 338, 397
Boncompagni, Archbishop Cristoforo, 247
Boncompagni, Cardinal Filippo, 133, 145, 151, 158, 160, 163, 164, 165, 177, 397
Boncompagni, Cardinal Ugo (See also Gregory XIII, Pope), 102, 103, 104, 123, 271
Boncompagni, Cristoforo, 133
Boncompagni, Giacomo, 133, 138, 141, 160
Bonelli, Cardinal Carlo Michele (See also Cardinal Alessandrino), 120, 135, 148, 149, 150, 158, 160, 163, 171, 397
Boniface VIII, Pope, 362
Bonucci, Cardinal Stefano, 264, 266, 267, 268, 269, 271
Booth, M., 95
Borromeo, Cardinal Federico, 99, 264, 265, 267, 269

Borromeo, St Charles, 99, 100, 102, 104, 105, 124, 125, 126, 127, 152, 156, 157, 203, 247, 270, 275, 278, 297, 309, 373, 397
Boschi, Count, 187
Botio, Sigismondo, 42, 81
Botticelli, Sandro, 142
Bourbon del Monte Santa Maria, Cardinal Francesco Maria, 265, 266
Bourbon-Vendôme, Cardinal François de, 146
Bramante, Donato di Pascuccio d'Antonio, 221
Braudel, F., 341, 392
Brodrick, J., 337, 340, 341, 342
Brooke, R. B., 134, 341
Brown, H. F., 89, 90
Brumani, Mgr Matteo, 393

# C

Caetani, Cardinal Enrico, 271, 316
Caetani, Cardinal Niccolò, 215
Cajetan, St, 301
Caligula, Emperor, 223
Callixtus I, Pope St, 230
Calvin, John, 11, 15
Cano, Fr Melchior, 313, 315
Carafa, Cardinal Antonio, 148, 191, 276, 284, 285, 288
Carafa, Cardinal Carlo, 397
Carafa, Cardinal Giovanni Pietro (See also Paul IV, Pope), 10, 30, 31, 32, 39, 56, 85, 109, 301
Carandente, Giovanni, 337
Caravia, Alessandro, 58
Cardella, L., 136, 217, 336, 337

*Index of names*

Carpi, Cardinal Rodolfo Pioda, 16, 18, 19, 21, 22, 23, 29, 31, 32, 41, 42, 53, 57, 58, 60, 65, 66, 67, 68, 70, 71, 72, 74, 79, 80, 81, 82, 83, 84, 85, 86, 87, 89, 92, 95, 96, 109, 132, 271
Carranza, Archbishop Bartolomé, 102, 103, 120, 124, 174, 271, 336
Castagna, Archbishop Giovanni Battista (See also Urban VII, Pope), 102, 276
Castro Osorio, Cardinal Rodrigo de, 146
Castrucci, Cardinal Giovanni Battista, 269, 271
Catherine of Spain, Infanta, 384
Cavallo, Luigi, 58
Cecchetti, G., 89, 92
Cecilia Metella, 399
Cervini degli Spannochi, Cardinal Marcello (See also Pope Marcellus II), 156, 283
Cesi, Cardinal Pier Donato, 146, 298
Chadwick, Owen, 337, 341, 342
Chambers, D. S., 87, 88, 89
Charles Albert, Duke of Savoy, 384
Charles Emmanuel, Duke of Savoy, 384, 385, 386, 388
Charles IX, King of France, 280, 382
Charles of Austria, Archduke, 309
Charles V, Emperor, 16, 20, 36, 39, 40, 41
Chaves, Fr Diego de, 313
Cherubino da Maria, fra, 17
Chesterton, G. K., 179
Chigi, Agostino, 231
Christina of Lorraine, 383
Churchill, Sir Winston, 115
Cicero, 9
Claude of Valois, 383
Clement VI, Pope, xi

Clement VII, Pope, 84, 197, 226, 232, 388
Clement VIII, Pope (See also Aldobrandini, Cardinal Ippolito), 103, 286
Coccia, A., 339, 342
Colonna, admiral Marcantonio, 122
Colonna, Cardinal Ascanio, 264, 265, 266, 267, 276, 280, 281, 284
Colonna, Cardinal Marcantonio, 36, 122, 140, 149, 187, 191, 215, 280
Colonna, Marco Antonio, 195
Colonna, Prosper, 140
Concleusis, Bishop, 105
Constantine the Great, Emperor, 220, 243
Contarini, Gasparo, 292
Corgna, Cardinal Fulvio Giulio della, 31
Cornaro, Cardinal Federico, 201, 267, 268, 269, 270
Cosimo I, Grand-Duke of Tuscany, 152
Cremanchi, G., 177
Creswell, Fr Joseph, 325
Crispi, Gaspare de, 82
Crispo, Giovanni Battista, 369
Cugnoni, Giuseppe, 23, 87, 88, 89, 90, 135, 137, 337
Cupis, Bishop Bernardino de, 363
Cusani, Cardinal Agostino, 267, 269

**D**

Damasceni, Fabio, 118
Dandini, Cardinal Girolamo, 31
Davidson, N. S., 399
De Seta, C., 378
Dei, Guglielmo, 200
Dei, Leonardo, 200
Delfini, Giovanni Antonio, 66, 67, 80, 81, 82, 91

Delumeau, Jean, 87, 97, 135, 136, 137, 176, 177, 216, 217, 218, 253, 254, 336, 337, 349, 377, 378, 379, 392
Demosthenes, 9
Deza, Cardinal Pedro de, 146, 147, 149, 276
Di Fonzo, L., 340
Didacus, St, 290
Diego of Alcalá, St, 397
Divo, Cornelio, 53, 60, 62, 77, 91
Dominic, St, 301
Drascovics, Cardinal György, 264, 265, 269, 270
Duffy, Eamon, xiv
d'Este, Cardinal Ippolito, 85
d'Este, Cardinal Ludovico, 146, 149, 157, 159, 161, 162, 163, 164, 165, 172, 376, 385

# E

Earle, P., 378
Edward VI, King, 15
Egger, H., 176
Ehrle, F., 176
Elizabeth I, Queen of England, 281, 389, 390, 398
Elliott, J. H., 336
Elliott, L., 217, 340
Emmanuel Philibert, Duke of Savoy, 384, 385, 386
Erasmus, Desiderius, 58, 61
Ercole II, Duke of Ferrara, 161
Eugenius III, Pope, xi

# F

Facchinetti de Nuce, Cardinal Giovanni Antonio (See also Urban IX, Pope), 148, 149, 164, 275, 278, 299

Farnese, Alessandro Duke of Parma, 374
Farnese, Cardinal Alessandro, 120, 131, 142, 146, 148, 151, 154, 159, 161, 165, 166, 167, 171, 177, 189, 276, 336, 363
Fauni da Costacciaro, Bonaventura Pio, 18
Fenizi, Ascanio, 197
Feo, Italo de, xi, 254
Ferdinand of Austria, 147, 158
Fermani, Bishop Cornelio, 363
Fermo, Diana, 5
Fermo, Ludovico Vecchi da, 5
Ferneto, V. da Montedinove, 9
Ferratini, Bishop Bartolomeo, 225
Ferrero, Cardinal Guido Luca, 163, 164
Fiammetta, 40, 87
Filarete, N. da S. Vittoria, 9
Flacius Illyricus, Matthias, 286, 287
Fontana, Domenico, 128, 129, 204, 217, 221, 223, 224, 226, 230, 233, 234, 241, 244, 245, 253, 391, 396
Fonzio, Fra Bartolomeo, 59, 90
Fossombre, Captain, 186
Francis de Paola, St, 290, 307
Francis of Assisi, St, 7, 10, 15, 269, 317
Frederick II, Emperor, 371
Fried, R. C., 216, 254

# G

Gabriel, St Archangel, 346
Gabrielli, Magino, 202
Gaetani, Cardinal Enrico, 269
Galli, Cardinal Antonio Maria, 157, 160, 271, 292, 293
Galli, P. A., 135, 137
Gàmbara, Cardinal Gianfrancesco, 151
Gaspare de Crispi, 82
Gatti, I. L., 88, 89, 90, 91, 92, 93

Gasquet, Cardinal F. N. A., 342, 377
Gelasius II, Pope, xi
Gervaso, R., 379, 392
Gesualdo, Cardinal Afonso, 160
Ghislieri, Cardinal Michele (See also Pius V, Pope St)See also Pope Pius V, 29, 30, 42, 53, 56, 59, 61, 62, 63, 64, 65, 68, 73, 78, 79, 85, 89, 96, 97, 102, 104, 109, 141, 152, 157
Gibbon, Edward, 216
Giovanni da Correggio, 14
Giovanni della Casa, 61
Giovannini, Bishop Paolo Emilio, 378
Giulio da Piacenza, 50
Giuseppe da Fermo, fra, 17
Giustiniani, Cardinal Benedetto, 288, 393
Glorieri, Archbishop Alessandro, 370
Golfi da Pergola, Bartolomeo, 14
Gondi, Cardinal Pierre de, 269, 270
Gonzaga, Cardinal Giovanni Vincenzo, 164
Gonzaga, Cardinal Scipione, 265, 267, 271, 288
Gonzaga, Count Alfonso, 373
Gonzaga, Gaspare di, 373
Granvelle, Cardinal Antoine Perrenot de, 146, 152
Graziani, Antonio Maria, 75, 176
Gregory IX, Pope, 231
Gregory Nazianzen, St, 290
Gregory the Great, Pope St, 290, 395, 399
Gregory VII, Pope, 317
Gregory XIII, Pope (See also Boncompagni, Cardinal Ugo), 103, 123, 124, 126, 128, 131, 132, 133, 134, 136, 139, 140, 144, 146, 147, 148, 149, 150, 151, 152, 154, 158, 159, 160, 162, 164, 171, 173, 174, 188, 191, 196, 201, 205, 228, 231, 233, 239, 240, 258, 263, 271, 282, 303, 311, 313, 314, 317, 318, 319, 322, 333, 338, 360, 383, 397, 398
Grendler, P. F., 90, 91, 92, 93
Grimani, Cardinal Giovanni, 98, 99
Guastavillani, Cardinal Filippo, 133, 140, 150, 160, 161, 164, 188, 363, 364
Guercino, priest, 187
Guise, Louis II Cardinal of, 316
Gàmbara, Cardinal Gian Francesco, 149

# H

Hadrian IV, Pope, xi
Hale, J., 90, 377
Hanlon, G., 377
Harman, A. M., 136
Heemskirk, Martin van, 253
Helena, St, 227, 230
Henry II, King of France, 280, 382
Henry III, King of France, xii, 161, 263, 316, 385, 386, 387
Henry IV, King of France, 383, 384, 385, 397
Henry of Navarre (See also Henry IV, King of France), 385
Henry VIII, King of England, 12
Holt, Fr William, 325
Hübner, A. von, xi, 135, 136, 137, 176, 177, 178, 216, 217, 340, 342, 391, 393, 396, 397, 399

# I

Incoronate, Marco Antonio, 188
Innocent III, Pope, 317, 371
Innocent V, Pope, xi
Innocent VIII, Pope, 226, 384

Isabella de Medici, 127

## J

Januarius, St, 290, 291
Jerome, St, 283, 290
John Chrysostom, St, 290
John III, King of Sweden, 125
John of Gaunt, 324
John of God, St, 307
John XXIII, Pope Bl, xiii, 262, 397
Johnson, Samuel, xiii, xiv
Joyeuse, Cardinal François de, 146, 215, 288
Julius II, Pope, xi, xii, 151, 214, 267, 352
Julius III, Pope, 31, 302
Jung, W., 399

## K

Kelly, H., xiv

## L

Lainez, Fr Diego, 310
Lancellotti, Cardinal Scipione, 363
Landini, Taddeo, 392
Laurenti, Tommaso, 227
Ledesma, Diego, 313
Lees-Milne, J., 252, 253
Leo X, Pope, 5, 11, 262, 321
Leonardo da Vinci, 197
Lessius, Fr Leonard, 315
Leti, Gregory, xi, xiv, 393
Lewis, Dr Owen, 323, 325
Logan, F. D., 88, 91
Logan, O. M. T., 338
Lollo, Andrea, 135
Lorenzo di Toledo, 27
Lorenzo the Magnificent, 382

Lorraine-Vaudémont, Cardinal Charles III de, 264, 267
Loyola, St Ignatius, 33, 34, 36, 302, 308
Lucius III, Pope, xi
Luque, Hernando de, 327
Luther, Martin, 31, 33
Lénoncourt, Cardinal Philippe de, 265, 280

## M

Machiavelli, Niccolò, 61
Maderno, Carlo, 222, 225
Madruzzo, Cardinal Cristoforo, 89
Madruzzo, Cardinal Ludovico, 146, 147, 148, 162, 163, 278
Maggiorano, Nicolo, 283
Magnani, Giulio, 22, 36
Magnano, Bernardino da, 193
Malatesta, Lamberto, 188, 382
Mangone, Benedetto, 370
Manutius, Aldus the Younger, 283, 337
Marcellus II, Pope (See also Cervini degli Spannochi, Cardinal Marcello), 156, 283
Marco Antonio da Luga, 74
Marcus Aurelius, Emperor, 235, 247
Margaret of Valois, Duchess of Berry, 384
Maria of Portugal, Infanta, 374
Mariana da Frontillo, 6
Martin, J. J., 377
Mary, Mother of God, 230, 290, 301, 303, 346, 347, 363
Mary I, Queen of England, 51
Mary, Queen of Scots, 324, 345, 390
Massimo Taparelli, Marchese Azeglio, 253, 254
Mattei, Cardinal Girolamo, 269
Matteo di Bassi, 12

*Index of names*  427

Maximilian III, Archduke of Austria, 391
Medici, Cardinal Alessandro de', 177
Medici, Cardinal Ferdinando de' (See also Medici, Grand Duke Ferdinando I de'), 140, 146, 147, 148, 150, 151, 152, 153, 158, 159, 160, 161, 162, 163, 164, 165, 168, 171, 172, 176, 189, 263, 336, 363, 382, 383
Medici, Cardinal Giovanni de', 153
Medici, Catherine de', 382, 383
Medici, Francesco I de', 381, 382
Medici, Grand Duke Ferdinando I de' (See also Medici, Cardinal Ferdinando de'), 393
Mendoza, Cardinal Juan Hurtado de, 265
Merlo, Giovanni Antonio, 291
Mercati, Giovanni, 233
Michelangelo di Lodovico Buonarroti Simoni, 26, 28, 83, 84, 210
Michael, Melchior, 72
Michele della Torre, Bishop, 91
Miele, M., 379
Mignucci, Santone, 41
Mignura, Giovanni Battista, 16
Mocenigo, Giovanni, 68, 72
Molina, Fr Luis de, 315
Montaigne, Michel de, 375, 376, 379
Montanelli, I., 379, 392
Monte Lupone, Marmilio Adamantino da, 101
Morosini, Cardinal Gianfrancesco, 266, 267, 269
Moses, 329
Mula, Cardinal Marco Antonio da, 72, 75, 92, 99
Muratori, Giovanni Antonio, 80, 91
Muret, Marc'Antonio, 139

Musso da Piacenza, Cornelio, 99, 108, 123

**N**

Narducci, E., 134
Neale, J. E., 393
Neri, St Philip, 34–35, 123, 126, 203, 205, 209, 228, 247, 265, 269, 286, 302, 322
Nero, Emperor, 223, 231
Newman, Bl John Henry, 379
Nicholas IV, Pope, xi, 178, 224
Nicholas of Tolentino, St, 290
Nicholas V, Pope, 221, 222, 226
Nille, K., 399
Norwich, J. J., 25, 88

**O**

Ochino, Bernardino, 33, 40, 85
Odoardi, G., 340
Olivares, Enrique de Guzmán y Ribera, second count of, 146, 167
Onofrio, Cesare d', 396
Orbaan, J. A. F., 135, 218, 253, 254
Origoni da Varese, Tommaso, 102, 104, 105, 112
Orsini, Antonio, 385
Orsini, Latino, 131
Orsini, Ludovico, 186
Orsini, Paolo Giordano, 127, 130, 131, 138, 165, 166, 186, 195
Ottinelli, Bishop Giulio, 293

**P**

Pachini, Professor, 337
Pagano, Paolo, 135

Paleotti, Cardinal Gabriele, 263, 274, 275, 295, 297, 338
Palestrina, Giovanni Pierluigi da, 167, 291, 292
Pallenrieri, 130
Pallotta, Cardinal Giovanni Evangelista, 247, 266, 267, 271
Parsons, Fr Robert, 325
Partner, P., 377
Paschini, P., 89, 90, 91, 92, 134, 136, 339
Passeni, Iohannes Iacobus, 19
Pastor, Ludwig von, 2, 23, 87, 90, 91, 92, 93, 130, 134, 135, 136, 137, 138, 139, 151, 175, 216, 217, 218, 253, 254, 274, 336, 337, 338, 339, 340, 341, 342, 343, 377, 378, 379
Paul II, Pope, 346
Paul III, Pope, 16, 31, 57, 142, 149, 151, 163, 262, 360
Paul IV, Pope, 10, 30, 41, 42, 52, 60, 61, 65, 68, 80, 85, 97, 149, 151, 156, 170, 256, 276, 280, 282, 301, 305, 360, 367, 396
Paul, St, 247
Pecchiai, P., 87, 136, 137, 191, 216, 253, 377
Pedro di Toledo, Don, 38, 39
Pelagius, 314
Pellevé, Cardinal Nicolas de, 146, 147
Penzola, Tommaso Marconi da, 58
Pepoli, Cardinal Guido, 264, 269
Pepoli, Giovanni, 187
Peretti Damasceni, Alessandro, 135
Peretti Damasceni, Flavia, 131, 195
Peretti Damasceni, Michele, 214, 374
Peretti Damasceni, Ursula, 195
Peretti Mignucci, Francesco, 135, 137
Peretti, Camilla, 6, 16, 81, 118, 119, 128, 132, 135, 137, 173, 226, 260, 374, 393

Peretti, Cardinal Alessandro, 259, 262, 264, 336, 393
Peretti, Flora, 81
Peretti, Francesco Damasceni, 81, 127, 130, 165, 230
Peretti, Maria, 81
Peretti, Maria-Felice, 118, 119, 128
Peretti, Piergentile di Giacomo, 4, 5, 6, 17, 23
Peretti, Prospero, 80
Persico of Calabria, 18, 85
Perugino, Pietro di Cristoforo Vannucci, 142
Peter the Martyr, St, 290
Peter, St, 247
Petrarch, Francesco, 40
Petrocchini, Cardinal Gregorio, 266, 268
Petrozani, Tullio, 393
Petruccelli della Gattina, F., 175, 176, 177, 178
Philip II, King of Spain, 41, 51, 52, 103, 124, 146, 163, 167, 256, 263, 277, 312, 313, 314, 316, 317, 318, 319, 324, 325, 326, 331, 332, 349, 350, 372, 373, 376, 383, 384, 385, 389, 390, 397, 398
Picco, Giovanni Battista di, 135
Piccolomini, Alfonso Duke of Montemarciano, 188, 193, 382
Pierbenedetti, Cardinal Mariano, 191, 265, 267, 271
Pinelli, Cardinal Domenico, 267, 268, 269, 271, 393
Pinturicchio, Bernardino di Betto Betti, 142
Pirie, Valérie, 219, 399
Pistolesi, F., 23, 91, 135, 136, 137, 342, 378

Pius IV, Pope, 65, 72, 73, 79, 97, 99, 100, 102, 103, 104, 119, 121, 141, 149, 150, 151, 154, 156, 160, 161, 163, 172, 232, 233, 249, 262, 289
Pius V, Pope St (See also Ghislieri, Cardinal Michele), xi, xii, 29, 105, 106, 111, 120, 121, 123, 128, 131, 132, 133, 148, 149, 150, 152, 154, 160, 163, 166, 170, 172, 174, 181, 197, 201, 205, 212, 228, 230, 258, 262, 283, 290, 299, 301, 303, 305, 306, 307, 311, 314, 319, 390, 392
Pius X, Pope St (See also Sarto, Cardinal Giuseppe), 381, 392
Pizarro, Francisco, 327
Placid, St, 290, 291
Poggio Bracciolini, Giovanni Francesco, 61
Pole, Cardinal Reginald, 176
Pompei, A., 340
Porta, Giacomo della, 221
Prete Braudel, Serafino, 378
Priuli, Lorenzo, Doge of Venice, 44, 178
Prodi, Paolo, 336, 338, 339
Pullan, B., 87, 88

## Q

Quintillian, 9
Quiroga y Vela, Cardinal Gaspar de, 146, 308

## R

Rabelais, François, 61
Radziwill, Cardinal Jerzy, 147
Rambouillet, Cardinal Charles d'Angennes de, 147
Ramsden, John, 345
Ranke, L. von, 2, 217

Raphael Sanzio da Urbino, 231
Rebaschi Carotti, L., 175
Rehoboam, 186
Renwick, A. M., 136
Reynolds, S., 341
Riario, Cardinal Alessandro, 144, 147, 164
Rogatus Rosatius, 9
Romani, M., 217
Ronga, Luigi, 338
Rossi, Cardinal Ippolito de', 265, 266, 269
Rossino, Archbishop Giulio, 370
Rovere, Cardinal Girolamo della, 266, 267, 269, 270, 280
Rovere, Francesca Maria della, 5
Rudolph II, Emperor, 146, 264
Rusticucci, Cardinal Girolamo, 131

## S

Salvatore da Frontillo, fra, 7, 9
Salviata, Lucrezia, 131
Salviati, Cardinal Antonmaria, 187, 191
Sambuco, Curzietto dal, 187
San Giorgio, Cardinal Gian Francesco Biandrate Aldobrandini di, 191, 363
Sangalletto, Papal chamberlain, 393
Santacroce, Cardinal Prospero, 147, 307
Santori, A., 88
Santorio, Cardinal Giulio Antonio, 263, 299
Sapienti d'Augusta, Antonio, 67, 81, 82, 83, 95, 102, 104
Sarnano, Cardinal Costanzo da (Also known as Boccafuoco), 267, 268, 279, 287, 288, 292, 299
Sarno, Count, 385

Sarto, Cardinal Giuseppe (See also Pius X, Pope St), 381
Sauli, Cardinal Antonmaria, 266, 269
Savelli, Cardinal Giacomo, 147, 148, 149, 159, 183, 189, 370
Savonarola, Girolamo, 33, 82
Schroeder, H. J., 135, 339
Sciarra, Marco, 370
Scudi, Mgr, 371
Sebastian, St, 230
Selley, W. T., xii, xiii
Septimus Severus, 396
Serbelloni, Cardinal Giovanni Antonio, 247
Sereni da Capodistria, Agostino, 59
Sforza di Santa Fiora, Cardinal Francesco, 147, 148, 189
Sforza, Ascanio, 188
Short, J. R., 254
Sigismund III Vasa, Prince of Sweden, 391
Simoncelli, Cardinal Girolamo, 148, 149
Sirleto, Cardinal Guglielmo, 147, 156, 157, 162, 166, 275, 276, 281, 283, 284
Sixtus IV, Pope, xi, xii, 27, 119, 178, 181, 197, 231, 267, 395
Smith, R., 376
Sparacio, D., 90
Speciani, Bishop Cesare, 278
Spinazzola, Marchese di, 178
Spinola, Cardinal Filippo, 176, 299
Stella, D., 88, 89
Stella, Francesco, 59, 68, 70, 71
Suarez, Fr Francisco, 312
Sylvester I, Pope, 227

## T

Tagliaventi, F., 1, 216
Tagliavia d'Aragonia, Cardinal Simeone, 146
Tancredi, Giovanni, 115
Tasso, Torquato, 162, 375
Telesio, 18
Tempesti, C. L., 23, 135, 136, 138, 177, 216, 217, 339, 393
Teresa of Avila, St, 125, 318
Tiepolo, Antonio, 395
Toledo Herrera, Francisco de, 263
Toman, R., 399
Tommaso da Vicenza, 92
Torre, Cardinal Michele della, 158, 159, 160
Trajan, Emperor, 235, 237, 239, 247, 399
Truchsess, Cardinal Otto von Waldburg, 89
Tucci, Stefano, 139

## U

Umili, P. O. da Patrignone, 9
Urban IX, Pope (See also Facchinetti de Nuce, Cardinal Giovanni Antonio), 299
Urban V, Pope, xi
Urban VII, Pope (See also Castagna, Archbishop Giovanni Battista), 103, 316, 383

## V

Valdès, Alfonso de, 40, 58
Valenti, Giovanni, 188
Valentino, Pietro, 202
Vergerio, Aurelio, 57, 58
Vergerio, bishop Pier Paolo, 57, 59

*Index of names*

## W

Willis, M., 23, 337, 341
Wren, Sir Christopher, xiii

## X

Xavier, St Francis, 328, 390
Ximénes de Cisneros, Cardinal Francisco, 106, 317

## Z

Zanettini, Bishop Sigismondo, 366
Zwingli, Ulrich, 11
Zúñiga y Avellaneda, Juan de, 187, 369

www.ingramcontent.com/pod-product-compliance
Lightning Source LLC
Chambersburg PA
CBHW050426240426
43661CB00055B/2283